ISBN 978-1-332-21696-3
PIBN 10299634

1 MONTH OF FREE READING

at
www.ForgottenBooks.com

By purchasing this book you are eligible for one month membership to ForgottenBooks.com, giving you unlimited access to our entire collection of over 700,000 titles via our web site and mobile apps.

To claim your free month visit:
www.forgottenbooks.com/free299634

English
Français
Deutsche
Italiano
Español
Português

www.forgottenbooks.com

Mythology Photography **Fiction**
Fishing Christianity **Art** Cooking
Essays Buddhism Freemasonry
Medicine **Biology** Music **Ancient
Egypt** Evolution Carpentry Physics
Dance Geology **Mathematics** Fitness
Shakespeare **Folklore** Yoga Marketing
Confidence Immortality Biographies
Poetry **Psychology** Witchcraft
Electronics Chemistry History **Law**
Accounting **Philosophy** Anthropology
Alchemy Drama Quantum Mechanics
Atheism Sexual Health **Ancient History**
Entrepreneurship Languages Sport
Paleontology Needlework Islam
Metaphysics Investment Archaeology
Parenting Statistics Criminology
Motivational

M

Thirty-ninth Annual Report

Woman's Foreign Missionary Society

Of the Methodist Episcopal Church

Nineteen Hundred and Eight

CONTENTS

MRS. ANNIE RYDER GRACEY

Translated February 16, 1908

*Recording Secretary of the Woman's Foreign
Missionary Society 1882-1905*

"Throughly furnished unto all good works."

Motto: "SAVED FOR SERVICE."

THIRTY-NINTH ANNUAL REPORT

OF THE

WOMAN'S FOREIGN MISSIONARY SOCIETY

OF THE

METHODIST EPISCOPAL CHURCH.

ORGANIZED 1869.
INCORPORATED 1884.

1908.

GENERAL OFFICE:
ROOM 611, 150 FIFTH AVENUE, NEW YORK.
PUBLICATION OFFICE:
36 BROMFIELD STREET, BOSTON, MASS.

SESSIONS OF THE GENERAL EXECUTIVE COMMITTEE.

Date	PLACE	PRESIDENT	SECRETARY	Receipts
1870	Boston, Mass	Mrs. Dr. Patten	Mrs. W. F. Warren	$4,546 86
1871	Chicago, Ill	" Bishop Kingsley	" W. F. Warren	22,397 99
1872	New York City	" Bishop Clark	" W. F. Warren	44,477 46
1873	Cincinnati, O	" L. D. McCabe	" R. Meredith	54,834 87
1874	Philadelphia, Pa	" F. G. Hibbard	" J. H. Knowles	64,809 25
1875	Baltimore, Md	" F. A. Crook	" R. R. Battee	61,492 19
1876	Washington, D. C	" F. G. Hibbard	" W. F. Warren	55,276 06
1877	Minneapolis, Minn	" Dr. Goodrich	" Delia Williams	72,464 30
1878	Boston, Mass	" W. F. Warren	" J. T. Gracey	68,063 52
1879	Chicago, Ill	" S. J. Steele	" L. H. Daggett	66,843 69
1880	Columbus, O	" W. F. Warren	" J. T. Gracey	76,276 43
1881	Buffalo, N. Y	" F. G. Hibbard	" Mary C. Nind	107,932 54
1882	Philadelphia, Pa	" W. F. Warren	" J. T. Gracey	195,678 50
1883	Des Moines, Ia	" L. G. Murphy	" J. T. Gracey	126,823 33
1884	Baltimore, Md	" W. F. Warren	" J. T. Gracey	148,199 14
1885	Evanston, Ill	" I. R. Hitt	" F. P. Crandon	157,442 66
1886	Providence, R. I	" W. F. Warren	" J. H. Knowles	167,098 85
1887	Lincoln, Neb	Miss P. L. Elliott	" J. T. Gracey	191,158 13
1888	Cincinnati, O	Mrs. Bishop Clark	" J. T. Gracey	206,308 69
1889	Detroit, Mich	" I. N. Danforth	" J. T. Gracey	226,496 15
1890	Wilkesbarre, Pa	" W. F. Warren	" J. T. Gracey	220,329 96
1891	Kansas City, Mo	" J. J. Imhoff	" J. T. Gracey	263,660 69
1892	Springfield, Mass	" W. F. Warren	" J. T. Gracey	265,242 15
1893	St. Paul, Minn	" W. Couch	" J. T. Gracey	277,803 79
1894	Washington, D. C	" A. H. Eaton	" J. T. Gracey	311,925 96
1895	St. Louis, Mo	Miss E. Pearson	" J. T. Gracey	289,227 00
1896	Rochester, N. Y	Mrs. S. L. Baldwin	" J. T. Gracey	285,823 94
1897	Denver, Colo	" C. D. Foss	" J. T. Gracey	313,987 86
1898	Indianapolis, Ind	" C. D. Foss	" J. T. Gracey	328,488 75
1899	Cleveland, O	" C. D. Foss	" J. T. Gracey	360,388 63
1900	Worcester, Mass	" C. D. Foss	" J. T. Gracey	414,531 33
1901	Philadelphia, Pa	" C. D. Foss	" J. T. Gracey	426,795 28
1902	Minneapolis, Minn	" C. D. Foss	" J. T. Gracey	478,236 03
1903	Baltimore, Md	" C. D. Foss	" J. T. Gracey	491,391 75
1904	Kansas City, Mo	" C. D. Foss	" J. H. Knowles	534,040 17
1905	New York City	" C. D. Foss	" C. S. Nutter	548,943 55
1906	Omaha, Neb	" A. W. Patten	" C. W. Barnes	616,457 71
1907	Springfield, Ill	" C. D. Foss	" C. W. Barnes	692,490 07
1908	Cincinnati, O	" C. D. Foss	" C. W. Barnes	673,400 04

Total since organization..$9,905,685 27

OFFICERS

of the

Woman's Foreign Missionary Society

of the

METHODIST EPISCOPAL CHURCH.

PRESIDENT EMERITUS.
MRS. C. D. FOSS, 2043 Arch St., Philadelphia, Pa.

PRESIDENT.
MRS. W. F. McDOWELL, 1936 Sheridan Road, Evanston, Ill.

VICE-PRESIDENT.
MRS. A. W. PATTEN, 616 Foster St., Evanston, Ill.

SECRETARY.
MRS. C. W. BARNES, 12 N. Franklin St., Delaware, Ohio.

TREASURER.
MISS FLORENCE HOOPER, 2201 Maryland Ave., Baltimore, Md.

GENERAL COUNSEL.
LEMUEL SKIDMORE, 67 Wall St., New York City.

CORRESPONDING SECRETARIES.
MISS MARY E. HOLT, 4 Berwick Park, Boston, Mass.

MRS. J. M. CORNELL, Seabright, N. J.

MISS C. J. CARNAHAN, Shady Ave. and Walnut St. E., E. Pittsburg, Pa.

MRS. E. D. HUNTLEY, "The Portner," Washington, D. C.

MRS. R. L. THOMAS, 792 E. McMillan St., Walnut Hills, Cincinnati, Ohio.

MRS. F. P. CRANDON, 1414 Forest Ave., Evanston, Ill.

MRS. W. B. THOMPSON, 1018 Des Moines St., Des Moines, Iowa.

MRS. F. F. LINDSAY, 25 Seymour Ave., Minneapolis, Minn.

MISS ELLA M. WATSON, 1701 S. 17th St., Lincoln, Neb.

MRS. S. F. JOHNSON, 520 Oakland Ave., Pasadena, Cal.

MRS. A. N. FISHER, 214 Twelfth St., Portland, Ore.

GENERAL SECRETARIES.
German Work.—MISS LOUISE C. ROTHWEILER, 1190 Mozart St., Columbus, Ohio.

Scandinavian Work.—MRS. HANNA HENSCHEN, 2830 N. Hermitage Ave., Chicago, Ill.

Young People's Work.—MISS WINIFRED SPAULDING, 4449 Columbia Ave., Madisonville, Ohio.

Children's Work.—MRS. LUCIE F. HARRISON, 497 S. El Molino Ave., Pasadena, Cal.

EDITORS OF PERIODICALS.

WOMAN'S MISSIONARY FRIEND.
MISS ELIZABETH C. NORTHUP, 77 Crescent St., Waltham, Mass

DER FRAUEN-MISSIONS FREUND.
MISS AMALIA M. ACHARD, 344 Wabash St., Elgin, Ill.

CHILDREN'S MISSIONARY FRIEND.
MRS. O. W. SCOTT, 86 Highland Ave., Fitchburg, Mass.

THE STUDY.
MRS. MARY ISHAM, University Place, Lincoln, Neb.

GENERAL LITERATURE.
MISS ELIZABETH C. NORTHUP, 77 Crescent St., Waltham, Mass.

PUBLISHER.
MISS ANNIE G. BAILEY, 36 Bromfield St., Boston, Mass.

SECRETARY OF GENERAL OFFICE.
MISS ELIZABETH R. BENDER, Room 611, 150 Fifth Ave., New York.

OFFICIAL CORRESPONDENTS.
North China and South America.—Miss M. E. Holt.
Central China.—Mrs. J. M. Cornell.
Korea, Germany, and Switzerland.—Miss L. C. Rothweiler.
Mexico and Japan.—Miss C. J. Carnahan.
Foochow and South India.—Mrs. E. D. Huntley.
North India and South Japan.—Mrs. R. L. Thomas.
Italy, Bulgaria, and West China.—Mrs. F. P. Crandon.
Bombay and Burma.—Mrs. W. B. Thompson.
Malaysia and Philippine Islands.—Mrs. F. F. Lindsay.
Northwest India.—Miss E. M. Watson.
Africa and Bengal.—Mrs. S. F. Johnson.
Central Provinces and Hing Hua.—Mrs. A. N. Fisher.

TREASURERS IN FOREIGN FIELDS.
North India.—Mrs. A. H. Briggs, Lucknow, India.
Northwest India.—Miss M. A. Livermore, Meerut, India.
South India.—Miss Catherine Wood, Haiderabad, Deccan, India.
Central Provinces.—Mrs. Alma H. Holland, Hawa Bagh, Jabalpur, India.
Bombay.—Miss A. A. Abbott, Thoburn House, Apollo-Bunder, Bombay, India.
Bengal.—Miss Elizabeth Maxey, 150 Dharamtala St., Calcutta, India.
Burma.—Miss Luella Rigby, Methodist Mission, Rangoon, Burma.
Malaysia.—Mrs. W. T. Cherry, Singapore, Sts. Settlement.
Philippines.—Miss Marguerite Decker, 203 Calle Cervantes, Manila, P. I.
North China.—Mrs. Charlotte M. Jewell, Peking, China.
Central China.—Miss Clara E. Merrill, Kiu Kiang, China.

TREASURERS IN FOREIGN FIELDS.—Continued.

West China.—Miss Ella Manning, Tsicheo, via Hankow, China.

Foochow.—Miss Elizabeth M. Strow, Foochow, China.

Hing Hua.—Miss Lizzie Varney, Hing Hua, via Foochow, China.

.Korea.—Miss Josephine O. Paine, Chemulpo, Korea,

North Japan.—Miss Augusta Dickerson, Hakodate, Japan.

Central Japan.—Mrs. Charles Bishop, 15 Akashi-cho, Tsukiji, Tokyo, Japan.

South Japan.—Miss Mariana Young, Nagasaki, Japan.

Mexico.—Miss Laura Temple, Apartado 1340, Mexico City, Mexico.

Argentina, S. A.—Miss Bertha E. Kneeland, 1449 Calle Laprida, Rosario de Santa Fe, Argentine Republic, S. A.

Montevideo.—Miss Lizzie Hewett, 257 Calle San José, Montevideo, Uruguay, S. A.

Peru.—Miss Elsie Wood, Inquisition Plaza 559, Lima, Peru, S. A.

Bulgaria.—Miss Kate B. Blackburn, Lovetch, Bulgaria.

Italy.—Miss Edith.Burt, Crandon Hall, via Veneto, Rome, Italy.

Africa.—Miss Susan Collins (Quessua), Malange, Angola, Africa.

East Africa.—Mrs. Virginia S. Coffin, Old Umtali, Rhodesia, Africa.

Switzerland.—Mrs. Anna Spoerri, Zeltweg, Zurich, Switzerland.

North Germany.—Mrs. C. Wunderlich, Glauchäuer Strasse 44, Zwickau, Germany.

THE FOREIGN DEPARTMENT.

The President of the Society and the Corresponding Secretaries of the several Branches constitute the Foreign Department.

All communications to be brought before the Woman's Foreign Missionary Society in the interim of the General Executive Committee, should be addressed to the Secretary of this department, Miss Ella M. Watson, 1701 S. 17th St., Lincoln, Neb.

THE HOME DEPARTMENT.

The Vice-President of the Society and the Associate Secretaries of the several Branches constitute the Home Department. Secretary of this department, Mrs. Chas. W. Fowler, 208 Fremont St., Chicago, Ill.

OFFICERS AND DELEGATES

OF THE

GENERAL EXECUTIVE COMMITTEE

OF THE

Woman's Foreign Missionary Society,

1908.

PRESIDENT.
MRS. CYRUS D. FOSS.

SECRETARY.
MRS. C. W. BARNES.

NEW ENGLAND BRANCH.
MISS MARY E. HOLT. MRS. JOHN LEGG. MRS. C. S. NUTTER.

NEW YORK BRANCH.
MRS. J. M. CORNELL. MRS. CHAS. L. MEAD. MRS. J. SUMNER STONE.

PHILADELPHIA BRANCH.
MISS C. CARNAHAN. MRS. H. C. SHEAFER. MISS EMMA A. FOWLER.

BALTIMORE BRANCH.
MRS. E. D. HUNTLEY. MRS. J. T. KING. MRS. E. L. HARVEY.
MISS LULU P. HOOPER (*Alternate*).

NORTHWESTERN BRANCH.
MRS. F. P. CRANDON. MRS. J. B. INMAN. MRS. ANNA B. ADAMS.

DES MOINES BRANCH.
MRS. W. B. THOMPSON. MISS ELIZABETH PEARSON. MRS PEARL R. CAMPBELL.

MINNEAPOLIS BRANCH.
MRS. F. F. LINDSAY. MRS. C. A. SAUTER. MRS. A. J. THORNE.

TOPEKA BRANCH.
MISS ELLA WATSON. MRS. R. S. FREEMAN. MISS MATILDA WATSON.

CINCINNATI BRANCH.
MRS. R. L. THOMAS. MRS. A. J. CLARKE. MRS. J. E. McGEE.

PACIFIC BRANCH.
MRS. S. F. JOHNSON. MRS. W. H. WALLACE. MRS. W. C. SCHMUTZLER.

COLUMBIA RIVER BRANCH.
MRS. A. N. FISHER, MRS. J. D. McLEAN. MRS. J. W. WISEMAN.

SECRETARY OF THE GERMAN WORK.
MISS LOUISE ROTHWEILER.

SECRETARY OF SCANDINAVIAN WORK.
MRS. HANNA HENSCHEN.

LITERATURE COMMITTEE.
MRS. J. H. KNOWLES. MRS. L. T. M. SLOCUM. MISS LULU HEACOCK.

COMMITTEES FOR 1908-1909.

FOREIGN DEPARTMENT.
MRS. W. F. McDOWELL, Chairman, 1936 Sheridan Road, Evanston, Ill.
MISS ELLA WATSON, Secretary, 1701 S. 17th St., Lincoln, Neb.

HOME DEPARTMENT.
MRS. A. W. PATTEN, Chairman, 616 Foster St., Evanston, Ill.
MRS. CHAS. W. FOWLER, Secretary, 208 Fremont St., Chicago, Ill.

COMMITTEE ON BY-LAWS.
MRS. C. W. BARNES.   MRS. JOHN LEGG.   MRS. W. B. THOMPSON.
MRS. S. J. HERBEN.

COMMITTEE ON REAL ESTATE AND TITLES.
MRS. W. B. DAVIS, Clifton, Cincinnati, O.   MRS. C. D. FOSS.
MISS PAULINE J. WALDEN.

COMMITTEE ON MISSIONARY EDUCATION IN METHODIST COLLEGES.
MRS. MARY ISHAM, University Place, Neb.
MISS LOUISE MANNING HODGKINS, Wilbraham, Mass.
MRS. A. W. PATTEN, Evanston, Ill.

COMMITTEE ON GENERAL OFFICE.
MRS. W. B. DAVIS, Chairman.   MRS. CYRUS D. FOSS.   MRS. JOHN LEGG.
MRS. J. M. CORNELL.   MRS. F. P. CRANDON.   MRS. J. E. LEAYCRAFT.

COMMITTEE ON RETIREMENT FUND.
MRS. C. D. FOSS.   MISS ELIZABETH PIERCE.   *MRS. E. D. NORTH.   MISS ELLA
CARNAHAN, and the Treasurer of the Woman's Foreign Missionary Society.

GENERAL STATEMENT FOR THE YEAR OCTOBER 1, 1907— OCTOBER 1, 1908.

RECEIPTS.

Balance on hand, October 1, 1907			$72,350 13
*Regular receipts	$671,303 90		
Transferred from Invested Fund	1,700 00		
Annuities	2,500 00		
Bequests and special gifts	7,596 04		
		683,099 94	
Overdraft in one Branch		247 35	
			$755,697 42

DISBURSEMENTS.

†Regular disbursements	$696,569 53		
Transferred to Annuity Funds	4,194 70		
Transferred to Trust Funds	6,584 00		
		$707,348 23	
Balance on hand October 1, 1908		48,349 19	
			$755,697 42

---

*For receipts by Branches, refer to page 12.
† For disbursements by Branches, refer to pages 186–188.

OFFICIAL MINUTES

OF THE

General Executive Committee

OF THE

Woman's Foreign Missionary Society

OF THE

METHODIST EPISCOPAL CHURCH.

Thirty-Ninth Session.

THURSDAY, OCTOBER 29, 1908.

The Thirty-ninth Annual Session of the General Executive Committee of the Woman's Foreign Missionary Society of the Methodist Episcopal Church convened in Trinity Methodist Episcopal Church, Cincinnati, Ohio, on Thursday morning, October 29, 1908, at 9 o'clock.

The meeting was called to order by the President, Mrs. C. D. Foss. The devotional service was conducted by Mrs. F. P. Crandon, Corresponding Secretary of the Northwestern Branch. After the hymn, "O, for a thousand tongues to sing," Mrs. Crandon read as the Scripture lesson Psalm 98 and verses from 1 Peter i. Prayer was offered by Miss Pauline Walden and the devotional service closed with the hymn, "All praise to our redeeming Lord."

The roll was called by the Secretary as follows:

President—Mrs. Cyrus D. Foss.   *Secretary*—Mrs. C. W. Barnes.

NEW ENGLAND BRANCH.
Miss Mary E. Holt,
Mrs. John Legg,
Mrs. C. S. Nutter.

NEW YORK BRANCH.
Mrs. J. M. Cornell,
Mrs. Charles L. Mead,
Mrs. J. Sumner Stone.

PHILADELPHIA BRANCH.
Miss C. J. Carnahan,
Mrs. H. C. Sheafer.
Miss Emma A. Fowler.

BALTIMORE BRANCH.
Mrs. E. D. Huntley,
Mrs. J. T. King,
Mrs. E. L. Harvey.

CINCINNATI BRANCH.
Mrs. R. L. Thomas,
Mrs. A. J. Clarke,
Mrs. J. E. McGee.

NORTHWESTERN BRANCH.
Mrs. F. P. Crandon,
Mrs. J. B. Inman,
Mrs. Anna B. Adams.

9

DES MOINES BRANCH.
Mrs. W. B. Thompson,
Miss Elizabeth Pearson.
Mrs. Pearl R. Campbell.

MINNEAPOLIS BRANCH.
Mrs. F. F. Lindsay,
Mrs. C. H. Sauter,
Mrs. A. J. Thorne.

TOPEKA BRANCH.
Miss Ella Watson,
Mrs. R. S. Freeman,
Miss Matilda Watson.

PACIFIC BRANCH.
Mrs. S. F. Johnson,
Mrs. W. H. Wallace,
Mrs. W. C. Schmutzler.

COLUMBIA RIVER BRANCH.
Mrs. A. N. Fisher,
Mrs. J. D. McLean,
Mrs. J. W. Wiseman.

GENERAL SECRETARIES.
Miss Louise Rothweiler,
Secretary of German Work;
Mrs. Hanna Henschen,
Secretary of Scandinavian Work.

LITERATURE COMMITTEE.
Mrs. J. H. Knowles,
Mrs. L. T. M. Slocum,
Miss Lulu Heacock.

The seating of the delegates was next in order, and was arranged according to the usual custom.

Mrs. R. L. Thomas, Corresponding Secretary of the Cincinnati Branch, the entertaining Branch, gave a brief but cordial welcome to the General Executive Committee. Mrs. C. D. Foss responded, and a letter of greeting from Bishop Moore was read by the Recording Secretary.

Miss Ella Watson, Secretary of the Reference Committee, announced the following standing committees:

PUBLICATION COMMITTEE.
New England—Mrs. John Legg.
New York—Mrs. J. S. Stone.
Philadelphia—Miss Emma A. Fowler.
Baltimore—Mrs. J. T. King.
Cincinnati—Mrs. J. E. McGee.
Northwestern—Mrs. Anna B. Adams.
Des Moines—
  Miss Elizabeth Pearson.
Minneapolis—Mrs. C. H. Sauter.
Topeka—Miss Matilda Watson.
Pacific—Mrs. W. H. Wallace.
Columbia River—Mrs. J. D. McLean.

MISSIONARY CANDIDATES.
New England—Mrs. C. S. Nutter.
New York—Mrs. C. L. Mead.
Philadelphia—Mrs. H. C. Sheafer.
Baltimore—Mrs. E. L. Harvey
Cincinnati—Mrs. A. J. Clarke.
Northwestern—Mrs. J. B. Inman.
Des Moines—
  Mrs. Pearl R. Campbell.
Minneapolis—Mrs. A. J. Thorne.
Topeka—Mrs. R. S. Freeman.
Pacific—Mrs. W. C. Schmutzler.
Columbia River—
  Mrs. J. W. Wiseman.

The Finance Committee, consisting of the Corresponding Secretaries.

The program prepared by the local committee was accepted.

Memorials were received as follows:

From the New York Branch.—The New York Branch memorializes the General Executive Committee to request the Editor of the *Woman's Missionary Friend* to prepare a program for general use on the Day of Prayer, to be printed in the January, 1909, issue of the magazine.

(2) The New York Branch memorializes the General Executive to

change the boundaries of the Branches from State lines to Conference lines.

(3) The New York Branch memorializes the General Executive Committee to defer action on constitutional changes, for further deliberation.

(4) *Pacific Branch:* WHEREAS, The long-established custom of having Branch Home Secretaries has proved so successful and harmonious an arrangement, we beg that the relation between the Branch Corresponding Secretary and the Branch Home Secretary be continued as it now exists. We furthermore ask that the Branch Home Secretaries be made *ex-officio* members of the General Executive Committee, and that they shall, during the annual session of the General Executive, act as a Committee on the Home affairs of the Woman's Foreign Missionary Society.

During the interim, we ask that they devote themselves to the interests of their respective Branches, as they have done in the past, their joint official relation ceasing on the adjournment of the annual meeting of the General Executive Committee.

We most heartily protest against the plan for creating two Boards with co-ordinate powers, and beg that the relation of the Branch Corresponding Secretary and the Branch Home Secretary, as it now exists, remain unchanged.

We also protest against the proposed plan of choosing delegates to the General Executive Committee in proportion to the membership or receipts of a Branch.

We also ask that the representation at General Executive Committee meeting shall never fall below two delegates at large from each Branch, in addition to the Branch Corresponding Secretary and the Branch Home Secretary.

(5) *Minneapolis Branch:* The memorial of the Pacific Branch was presented to the Minneapolis Branch at its recent annual meeting and was found to be in such full accord with its wish upon the questions involved that it seemed unnecessary to repeat it in words. We therefore only state that the memorial from the Pacific Branch is most heartily endorsed by the Minneapolis Branch.

These memorials were referred to a committee to be appointed by the chair.

The reports of the Home Work were presented by the Branch Corresponding Secretaries. (See Reports.) These reports were supplemented by the introduction of the out-going missionaries: Miss Alethea Tracey, from New York Branch, for Central China; Miss Helen Santee, from Philadelphia Branch, for Japan; Miss Flora Carncross, from Northwestern Branch, for Central China; Miss Myra Jaquet, from Northwestern Branch, for North China; Miss Edith Fonda, Northwestern Branch, for Hing Hua; Miss Mary Voigt, Northwestern Branch, for India; Miss Jessie Ankeney, Des Moines Branch, for South China; Miss Winifred

Gabrielson, Topeka Branch, for India; Miss Minnie Gardner, Topeka Branch, for Japan; Miss Laura Frazey, Topeka Branch, for Foochow.

The receipts for the year were as follows:

New England Branch	$53,487 18
New York Branch	98,456 78
Philadelphia Branch	62,049 56
Baltimore Branch	21,751 41
Cincinnati Branch	84,227 31
Northwestern Branch	150,585 73
Des Moines Branch	65,681 39
Minneapolis Branch	38,967 48
Topeka Branch	46,657 64
Pacific Branch	37,240 00
Columbia River Branch	14,295 56
Total amount received	$673,400 04
Total amount received 1906-07	692,490 07
Decrease	$19,090 03

This decrease was explained by the large amounts received in 1906-07 as bequests and special gifts.

Miss Carnahan announced a telegram saying that the Emory Church, Pittsburg, would invite the General Executive Committee to hold its Annual Meeting, 1909, in that church.

Miss Watson presented a partial report from the Reference Committee.

The following missionaries were introduced:

From India—Misses Joan Davis, Anna Lawson, Julia Wisner, Kate Blair, Lilavati Singh, Florence Nichols, Francis Scott, and Ada Pugh.

From Japan—Misses Rebecca Watson, M. B. Griffiths, Georgia Weaver, Matilda Spencer, and Anna Sears.

From China—Rachel R. Benn, M. D., Misses Sarah Peters and Julia Bonafield.

From South America—Miss Mary F. Swaney.

From Malaysia—Mrs. Bishop Oldham.

From Italy—Miss Eva Odgers.

From Korea—Miss Henrietta Robbins.

The following ministers were presented: Bishop Harris, Japan; Dr. McCartney, West China; Dr. Rader, Philippines; Dr. H. D. Ketcham, pastor of Trinity Church, Cincinnati.

After announcements, Dr. Ketcham led in a closing prayer and pronounced the benediction.

Memorial Service.

On Thursday afternoon at 3 o'clock a service was held in memory of Mrs. J. T. Gracey, Miss Catharine O. Curts, and Mrs. L. A. Alderman.

Mrs. C. D. Foss presided, the Scripture lesson, John xiv, was read by Miss Matilda Watson, prayer was offered by Mrs. W. B. Thompson, and Rev. and Mrs. Clifford Myers sang effectively "Forever with the Lord."

Miss M. E. Holt paid tribute to Mrs. Alderman and her work. For almost twenty-five years she was Corresponding Secretary of the New England Branch; a woman of prayer, of painstaking care, and of loving thoughtfulness, she faithfully discharged every detail of her heavy duties.

Mrs. B. R. Cowen told of her helpful associations with Mrs. Alderman and also with Mrs. J. T. Gracey.

Mrs. J. H. Knowles gave a most tender and affectionate tribute to Mrs. Gracey: "In all the various offices which the latter held, she shone; but in her home she was resplendent. Her great brilliancy of mind and her broad knowledge of missionary matters made her a tower of strength to the Woman's Foreign Missionary Society."

Miss Anna Lawson spoke of the life of Miss Kate O. Curts, who died at Godhra, January 3, 1908: "Of sound judgment, practical ability, quiet, strong personality, she was 'saved for service.'" The benediction closed the service.

FRIDAY, OCTOBER 30.

Session opened at 9 o'clock, Mrs. C. D. Foss presiding, and Mrs. E. D. Huntley, of the Baltimore Branch, in charge of the devotional hour. After the hymn "Faith of our fathers," Mrs. S. J. Herben read Isaiah xl, Mrs. John Legg led in prayer, and the hymn "My Jesus, as Thou wilt," closed the devotional hour.

The roll was called and the minutes of the Thursday morning session were read and approved.

The officers, visitors, and missionaries were invited to sit in close proximity to the representatives of their respective Branches.

The President announced the Committee on Memorials, as follows: Mrs. C. S. Nutter, Mrs. H. C. Sheafer, and Mrs. E. L. Harvey.

Miss Watson read the remaining portion of the report of the Reference Committee. The report was accepted with a provision that matters demanding action should be brought up later in the meeting.

Mrs. J. M. Cornell presented her report as General Treasurer. Accepted.

Miss Elizabeth R. Bender, Secretary of General Office, presented her report. The report was accepted, and two requests which she made were granted:

First—That the General Executive Committee shall authorize the Secretary of the General Office to select a cable address and have it entered in the cable offices at New York.

Second—That the Corresponding Secretaries, if practicable, shall plan to send out the missionaries in one or more parties during the year.

Miss Louise Rothweiler presented her report as Secretary of the German Department; Mrs. Hannah Henschen, of the Scandinavian Department, and Miss Winifred Spaulding, of the Young People's Work. Accepted.

Bishop Thoburn was introduced.

Reporters of this meeting for the various Church papers were appointed as follows.

Zion's Herald, Mrs. O. W. Scott.
Northwestern Christian Advocate, Miss Frances Baker.
Epworth Herald, Mrs. S. J. Herben.
Christian Advocate, Mrs. J. H. Knowles.
Pacific Christian Advocate, Mrs. J. D. McLean.
California Christian Advocate, Miss Lulu Heacock.
Pittsburg Christian Advocate, Mrs. C. E. Davis.
Philadelphia Methodist, Mrs. H. C. Sheafer.
Baltimore Methodist, Mrs. J. T. King.
Western Christian Advocate, Mrs. Wm. A. Gamble.
Methodist Advocate-Journal, Mrs. A. J. Clarke.
Christliche Apologete, Mrs. J. T. Endriss.
Central Christian Advocate, Mrs. Mary Isham.
World-Wide Missions, Mrs. Lena Leonard Fisher.

Dr. Levi Gilbert and Dr. Sheridan Bell were introduced.

The following missionaries were presented:

From India—Misses Christina Lawson, Grace Woods, Mrs. Stephens, and Dr. Lewis.
From Burmah—Misses Grace Stockwell and Josephine Stahl.
From China—Miss Gertrude Howe.
From Japan—Misses Anna Slate, Harriet Alling, Mabel Seeds, Leonora Seeds, Bessie Alexander.
From Italy—Miss Ella Vickery and Miss Llewellyn.
From Mexico—Miss Ida Bohannon.
Missionary Candidates—Misses Winifred Muir, Linnie Terrell, and Lulu Gorlisch.

The following reports were presented, accepted, and referred to the Publication Committee: Of the *Children's Missionary Friend,* by Mrs. O. W. Scott, editor; *Woman's Missionary Friend,* by Elizabeth Northup, editor; *Der Frauen Missions-Freund,* by Miss M. Achard, editor; of the Zenana paper, by Miss Mary E. Holt; of *The Study,* by Mrs. Mary Isham, editor; for the Literature Committee, by Mrs. J. H. Knowles, Chairman, and the financial statement of the Literature Committee, by Miss Walden.

The beautiful hymn of Miss Hodgkins, "One Heart, One Way," was sung.

Mrs. Lucy Ryder Meyer, Superintendent of Chicago Training-school, was introduced, and brought cheering words.

On motion of Mrs. R. L. Thomas, the question of the German Branch was made the order of the day for 10.30 A. M. Monday.

Mrs. Wm. B. Davis, chairman of the Program Committee, made a plea for subscriptions to the *Daily Bulletin,* commended Miss Hodgkins's hymn, "One Heart, One Way," and expressed appreciation of the kindness of the Methodist Book Concern in donating 1,500 programs.

The following were introduced: Dr. J. C. Butcher, Dr. Christian Golder, Superintendent of the German Deaconess Work in Cincinnati; Bishop Scott, of Africa, and Dr. J. G. Vaughan, a Field Secretary of the Board of Foreign Missions.

After announcements, the Rev. Adna Leonard led in prayer and pronounced the benediction.

SATURDAY, OCTOBER 31.

Session opened at 9 o'clock, Mrs. Foss presiding, and Miss M. E. Holt, of the New England Branch, in charge of the devotional hour. After the hymn "All Hail the Power of Jesus' Name," Miss Clementina Butler read Isaiah xxxv, Mrs. A. S. Nutter led in prayer, and the hymn "O, for a closer walk with God" was sung.

Mrs. Huntley announced that Mrs. E. L. Harvey had been called home on account of illness and Miss Lulu Hooper would take her place as delegate and also on the Missionary Candidate Committee.

The roll was called and the minutes of Friday morning's session were read and approved.

Miss Ella Watson presented an additional report from the Reference Committee. Accepted.

Miss Pearson was appointed to take the place of Mrs. Harvey on the Committee on Memorials.

The Official Correspondence was next in order. Mrs. F. P. Crandon, Official Correspondent, presented a report from Bulgaria, and Miss C. J. Carnahan, Official Correspondent, presented a report from Mexico. At the request of Mrs. W. B. Thompson, Official Correspondent, Miss Stahl represented the English work in Burmah, and Miss Stockwell the Burmese work. Miss Gertrude Howe represented the work in Central China, and Bishop Hartzell in Africa, by the request of Mrs. J. M. Cornell and Mrs. S. F. Johnson, Official Correspondents, respectively.

Miss Watson presented the following, which was adopted:

Resolved, That we heartily commend the plan that was presented to us by Bishop Hartzell for the Africa Diamond Jubilee, in its purpose to raise $300,000 for the work in that great continent, because of the unprecedented opportunities there to turn the heart of the people to Christ. We further recommend that our aim shall be to raise $50,000 as our Jubilee offering for Africa, and that each Branch shall appoint a committee to distribute literature and in other ways further this work.

At the request of Mrs. F. F. Lindsay, Official Correspondent, Mrs. Bishop Oldham represented Malaysia, and Dr. M. A. Rader, the Philippine Islands; and Bishop Robinson, North India, at the request of Mrs. R. L. Thomas, Official Correspondent.

"The Story Must be Told" was sung effectively by Mrs. Lena Fisher and Miss Woods.

Mrs. Bishop Oldham made a strong plea for money for opening work in new fields, and received subscriptions amounting to $8,275.

At the request of Mrs. E. D. Huntley, Official Correspondent, Miss Julia Bonafield represented the Foochow Conference.

Mrs. Foss stated that, on account of other heavy duties, it would be impossible for her to serve again as President of the Woman's Foreign Missionary Society, and appointed the following Committee on Nomination of General Officers; Miss Holt,' Mrs. Crandon, and Miss Matilda Watson.

The following were introduced: Mrs. Bishop Walden, Mrs. Bishop Moore, Cincinnati; Dr. Heber Jones, Korea; Miss Fannie Fisher, Kolar; Miss Elizabeth Wells, Vikarabad; Mrs. James Cowen, formerly of Japan; Mrs. Mary Carr Curtis, formerly of Malaysia, and Miss Pauline Westcott, Hing Hua.

After announcements, Dr. Walter Cole led in prayer and pronounced the benediction.

SUNDAY, NOVEMBER 1.

AFTERNOON SESSION.

A Service of Commission for out-going missionaries was held at 3 o'clock.' As Mrs. Foss's voice had entirely failed her, Mrs. A. J. Clarke presided. After the hymn "Go forth, ye heralds, in My name," Dr. George Heber Jones, of Korea, read the Scripture lesson and Bishop John E. Robinson, of India, led in prayer.

Mrs. A. J. Clarke presented the following candidates: Miss Alethea W. Tracey, from New York Branch, to Central China; Miss Helen C. Santee, Philadelphia Branch, to Central Japan; Miss Linnie Terrell, Cincinnati Branch, to India; Miss Winifred Muir and Miss Myra Jaquet, Northwestern Branch, to China; Miss Mary Voigt, Northwestern Branch, to India; Misses Flora Carncross and Edith Fonda, Northwestern Branch, places not determined; Misses Winnie Gabrielson, Minnie Gardner, Laura Frazey, Topeka Branch, to India, China, and Japan respectively. Each missionary spoke briefly of her call to the work.

Mrs. W. W. Davison sang very beautifully "Hold them close, dear Father."

Responses were given on behalf of the Woman's Foreign Missionary Society by Mrs. A. N. Fisher, of the native Christians by Tomi Furuta, and welcome to the missionary ranks was expressed by Miss Gertrude Howe. The presentation of commissions was made by Bishop J. M. Thoburn, who also led in the prayer of consecration, and, after the hymn "Arise, ye saints, arise!" pronounced the benediction.

The Thirty-ninth Anniversary Service opened at 7.45 P. M., Mrs. A. J. Clarke presiding. The deaconesses from the Elizabeth Gamble Deaconess Home sang an opening hymn, after which the Rev. H. D. Ketcham led in prayer. An anthem, "Send forth reapers," was sung, and Mrs. C. W. Barnes presented the thirty-ninth annual report. The address of the evening was given by Miss Lilavati Singh, Professor of English Literature in the Isabel Thoburn College, Lucknow, India.

Mrs. Bishop Oldham presented an earnest plea for a generous collection, and Bishop Thoburn supplemented this plea with stirring words.

After another song by the deaconesses, the benediction was pronounced by the Rev. Heber D. Ketcham.

MONDAY, NOVEMBER 2.

Session opened at 9 o'clock, Mrs. Foss presiding and Mrs. J. Sumner Stone in charge of the devotional hour. After the singing of the hymn "Glorious things of Thee are spoken," Miss W. R. Lewis read Isaiah lxii, and Mrs. Charles Spaeth led in prayer. The hymn "Walk in the light" closed the devotional hour.

The roll was called, and minutes of Saturday morning session were read and approved.

Mrs. Harrison presented her report as Secretary of Children's Work. Accepted.

Miss Pauline Walden presented her report as Publisher. The report was accepted and referred to the Publication Committee. Hearty appreciation of all her labors and regret at her retirement, were expressed.

Mrs. A. E. Sanford, the new President of Folts' Mission Institute, presented her report. Accepted, and referred to Committee on Missionary Candidates.

The order of business was called for; namely, the consideration of the proposed change of Constitution, notice of which was given last year, and which looked to the formation of a German Branch; viz.: That article VII, section 1, shall be changed, by inserting in the first sentence immediately following the words "general plan for districting the territory of the Churches," the words "except the German Conferences." Also by inserting after the enumeration of Branches, the words "German Branch— All German Conferences in the Methodist Episcopal Church." After discussion, in which Miss Rothweiler and Mrs. Thomas spoke in favor of the change, and Mrs. Sauter, Mrs. Schmutzler, Mrs. Lindsay, and Mrs. Johnson against it, the privilege of the floor was granted to Dr. Nast, who spoke in favor of the change. Miss Watson reported that the German Conferences in the Topeka Branch were in favor of the change, and Mrs. J. T. King and Mrs. Fisher, that the Germans of the Baltimore and Columbia River Branches were against it.

2

The previous question having been called for, Mrs. Wallace, Mrs. McLean, and Mrs. Inman were appointed tellers, and the vote was taken: 39 votes cast; 30 against the change, and 9 for it. The proposed change was therefore lost.

The following Committee on Resolutions was appointed: Mrs. Reba S. Freeman, Mrs. Charles L. Mead, and Miss Lulu Hooper.

The amendment to the charter of the Woman's Foreign Missionary Society, as passed by the Legislature of New York during last winter, was read and confirmed. (See printed amendment.)

Dr. Drees and Mrs. Craver, of South America, were introduced, and the Rev. Davis W. Clark, D. D., presented greetings from the Methodist Preachers' Association of Cincinnati, and pronounced the benediction.

TUESDAY, NOVEMBER 3.

Session opened at 9 o'clock, Mrs. Foss presiding, and Mrs. Harrison in charge of the devotional hour. After the hymn "How firm a foundation," Mrs. Schmutzler read a porition of Romans viii, and Mrs. W. H. Wallace led in prayer. The hymn "More love to Thee, O Christ," closed the devotional hour.

The roll was called, and the minutes of Monday morning session were read and approved.

The following memorial from Mrs. Harrison was referred to the Committee on Memorials:

Upon consultation with many of the workers, we find it is the opinion of a large majority, that more children could be added to the Little Light Bearers with the annual dues at ten cents, and greater good result;

Therefore, I would memorialize the General Executive Committee to make ten cents the membership dues for the Little Light Bearers.

The following legal documents were attended to:

First—Regarding a piece of property at Mt. Holly, New Jersey, upon which repairs are needed. The following resolution was adopted:

Resolved, That the Woman's Foreign Missionary Society of the Methodist Episcopal Church do consent that a mortgage, to secure a loan of $1,200, be placed upon the house and parcel of land No. 7 Brainerd Street, Mt. Holly, New Jersey, by the other parties interested in said property, under the will of Mrs. A. L. Buckley, deceased, and the President is authorized to execute, in the name and under the corporate seal of the Society, any legal documents which may be necessary for the placing of such mortgage.

Second—Regarding the assignment to Josiah D. Payne, upon the payment of $2,000 to the Woman's Foreign Missionary Society, all right, title, and interest of said corporation in and to the estate of J. D. Payne, deceased.

A resolution was adopted in accordance with the above.

Mrs. Pearl R. Campbell, as Secretary, presented the report of the Committee on Missionary Candidates, which was accepted and considered item by item.

The Misses Wilhelmina Erbst, Mary E. Shannon, and Agnes Ashwell were recommended for acceptance. Miss Daisy Creighton, recommended and left under the care of the Baltimore Branch. Miss Kathryn Willis and Miss Grace Davis, recommended for acceptance on condition that their certificates of health are satisfactory. Report adopted as a whole.

Mrs. Sheafer presented the report of the Committee on Memorials, which was accepted and considered item by item.

First Item—Memorial from the New York Branch regarding a change of boundary from State lines to Conference lines. No action recommended, nor taken on this.

Second Item—Memorial from New York Branch regarding a program for general use on the Day of Prayer. Referred to the Publication Committee.

Third Item—Memorial from New York Branch asking that action be deferred on proposed change of Constitution. No action recommended nor taken upon this.

Fourth Item—Memorial from the Pacific Branch regarding the position of Home Secretaries in the General Executive Committee. Referred to the By-law Committee.

Fifth Item—Memorial from the Minneapolis Branch endorsing memorial No. 4. Referred to the By-law Committee.

Sixth Item—Memorial from Mrs. Harrison regarding dues of Little Light Bearers. Recommended to be adopted, but, after discussion, not adopted.

Report adopted as a whole.

Dr. Heber Jones presented Korea, at the request of Miss Rothweiler, Official Correspondent.

On motion of Mrs. Thompson, further reading of foreign reports was deferred, in order that miscellaneous business might be considered.

Mrs. Johnson presented the proposed change of Constitution, notice of which was given last year, viz.: "That the first sentence in Article V, section 1, reading as follows: 'The management and general administration of the affairs of the Society shall be vested in a General Executive Committee, consisting of a President, Recording Secretary, Treasurer, the Corresponding Secretary, and two delegates from each Branch, Secretary of German Work, and Secretary of Scandinavian Work,' shall be so changed as to read, 'The management and general administration of the affairs of the Society shall be vested in an Executive Committee consisting of a President, Vice-president, Recording Secretary, Treasurer, Corresponding Secretary, the member of the Home Board and two delegates from each Branch, or such other persons as the Constitution of said Society shall hereafter from time to time provide.'" After earnest discussion, in which Mrs. Johnson, Mrs. Knowles, Mrs. Legg, Mrs. Sheafer, and Mrs. Thompson participated, the proposed change was adopted.

Mrs. Thompson, as Chairman, presented a report from the By-law Committee, which was accepted and considered item by item. (See By-laws as adopted, in Constitution and By-laws.)

By-law No. 3, treating of the division of the General Executive Committee into a Foreign Department, consisting of the President and Corresponding Secretaries, and of a Home Department, consisting of the Vice-president and the Associate Secretaries, elicited much discussion. The name Associate Secretary was adopted by a vote of 25 ayes and 8 nays.

The proposed duties of the Associate Secretary caused earnest discussion, in which Mrs. Knowles, Mrs. Thompson, Mrs. Thomas, Mrs. Stone, Mrs. Huntley, and Mrs. Herben, by permission of the committee, took part.

Fraternal delegates from the Woman's Home Missionary Society were introduced: Mrs. William Christie Herron, First Vice-president, and Mrs. F. A. Aiken, Recording Secretary. Mrs. Aiken, in well-chosen words, brought loving greetings and encouragements from this sister organization, to which Mrs. Barnes responded. The hymn "Blest be the tie that binds" was sung.

Dr. and Mrs. Byers, of Asansol, sang effectively in Hindustani, a song of victory.

On the request of Miss Watson, Official Correspondent, Miss Anna Lawson represented the Northwest India Conference.

Miss Fowler called attention to the literature on sale, and Mrs. McGee to the missionary exhibit.

Dr. D. Lee Aultman led in a short prayer and pronounced the benediction.

WEDNESDAY, NOVEMBER 4.

Session opened at 9 o'clock, Mrs. Foss presiding and Mrs. C. F. Blume in charge of the devotional hour. After the hymn "Jesus shall reign where'er the sun," Mrs. A. J. Thorne read Psalm lxxii. Mrs. Bishop Oldham led in prayer, and the hymn "Ye servants of God, your Master proclaim," closed the devotional hour.

The roll was called and the minutes of the Tuesday morning session were read and, after corrections, approved.

Mrs. Pearl Campbell presented the final report of the Committee on Missionary Candidates. It was as follows: "We have carefully considered the reports of Folts Institute and find nothing therein that requires any action by this committee." Accepted, and the report adopted as a whole.

Mrs. J. D. McLean presented the report of the Publication Committee, which was accepted and considered item by item.

First Item—Endorsing our publications. Adopted.

Second Item—Regarding editors and publisher and their salaries. Adopted.

Third Item—Expressing regret at the resignation of Miss Walden, and recommending Miss Annie G. Bailey for publisher. Adopted.

Fourth Item—Approving the *Daily Bulletin.* Adopted.

Fifth Item—Recommending the appropriations for special contributions. Adopted.

Sixth Item—Recommending funds for Scandinavian work. Adopted.

Seventh Item—Regarding the issue of 30,000 copies of the Recording Secretary's Annual Report. Adopted.

Report of the Publication Committee was adopted as a whole.

On request of Mrs. W. B. Thompson, Official Correspondent, the Bombay Conference was represented by Miss Davis and Miss Christina Lawson. Miss Spencer represented Japan Conference, Miss Swaney the South America Conference, and Miss Westcott the Hing Hua, on request of the Official Correspondents.

The following resolution was adopted:

Resolved, That the representatives of the German Conferences here assembled, shall be appointed a committee to formulate plans for simplifying the German work, and report to this body.

On motion of Mrs. Thompson, the General Executive Committee proceeded to the election of the officers, and to miscellaneous business.

Miss Holt stated that Mrs. Foss was compelled to give up the position as President not because she was not able nor willing longer to fill it, but on account of the pressure of other duties. Miss Holt paid tribute to Mrs. Foss's character and work, and the latter briefly and fittingly responded.

The following nominations were presented by Miss Holt: For President Emeritus, Mrs. Cyrus D. Foss; President, Mrs. W. F. McDowell; Vice-president, Mrs. A. W. Patten; Recording Secretary, Mrs. C. W. Barnes; Treasurer, Miss Florence Hooper. Mrs. Mead, Mrs. King, and Mrs. Thorne were appointed tellers, and the vote was taken.

Miss Fowler invited the General Executive Committee to meet in Emory Church, Pittsburg, one year hence. Accepted with thanks.

The following telegram was read: "In appreciation of the flowers so often placed on mother's desk, by members of the Executive Committee, on her birthday, November 4th, please accept check for $25, following by mail, for the Anna Ryder Gracey Home, Sitapur. (Signed) Lilly Ryder Gracey."

The Secretary was instructed to send a telegram of loving sympathy to Dr. and the Misses Gracey.

Mrs. Thompson, Chairman, resumed the presentation of the report of the By-law Committee, which was considered item by item. (See By-laws as adopted, in Constitution and By-laws.)

Mrs. Thompson recalled the fact that a notice of a proposed change of Constitution had been given in the meeting of 1905, by which the words "Literature Committee" should be omitted from Article V of the Constitution. This proposed change was adopted in 1906, 29 ayes and 7 nays; but as this action was found to be illegal on account of the phrasing of our charter, the words "Literature Committee" had been replaced in the Constitution until a new amendment to the charter could be obtained. As this new amendment had been passed by the Legislature of New York during the last year, it was moved that the vote of two years ago be confirmed, which was done, and the words "Literature Committee" were therefore dropped from Article V of the Constitution.

Mrs. Knowles presented the offer of Mr. Ninde to donate five hundred copies of the memorial volume of Mrs. Mary C. Ninde, free of charge, to the Woman's Foreign Missionary Society. This offer was accepted, and Mrs. Knowles was asked to express appreciation, and to inform Mr. Ninde where to send the books.

On motion, the records of the Literature Committee were given into the keeping of the Secretary of the Woman's Foreign Missionary Society.

Mrs. Cyrus D. Foss was elected President Emeritus by acclamation; and the general officers, as nominated, were elected.

Miss Elizabeth F. Pierce presented a plan for the care of retired missionaries. Report adopted, and Mrs. Foss, Miss Elizabeth Pierce, Mrs. E. D. North, Miss Ella Carnahan, and the Treasurer of the Woman's Foreign Missionary Society were appointed as the Committee on the Retirement Fund.

Miss Northup presented the literature on sale.

Mrs. Isham presented her report on Mission Study in Colleges. Accepted.

The resignation of Miss Jontz, of the Committee on Mission Study in the Colleges, was accepted, and Mrs. A. W. Patten was appointed, the committee, therefore, being Mrs. Isham, Miss Hodgkins, and Mrs. Patten.

The Secretary was instructed to send telegrams to Mrs. McDowell, Mrs. Patten, and Miss Florence Hooper, informing them of their election.

Mention was made of the kindness of the girls of the Sunshine Society in providing pads and blotters for the Corresponding Secretaries, and a letter was read from Dr. Heber Ketcham expressing regret at enforced absence.

Dr. Peale led in prayer and pronounced the benediction.

THURSDAY, NOVEMBER 5.

Session opened at 9 o'clock, Mrs. Foss presiding, and Mrs. Sheafer in charge of the devotional hour. After the hymn "In the cross of Christ I glory," Mrs. Sheafer read Scripture selections and led in prayer, and the Standard Bearers' hymn closed the devotional hour.

The roll was called, and the minutes of the Wednesday morning session were read, corrected, and accepted.

Miss Rothweiler, Official Correspondent, presented the work in Germany and Switzerland.

On request of Mrs. S. F. Johnson, Official Correspondent, Miss Wisner represented the Bengal Conference.

The Rev. and Mrs. Byers sang in Bengali "Jesus, I make Thee King in my heart," and followed with an English song.

At the request of Miss Holt, Official Correspondent, Dr. Benn represented the North China Conference.

In behalf of the Reference Committee, Miss Watson spoke of the heart-stirring appeals made by the foreign Bishops and missionaries for an enlargement of our work, and on motion of Mrs. Johnson a collection was taken, which amounted to $78.75.

Lilavati Singh was introduced, and brought greetings from India.

The General Executive Committee was favored by a visit from President-elect Taft, who entered, escorted by Bishop Hartzell. After his introduction to the Woman's Foreign Missionary Society, the President-elect gave an address upon missionary work in the Philippines, strongly commending it, and congratulated the Society on what had been accomplished. Mrs. Knowles eloquently responded, and the audience joined in singing "My country, 't is of thee," as Mr. Taft passed out.

Mrs. Bishop Cranston was introduced.

Mrs. Thompson presented the final report of the By-law Committee, which was considered and acted upon item by item. The report as a whole was adopted. (See report as adopted, in Constitution and By-laws.)

Miss Pierce made a plea for contributions to the fund for retired missionaries.

It was ordered that the reports of the Official Correspondents be received and printed.

Miss Watson, from the Reference Committee, nominated the following: For Secretary of General Office, Miss Elizabeth Bender, salary $900, office expenses, $500; Secretary of Young People's Work, Miss Winifred Spaulding; Secretary of Children's Work, Mrs. Lucie Harrison; Secretary of German Work, Miss Louise Rothweiler; Secretary of Scandinavian Work, Mrs. Hannah Henschen. The Recording Secretary was instructed to cast the ballot for the above-named officers, which she accordingly did, and they were duly elected.

Miss Bender was appointed to have charge of our endowed room at Clifton Springs.

The following appointments were made: As the Methodist member of the Committee on International Conference of Woman's Missionary Boards, to be held in Boston next February, Mrs. J. Sumner Stone; as delegates to the same, Miss M. E. Holt, Miss Juliette Smith, Miss Clemeutina Butler, Mrs. John Legg, Mrs. J. H. Knowles, Mrs. J. M. Cornell, and Miss E. C. Northup; as Committee on Program for the Summer School for Foreign Missions at Northfield, Miss W. R. Lewis; as the Methodist member of the Committee on United Study of Missions, Miss Northup.

It was voted to send representatives to the Students' Conferences of the Young Woman's Christian Association, in 1909, which are to be held at Silver Bay; Mt. Lake Park, Maryland; Lake Geneva, Wisconsin; Cascade, Colorado; Seaside, Oregon, and Capitola, California. The expenses of the representative to Silver Bay to be paid by the New York and New England Branches; to Mt. Lake Park by the Baltimore and Cincinnati Branches, and the expenses of the other delegates by the Branches in

whose boundaries the Conferences are held. Representatives to be nominated by the Corresponding Secretaries of the Branches in which the
Conferences are located.

Miss Walden highly commended her successor, Miss Annie G. Bailey.

The following were elected Directors of Folts Mission Institute:
Directors whose terms expire 1909—Mrs. S. L. Baldwin, Brooklyn, N. Y.;
Rev. Wm. D. Marsh, Little Falls, N. Y.; Miss Louise Manning Hodgkins,
Wilbraham, Mass.; Miss Mary E. Holt, Boston, Mass.; Charles S. Mil-
lington, Herkimer, N. Y.; George R. Blount, Lacona, N. Y., and Bishop
Daniel A. Goodsell, for vacancy caused by the death of Bishop E. G.
Andrews, whose term would have expired 1910.

Telegrams of acceptance were read from the newly elected officers,
Mrs. W. F. McDowell, Mrs. A. W. Patten, Miss Florence Hooper, and
Miss Annie G. Bailey.

Mrs. W. B. Davis presented a verbal report of the Committee on Real
Estate, and requested that Miss Walden be added to the committee.

The following were appointed as auditors for the accounts of the
General Treasurer: Mrs. J. E. Leaycraft and Mrs. F. M. North.

Miss Spaulding, Secretary of Young People's Work, presented resolutions from the Young People's Superintendents present at this session,
which were received, and acted upon item by item.

First Item—Regarding a financial age limit. Adopted.

Second Item—Regarding Young People's organizations paying $1 dues.
Adopted.

Third Item—Regarding the use of the dues of the Young People's
organizations to support Young People's missionaries. Adopted.

Fourth Item—Regarding the employment by each Branch of a Field
Secretary of Young People's Work. No action taken.

Fifth Item—Regarding uniform blanks. Adopted.

Sixth Item—Regarding Contingent Fund of the Young People's Society. Adopted.

Seventh Item—Regarding an Auxiliary Supervisor of Young People's
Work. Adopted.

Eighth Item—Regarding free literature for inaugurating Young
People's Work. Adopted.

Ninth Item—Regarding the representing of Young People's Work in
the *Woman's Missionary Friend.* Referred to the Home Department.
(See Report of Young People's Superintendents.)

On motion, it was decided to adjourn, to meet at 2 P. M.

Miss Anna Bing, Sappora, Japan, and Miss Hardy, Lucknow, were introduced.

Dr. S. F. Oliver led in prayer and pronounced the benediction.

AFTERNOON SESSION.

The adjourned session reopened at 2 o'clock, Mrs. Foss presiding.
After the hymn "All hail the power of Jesus' name," Rev. J. E. McGee
conducted the devotional hour.

The roll was called, and the minutes of the morning session were read
and approved.

The Committees on General Office and Real Estate were appointed.

The following notices of proposed changes in Constitution were presented:

First—From the Cincinnati Branch—That Article VII, Section 1, shall be changed by inserting in the first sentence, immediately following the words "general plan for districting the territory of the Church," "except the German Conferences desiring a German Branch;" also by inserting after the enumeration of Branches the words "German Branch—All German Conferences of the Methodist Church desiring a German Branch."

Second—From the Topeka Branch—That in the Constitution for Auxiliary societies, Article V, the words "supervisor of Young People's Work" be inserted after the words "a Treasurer." So this article shall read, "a President, etc., and Treasurer, and Supervisor of Young People's Work," etc.

Third—From the Des Moines Branch—That that portion of Article VI, "Permanent Committee of the Woman's Foreign Missionary Society," entitled "Reference Committee," be stricken out.

The following Committee on Constitution and By-laws was appointed: Mrs. C. W. Barnes, Mrs. John Legg, Mrs. W. B. Thompson, and Mrs. S. J. Herben.

Miss Walden, as one of the Special Committee, reported that it would be impossible to obtain a copyright or patent on our badge. Report accepted and committee dismissed.

Miss Rothweiler presented a report from the committee to formulate plans for simplifying the German work, which was accepted. (See printed report.)

On motion of Mrs. Knowles a rising vote of thanks and of appreciation was given Miss Baker for her arduous work upon the *Daily Bulletin,* and she was requested to finish the edition by preparing an issue of the proceedings of this last day of the session. The debt incurred by issuing the *Bulletin* was ordered paid from the general treasury.

Mrs. Henschen presented a plan regarding the reports from the Swedish Conferences, similar to that adopted regarding the German Conferences. Adopted.

The following were appointed as Committee on General Office: Mrs. W. B. Davis, Mrs. Cyrus D. Foss, Mrs. John Legg, Mrs. Leaycraft, the Associate Secretary of the New York Branch, and the Associate Secretary of the Northwestern Branch.

The report of the Registration Committee was as follows: Total registration, 187. Officers, 2; Corresponding Secretaries, 11; Delegates, 22; General Secretaries, 4; Literature Committee, 3; Editors, 5; Publisher, 1; Office Secretary, 1; Missionaries, 70; of whom 37 are of the Woman's Foreign Missionary Society on home leave; 14 are new missionaries; 2, missionary candidates; 17 from the Board of Foreign Missions; and 68 visitors from out of town.

Miss Watson presented the final report from the Reference Committee, which was accepted.

Miss Hooper presented the report of the. Committee on Resolutions, which was adopted by a rising vote. (See Resolutions.)

After the singing of Miss Hodgkins's beautiful hymn, "One Heart, One Way," the appropriations for the coming year were read and adopted, as follows:

New England Branch	$44,000
New York Branch	100,000
Philadelphia Branch	62,778
Baltimore Branch	19,000
Cincinnati Branch	75,523
Northwestern Branch	150,000
Des Moines Branch	65,767
Minneapolis Branch	25,600
Topeka Branch	46,000
Pacific Branch	40,000
Columbia River Branch	14,000
Total	$642,668.

An advance over appropriations of last year of $30,386.

The business of the General Executive Committee having been concluded, Mrs. J. H. Knowles conducted the closing service. After the hymn "Thou Shepherd of Israel and mine," she read a Scripture lesson from St. Paul's Epistles to the Colossians, with appropriate comments, and led in prayer; after which the Thirty-ninth Session of the General Executive Committee adjourned.

Mrs. C. W. Barnes, *Recording Secretary.*

PROPOSED CHANGES OF CONSTITUTION.

At the General Executive Committee meeting for 1909 the following changes of Constitution for the Woman's Foreign Missionary Society of the Methodist Episcopal Church will be asked for, namely:

That Article VII, Section 1, shall be changed by inserting in the first sentence, immediately following the words "General plan for districting the territory of the Church," "except the German Conferences desiring a German Branch;" also by inserting after the enumeration of Branches the words, "German Branch—All German Conferences of the Methodist Episcopal Church desiring a German Branch."—Cincinnati Branch.

That that portion of Article VI, "Permanent Committees of the Woman's Foreign Missionary Society," entitled "Reference Committee," be stricken out.—Des Moines Branch.

That in the Constitution for Auxiliary Societies, Article V, the words "Supervisor of Young People's Work" shall be inserted after the words "a Treasurer." So this article shall read "a President, etc., a Treasurer, a Supervisor of Young People's Work," etc.—Topeka Branch.

RESOLUTIONS ADOPTED AT VARIOUS SESSIONS OF THE GENERAL EXECUTIVE COMMITTEE.

OUR SPECIAL WORK.

WHEREAS, We, your representatives on the foreign field, recognize that close personal touch is necessary in order to awaken and continue interest in mission work; and

WHEREAS, The present method of carrying on one form of special work, namely, the attachment of individual givers at home to an individual protege on the foreign field, is often productive of many harmful influences and results, both upon the givers at home and the proteges on the foreign field, aside from the great labor involved in the necessary correspondence; and

WHEREAS, This system is detrimental to the fundamental principles of our Christian service, in that such gifts frequently prove to have been of a merely temporal and philanthropic character, instead of being offerings made to the Lord Christ and to the general advancement of His kingdom; therefore,

Resolved, 1. That the missionary be made the living link between the givers at home and the foreign field, whose support shall be assigned to the various Conferences and Districts, and whose duty it shall be to write regularly to her constituency, letters which may be multiplied and sent to each Auxiliary.

2. That Bible readers, teachers, and scholarships, so far as possible, be paid from the regular funds as apportioned to the different Branches and Conferences.

Signed by missionaries.

Adopted by General Executive Committee. (1901.)

REPORTS.

Resolved, That reports presented by the various committees and individuals, authorized by the General Executive Committee, shall be limited to ten minutes in time of reading. (1902.)

TREASURER'S REPORT.

Mrs. J. M. Cornell, *in account with the Woman's Foreign Missionary Society.*

Receipts.

October 1, 1907, balance on hand............................ $2,157 87

From assessment of 1 per cent on receipts—
New England Branch..........................	$843 00	
New York Branch............................	967 00	
Philadelphia Branch	644 00	
Baltimore Branch	188 00	
Cincinnati Branch	888 00	
Northwestern Branch	1,529 00	
Des Moines Branch	674 00	
Minneapolis Branch	282 00	
Topeka Branch ....,	420 00	
Pacific Branch ...., ...	332 00	
Columbia River Branch......................	64 00	
		6,831 00

Special gift for assistance in General Office, from Mrs. Bashford,   200 00

$9,188 87

Disbursements.

Traveling expenses to General Executive Meeting, Springfield, Illinois, October, 1907.

President ...., ...	$55 40
Recording Secretary	27 70
New England: Secretary, 2 delegates, 2 missionaries.	259 98
New York: Secretary, 2 delegates, 4 missionaries....	330 54
Philadelphia: Secretary, 2 delegates, 2 missionaries...	179 48
Baltimore: Secretary, 2 delegates...................	156 75
Cincinnati: Secretary, 2 delegates..................	56 50
Northwestern: Secretary, 2 delegates, 6 missionaries.	65 50
Des Moines: Secretary, 2 delegates, 4 missionaries...	74 68
Minneapolis: Secretary, 2 delegates.................	95 30
Topeka: Secretary, 2 delegates, 3 missionaries.......	140 00
Pacific: Secretary, 2 delegates, 1 missionary:........	464 85
Columbia River: Secretary, 1 delegate..............	257 00
Secretary of German Work........................	16 25
Secretary of Swedish Work........................	7 40
Secretaries of Young Woman's Work..............	21 25
Secretary of Children's Work.....................	64 44
	$2,273 02

Expenses of officers—

Recording Secretary—postage, printing, etc., 1907.........	14	75
Secretary of Young Woman's Work, 1907.................	18	00
Secretary of Young Woman's Work, 1908.................	150	00
Secretary of Children's Work.............................	39	20

$2,494 97

Traveling expenses to Reference Committee Meeting in Baltimore, May, 1908:

Acting Chairman	$46 00	
New England		
New York		
Philadelphia		
Baltimore	2 00	
Cincinnati	35 00	
Northwestern		
Des Moines	61 00	
Minneapolis	64 00	
Topeka	80 00	
Pacific	134 50	
		422 50

Stenographer and typewriting................................	12 40
Recording Secretary's expenses to General Conference Anniversary	24 50

Expenses of General Office.

Office rent, October 1, 1907, to October 1, 1908.......	$525 00	
Secretary, salary....................................	900 00	
Secretary, travel, Baltimore Executive Committee meeting $6 45		
Pittsburg, convention 9 85		
Silver Bay, convention 21 95		
	38 25	
Office help and running expenses....................	300 00	
Office help, special gift from Mrs. Bashford.........	200 00	
		1,963 25

Young People's Work, deaconess allowance..........	120 00	
Expenses of Secretary to Pittsburg Convention.....	15 75	
		135 75

Printing Quadrennial Report in General Conference Handbook	46 82
Japan, legal expenses of procuring deeds for Omura property	60 00
Folts Mission Institute, running expenses..........	500 00

		$5,660 19
Balance on hand October 1, 1908...................		3,528 68
Total receipts		$9,188 87

Examined and found correct.

CAROLINE C. LEAYCRAFT,
LOUISE M. NORTH.

REPORT OF THE REFERENCE COMMITTEE.

Prior to the mid-year meeeting of the Reference Committee consent was given for the return home of Misses Anna E. Lawson, Joan Davis, Grace Stockwell, Kate Blair, Georgiana Weaver, Bessie Alexander, Gertrude Howe, Helen Robinson, Christina Lawson, and Florence Nichols; to Miss Ada Holmes for a furlough in Europe, and to Miss Ida Kahn, in the United States. Consent was given for the return to the field of Misses Mary Williams, Mabel Allen, Harriet Alling, Kate Ogborn, Eliza Parks, and Minnie Wilson.

The following missionaries were appointed: Miss Lena Hatfield, M. D., to Foochow; Melissa Manderson, North China; Helen Santee, Yokohama; Estie T. Boddy, North China; Alethea Tracey, Kiukiang; Luella Huelster, Central China; and Miss Daisy Byron Sutton, Nagasaki, Japan.

The following missionary candidates were accepted: Miss Paula Seidlmann, appointed to Sieng Iu; Lulu Golisch, Hortense R. Robbins, Edith Lois Fonda, and Flora M. Carncross.

One hundred and fifty dollars was allowed for the expense of the Young People's Department.

Consent was given to exchange the Crandon Hall property in Rome for a larger and more desirable one, the Society to pay a difference not to exceed $10,000.

Miss Winifred Spaulding was appointed a delegate to the International Convention, under the Young People's Missionary Movement, in Pittsburg, March 10th to 13th.

Mrs. Barnes was instructed to issue a booklet containing the Quadrennial Report, for distribution during the General Conference.

The Society agreed to pay the expense, *pro rata,* of the Quadrennial Report in the General Conference Handbook.

The name of the training-school in Manila was changed to the Harris Memorial Deaconess Training-school.

Official Correspondents and Foreign Treasurers were elected for the coming year.

Dr. Margaret Lewis was given permission to present the need for a new building for Bareilly Hospital.

The mid-year meeting of the Reference Committee convened in First Church, Baltimore, May 7, 1908, Mrs. A. W. Patten presiding, and all members present except Mrs. A. N. Fisher.

The following missionaries appeared before the committee and presented the claims of their respective fields: Bishops Bashford, Burt, Harris, Oldham, Robinson, Warne, Hartzell, and the Reverend Doctors George Heber Jones, Drees, Tallon, Goucher, Butler, and Johansson; also Mrs. Bashford, Mrs. Springer, Miss Trimble, and Miss Bonafield.

Pro rata pledges were made for the sending of Miss Donaldson to Africa; for the Bareilly roof; the outgoing expenses of Mrs. Fox to the school in Poona; to reimburse the Rosario Building Fund; for the completion of the Shajahanpur roof, and for the payment of land for the Kiukiang Hospital.

On motion, it was decided that the Reference Committee of each Foreign Conference shall decide immediately upon the departure of a missionary on furlough, whether or not her return to the field is desired, and shall communicate decision to the Branch which is supporting her.

The Woman's Conference at Korea, having voted to join with the ladies of the Methodist Episcopal Church, South, in a Woman's Training-school, asked the sanction of the Reference Committee to the action. Sanction was given.

A resolution having been received from the Woman's Conference of Korea, asking permission to raise $10,000 for buildings and equipment for a school of higher grade in Pyeng Yeng, permission was given to ask individuals for amounts not less than $500, but approval was denied for a general appeal.

It was voted not to sell the West Gate site in Seoul, at present.

The following was adopted:

Resolved, That for the present the relations existing between the Woman's Foreign Missionary Society and the Folts Mission Institute remain as heretofore. This committee agrees to give to the Institute its moral support and to exert its influence towards securing students, but the Society does not assume any financial obligation. It is the judgment of the committee that, for the best interest of the school, the President shall be a member of the Methodist Church.

It was decided to present a memorial to the General Conference asking that the Presidents ·of the Auxiliaries of the Woman's Foreign Missionary Society be made members of the Quarterly Conferences.

The following resolutions were adopted:

First, recognizing the urgent need of strengthening the work for women in the Philippines—

Resolved, That we, the Reference Committee of the Woman's Foreign Missionary Society, heartily endorse the project presented by Miss Decker of erecting a high school dormitory for girls, providing that the Society shall not be asked to raise the additional $4,000 needed for this enterprise.

Second—

Resolved, That when Miss Fenderick returns on furlough, we request our Bishop not to appoint another missionary in her place, as we do not promise to make an appropriation for building in Bidar.

Approval was given to the action of the Central Conference, India, appointing Miss Kate Blair as the editor of the history of the Woman's Foreign Missionary Society in India; and of appointing a committee to prepare a Manual for the Woman's Conference in India.

A Committee on Curriculum for Foreign Schools was appointed as follows: Mrs. Barnes, Mrs. Patten, and Miss Bender.

The following resolutions were adopted:

Resolved, That a farewell service, to be known as a Service of Commission, be included in our program at each General Executive session. Second, That a formal commission, duly signed, be given to each outgoing missionary.

Mrs. Lindsay and Mrs. Thomas were appointed a committee to prepare a farewell service, and certificates for outgoing missionaries.

Mrs. Oldham was requested to organize the work of our Society during her stay in Sweden.

It was voted to recommend that each Branch shall have one delegate for 5,000 members, a second delegate when the membership shall have attained to 10,000, and one additional delegate for each succeeding 10,000.

The Asakusa Day School, Tokyo, was selected as the object for the Children's Thank-offering for 1909.

It was decided to undertake, in the near future, the erection of a high-school building at Lucknow, as a memorial to Mrs. Lois Parker.

Miss Bender, Mrs. Northup, and Miss Spaulding were appointed a committee to confer with leaders of Young People's Work, and various Young People's organizations, concerning co-operation in the several lines of work.

Aoyama was selected as the object for the Young People's Thank-offering for 1909.

Mrs. Crandon, Miss Holt, and Mrs. Lindsay were appointed a committee for the readjustment of the salaries of missionaries.

Consent was given for the home-coming of Misses Soper, Bing, Fenderick, Dr. Taft, Misses Temple, Hampton, and Plum.

Consent was also given for the return to the field, in case satisfactory health certificates were furnished, of Misses Robbins, Miller, Wells, Wilson, Ellicker, Williams, Gheer, Scott, Heaton, Shaw, Melton, McKnight, Mabel Seeds, Dr. Lewis, Dr. Stevenson, and Miss Young.

The following candidates were appointed: Misses Winifred Muir, China; Myra Jaquet, China; Thirza E. Bunce, China; Mary S. Voigt, India; Adella M. Ashbaugh, Japan; Helen Santee, Yokohama; Laura Frazey, China; Roxanna Oldroyd, Lucknow; Minnie Gardner, Japan; Linnie Terrell, India; and Grace McClurg.

At the meetings in connection with the General Executive Committee, the following resolutions were adopted:

1. In view of the fact that missionaries are so badly needed in other stations, and in view of our limited finances, we are not able either to enlarge the work at Allahabad or to sustain a missionary at this station.

2. *Resolved,* That the corner-stone of the Lois Parker High School at Lucknow be laid August 21, 1909, in celebration of the fiftieth anniversary of Mrs. Parker's arrival in India; that the work on the building shall not be begun until notification is received and the funds are in hand; that $20,000 shall cover the entire amount to be paid by the Woman's Foreign Missionary Society.

3. *Resolved,* That, having heard of the attempt to make the school at Baroda co-educational, it is our judgment that the time has not yet arrived in India when our schools should be placed upon this basis, and therefore instruct our missionaries not to enter into such an arrangement.

4. *Resolved,* That we co-operate with Miss Northup in the preparation of two leaflets for distribution at Summer Students' Conferences: one based on Miss Thoburn's "An Open Letter to Missionary Candidates" (see *The Friend,* September, 1896), and the other, a leaflet to be used, in the Spring, stating immediate and pressing needs on the foreign field.

5. *Resolved,* That we acknowledge the receipt of the letter regarding the endowed room at Clifton Springs Sanitarium, accept the conditions therein stated, and approve the appointment of Miss Bender to attend to all business connected with the room.

It was decided to purchase four and one-half acres' of land at Aoyama, Tokyo, the price of same being $21,250. Five thousand dollars will be taken as the Young People's Thank-offering of 1909.

Mrs. Thompson and Mrs. Johnson were appointed a committee on the composition and authority of the Field Reference Committee.

The Topeka Branch was authorized to send Miss Gabrielson to India via Sweden, for the purpose of organizing Woman's Foreign Missionary Society Auxiliaries in that country. Organizations to be affiliated with the Topeka Branch.

Fifteen hundred dollars for the Rosario building was selected as the object for the Children's Thank-offering for 1909.

Twenty thousand dollars for the Lois Parker High School building was pro rated, and $13,000 for the Isabella Thoburn College.

The recommendation making an appropriation of one cent per Auxiliary member for the Retirement Fund was accepted. This amount to be paid annually to the Treasurer of the Woman's Foreign Missionary Society on the first day of May.

Committee on Unification of Course of Study in Our Mission Schools reported. The report was accepted and the committee discharged.

Fifteen thousand dollars toward the Lillian Harris Memorial Hospital of Seoul, Korea, was decided upon as the object for the Thank-offering of the German Conferences.

In view of the fact that it is impossible to secure reduced railroad rates, it was decided that it was unnecessary to elect a railroad committee. A vote of thanks was given to Mrs. Clark and Miss Walden for their faithful and efficient work.

REPORTS OF COMMITTEES.

PUBLICATION.

WHEREAS, We heartily appreciate the management of our publications in charge of the editors of the *Woman's Missionary Friend*, the *Children's Missionary Friend, Der Frauen Missions-Freund*, the *Study*, the Tokiwa and Zenana papers; therefore,

Resolved, That it is our pleasure to make the following nominations: As Editor of the *Woman's Missionary Friend*, Miss Elizabeth C. Northup, at a salary of $700; of the *Children's Missionary Friend*, Mrs. O. W. Scott, at a salary of $300; of *Der Frauen Missions-Freund*, Miss A. W. Achard, at a salary of $250; of the *Study*, Mrs. Mary Isham, at a salary of $100; as Editor of Literature, Miss Elizabeth C. Northup, at a salary of $300; as Publisher, Miss Annie G. Bailey, at a salary of $700; and as Auditor, Mr. George E. Whittaker.

Resolved, It is with sincere regret that we learn of the resignation of Miss Pauline J. Walden, who during the past twenty-six years has held the responsible position of Publisher for the Woman's Foreign Missionary Society. Her marked ability, sweet patience, unwavering faithfulness, and deep spirituality have endeared her to all our hearts, and made the publishing department of our work a pronounced success.

Resolved, That we most heartily commend and appreciate the *Daily Bulletin*, and trust it may become a permanent feature of the General Executive Committee meetings.

Resolved, That we recommend the appropriations for special contributions be as follows: To Editor of *Friend*, $75; to the Editor of Literature, $50; to Editor of *Children's Missionary Friend*, $25.

Resolved, That we recommend that the Secretary of Scandinavian Work be authorized to draw $150, in quarterly installments, from the funds of the publishing house, to be used in interest of literature for Scandinavian Work, and to be expended at the orders of a committee, to be composed of the Corresponding Secretary of the Northwestern Branch and Secretary of Scandinavian Work.

WHEREAS, The Woman's Foreign Missionary Society is to be organized in Sweden this year;

Resolved, We allow $50 for this work.

Resolved, That we recommend the issuing of 30,000 copies of the Secretary's Annual Report, to be distributed as free leaflets to Auxiliaries; pastors also being furnished with a copy.

SARAH C. LEGG, Chairman.
KATHRYN S. McLEAN, Secretary.

MISSIONARY CANDIDATES.

We have examined the testimonials of the following candidates and recommend them for acceptance and appointment:

Cincinnati Branch—Miss Agnes Ashwill, Batavia, Ohio.

Minneapolis Branch—Miss Wilhemina Erbst, St. Paul, Minn.

Baltimore Branch—Miss Daisy L. Creighton, Baltimore, Md., testimonials satisfactory except that further training is recommended.

Baltimore Branch—Miss Katherine Willis, Baltimore, Md., acceptance recommended when a clear health certificate can be obtained.

Cincinnati Branch—Miss Grace C. Davis, Upper Sandusky, Ohio, acceptance recommended when a clear health certificate can be obtained.

Topeka Branch—Miss Mary E. Shannon, Baldwin, Kan., appointment recommended at the end of her college course.

Also, we have carefully considered the report of Folts Mission Institute and find nothing therein that requires any action to be taken by this committee.

MRS. C. S. NUTTER, Chairman.
MRS. PEARL R. CAMPBELL, Secretary.

MEMORIALS.

Six memorials were referred to the committee: three from New York Branch, one from Pacific Branch, one from Minneapolis Branch, one from Mrs. Harrison, Secretary of Children's Work.

1. The committee recommends that the request of the New York Branch, with reference to a program for a Day of Prayer, be referred to the Publication Committee.

2, 3. We recommend that the memorial from the Pacific Branch and its endorsement by the Minneapolis Branch, which would necessitate changes in the By-laws, be referred to the Committee on By-laws.

4. We recommend that no action be taken on the memorial from the New York Branch with regard to change of boundaries.

5. We recommend that no action be taken on the memorial on deferring action on constitutional changes.

6. We recommend that the memorial presented by Mrs. Harrison with regard to dues of Little Light Bearers be accepted.

MRS. C. S. NUTTER,
MISS E. PEARSON,
MRS. H. C. SHEAFER,
Committee.

RESOLUTIONS.

WHEREAS, Our beloved President feels that she must retire from active duty in the Society,

Resolved, That it is with sincere regret we accept her decision, and assure her of our love and appreciation of her services.

WHEREAS, In the judgment of the Executive Committee it has seemed wise to discontinue the Literature Committee,

Resolved, That we express our appreciation of their efficient service.

WHEREAS, The Executive Committee has been highly favored in having the President-elect of the United States, Wm. H. Taft, address this body,

Resolved, We thank him and the committee who planned his coming, and ask Divine guidance for him in the performance of his new duties.

The meeting of the General Executive Committee of 1908 will be held in happy remembrance by all who have had the pleasure of attendance upon its sessions.

We can scarcely say enough of the excellent arrangements for our pleasure and comfort. We express our grateful appreciation to the Cincinnati Branch for their generous invitation to the Secretaries and visitors, not members of the Committee, whose presence, with that of our beloved missionaries, has added much to the interest and profit of the occasion; to the pastor and officiary of the Church for their hospitality in use of church, and to the sexton for his considerate attentions; to the organist and singers for the inspiration of their music; to the various committees who have planned and executed so successfully the details of the entertainment; to the hostesses who have made us feel so delightfully at home; to Mr. Jas N. Gamble, through whose courtesy the hospitality of the Elizabeth Gamble Deaconess Home and Training-school has been enjoyed; to the members of the Cincinnati Preachers' Meeting for their cordial greetings to us as their guests and fellow-workers; to the Methodist Book Concern for the gift of the beautiful programs; to Miss Baker and her co-workers for editing the *Daily Bulletin,* which has been so helpful a factor; to the Press for all courtesies extended; to those who, with great care and pains, have arranged the unusually interesting missionary exhibit; and to all who have in so many gracious ways shown the spirit of the Master in loving service.
REBA S. FREEMAN.
ELINOR S. MEAD.
LULU P. HOOPER.

BY-LAWS.

(See report as adopted, in Constitution and By-laws.)

REAL ESTATE.

The Committee on Real Estate reported progress, and asked that the Committee be enlarged by the addition of Miss Pauline J. Walden.

The Committee desire that the Corresponding Secretaries report to them any new purchase of land, and order their foreign correspondents to forward to the Committee on Real Estate the size and location of purchase, date of purchase, value of land in gold, to whom deeded, and any other facts of interest, to be recorded by Committee.
MRS. WM. B. DAVIS,
MRS. CYRUS D. FOSS.

GENERAL OFFICE.

In pursuance of the expressed purpose of the General Office, an effort has been made to make available all possible information concerning our Society. The files of the *Woman's Missionary Friend* and the Annual Report are complete; those of the Branches and foreign Conferences are not yet full. The biographical and photographic files of the missionaries are growing. To answer calls for current information, clippings are made from our mission and church papers, and blanks have been prepared and sent to each Corresponding Secretary with the thought of having information received monthly. Items of news have been sent to the *Wo-*

man's Missionary Friend, the *Christian Advocate,* and other church papers.

Another department of work has been that of service given to the Branches and the missionaries. The number of boxes shipped through the General Office to our workers on the foreign field has been 266, coming from nine Branches and representing $650 in freight charges. Passage has been arranged for twenty-three missionaries (representing five Branches) ; fifteen missionaries have been assisted in New York (representing six Branches) ; service has been given to sixteen on the foreign field (representing seven Branches), and assistance has been rendered six foreign young women—Chinese, Japanese, Hindu, Italian, Bulgarian, and Mexican. Cablegrams have been received and transmitted. Full information concerning routes of travel for our missionaries has been secured from railroad and steamship offices; other Mission Boards have been communicated with in order to learn their methods of transportation and the experience *en route* of missionaries has been gleaned as far as possible. All this has been compiled, and a copy of it sent to each Branch Corresponding Secretary. A list of hotels in the principal ports which our missionaries touch in their travels has been procured and placed on file, also suggestions as to outfits for new missionaries. The purpose and work of the General Office have been presented to fourteen foreign Conferences, and in six of these Conferences a missionary has been appointed to co-operate with the Secretary in making the office an effective means of service to our foreign workers. The assignment of our semi-endowed room in Clifton Springs Sanitarium has been placed in the hands of the Secretary of the General Office. The fact that our Society owns a lot in Maple Grove Cemetery, near New York, has been brought to the attention of the Ways and Means Committee of the New York Branch, and a local committee appointed by them to visit the place and report annually. The only one buried in the lot is Ann Wilkins.

A third line of work has been that which belongs to the Office as a point of contact between our own Society and other organizations. The closest touch has been with the Board of Foreign Missions. Contributions to our Society to the amount of $2,274.22 have been received from this Board, and forwarded to the Branches. By means of frequent interviews and close touch, at every point where this has been possible, the effort has been made to make the Office a means of promoting sympathetic understanding and helpful co-operation between the two Boards. There have been frequent conferences with the officers of the Young Women's Christian Association concerning matters of mutual interest, especially the summer student conventions, to which we were invited to send representatives. There were six such conventions, at all of which there were representatives of our Society. The Student Volunteer leaders have been helpful, Dr. Zwimer keeping us informed of volunteers belonging to our Church.

The Secretary of the General Office has attended two conventions as representative of the Woman's Foreign Missionary Society—that of the Young People's Missionary Movement in Pittsburg in March, and the Young Women's Christian Association Student Conference at Silver Bay in June. Reports of these were duly presented to the Branches. The Secretary has also served on two committees.

The Transit Committee in New York has given most valuable assistance to twenty-one missionaries passing through the city, and has attended to shopping for six on the foreign field. A similar committee has been appointed in Philadelphia, and has rendered helpful service to our workers.

Grateful recognition of the help of those interested in the General Office is in place, especially of the volunteer assistance given by Miss J.

F. Bango and Miss A. A. Brennen, and the generous gift of $200 made to the Office by Mrs. Bishop Bashford.

The following recommendations are respectfully submitted:

1. That the Committee on the General Office be authorized to adopt a suitable cable address for our Society, and have it registered at one or more of the cable offices in New York.

2. That such an understanding be had with the foreign Conferences and such arrangements made by those having in charge the sending of missionaries to the field, that they may be sent in parties once or twice a year. This recommendation expresses the feeling of members of the Transit Committee in New York and the Secretary of the General Office, and receives the endorsement of the Committee on the Office.

Respectfully submitted,

ELIZABETH R. BENDER, *Secretary of General Office.*

LITERATURE.

It looks like a little matter, this amiable collection of typewritten papers, but it represents hours and days of thought and extensive use of the United States Postoffice service. It was thought not necessary to have a mid-year meeting of the Literature Committee, as most of the leaflets needed for the Study Course were arranged for, during the session of the General Executive Committee at Springfield; and in view of the financial pressure it seemed best to issue few other new leaflets. A tentative outline for the monthly study was prepared by Miss Northup, and sent to each member of the Literature Committee for criticism and suggestion; also the Young People's Study Course, arranged by Miss Spaulding. This proved, in results, apparently as good a way as to have the Committee spend days together in consultation. The new leaflets were submitted in manuscript to each member of the Committee, and received their endorsement before printing.

We present first, prosaic figures, always remembering that we never count them to have "apprehended," but only "reaching forth" towards the truth. The Publisher's statistics, since they are on a gold basis, are reliable.

Issue of new leaflets	15
Number printed	175,750
Leaflet report	30,000
Free advertising leaflets	6
Number printed	79,300
New leaflets	284,050
Children's leaflets (new)	17
Number printed	114,000
Reprints	26
Number printed	193,450
Total output from publishing office, copies	591,500
Pages	4,469,200

From the Publisher we learn that many of our old leaflets continue to be favorites. Notably, "If They Only Knew," which has had ten or twelve issues, and others almost as many. The children's leaflets are nearly all from Mrs. Scott's fruitful pen, and from the children's magician, Mrs. Harrison. We are indebted to the American Bible Society, through its Secretary, Rev. Dr. W. I. Haven, for free use of their leaflets on Siam, and to the Presbyterian Woman's Board for leaflets on the same subject, purchased by us at wholesale price. Many excellent prints have been issued by the various Branches on appeals, thank-offering, local themes, etc., also leaflets that would be useful for general circulation, such as, "Mites and Mights," and "How to make our Missionary Societies More Effective," by Philadelphia Branch, and the Mystery Box, from North-western Branch, such a fine revealer of the excellencies of the *Friend,* and "Two Dolls and a Bear," and "How the Babies were Saved," from Cincinnati Branch. The printed letters sent out by Conference and District Secretaries should be counted among our very effective leaflets; also the German prints, which are particularly attractive. The statistical table shows the following Auxiliaries using topics printed in the *Friend:* Des Moines stands first, Cincinnati and Topeka next. Using printed programs: Northwestern first, Cincinnati next, Des Moines next. Using Loan Library: New York alone reports—28. Completing the Reading Course: Des Moines first, New York next. Using Reference Library: New York and Des Moines lead. Missionary books in Churches: North-western first, New York next, New England third. *Children's Friend* in · Sunday-schools: New York first, Minnesota and Pacific next. Receipts from sales of literature: Northwestern first, Topeka next, New York third. Number of Study books sold: Northwestern first, Cincinnati next.

Early in June a letter was sent from the Chairman of this Committee to each Branch Secretary of Literature, with a schedule of questions to be answered by reports from the Auxiliaries, through the District Secretaries of Literature. A request was also made for suggestions and plans for the efficiency of this department of the Woman's Foreign Missionary Society.

And now we will take our dessert at this table of information; not ice-cream—that is too cold—but plum pudding, with "sugar and spice, and all that's nice."

It has been a joy to receive the letters in reply. They have shown much enthusiasm and careful interest. Every one expresses the conviction that the preparation and circulation of our literature is a vital factor in our success. Those who are most closely in touch with it believe that here, in a large measure, lies the answer to the stirring question, "How shall we strengthen our department of home supplies to keep pace with the development in the foreign field?" Des Moines says: "Our literature and our Reading Course are up-to-date, and no woman who reads it can be indifferent to the call to give 'her money or her life.'" In this Branch there is a copy of the *Friend* in every Methodist college, acknowledged by the librarian, with the assurance that it will be read. In many of the Branches personal letters have accompanied the leaflets sent, not only to District Secretaries, but to Auxiliaries and individuals. Instances are given where this has resulted in special gifts to the Society. In some districts a sum is voted from the District Contingent Fund to send litera-ture to Auxiliaries that have not yet learned their need of it, and to un-organized Churches, and to persons who, sad to say, are not yet as "extinct as the dodo," and who still sing the refrain floating from the dark eight-eenth century, "I do not believe in foreign missions." This manner of dis-tributing we strongly recommend.

In the Philadelphia Branch printed slips were sent out offering a book worth $1.50 to the Society reporting the largest number completing the Reading Course between November, 1907, and June, 1908; a book worth $1.00 to the Society with the next highest number. To Junior Societies similarly reporting on the Junior Reading Course, a book worth $1.00, and another worth 50 cents were offered. The union of Foreign and Home Societies in some places, it is said, prevents the use of the United Study books, also of the skeleton program, and the question is asked, Would it be possible to prepare a skeleton program that could be used in a union Society? This program has been found very useful, and in one instance the figures are given to show how much expense it has saved the Auxiliaries.

It is suggested that a list of books in the Loan Library, the Reference Library, and the Reading Course should be sent to each Auxiliary, because, from some places (not confined to rural districts), they write: "We do not even know what you mean by your questions concerning these books." We believe the present plan of conducting the Literature Department, although not perfect, is far from being a failure. Nothing, we believe, can be better than the method of a Secretary of Literature in each Branch, a Secretary of Literature in each district (not each Conference), and a Secretary of Literature in each Auxiliary. The plan is perfectly practicable. This year's report shows that it is constantly more appreciated and better carried out. The Branch Secretaries are feeling more than ever their responsibilities, and are communicating this consciousness to the districts and Auxiliaries. If we practice the plan, results will tell the story. It requires work; *everything of value costs something.* By permission of Dr. Isaac Watts we say of every worker of the Woman's Foreign Missionary Society:

> How doth her little busy brain
> Improve each shining hour,
> And gather ideas all the day,
> With all her might and power.

> How skillfully she wields her pen;'
> How great the pains she takes,
> And labors hard to bring out well
> The canny plans she makes.

And to all who sit by and eat her honey while she busily buzzes, we would say:

> In works of labor or of skill
> You must be busy, too,
> For, O, there are so many things
> For brains and hearts to do.

Mrs. J. H. Knowles, *Chairman,*
Mrs. L. T. M. Slocum,
Lulu Heacock,
Literature Committee.

FINANCIAL REPORT.

From October 1, 1907, to October 1, 1908.

By Cash Paid for—

Printing Leaflets	$2,175 05	
Manuscript	17 00	
Cuts	23 44	
		$2,215 49
Printing Leaflet Report	$94 00	
Postage and express	50 00	
		144 00
S. B. Supplies	$369 73	
L. L. B. Supplies	181 66	
K. H. Supplies	258 33	
		809 72

Catalogues	$128 50	
Helps and Books (United Study Books, 4,135)..	1,119 19	
Illustrated Post Cards	171 50	
		1,419 19
Office Rent	$300 08	
Office Help	890 58	
W. Paper, Twine, etc..........................	98 08	
Postage and Express	786 09	
		2,074 83
Editor's Salary and Postage....................	$307 00	
Preparing Children's Literature	100 00	
Traveling Expenses of Committee	93 20	
		500 20
Total Expenses		$7,163 43

To Cash Received for—		
Literature	$5,414 55	
S. B. Supplies	546 29	
L. L. B. Supplies.............................	476 36	
K. H. Supplies	408 36	
Leaflet Report	144 78	
		6,981 34
Cash Deficit		$182 09

Bills due on Literature	$587 50	
Literature on hand, 1907-1908.....................	1,230 00	
		$1,817 50
Cash Deficit		182 09
Net Balance		$1,635 41

PAULINE J. WALDEN, *Publisher.*

REPORT OF BRANCH LITERATURE DEPARTMENT.

Total Receipts from Branch Departments of Supplies..........	$16,047 29
Total Receipts from Study Books in Branches................	14,571 00
Total Number of Branch Reports............................	22,500
Total Number having completed Reading Course............	284

REPORT OF GERMAN LITERATURE.
1907—1908.

There have been issued during the year—

4,000 Copies of German Annual Report.............44 pp. =	176,000 pp.
1,200 Copies of a condensed translation of "Gloria Christi," under the name of "Christus der Wohltäter ....48 pp. =	57,600 pp.
1,500 Copies of a Thank-offering program....:..... 8 pp. =	12,000 pp.
6,500 Copies of four new Leaflets, two for general use, two for the Study of the coming year...	47,000 pp.
2,000 Copies of one Reprint	16,000 pp.
500 Copies of a Price List	1,000 pp.
A total output of...........................	309,600 pp.
At a cost of..	$222 20

This is probably the largest output of any year in the history of the German Work.

Besides this, we purchased other—

German Publications for	$3	50
English Publications for	18	29
Pins, etc.	69	77
Office Expenses amounted to	41	60
Total	$355	36
Cash Balance on hand	41	54
Total	$396	90
Our sales amounted to	$303	30
Cash and receipts from other sources	93	60
	$396	90

Respectfully submitted,
LOUISA C. ROTHWEILER, *Secretary of German Work.*

PUBLICATIONS IN JAPANESE.

October, 1907, to September, 1908.

Books and Tracts.	Copies.	Pages.
Pilgrim's Progress for Children, Second Edition	1,500	183,000
Life of Jesus for Children, Second Edition	2,000	256,000
Life of Jesus, Tract Edition	5,000	470,000
Tokiwa Cook Book, Third Edition	2,000	370,000
The Lord's Supper, Third Edition	2,000	44,000
The Lord's Prayer, Second Edition	2,000	30,000
Not a Sinner, Fourth Edition	5,000	35,000
	19,500	1,388,000

Cards.	Copies.
Jesus at Twelve, Third Edition	3,000
Seeing, Hearing, and Speaking no Evil, Third Edition	2,000
Tokiwa Calendar for 1908	1,000
Sunday-school Reward Cards, Second Edition	25,000
	31,000

Our magazine for women, the Tokiwa, has been issued as usual each month, making a total for the year of ten thousand four hundred and twenty-five copies. Printers' prices have advanced considerably since the war, and we have been obliged to raise our prices a little in consequence. But our subscribers and patrons remain loyal, and all our publications seem to be in as high favor as ever. Miss Daniel did excellent work during our absence, and we have but one complaint against her. She sold too many of our publications out of stock, making our first work almost entirely that of revising and reprinting. But we have a few new publications now under way, and are advancing as rapidly as the slow movements of translators and printers will permit. We have not ventured yet into the unknown depths of Korean literature, for the needed funds and helper have not been forthcoming; so we stand only on the brink, hoping yet dreading to have the pillar of cloud move in that direction.

EMMA E. DICKINSON.
GEORGIANA BAUCUS.

WOMAN'S MISSIONARY FRIEND.

One year ago when financial clouds lowered over the country it was feared by many that the economizing of our constituency would begin in their subscriptions to missionary periodicals. The returns show, however, that such fears were not justified, for the *Friend* has now the largest subscription list in its history, a total of 25,535, with an advance of 878 over last year's report. The nearest approach to this was in 1874, when the list was 25,000. The statistical returns by Branches are as follows:

		In- crease.	De- crease.
New England	1,961	...	113
New York	3,206	129	...
Philadelphia	3,233	178	...
Baltimore	706	...	108
Cincinnati	2,789	...	48
Northwestern	6,136	406	...
Des Moines	2,773	99	...
Minneapolis	843	21	...
Topeka	1,497	132	...
Pacific	959	147	...
Columbia River	641	123	...

It will be noted that the decrease in three Branches is not heavy, and it is entirely probable that most of it is due to failure to look after renewals. In some of the Branches a splendid advance has been made. For the coming year it is suggested that we take as our aim, 27,000 subscribers, and that our motto be:

All old subscribers retained,
Fifteen hundred new ones gained.

To cover this advance, making due allowance for possible shrinkage, the Branches are urged to make special effort for a given number of subscribers, each on a pro rata plan based roughly on membership and what former efforts indicate, as within their ability. The proposed figures are as follows. New England, 75; New York, 200; Philadelphia, 150; Baltimore, 80; Cincinnati, 40; Northwestern, 500; Des Moines, 150; Minneapolis, 75; Topeka, 150; Pacific, 200; Columbia River, 150. Set this as a definite aim, and we shall surely move toward our coveted 30,000; we ought at least to compass 27,000.

A study of the foreign field as covered by the *Friend* during the year shows that India has had 30 articles; China, 32; the Philippines, 12; Korea, 11; Mexico, 10; Japan, 9; Burma, 7; Africa, 6; the Moslem world, 6; Malaysia, 5; South America, 3; Bulgaria and the Island world, one each. The only field not heard from has been Italy. From missionaries and bishops and their wives, there have been 135 contributions; from home workers, 38. Of the leading articles, 64 have been devoted to the foreign field and 32 to the home base. The usefulness of articles depends on their timeliness, accompanying pictures, and the amount on hand or recently used concerning a given field. Articles are sometimes held over because they will "keep," and it is always necessary to study balance of material.

The year has witnessed the completion of the China Centennial Fund, to which the Woman's Foreign Missionary Society, aiming for $100,000, reported, through the *Friend*, $175,000. Liberal space has also been given to the discussion of constitutional changes of large importance to the Society in this, its transition period. Five special numbers have been issued, covering Burma, Mexico, Philanthropic Missions, Medical Missions, and the June number for young people. During the coming year, program material will be issued two months in advance, to accommodate Societies that hold meetings the first week in the month.

The Magazine Fund, in whose card catalogue is kept a record of magazines sent to missionaries by individuals and Societies—either direct or through the *Friend*—shows a list of 320, as against 211 last year. In most instances the givers prefer to remain anonymous, but it is suggested that missionaries send a word of acknowledgment to the Editor of the *Friend*, who will gladly transmit it.

A new feature used with much success in various parts of the country, has been the Mystery Box, which has been aptly termed a revealer of the contents of the *Friend*. It is commended as an aid in securing new subscribers at District and Auxiliary meetings, and as a method of adding spice to missionary programs. The Mystery Box "Sphinx" and "Pyramid" will be explained in the *Friend*.

Renewed appreciation of the work of Auxiliary agents is once again expressed. Secretaries of Literature and Periodicals and missionary speakers are urged to present the claims of the *Friend* on every possible occasion. This is a well-tested principle of business advertising, and we can not afford to neglect it or to fail to take care of the leaks that occur when renewals are not looked after. Only in this way can we approximate toward the record of a certain "auxiliary" consisting of one member, who subscribed for two *"Friends"* and raised $300 a year!

To contributors, associate editors, and all who have sent encouraging messages, heartiest thanks are extended.

Respectfully submitted,

ELIZABETH C. NORTHUP, *Editor.*

TABLE OF SUBSCRIPTIONS TO THE WOMAN'S MISSIONARY FRIEND
FROM 1869 TO 1908

Year	Subscriptions
1870	3,000
1871	21 000
1872	22,000
1873	24,000
1874	25,000
1875	16,000
1876	17,313
1877	16,000
1878	14,074
1879	13,388
1880	15,606
1881	18,007
1882	20,020
1883	19,571
1884	20,045
1885	19,816
1886	19,456
1887	19,987
1888	19,907
1889	19,834
1890	19,236
1891	20,401
1892	21,512
1893	21,529
1894	21,617
1895	20,411
1896	19,146
1897	19,026

```
1898————————————————————————————20,858
1899————————————————————————————21,812
1900——————————————————————————————22,720
1901————————————————————————————21,447
1902——————————————————————————————23,538
1903————————————————————————————————24,120
1904————————————————————————————————24,184
1905——————————————————————————————23,402
1906—————————————————————————————23,627
1907—————————————————————————————————24,657
1908——————————————————————————————————25,535
```

THE CHILDREN'S MISSIONARY FRIEND.

Another twelve-month of wonderful missionary history brings us to the time when an inventory must be taken. But as the real standing of a periodical depends upon its subscriptions, our record can never be completed until the publisher's figures arrive. Our special anxiety was relieved when a few weeks ago she wrote: "I hasten to tell you that the number of subscribers to the *Children's Missionary Friend* is 36,415, a gain of 3,630." You all rejoice in this gain we are sure, but special credit for it belongs to those Branch Superintendents of Children's Work who met in Springfield one year ago, and in conference with Mrs. Harrison, made the first definite plan to increase the subscriptions. To them our thanks are due, and we trust the "plan" may be indefinitely extended.

Meanwhile the little *Friend* has tried to deserve its increased prosperity. Your Editor was interested in a letter which came last winter from the Foreign Missions Library in New York. In it was this question: "Are you satisfied that it is better to publish a separate magazine for children rather than to have a children's department in your woman's magazine?" In response we gave a summary of its subscription list, its lesson scheme, Thank-offering, and life member income, which must have been interpreted as an affirmative answer!

It would be *impossible* to crowd the *Children's Friend* back into its former nut-shell, and we trust this mistaken policy—adopted by at least one denomination to the extinction of its young people's periodical—may never prevail in our Society.

Our general Thank-offering for 1908 has been, as during the previous year, for the Industrial School in Mexico, and amounts to $873.59, making a total for the two years of $1,845.59. Had all gifts been reported, $2,000 would undoubtedly have been realized.

Our new Thank-offering is $1,500 for the new school building in Rosario, South America.

Our Little Life Members form an ever increasing army of infantile happiness, flanked by a splendid contingent of King's Heralds.

This year, counting the December photographs, we have had 315, making a grand total of 946 since little Ruth Josephine Brown started the procession in 1902. This number does not include those whose pictures have not been sent to the paper. When we think what this means in big round dollars—more than 9,000 of them—on both sides of the ocean, we must call it a phenomenal success!

Our thanks are again extended, as in by-gone years, to the dear missionaries abroad and on home leave, who have sent so many excellent contributions. We pity those who have not read them. Photographs have also been generously supplied, and it is an unprecedented fact that a few are left over for another year! And speaking of "excellent contributions," have you observed that missionary literature for children has been largely *created* since our little paper began its pilgrimage? In 1889 we asked Mrs. Warren, then Editor of the *Woman's Friend,* where we· were to secure material for the new venture, and she laughingly replied: "Write it." She had but two manuscripts to contribute from the "Children's Department." Miss Walden supplemented these with a bound volume of "Children's Work for Children," and this was our capital.

As late as 1900 no suitable book could be found for a Reading Course, but now there are many fascinating volumes. Our children's societies, with text-book, paper, leaflets, and this large variety of books, are as well equipped as our Auxiliaries, which is exactly as it should be. It remains for us to see that books and readers are made happily acquainted.

We looked forward with some anxiety to the study of the Moslem World for children, but it proves remarkably interesting. An illuminating thought is in this incident from the North India Report. A missionary says:

"One day while in Joa we saw the door of one of the houses open ever so slightly and a woman's hand was thrust out. This hand kept beckoning to us, and finally we drew near and caught a glimpse of a young and beautiful Mohammedan woman. She asked us in, and squeezing through the crack in the door we found ourselves in the zenana of an official. The woman fairly cried with joy to see us. It was a pleasure to tell her about Christ, for she seemed to have a real spiritual hunger. She said, 'I am a very sad woman; I have been sad all my life. These words give me hope.'"

Since reading this I have thought of this year's study as "the call of the beckoning hand." It seemed all at once that the Orient was full of beckoning hands, and some of them very, very small. Shall we help our King's Heralds to see the tiny hands of Mohammedan children, as well as those in our special mission fields, and answer their call?

We can not close this report without expressing personal sorrow over the resignation of our Publisher. We still have the telegram she sent, with the news of our election, and from that day to this her kindness and generous consideration and patience have been unfailing. There is but one word which sums up the nineteen years of official relationship—it is "Faithfulness."

If we strike that keynote in our service for Christ, what may we not accomplish? Respectfully submitted.

Mrs. O. W. Scott.

"FRAUEN-MISSIONS-FREUND."

The report of the Editor of a paper like the *Frauen-Missions-Freund* is naturally much the same year after year. We praise God for His ever-present help in this work for Him. We believe that the *Freund* is not only subscribed for, but read by most of our Auxiliary members, and it is extensively used in the Auxiliary meetings, as we embody the "Study" in it. Though during these last few years the cause of Missions is being presented much more frequently in our Church papers than formerly, we still have our place to fill, and know that there are many more places where the *Freund* might and ought to find new friends.

We have tried to crowd as much missionary information as possible into the small space we have for it, and have tried to keep in line with the "Study," supplementing it with helpful articles. The home side requires a little more space as we grow older and expand, and the question never arises, how to fill our pages, but how to get the most important things into them.

Our subscription list shows an increase of 121, being now 4,631.

That means that two-thirds of our members in. this country take the *Freund,* and since more than one member of one family often belong to the Woman's Foreign Missionary Society, we can say that in nearly every family where some one belongs to the Woman's Foreign Missionary Society, *Frauen-Missions-Freund* is read.

May God bless it and make it a power for the furtherance of the Kingdom! This is the wish of the Editor.

A. M. ACHARD.

"THE STUDY."

Yesterday we met for a tender memorial meeting in honor of one of the pioneers of our many-armed missionary service—Mrs. J. T. Gracey— who, at home and abroad, proved her devotion and God-given efficiency. This morning the editorship of the *Study* seems to us doubly a sacred trust, because it is the child of her brain, and she was its first Editor.

It still seeks to be, within its compass of 1,500 words a month, an interpreter of history of missions, a finger-board pointing to God's leadings among men and nations, a helper to the beginner in mission study, and to the post-graduate student. If it was needed in the beginning, when our Auxiliary meetings were devoted exclusively to the study of our own work, it is more necessary in these years, when the wide world and the enterprise of Christendom are to be compassed in the brief hours of our monthly Auxiliary meetings. Last year, Gloria Christi— the glory of Christ in the salvation of men—was traced through every land beneath the sun. Aside from the text-book, we had some unusual topics. The review of the General Executive Report and the study of Burma gave us living touch with our mission fields. "Rivers and Mountains" sent us to libraries, but showed us from an unusual viewpoint the sweetness and purity of our own faith, in contrast with pagan religions. The Mite-box month revived our interest in these practical gleaners.

This year we have new fields of study in the Moslem world, which the Church has so long neglected. Yet with surprise and delight we find our sickles bright with service there. One of the earliest Girls' Schools in North India, was cared for by the wife of an early Mahommedan convert and preacher of Methodism. We have more Mohammedan preachers in India than any other mission. The Woman's Foreign Missionary Society stood fast and held Bulgaria, when the General Board would have abandoned the field.

We regret to announce a decrease in subscriptions to *The Study.* The subscription list on October first was 33,244. A little effort at Branch and district meetings could easily enable us to report 40,000, a year from now. The price is so low—10 cents for single subscription, 2½ cents in clubs of twelve—that every Auxiliary should have its help; every member should read it.

ZENANA PAPERS.

The Zenana Paper is published in five languages, as follows: Abla Hitkarak, Hindi; Rafig I., Niswan, Urdu, editor, Miss Lilavati Singh; Mathar Mithiri, Tamil, editor, Miss Grace Stephens; Mahili Bandhub, Bengali, editor, Mrs. J. P. Meik; Striyanchi Maitreen, Marathi, editor, Miss Helen E. Robinson. These are published in Lucknow, Calcutta, Madras, and Bombay.

Miss Robinson reports for the Marathi edition, as follows: This eight-page monthly has a circulation of about 350, mostly subscribed for by missionaries, but distributed among and read by a large number of Hindus and Indian Christians. The subscriptions do not quite cover the cost of a single monthly edition, but each year it steadily grows in favor. The weary editor is often at a loss for subjects, because no one ever contributes voluntarily, but once in a while an Indian Christian will try to express his or her appreciation of the paper by sending in a long article or a few verses, which we are not always able to publish, but which are responded to with gratitude. Manoramabai, the gifted daughter of the Pandita, just this morning offered the editor something from her own pen, and she accepted that without any hesitation.

The story of "The Transformation of Lachlan Campbell" has been dressed in Indian garb and made to speak in Marathi. If it will speak to the Marathi readers of the *Friend* as it has to the Scotch readers of Ian Maclaren, the editor will be glad.

We lack a gifted literary Indian man or woman who will express in his or her own tongue the messages that will reach the Hindu woman's heart, either through the medium of verse or good prose. We employ the best Christian translator we can get and he is a busy bank clerk. Till our Church is old enough to furnish a well-educated, Marathi-speaking Indian, devoted to literary work, this paper will never be as attractive as it should be.

Hindu women are not yet trained to be good, appreciative readers, because their education ends so soon, nor do they often try to express their thought or appreciation in conversation. As in conversation with most Indian women the talk is usually one-sided, so the editor feels in carrying on her work on the paper, that is all one-sided. How she would like to know what is in the other person's mind!

Miss Singh reports for the Hindi and Urdu editions.

The work of this paper has been carried on under disadvantages this year, as the unexpectedly heavy work of the editor in the college has left her scarcely any time to devote to writing.

Among the articles that have appeared during the year are a serial story by Miss Marston, and descriptions of the editor's trip to Japan. At the request of the Assistant Civil Surgeon, special articles on plague and methods of prevention, have been published, with headings in large type.

Valuable help has been given by Mrs. Chowfin, Miss Mudge, and also by Miss Buck up to the time of her death. The thanks of the editor are due to those who so kindly and promptly responded to her requests for articles.

The Sunday-school Times, of Philadelphia, has presented the paper with a set of cuts, which will greatly enhance its value.

While conscious of the unsatisfactory nature of the work accomplished, the editor has been gratified by receiving letters from women in different parts of India, telling what this paper has meant to them and the members of their families.

FINANCIAL STATEMENT ZENANA PAPER FUND.

October 1, 1907, balance............................		$1,218 52
Received from New England Branch...............	$798 05	
Received from Baltimore Branch....................	87 50	
Received from Northwestern Branch................	70 00	
Received from Topeka Branch.....................	60 00	
Received from New York, Philadelphia, Cincinnati, Des Moines, Northwestern, and Minneapolis Branches	1,270 62	
Received from interest on deposits...............	97 59	
		$2,383 76
		$3,602 28

Remitted to Lucknow, India...................... $1,370 00
Remitted to Bombay, India........................ 200 00
Collection checks................................ 47
                                                    ———————— $1,570 47

October, 1908, balance............................ $2,031 81

STATEMENT OF FUND (PRINCIPAL).

New England Branch investment................. $5,500 00
Baltimore Branch investment.................... 2,500 00
Northwestern Branch investment................. 1,400 00
Topeka Branch investment....................... 1,000 00
New York, Philadelphia, Cincinnati, Northwestern,
  Des Moines, Minneapolis Branches included in
  note of Garrett Biblical Institute, Evanston, Ill.. 11,700 00

  Total $22,100 00

MARY E. HOLT, *Treasurer*.

PUBLISHER'S REPORT.

One year ago I presented to this committee a twenty-five years' resumé of the publication work, so I will only give the past year's record.

The total subscriptions of the four periodicals are 99,825, making, for the twelve months, 1,349,791 copies; added to these, 591,500 leaflets, giving a total of 1,941,219 copies, or 27,250,960 pages of printed matter.

There are not many quiet moments with such a procession passing in and out of the office.

The life of a publisher is one of constant, unremitting care, not always smooth, however hard we try to make it so, for we have an immense constituency to serve, varied in their needs and demands.

I wish I could introduce to you, or better still, take you to the publication office that you might see my family of loyal helpers, one serving with unfailing devotion to the work for nineteen years; others twelve, eight, and six years. All giving faithful service. It has required some patience to wait for those things which, from the publisher's point of view, were necessary for the development of the work. With a constantly growing conviction that a children's paper was a necessity, we waited six years before our beautiful *Children's Friend* was sen forth on its mission of love and helpfulness to the children of our Church.

In 1897 the publisher sent to the Reference Committee this recommendation, "A permanent Board of Publication, selected with care, a representative from each Branch, to whom should be committed all the interests of the publication work—financial, literary, and the needs of the Society."

Through various forms it was brought before the Executive Committee, until 1900 it came in the form of a change of Constitution, which failed to pass by a small majority, and from that came the organization of the present Literature Committee, covering only a small part of the publication interests.

I am still waiting to see the desire of my heart, not having changed my conviction of its necessity, and trust something may be done at this meeting on this line.

Notwithstanding some misunderstandings and consequent disappointments which have come, and which have seemed to me to place limitations on the advancement of the work, the twenty-six years have been

filled with blessed service for Christ and the cause which is so near to
His great heart of love. I am filled with gratitude that through your
kindness, from year to year, this blessed work has been committed to me.
I have loved it, almost to a passion, have held it as a sacred trust, and
given to it *joyfully* the best there was in me to give. I dare not trust
myself to express all I feel, but I do thank the noble women of this
Society, in this land and across the sea, who have so generously expressed
their appreciation of the work which, by the help of the Lord, I have been
able to do when sending their regrets at my retirement. I would also
thank my co-laborers, the editors of the periodicals, and the Literature
Committee for their patience with me, and this Board of Secretaries for
their constant confidence and sympathy. My affection for this beloved
work will not cease with my retirement, but in the words of our dear
Mrs. Gracey, with whom for over twenty years I had sweet fellowship
and the most pleasant business relations, "I love the Woman's Foreign
Missionary Society, and will care for its interests while I have life and
being."   PAULINE J. WALDEN, *Publisher.*

PAULINE J. WALDEN, *Publisher, in account with Woman's Foreign Missionary Society, from October 1, 1907, to October 1, 1908.*

To cash on hand...........................		$2,838 08
Received for subscriptions to *Woman's Missionary*		
Friend	$12,216 71	
Received for subscriptions to *Children's Missionary*		
Friend	3,581 66	
Received for subscriptions to *Frauen Missions Freund*	1,115 56	
Received for subscriptions to *The Study*............	867 68	
		$17,781 61
Received for Literature...........................		6,981 34
Received for Annual Reports......................	$1,025 93	
Received for Woman's Foreign Missionary Badges..	846 82	
Received for advertising..........................	171 36	
Received for interest on loans and deposits..........	264 86	
Received for rebate on editor's telephone...........	9 00	
Received for sundries............................	13 47	2,331 44
Total receipts		$29,932 47
By cash paid for—		
Printing and mailing *Woman's Missionary Friend*..	$8,817 57	
Editor's salary and incidentals.....................	739 47	
Editor's secretary	400 02	
Editor's rent and telephone.......................	175 32	
		$10,132 38
Printing and mailing *Children's Missionary Friend*...	$3,381 46	
Editor's salary and incidentals.....................	326 05	
		3,707 51
Printing and mailing *Frauen Missions Freund*........	$975 93	
Editor's salary and incidentals.....................	256 10	
		1,232 03
Printing and mailing *The Study*.....................	$858 56	
Editor's salary and incidentals.....................	103 03	
		961 59
Printing and mailing Annual Reports...............	$1,144 60	
Editing Annual Report	50 00	
		1,194 60
Literature expenses		7,163 43

4

Publisher's salary	$700 00	
Office rent and expenses	593 15	
		1,293 15
Woman's Foreign Missionary Society badges		1,455 91
Little Light Bearer cuts	$52 20	
Insurance	322 00	
Auditor	10 00	
Incidentals	70 29	
		454 49
By order of General Executive Committee as follows:		
Swedish Translations	$100 00	
Quadrennial report	47 50	
Traveling expenses of Publisher and Editors to General Executive Committee	206 17	
		353 67
Cash on hand		1,983 71
		$29,932 47

ASSETS PUBLISHING INTERESTS, OCTOBER 1, 1908.

Five first mortgages	$3,300 00	
Deposit in Five Cent Savings Bank	500 11	
Deposit in Home Savings Bank	575 78	
Interest due on loans and deposits	89 87	
Cash on hand	1,983 71	
		$6,449 47
Type and furniture	$1,150 00	
Office furniture	325 00	
Value of stock on hand	5,575 00	
		7,050 00
		$13,499 47
Less amount due on unexpired subscriptions to *Woman's Missionary Friend, Children's Missionary Friend, Frauen-Missions-Freund,* and *The Study*		6,770 50
		$6,728 97

Receipts, expenditures and vouchers examined, and assets verified. The accounts are found correct.

October 24, 1908.   GEO. E. WHITAKER, *Auditor.*

SUBSCRIPTIONS TO PERIODICALS, OCTOBER 1, 1908.

	W. M. F.	C. M. F.	F. M. F.	The Study.
New England Branch	1,961	3,689	56	2,215
New York Branch	3,206	4,531	199	4,058
Philadelphia Branch	3,233	3,037	49	4,617
Baltimore Branch	706	1,298	65	963
Cincinnati Branch	2,789	3,795	258	4,708
Northwestern Branch	6,136	8,445	984	6,842
Des Moines Branch	2,773	4,219	729	4,060
Minneapolis Branch	843	1,241	655	1,221
Topeka Branch	1,497	2,360	764	2,562
Pacific Branch	959	2,325	182	984
Columbia River Branch	641	973	149	997

	W. M. F.	C. M. F.	F. M. F.	The Study.
Scattering	429	140	43	16
Foreign	362	362	498	1
October 1, 1908.............	25,535	36,415	4,631	33,244
October 1, 1907.............	24,657	32,785	4,510	35,644
Increase of	878	3,630	121	Dec. 2,400

MISSION STUDY IN COLLEGES.

Your Committee, re-appointed'at Springfield, Ill., in 1907, beg leave to submit the following report:

At the University Senate, held in Evanston in the interests of our colleges, it will be recalled, that the following reply was given the Committee of the Woman's Foreign Missionary Society relative to the introduction of courses of study in missions, as a part of the curricula of our Methodist Episcopal colleges:

"While we feel that many of our colleges would be embarrassed by a definite requirement at this time that such courses should be given, we still recognize the relation of missions to history and sociology, as well as to the religious life, and we recommend that, wherever our institutions are able to do so, they offer well-ordered and well-taught courses in missions so thoroughly organized, as to have an educational value on a par with that of other parts of the curriculum."

With this encouragement your Committee would like to be authorized to have printed, at the expense of the Woman's Foreign Missionary Society, a letter with suggestive courses or lists of subjects that might be profitably considered; not so elaborate as that now offered at Yale, but on the same general lines.

This printed letter, with a list of books of reference and the endorsement of the Executive Committee of the Woman's Foreign Missionary Society, we would send to each of our Methodist Episcopal colleges, with a copy of the vote of the University Senate, and the request that the matter be considered for the curriculum in each college for 1909-1910. The action of your body would give ample time for a consideration in the spring meetings of the various Faculties and Boards of Trustees.

Respectfully submitted,
LOUISE MANNING HODGKINS.
MARY ISHAM.
IDA V. JONTZ.

FOLTS MISSION INSTITUTE.

It is known to the most of you that during nearly all of last year the school was without either a President or a Field Secretary, consequently there was very little connection between the school and the outside world. Financially we did not suffer. We received special gifts amounting to $2,973.85. This included the $1,000 appropriation made by the General Executive, for which we are grateful. We also received gifts from Mr. G. P. Folts amounting to over $3,000, and $1,000 from the Remington estate for our Permanent Scholarship Fund. This fund now amounts to $6,800. We want to make it $50,000.

The work done in the school last year was better than might be expected under the circumstances, and a class of sixteen was graduated. This year we have had, for the first quarter, an enrollment of thirty-five; of these, five are residents of Herkimer, and thirty are regular boarding students. Ten States are represented, and we have six foreign students; also a missionary's daughter from India and one from Japan. We consider the foreign students a great help and blessing to our school. They are almost without exception among our most spiritual girls. They are earnest, diligent, and appreciative of the comforts and influences of the school, but always looking forward to work among and for their own people.

There are among our number girls from other denominations; one from the Dutch Reform, two from the Presbyterian, and one from the Baptist. Thirteen of our girls are Student Volunteers. Home life at the Institute is ideal; each member courteous, cheerful, industrious, and thankful. Our aim is not to produce weaklings, but stalwart Christians, physically, mentally, and spiritually strong. Special attention is given to health and to health exercises.

Our course of study comprises two schools: the Bible School and the Kindergarten Training-school, each of which requires two years to complete the course. In the Bible School one year is given to each of the following subjects: Old Testament, New Testament, Comparative Religions, Church History and History of Missions, Religious Pedagogy and Applied Christianity, Bookkeeping, Domestic Arts, and Domestic Science; also the following subjects, which are in common with the kindergartners: Psychology, Elocution, and Physical Culture. Lectures are given on Sociology.

The work done in the Kindergarten Training-school is an accredited course in the State of New York, and includes also, one year of study in the New Testament. The students do practice work in the kindergarten.

In the Old Testament, a careful study is made of the historical and poetical books, and the prophecies are studied exegetically. Some attention has also been given to criticism, but not to such an alarming extent as has by some been supposed. A course of lectures is given on the Pentateuch. The New Testament study comprehends the geography of Bible lands; a brief history of the period from the exile to the advent; the harmony of the four Gospels, giving the life and teachings of Jesus; the history of the Apostolic Church, recorded in the book of Acts, and a careful exegesis of the principal epistles.

Careful attention is given to the individual Christian experience of each and every girl. We want them to know God and Jesus Christ, whom He hath sent. Lectures are given upon the "Attributes of God," the "Mission of Jesus," the "Baptism of the Holy Spirit," and the "Great Commission."

Under this department a club for working girls has been organized, and the girls themselves have requested that the purpose of the club might be to study the Bible. In the class in Religious Pedagogy we also take up the work of the evangelist, the Bible School in all of its departments, the Epworth League, the Junior League, the Woman's Foreign Missionary Society, and all the important phases of Church work. We also study the Discipline, the history of Methodism, and the polity and doctrines of our Church.

From this brief and hurried outline of a part of our course of study you may get some idea of the character of the work which we are doing. The school has great possibilities. Will you help us to measure up to these possibilities? Stand by us; believe in us; pray for us; work with us. Not only send out the girls which we have trained, but send us girls for training.

Bishop Oldham writes, "The very best thing I can say about Folts

Institute is this: The product is eminently satisfactory. The young women you are sending to my mission fields are well trained and of the right spirit. I feel safe about the new missionary when she is from you. Send us many more."

MRS. A. E. SANFORD, *President.*

The following were nominated for Directors of Folts Institute: Directors whose term expires January, 1908: Mrs. S. L. Baldwin, Brooklyn, N. Y.; Rev. Wm. D. Marsh, Little Falls, N. Y; Miss Louise M. Hodgkins, Wilbraham, Mass.; Miss Mary E. Holt, Boston, Mass.; Charles S. Millington, Herkimer, N. Y.; George R. Blount, Lacona, N. Y.; also Bishop Daniel A. Goodsell for vacancy caused by death of Bishop Andrews, whose term would have expired 1910.

YOUNG PEOPLE'S SUPERINTENDENTS.

The Conference of Young People's Superintendents, assembled during the Executive session of the Woman's Foreign Missionary Society, meeting at Cincinnati, wish to present the following recommendations:

1. The adoption of a financial age limit, all from fourteen years to twenty-one years of age, inclusive, paying 60 cents a year, and all over twenty-one paying $1.00 a year. Adopted.

2. That organizations known as Young Woman's Foreign Missionary Societies, even when paying $1.00 dues, shall be reported as Young People's Work. Adopted.

3. That the dues of the Young Woman's Foreign Missionary Societies and the Standard Bearer Companies be devoted exclusively to the support of the young people's missionaries, and that in order to stimulate the interest of these societies as speedily as possible, a missionary be assigned for support to the young people of one or more Conferences. Adopted.

4. That wherever possible a Field Secretary or Organizer of Young People's Work be employed by each Branch. No action taken.

5. That we use uniform report blanks, to be published by our General Publishing Office. Adopted.

6. That the young people's societies be asked to pay a sum equal to 5 cents a year per member to the Branch Contingent Fund. Adopted.

7. That each Auxiliary appoint a Supervisor of Young People's Work. Adopted.

8. That each Branch instruct its depot of supplies to furnish to Superintendents and Organizers of Young People's Work, free, a definite allowance of leaflets, other than free literature, suitable for inaugurating new work or instructing young organizations. Adopted.

9. That as the interests of the Young People's Work seem to demand a larger consideration, we be granted four columns in the *Woman's Missionary Friend* for the use of the Young People's Department. Referred to the Home Department.

COMMITTEE ON RETIRED MISSIONARIES.

To the General Executive Committee:

Dear Sisters: The members of your Committee on Retired Missionaries have sought information from Missionary Societies of other than Methodist denomination in this country and in England, concerning their provision for retired missionaries.

The question before the Committee and before the Woman's Foreign Missionary Society is, Should women sent to the foreign fields to do the work to which every woman in the Church, by her profession of faith in Jesus, is committed, be merely provided with a bare living while they are doing that work, and be left to shift for themselves when sickness and the burden of years come on, or, shall the great sisterhood who stay at home amid the blessings which Christian civilization brings, take care of these women while they work and when they are worn out because of the work?

The plan presented by the Committee is to raise a "retirement fund" from the one dollar membership dues of Woman's Foreign Missionary Society women. One cent out of each dollar thus paid would, if cautiously handled, soon create a fund sufficient to provide for all our worn-out missionary sisters while they wait for the final "well done."

This fund, when established, will without doubt be increased from time to time by gifts and bequests. One such gift has already been reported, and is now drawing interest awaiting the adoption of a perfected plan.

It is not, however, right for us to commit our sacred obligations to our ordained missionary representatives, to the chance fulfillment of occasional gifts. The sources of the fund should be regular and permanent, as well as occasional and sympathetic. It should be administered with the greatest care and skill.

1. RETIREMENT FUND COMMITTEE.—We recommend that a special committee of five members be appointed by the Foreign Department, one of whom shall be the Treasurer of the Woman's Foreign Missionary Society, and also the Treasurer of the Retirement Fund, to be called the Retirement Fund Committee, said Committee to be authorized to take charge in full and in detail of the administration of the retirement fund for missionaries, as herein provided.

2. HOW TO CREATE THE FUND.—We recommend that each Branch make an appropriation of one cent per Auxiliary member; this amount to be paid annually to the Treasurer of the Woman's Foreign Missionary Society, on the first day of May.

The Retirement Fund Committee should be authorized to receive gifts or bequests for this special work. The Retirement Fund Committee should also be authorized to receive and invest appropriations, gifts, bequests, and to disburse the moneys thus gathered, to the persons retired by the Foreign Department. The Foreign Department should be the authority which retires, and the Retirement Fund Committee should execute the decisions of the Foreign Department.

CONCLUSIONS.

We offer certain conclusions from our study of the subject:

1. NO DIVISION OF RESPONSIBILITY.—We think any division of authority or responsibility might be unfair to the Branches and to the persons receiving or entitled to receive pensions. The tendency of a separation of interests is not good for the general work. Bear ye one another's burdens.

2. RETIREMENT ON HALF PAY.—We do not approve retirement on half pay. The pay of missionaries differs in different countries. The expense for maintenance in this country would presumably be uniform.

3. UNIFORM AGE.—We do not approve retirement at a uniform age. Some women "break" at an earlier age than others. Some women are more useful to the work on the foreign field, even though somewhat worn, than are other women in better health.

4. EACH CASE ON ITS MERITS.—We believe each case of retirement should be acted on by the Foreign Department on its own merits.

5. UNIFORM PENSION.—We do not approve of a uniform pension for all retired missionaries. A woman who breaks down after five years' service should not (other things being equal) receive as large a pension as one who has given her life to the service.

6. THE MISSIONARY BENEFIT ASSOCIATION.—It is possible that the Retirement Fund Committee could represent the interests of the missionaries who have already paid their money into the Missionary Benefit Association. There may or may not be money left in that fund to pay back to the depositors, when the Woman's Foreign Missionary Society Fund becomes available. These are matters of detail. The vital question is, Shall the great Woman's Foreign Missionary Society take care of its workers when they become worn out in the service, or shall they be left to shift for themselves, unless the chariot and the horses translate them in their labors as Miss Thoburn and Dr. Tuttle were translated.

MRS. CYRUS D. FOSS, Chairman Ex-officio.
ELISABETH F. PIERCE, Chairman.

REPORT REGARDING THE ADJUSTMENT OF THE GERMAN AND SCANDINAVIAN WORK.

Each foreign-speaking Conference may report to the one Branch with which it is most closely affiliated.

This plan results in the following Conference assignments:

GERMAN.

California German Conference..........................Pacific Branch.
Central German Conference........................Cincinnati Branch.
Chicago German Conference......................Northwestern Branch.
Northern German Conference.....................,.........Minneapolis Branch.
Northwestern German Conference.................Des Moines Branch.
Eastern German Conference........................New York Branch.
Pacific German Conference.....................·............Columbia River Branch.
St. Louis German Conference.........·..............Des Moines Branch.
Southern German Conference...........................Topeka Branch.
Western German Conference............·.....................Topeka Branch.

SCANDINAVIAN.

Northern Swedish Conference......................Minneapolis Branch.
Western Swedish Conference...........·.................Topeka Branch.
Central Swedish Conference......................Northwestern Branch.
Eastern Swedish Conference.......................New England Branch.
North Danish-Swedish Conference..................Minneapolis Branch.

The two Swedish Districts on the Pacific Coast to be arranged by Mrs. Fisher and Mrs. Johnson.

HOME WORK.

BRANCH OFFICERS.

I. NEW ENGLAND BRANCH.

NEW ENGLAND STATES.

President—Mrs. John Legg, 5 Claremont St., Worcester, Mass.
Corresponding Secretary—Miss Mary E. Holt, 4 Berwick Park, Boston, Mass.
Associate Secretary—Miss Clementina Butler, Newton Center, Mass.
Recording Secretary—Mrs. A. H. Nazarian, Chelsea, Mass.
Treasurer—Mrs. B. T. Williston, 3 Monmouth St., Somerville, Mass.

II. NEW YORK BRANCH.

NEW YORK AND NEW JERSEY.

President—Mrs. S. L. Baldwin, 1218 Pacific St., Brooklyn, N. Y.
Corresponding Secretary—Mrs. J. M. Cornell, Seabright, N. J.
Assistant Corresponding Secretary—Miss W. R. Lewis, 83 West Washington Place, New York City.
Associate Secretary—Mrs. Henry Waters, Scarsdale, N. Y.
Recording Secretary—Mrs. J. H. Knowles, Room 401, 150 Fifth Ave., New York City.
Treasurer—Mrs. J. Sumner Stone, 155 Pelham Road, New Rochelle, N. Y.
Secretary of Special Work—Mrs. Alfred I. Preston, 616 Nostrand Ave., Brooklyn, N. Y.

III. PHILADELPHIA BRANCH.

PENNSYLVANIA AND DELAWARE.

President—Miss Susan E. Lodge, 1720 Arch St., Philadelphia, Pa.
Corresponding Secretary—Miss Carrie J. Carnahan, Shady Ave. and Walnut St., Pittsburg, Pa.
Associate Secretary—Miss Emma A. Fowler, 722 N. Beatty St., East Pittsburg, Pa.
Recording Secretary—Mrs. Amos Wakelin, 200 Bullitt Building, Philadelphia, Pa.
Treasurer—Mrs. T. H. Wilson, Lawnhurst, Fox Chase, Philadelphia, Pa.

IV. BALTIMORE BRANCH.

MARYLAND, DISTRICT OF COLUMBIA, VIRGINIA, NORTH CAROLINA, SOUTH CAROLINA, GEORGIA, AND FLORIDA.

President—Mrs. A. H. Eaton, 807 Arlington Ave., Baltimore, Md.
Corresponding Secretary Emeritus—Mrs. E. B. Stevens, Baltimore, Md.

Corresponding Secretary—Mrs. E. D. Huntley, "The Portner," Washington, D. C.

Associate Secretary—Mrs. John T. King, 1425 Eutaw Place, Baltimore, Maryland.

Recording Secretary—Mrs. D. C. Morgan, Bloomingdale Road, S. Walbrook, Baltimore, Md.

Treasurer—Mrs. J. S. Rawlings, 206 Woodlawn Road, Roland Park, Md.

V. CINCINNATI BRANCH.

OHIO, WEST VIRGINIA, KENTUCKY, TENNESSEE, ALABAMA, AND MISSISSIPPI.

President Emeritus—Mrs. Wm. B. Davis, Clifton, Cincinnati, O.

President—Mrs. A. J. Clarke, 925 Main St., Wheeling, W. Va.

Corresponding Secretary Emeritus—Mrs. B. R. Cowen, Walnut Hills, Cincinnati, O.

Corresponding Secretary—Mrs. R. L. Thomas, 792 East McMillan St., Cincinnati, O.

Associate Secretary—Mrs. J. Ellington McGee, Pleasant Ridge, O.

Recording Secretary—Mrs. L. L. Townley, 237 Burns Ave., Wyoming, O.

Treasurer—Mrs. J. C. Kunz, 511 Broadway, Cincinnati, O.

VI. NORTHWESTERN BRANCH.

ILLINOIS, INDIANA, MICHIGAN, AND WISCONSIN.

President Emeritus—Mrs. Isaac R. Hitt, Washington, D. C.

President—Mrs. A. W. Patten, 616 Foster St., Evanston, Ill.

Corresponding Secretary—Mrs. Frank P. Crandon, 1414 Forest Ave., Evanston, Ill.

Assistant Corresponding Secretary—Mrs. Frank T. Kuhl, 800 S. 7th St., Springfield, Ill.

Associate Secretary—Mrs. Charles W. Fowler, 208 Fremont St., Chicago, Ill.

Recording Secretary—Mrs. L. H. Jennings, 2311 Kenmore Ave., Chicago, Ill.

Treasurer—Mrs. J. B. Inman, 310 S. State St., Springfield, Ill.

VII. DES MOINES BRANCH.

IOWA, MISSOURI, ARKANSAS, AND LOUISIANA.

President—Miss Elizabeth Pearson, 1100 High St., Des Moines, Ia.

Corresponding Secretary—Mrs. William B. Thompson, 1018 Des Moines St., Des Moines, Ia.

Associate Secretary—Miss May Villa Patten, 406 Iowa Ave., Muscatine, Ia.

Recording Secretary—Mrs. J. I. Compton, 400 Wabash Ave., Kansas City, Mo.

Treasurer Emeritus—Mrs. E. K. Stanley, 627 Fortieth St., Des Moines, Ia.

Treasurer—Mrs. W. H. Arnold, 1032 West Twentieth St., Des Moines, Ia.

Secretary of Special Work—Miss Kate E. Moss, 3145 Olive St., Kansas City, Mo.

VIII. MINNEAPOLIS BRANCH.

MINNESOTA, NORTH DAKOTA, AND SOUTH DAKOTA.

President—Mrs. C. N. Stowers, 3448 Emerson Ave., South Minneapolis, Minn.
Corresponding Secretary Emeritus—Mrs. C. S. Winchell, 113 State St., Minneapolis, Minn.
Corresponding Secretary—Mrs. F. F. Lindsay, 25 Seymour Ave., S. E., Minneapolis, Minn.
Recording Secretary—Mrs. A. J. Thorne, 628 Eighth Ave., S. E., Minneapolis, Minn.
Treasurer—Mrs. C. W. Hall, 3206 Second Ave., S., Minneapolis, Minn.

IX. TOPEKA BRANCH.

KANSAS, NEBRASKA, COLORADO, WYOMING, UTAH, NEW MEXICO, OKLAHOMA, AND TEXAS.

President—Mrs. Emma A. Imboden, 215 North Emporia Ave., Wichita, Kan.
Corresponding Secretary—Miss Ella M. Watson, 1701 South Seventeenth St., Lincoln, Neb.
Recording Secretary—Mrs. Mary M. Torrington, 203 Clay St., Topeka, Kan.
Treasurer—Mrs. I. E. McEntire, 704 Taylor St., Topeka, Kan.

X. PACIFIC BRANCH.

CALIFORNIA, NEVADA, ARIZONA, AND HAWAII.

President—Mrs. George B. Smyth, 2605 Hearst Ave., Berkeley, Cal.
Corresponding Secretary—Mrs. S. F. Johnson, 520 Oakland Ave., Pasadena, Cal.
Assistant Corresponding Secretary—Mrs. Charlotte O'Neal, 1460 N. Marengo Ave., Pasadena, Cal.
Associate Secretary—Mrs. Belle F. Anderson, Box 67, Dolgeville, Cal.
Recording Secretary—Mrs. J. R. Umsted, 3036 Hoover St., Los Angeles, Cal.
Treasurer—Mrs. Z. L. Parmelee, South Pasadena, Cal.

XI. COLUMBIA RIVER BRANCH.

MONTANA, IDAHO, WASHINGTON, AND OREGON.

President—Mrs. M. C. Wire, 205 W. Tenth St., Eugene, Ore.
Corresponding Secretary—Mrs. A. N. Fisher, 214 Twelfth St., Portland, Ore.
Recording Secretary—Mrs. W. H. Saylor, 871 South First St., Portland, Ore.
Treasurer—Miss Nettie M. Whitney, 704 South I St., Tacoma, Wash.

Reports of the Home Work.

NEW ENGLAND BRANCH.

The fact that we have not accomplished all we desired should not blind us to the greater fact that we have done wonderful things, considering the adverse conditions which have prevailed during the past twelve months. Perhaps no part of the country was so severely affected by the panic as New England, with its large manufacturing interests. It would not have been surprising if we had come up with a large deficit, but the fact that we have been able to bring all but $3,500 of the amount appropriated fills our hearts with profound gratitude. While we acknowledge a disappointment that we did not reach the entire amount, we remember that God asks our perfect love and service, and that the increase cometh from Him. For the opening year we have confidence in the Almighty power and will go forth in this strength.

Our anonymous friend has this year again given for buildings for children's educational work, and our treasury is richer by $9,500. We are not able to express to this generous donor our thanks, but acknowledge here our great indebtedness for this help.

During the year our hearts have sympathized with our Recording Secretary, Mrs. A. H. Nazarian, in the trial by fire, which has twice destroyed her home and imperiled the lives of her dear ones.

Mrs. Mary Pomeroy Donaldson, for twenty-seven years a Secretary of the Branch, has been obliged to relinquish her work. For sixteen years she held the position of District Secretary and for the past eleven years that of Conference Secretary of Vermont Conference. To her untiring labors the present prosperity of the work in that State is largely due.

Our Secretary of Young People's Work, Mrs. Stackpole, and Mrs. Stowell, Secretary of Children's Work, have been active during the year maturing plans which, we trust, will work out successfully during the coming twelve months.

The Northfield Summer School of Missions had a larger Methodist registration than ever before, and a most profitable session. An inter-denominational institute, in which the text-book for the coming year was presented, was held in Boston late in the year, and called out a large number of missionary workers, who were privileged to listen to brilliant addresses by the authors, Drs. Zwemer and Brown.

The Report from Silver Bay Conference mentioned several volunteers from our territory.

Our missionaries are continually held before God in our prayers, but particularly have we been touched for Miss Ada Mudge, as she learned in far-away Lucknow that she would see her mother's face no more on earth. Mrs. James Mudge was long a Vice-president of this Branch, and, because of her years of missionary service in India, bore a peculiar relation to the Board, and gave her daughter with gladness to serve in the land of her birth.

In November last we bade Godspeed to Miss Harvey as she sailed for her third term of service in India. She is now stationed at Raipur.

In January, Miss Kneeland was enabled to return to her field of labor in South America, through a special gift from a generous friend.

She is busy looking after the erection of the new school building in Rosario.

Miss Ruddick sailed in February, and on arrival in India resumed her work in Budaon.

In August, Miss Young returned to North China and it is thought that she may be appointed to Fai Au Fu, in the Shantung district.

Miss Nichols, on account of ill-health, has returned home. We regret that she may be unable to take up again her work in the Isabella Thoburn College, where she has been such a faithful leader since the death of Miss Thoburn. A reception was tendered to her and Miss Singh in Jacob Sleeper Hall, Boston University, which was largely attended.

Miss Knowles still remains in the homeland, but her heart is in India.

The remaining members of our missionary family are pushing their work in their respective fields, and faithfully holding aloft the banner of the Savior of the world.

Our annual meeting was one of the best in our history and was full of inspiration, notwithstanding the deficit reported and a decrease in membership being noted. A few days after this meeting came the news of the translation of our Corresponding Secretary Emeritus, Mrs. Lucy A. Alderman. For twenty-five years she led our forces and prevailed with God in prayer, for the work committed to us. During the past six years, in great feebleness of body, she has awaited her Master's call, and we are sure that His "well done" greeted her as she entered the Heavenly mansion. We thank God for her life of devoted service.

MARY E. HOLT, *Corresponding Secretary.*

TREASURER'S REPORT.

Balance, October 1, 1907.................................... $23,995 26
Total receipts 53,487 18

Grand total $77,482 44
Total disbursements 64,845 92

$12,636 52
Transfer of Annuity Funds 1,694 70

Balance, October 1, 1908.................................. $10,941 82

BELLE A. WILLISTON, *Treasurer.*

NEW YORK BRANCH.

The future looked dark to us of the New York Branch when we separated at Springfield a year ago. Word had come of the failure of the bank in which we had just deposited the ingatherings of fourth quarter, to meet the foreign remittance, of over $20,000.

We were enheartened by the ready sympathy, the strong sense of united interest that moved the General Executive Committee, at its closing session, to authorize the Treasurer to borrow the needed sum on a note of the Woman's Foreign Missionary Society. The financial panic proved more serious than we had thought—we found it impossible to borrow from any bank. Even the Treasurer of the Board of Foreign Missions could not aid us; our checks were coming in from the foreign field, and one or two were protested before we could gather funds to meet them, but the representatives of the foreign banks realized the solvency of the Society and gave us time.

Then our sisters farther West came to our help. Northwestern Branch loaned us $6,000 from their own treasury; Columbia River offered us help from their invested funds; we borrowed from members of our own Branch $5,500, and a few small gifts came from individuals scattered through several of the Branches. We wrote, and talked, and worked, and prayed, and as a result over $6,000 has come into the Branch treasury, during the year, for this special emergency. We have paid every dollar of our appropriation for regular work and almost all of our Thank-offering pledges.

Our Treasurer, Mrs. Stone, has done valiantly throughout the whole trying year, showing quick wit and fertility of resource in meeting sudden emergencies. When she balanced the figures for the current year and found a deficit of over $1,700, she brought it to the Annual Meeting with strong faith and purpose, that it should be raised before the close of the session, and her faith and work were honored, making our receipts for this year of panic a little greater than ever before. Knickerbocker Trust Co. has resumed payment and has paid $4,800 up to the present, and will eventually pay the whole amount. With the Psalmist we sing, "I was brought low, and He helped me. Return unto thy rest, O my soul; for the Lord hath dealt bountifully with thee."

The year has brought us a great sorrow in the death of Mrs. J. T. Gracey. Although closely associated with many of the larger interests of the general work of missions, she found time to serve as a Conference Secretary, and for twenty-three years was the leader of Genesee Conference. As a tribute of love, and in recognition of her labors in opening the work in Sitapur, India, Genesee Conference had given to the missionary Home built by them in that place, the name of Annie Ryder Gracey. We are glad that Mrs. Gracey knew of this expression of the love of her friends before she went to her heavenly home.

Our hearts were saddened by the news, early in January, of the death of Miss Kate O. Curts, of Godhra, India. She carried heavy responsibility in the great boarding school at Godhra, but was always faithful and cheerful, happy in the belief that she was where God would have her be.

Of our missionaries, Miss Lula Miller, of Korea, and Miss Phebe Wells, of Foochow, refreshed by their sojourn at home among friends, have returned to their fields of labor. Mrs Robert Sharp who, as Miss Alice Hammond, went first to Korea in 1900, sailed with Miss Miller in August. Miss Henrietta Robbins reached New York last December for her furlough, and plans to be back in Pyeng Yang again for her December classes. Miss Gheer, of South Japan; Miss Travis, of Foochow, and Miss Moyer, of Bengal, tarry with us a little longer. Miss Alethea Tracy, a candidate accepted last year, but delayed because of the condition of our treasury, is to sail for Central China within a few weeks.

After a few months of arduous work in Foochow, Miss Plumb was ordered home by her physician, and since her return has been in the sanitarium at Clifton Springs. She is slowly recovering and hopes to be able to go again to her China home. Our beloved Annie Budden, so long and so faithfully associated with the work at Pithoragarh, has been obliged to give up her labors for a season, owing to a serious break in health. She is taking her rest in Naini Tal, where we hope she will find the strength she needs, to return to the women to whom she has devoted her life. We are glad to have with us for the coming year, Miss Christina Lawson, of India; Miss Weaver, of Japan, and Dr. Carleton, of China, all of whom have returned within a few weeks.

Realizing our responsibility to Malaysia and not having found the promised teacher within the boundaries of New York Branch, we have adopted Miss Jessie Brooks, who went out from the Minneapolis Branch last year, and is in charge of the school in Malacca.

Interest and enthusiasm have been aroused by our Field Secretary, Miss Queal, and other speakers. We are indebted to Miss Clara Cushman, Mrs. John Springer, Mrs. Homer Stuntz, Miss Grace Todd, and to our own missionaries for 1,478 new members and for $3,950 in money. The Secretary of our Home Department, Miss Lewis, has visited many Auxiliary and District meetings, telling them what her eyes had seen on the mission field, inspiring them with the enthusiasm awakened in her own heart, by the noble deeds of our workers and the successes of our work.

The question is often asked, Does Special Work pay? New York Branch is constrained to say that it does. In the year just closed gifts amounting to $34,920 have gone out through the channels of Special Work. Who can estimate the inspiration and enthusiasm created by the close touch, one with another, the friendly interest, and the heartfelt prayers for the object of care—of Bible women and orphaned children, for their friend. Thirty-seven new orphans and scholarships add to the record for this year, besides Bible women, shares in hospital and leper work, and in hospital beds.

The Literature Department, because of the protracted illness of its Secretary, has been for two years without a Secretary. Without her to suggest and inspire, the work has suffered, and much less literature has been sold during the past year than during the preceding year. In the election of Mrs. Robert J. Cole to the office of Branch Secretary of Literature, we feel encouraged to believe that we have found the right woman to be Mrs. Turner's successor. Mrs. Cole has shown marked ability in taking hold of the work. She believes that enthusiasm for missions must come through comprehension of the subject, and that comprehension must come largely through our literature.

The young women reported 297 societies, with an estimated membership of 7,628, a loss of thirteen organizations and 551 members—on the whole a healthy loss, for nearly all were those which had a name to live, but were dead. One loss is gladly noted, that of "Avon" Young Woman's Society, which voluntarily became an Auxiliary. About five hundred letters from missionaries have been distributed, speaking to thousands of young women. Numerous boxes have been sent out, bringing joy to many in far-off lands. Miss Hughes writes of the ministry of dolls, and Dr. Li of the uplift given by clean bandages and soap.

The Young People's Department feels the need of field workers and urgently wishes there might be a young woman whose sole business it would be to itinerate among the Churches in the interests of this department. There seems to be a clearer conviction of duty on the part of the officers, a greater responsibility, and a smoother working of the machinery. The Conference and District Superintendents are becoming trained leaders. Most of them are taking a vital interest in their work.

Twenty-one Methodist young women registered at the Northfield Summer School, among them girls whose hearts had only recently been opened to their privileges in this work for missions. They went home with a new vision of their opportunities, and with a holy purpose to do what they might for missions.

The report of the Children's Work shows an increase in members and in interest. As in the Young Women's Department, the lack of leaders is sadly felt, and an appeal is made to members of Auxiliaries to-show a deeper concern for the children, who are willing and eager to be led.

The Branch Annual Meeting was beautifully entertained by the Newark Conference. All the arrangements were admirably planned and carried out, to the comfort and pleasure of the delegates. We were fortunate in having with us Miss Lilavati Singh, of Lucknow, who addressed the young women at their rally. Because of the financial strain of the year, the Treasurer's report was awaited with intense interest. When Mrs. Stone gave the figures and we knew that the year's appropriations had been met, joy filled all hearts. The sense of answered prayer gave added courage, and as the Conferences were called in turn, each Secretary had faith to pledge for the coming year an amount larger than ever given before. May God give to us all zeal and wisdom to meet the demands of the ever-growing work.

SARAH K. CORNELL, *Corresponding Secretary.*

TREASURER'S REPORT.

Balance on hand October 1, 1907.............................. $32 60
Receipts for year closing September 30, 1908.................. 98,456 78

Total $98,489 38
Disbursements for the year 98,489 38

KATE E. STONE, *Treasurer.*

PHILADELPHIA BRANCH.

Some one has said: "The Duke of Wellington's great, characteristic was his imperative sense of duty. If there was a duty for him to perform, nothing on earth in the shape of danger, nor of embarrassment, nor of personal vexation deterred him from immediate acceptance of his lot. To carry on the king's (or queen's) business, to be punctual at every appointment, from taking the field at Waterloo to taking his post at a christening, he looked upon as his duty."

Philadelphia Branch has had many just such faithful workers carrying on the King's business during the past year; yet for the first time in fourteen years we have had a deficit in our Contingent Fund. By the wise forethought of our sainted Mrs. Keen, we had kept a good balance on hand each year, but for several years past great emergencies have arisen, necessitating drawing on this fund. The surplus has now been exhausted and we went to Branch Meeting with a deficit of some $76. A collection quickly wiped out the debt and left a small balance in the treasury. We trust many, during the coming year, will feel moved to raise the fund to its former size.

The panic in the business world has had a strong effect on various localities in our Branch. In many places where heretofore persons had been large givers, now through lack of employment they have had to receive help from their Churches. Nevertheless the work was the Lord's, and where one person could not give, He touched the heart of some other one and the money went into the treasury. We report nearly $2,500 more from Conferences than last year, but we have had no large bequests.

The following missionaries are now in the homeland: Miss Mathilda Spencer, Miss E. Maud Soper, Miss Florence Singer, Miss Anna B. Slate, Miss M. L. Guthapfel, and Dr. R. R. Benn. Miss Guthapfel was

Field Secretary last year, working in many parts of the Branch very successfully. She will serve as Secretary this year also.

Miss Mary E. Williams returned to her work in Baroda last August. She spoke as often as strength would permit when at home, and made friends for Baroda wherever she went. Many other missionaries have spoken within our bounds during the year, giving enlightenment concerning their fields of labor and encouragement for our future undertakings. They were Dr. and Mrs. Headland, Rev. Mr. and Mrs. Rykett, Miss Bonafield, Miss Cushman, Miss Moyer, Dr. and Mrs. Neeld, Mrs. Mary Carr Curtiss, Miss Palacios, Dr. and Mrs. Wright, and Mrs. Titus Lowe. Ten of these spoke at a meeting of the Pittsburg District, which was so full of interest as to be compared to a Branch meeting.

We have had an increase of thirty-eight Auxiliaries and 2,233 members. We long to enlist all the women of Methodism in this blessed work, and our hearts go out in desire to spread the knowledge of our work throughout the most remote parts of our Branch.

We report an increase of 178 subscribers to the *Friend*, and of 308 subscribers to *The Study*. We have not made the desired advance in subscribers to the *Children's Friend*. This work must be laid on the hearts of the mothers. Literature has been more systematically and thoroughly circulated than ever before.

The sales for the past year at the Branch depot of supplies, and Pittsburg Conference, amount to over $1,200. A valuable leaflet, written by Mrs. Daniel Dorchester, Jr., entitled, "How to Make Our Missionary Societies More Efficient," was issued by Pittsburg Conference and successfully used throughout the Branch. We can recommend it to all Branches. About sixteen thousand Thank-offering leaflets were sent out.

To simplify the work of the Home Secretary, a little quarterly paper, styled *The Message*, was started last July, the plan to be tried one year. Its mission is to circulate messages from Branch officers to Auxiliaries. It has met with success and many have expressed the wish that it might become monthly.

We have two young women now ready to go to the foreign field— Miss Helen C. Santee, to Yokohama, and Dr. Minnie Stryker, to Tai-au-fu, China.

Two Auxiliaries in Pittsburg Conference remain on the Honor Roll, for having one hundred or more subscribers to *The Friend*.

The Banner Auxiliary in the Branch in point of membership is at Uniontown, Pittsburg Conference, with an enrollment of over three hundred.

Three District Secretaries in Pittsburg Conference have been compelled to resign—Mrs. Wray Grayson, for twenty-seven years a District Secretary; Miss Mary Hunnings, after twenty-four years' service, and Mrs. Stephen Bayard, after twenty-two years' service. These women have laid the foundations strong and deep, and whatever is built thereon will stand firm.

We have 2 new life patrons; 28 new life members; 23 new life members in the King's Heralds; 8 new ones in the Little Light Bearers.

The Annual Branch Meeting was one of spiritual power. A revival in the Church following the meeting, the minister said, was "partly due to the noble band of women who had prayed in their midst the week before." Seventeen new members for the Woman's Foreign Missionary Society were received the following Sabbath, when Miss Guthapfel spoke. A company of Standard Bearers was organized after the last noon luncheon by Misses Guthapfel and Santee, and named in honor of Miss Santee.

· ·We yearn for the uninterested women in all our Churches and desire
an organization in every Church in the Branch. ·

This year, while we are learning the importance of lifting the Mohammedan women out of their degraded lives and drawing away the
veils of ignorance and superstition from their eyes, may we succeed in
unveiling the eyes of the indifferent women of our own Branch, enabling
them to have a hew vision of the Lord Christ saying to them; "Go preach
My gospel to every creature."

CARRIE J. CARNAHAN, *Corresponding Secretary.*

TREASURER'S REPORT.

Receipts from Conferences. $60,037 42
Annuities 1,000 00
Bequests, special gifts, etc. 1,012 04

Total $62,049 46
Balance, October 1, 1907. . . . ; 10,609 35

Grand total $72,658 81
Disbursements 66,295 54

Balance, October 1, 1908. . . . . $6,363 27

MRS. THOMAS H. WILSON, *Treasurer.*

BALTIMORE BRANCH.

The General Conference of 1908 was held within the bounds of the
Baltimore Branch.. Only the memory remains with us. The first ten
days seemed like one grand missionary convention. The reports given
by our General Superintendents, and the educational feature of the Exhibit, must bring forth much fruit.

The meeting of the Reference Committee, with "open doors," was
greatly appreciated by visitors. Money came to the Woman's Foreign
Missionary Society because of it. Cincinnati Branch is $1,000 richer be-
cause of this new order.

The work of the year has been good. While no large gifts have
come into our treasury, one friend contributed $450 for our Emergency
Fund; another gave us $100 to furnish a room in the hospital at Pyeng
Yang in memory of a sister; and a daughter sent $100 to furnish a room
at Raipur in memory of a dear mother. No bequests have come to us.
The Magaw property is still in the hands of the court. A decision is expected in November. We are hoping that this gift can be available in
the near future. ·

.Mrs. E. B. Stevens, our Secretary Emeritus, has given much time
and strength to our work, since her return from the Orient. The scenes
of India's needs are vividly pictured by her as she leads you from the
North to the South of that great empire. The delegates and guests at
the General Conference answered many calls to speak at Sunday services
and prayer-meetings. Early in the year Miss Guthapfel gave us two addresses replete with startling facts. Miss Bonafield, Miss Ruby Sia,
and Miss Mae Carlton were present at our Annual Meeting, representing
their beloved China. They seem like our very own. Miss Ruby Sia was

educated on a scholarship supported by one of our Baltimore children's bands. They can well be proud of this talented Chinese girl. Mrs. F. F. Hathaway brought us tidings from Rome, and Miss Elizabeth Goucher encouraging reports from Japan. At all of these places we need new buildings, more scholarships, better equipment, and more missionaries.

The working force of our young people has been a factor in our financial increase, and the membership roll of Little Light Bearers far outnumbers that of any previous year. Fifteen names of Little Light Bearers grace the roll of life members.

The serious illness of our Home Secretary, Mrs. S. A. Hill, has compelled her to lay aside all work for at least a year, and it is with genuine regret that we eliminate her name from our list of officers.

Mrs. J. S. Barnard, our Secretary for St. John's River Conference, Fla., has removed to Rochester, N. Y. She will be greatly missed, as well as her husband, Dr. Barnard, who has been for many years a warm friend of our Woman's Foreign Missionary Society.

Death and removals have greatly weakened our working forces, and new hands must assume responsibilities that have been carried so successfully during the past years. The Lord's message to Joshua is one that we need for these new workers, "Be strong and of a good courage; be not afraid, neither be thou dismayed: for the Lord thy God is with thee whithersoever thou goest."

Our constituents have been represented at Northfield, Silver Bay, and Mountain Lake Park. Fine collections were taken at Summit Grove, Mountain Lake Park, and Washington Grove. The work is hard, but results are good. More literature has been sold in the Branch than in any previous year. The study classes are starting with a larger enrollment and a promise of fine work. *The Baltimore Methodist*, our Church paper for this section, has given us a page in their paper every other week, and in many ways assisted in our work. Our membership, while not large, is slowly gaining. The work for the year has been marked by many signs of progress. Support of special work by individuals has increased. At each Branch, Quarterly and Annual Meeting, many patrons have assumed special work.

Baltimore Branch is very happy to present to the Executive this year the papers of two of the four candidates who have knocked at our doors —young, gifted, consecrated girls, desiring work on the foreign field. Both are contemplating further preparation before accepting a place among our workers.

Mrs. Susan A. Tippet is still in California seeking health. She does not lose courage and hopes some day to return to her beloved China. She says: "I am trying to keep a cheery face, so that by my daily life I may be helpful to those with whom I come in contact. I am learning many lessons that will be helpful to me when I return to China. Chief among them is, not to worry, but to cast away every care upon Him, the great burden bearer." Fourteen missionary boxes and thirty-eight magazines have found their way to the homes of our missionaries.

The letters from our missionaries on the foreign field have been helpful factors in keeping our people informed and interested. While we regret that it is necessary to impose this added burden on our missionaries, we would voice our thanks to them for the many messages that have come to us through these patron letters.

Respectfully submitted,
AMELIA H. HUNTLEY, *Corresponding Secretary.*

TREASURER'S REPORT.

Balance, October, 1907................................... $4,592 73
Receipts for year closing 1908.......................... 21,751 41

Total $26,344 14
Disbursements 23,415 70

Balance, October, 1908................................. $2,928 44
Contingent included in the above.

MRS. J. S. RAWLINGS, *Treasurer.*

CINCINNATI BRANCH.

"Praise ye the Lord; praise Him for His mighty acts."

This has been one of the difficult years for Cincinnati Branch. We began with a deficit, and it has continued all the way through, but our tried and true women have been heroic in their efforts to meet all obligations, and the record shows several thousand dollars increase from regular sources, all regular appropriations met, emergency calls which have severely taxed our treasury answered, three new missionaries in the field, and the debt decreased nearly two-thirds.

There has been a healthy growth everywhere save in the subscriptions to the *Woman's Missionary Friend,* where there is a decrease of fifty-eight. This we deplore, and promise to do better.

We have been favored by having the headquarters of the Young People's Work, with its General Secretary, Miss Winifred Spaulding, located in Cincinnati. Miss Spaulding has been of great help to the new Superintendent of Young People's Work, Miss Mary I. Scott, in her endeavors to promote the interests of the work. We have 115 Young Woman's Societies, with a membership of 1,073, and 77 Standard Bearer companies, with a membership of 2,923, giving us a total membership of 3,996—an increase of 33 organizations this year.

A great advance has also been made in the children's work. They have an increase of 48 societies and 910 members, and an increase of 685 subscriptions to the *Children's Missionary Friend,* and 51 Life Members. They have paid Miss Marker's salary in full, and have more than doubled their Thank-offering. This is all due to the earnest efforts and increasing enthusiasm of the Superintendent of Children's Work, Mrs. Lena Leonard Fisher. Conference and District Superintendents have been quite generally appointed in both the Children's and Young People's Work.

The new Secretary of Special Work, Mrs. Emma Moore Scott, found it impossible to retain the office, and was succeeded by Miss Cora Haines, who has faithfully endeavored to supply all Auxiliaries desiring special work with a satisfactory beneficiary.

The Home Secretary, Mrs. J. E. McGee, has been inventive in her endeavors to further the interests of the Branch. Two new Field Secretaries have been secured, a College Department inaugurated, an Honor Roll for Churches having the four organizations—Auxiliary, Young Woman's, King's Heralds, Little Light Bearers—established, and a "Workers' Council," held at Annual Meeting, where all Branch difficulties were faced; and large plans for the new year were considered, the most important of which was the doubling of the membership, a Christmas offering to equip and send a new missionary to Lucknow, and our Ruby Anniversary—the fortieth of our Branch history.

The receipts from the office sales amounted to $1,700,.with a profit of more than $300.

The reports of the missionaries on the foreign field are full of interest. God has blessed the faithful service of these workers. There have been many changes in our missionary family. Cincinnati Branch has sent during the year, Miss Ora May Tuttle to Kong Ju, Korea; Miss Daisy Byron Sutton and Adella M. Ashbaugh to Nagasaki, and Miss Paula Seidlmann to Sieng Iu, China, and returned to their respective fields, Misses Lucy Sullivan, Luella R. Anderson, and Mary Hillman. We have welcomed eight missionaries home for rest and recuperation of health—Misses Hardie, Bonafield, Blair, Alexander, Wisner, Edmunds, Galbreath, and Mrs. Eddy. Miss Frances Scott will return to India early in November, and Miss Leonora Seeds will return to Japan as soon as her health permits. Early in September, Miss Margaret Edmunds was married to Rev. Wm. Butler Harrison, of the Presbyterian Board, and Miss Bessie Galbreath returns to marry Rev. W. F. Clark.

Our work was well represented at all the camp-meetings and Annual Conferences. The Annual Meeting in Columbus was largely attended and enthusiastic. For the first time our new President, Mrs. A. J. Clarke, presided. The meeting will long be remembered for its spiritual power, its unusually large congregations, its enthusiastic children's and Standard Bearers' meetings, and the presence of six of our own missionaries, and Miss Lilavati Singh, of the Northwestern Branch, Dr. Stephens, of Poona, Mrs. Emma Moore Scott, and Dr. Freese and wife, of the Board of Foreign Missions.

Several special gifts and three bequests have helped the treasury. The bequest of Miss Lillian Gamble for $5,000 was given to the General Fund; a bequest of $100 was given to the Sarah E. Creighton Hospital in Brindiban; and there was also one of $210.05 from Mrs. Martha H. Brakefield, and one of $250 from the estate of Mrs. Stockton. The special gifts were as follows: from Mrs. A. J. Clarke, $1,000 for the salaries of Misses Russell and Leonora Seeds; $100 to Dr. Hu King Eng's hospital; $100 for painting the Nagasaki property, and the half salary of Miss Ashbaugh.

Mrs. Wm. A. Gamble, $1,000 for land in Tsicheo; $200 for school house in Kong Ju; $150 for painting the Chemulpo Home and for painting the Nagasaki property.

From Miss Hettie List: $300 for painting the Nagasaki property; $100 for Dr. Hu King Eng's hospital.

The total receipts are $84,227.31, gathered by 30,145 women, young ladies, and children in 1,091 organizations.

We enter the new year with increased courage and the conviction that the Lord, who commanded, "Go ye," will be with us, supplying all our needs. MRS. R. L. THOMAS, *Corresponding Secretary.*

TREASURER'S REPORT.

Balance on hand (Special Fund), October 9, 1907 .... $5,855 25
Total receipts 92,227 31

Grand total $98,082 56
Total disbursement 98,082 56

Deficit (Special Fund).. .... $2,050 00

NORTHWESTERN BRANCH.

A study of the statistical record of the past year shows a steady growth in all departments of the home side. The decrease of Auxiliaries in South Germany and Switzerland cause a decrease in total Auxiliary memberships, but there has been a gain of a thousand members in the Conferences in this country. The total number of organizations is 2,269, and the membership nearly 60,000.

Our Young Woman's and Standard Bearers' Societies are increasing, and the ever multiplying Mission Study Classes among the young people are creating an enthusiasm we have long needed. Mrs. D. C. Cook, our efficient Branch Superintendent, will continue her wise leadership another year.

The Secretary of our College Department, Mrs. Herben, is working to touch our Methodist young women in the colleges, to the end that they maykbe of service in the foreign field, or leaders in the home side of our wor .

The children have been doing a beautiful work under the supervision of Mrs. W. C. Whitcomb. The reports with the attractive pictures of Life Members, the letters from their missionary, and the Thank-offering programs have contributed largely to the success attained. We think we can claim the banner Little Light Bearers Circle in Muncie, Indiana, with 300 members, under the leadership of Mrs. Bucklin, and with receipts of $110 for the year. The King's Heralds and Little Light Bearers are 12,850 strong. Young lives being trained for future service in the missionary work of the Church. It pays to work with the children.

Our Special Work is growing, and by the appointment of a Secretary in each Conference we are hoping to bring the patrons into close touch with the missionaries and their work.

The Committee on Literature has again touched a high-water mark, $5,692 being the total receipts of the year, an increase of $1,387. The number of study books sold was 3,405. Mrs. E. W. Burke has given eight years of faithful, hard work to this department, which embraces not only our depot of supplies, but our headquarters. The office is in a splendid condition financially and has employed a Secretary and an assistant, constantly during the year. We have added a telephone, an Oliver typewriter, and a cabinet file to its equipment.

Five new missionaries have been sent to the front this year. Immediately after the meeting of the General Executive Committee, Miss Abbott returned to India and was stationed at the Bowen Church, Bombay. Miss Norberg and Miss Forsythe also sailed for India in November, for their fields in Asansol and Phalera, India.

In January we were glad to send to China two greatly needed physicians: Dr. Manderson to Peking, to reinforce Dr. Gloss, and Dr. Hatfield to Foochow, to be associated with Dr. Lyon.

This Branch has had an unusual number of applicants, first-class young women, college and normal school graduates. The cry from the mission-fields has been so importunate that, at the risk of lessening our gifts for buildings this coming year, we have accepted and appointed six new missionaries. One of these, Miss Thirza Bunce, sailed for Tai Peng, Malaysia, in September. Four others will go next month: Miss Voigt to India, Misses Fonda, Carncross, and Jaquet to China. Miss Muir will wait a little longer before leaving the home land. Others are still awaiting their appointments.

The missionaries on home furlough are Misses Bohannon, Seeds, Swift, Shaw, Singh, Woods, Westcott, Howe, Sarah Peters, Vickery,

Stahl, Heaton, Alling, Fisher, Melton, Martin, Odgers, Dr. Lewis and Dr.
Kahn. Of these Misses Shaw, Alling, Seeds, Heaton, and Dr. Lewis will
return in a few weeks.

. Two important Conferences have been held within the limits of our
Branch: the Summer School of Missions, at Winona Lake, Indiana, un-
der the auspices of the Inter-denominational Committee of Woman's
Boards of the Central West, and the Y. W. C. A. Students' Conference, at
Geneva Lake, Wisconsin. Delegates from our Board were sent to both
of these meetings.

Our Branch Annual Meeting was entertained in a truly royal way at
Danville, Illinois. Seven hundred and fifty ladies were registered, and
the sales of literature were $453—the largest attendance and the largest
sales yet recorded. Miss Gertrude Howe, our veteran missionary, Dr. Ida
Kahn, and Professor Lilavati Singh added greatly to the interest, as did
the presence and words of all the missionaries. This meeting closed a
term of fourteen years of service of our Branch Treasurer, Mrs. B. D.
York, during which she has handled nearly a million and a half of dollars,
and inaugurated many plans for the disbursement of money, which have
been adopted by most of the Branches. We regret to part with her, but
her mantle falls on the shoulders of a worthy and experienced successor,
Mrs. J. B. Inman, of Springfield, Ill.

A new departure was made this year in the election of an Assistant
Corresponding Secretary, who shall share the responsibilities and the blessings that come to every Secretary. Mrs. Frank T. Kuhl, of Springfield,
Ill., has been chosen for this position, a Conference Secretary, who has
led her Conference to double its contributions in the last six years. We
are sure she will prove a valuable addition to our Branch officers.

Our total receipts for the year show a decrease, but this is owing to
the fact that we received no large gifts or bequests.

One of the most prominent and oft-repeated needs of our Home side
of the Branch is that of leaders, particularly in the Young People's and
Children's Departments. To meet the marvelous growth of our work
afar we must have a large increase in our active members at home,
women who will work diligently.

The closing hour of our Branch meeting was a consecration service,
wherein all present consecrated themselves anew, and pledged more faithful service to carry His love to the uttermost parts of the earth.

Mrs. F. P. Crandon, *Corresponding Secretary.*

TREASURER'S REPORT.

Balance in General Fund, October 1, 1907.........$11,117 07
Total receipts for the year........................ 150,585 73

Total $161,702 80
Transferred from Invested Fund.................. 1,700 00

Grand total $163,402 80
Total disbursements for 1907-08................. 153,874 48

Balance in General Fund, October 1, 1908....... $9,528 32

Mrs. Bertrand D. York,
Mrs. Laura C. Dunn,
Treasurers.

DES MOINES BRANCH.

An old song represents gleaners returning from the labor of the day with its varied results. One came "with empty hands and clouded brow," and the question is asked, "Where, O, where hast thou gleaned to-day?"

"All day long 'mid shady bowers
I've gayly sought earth's fairest flowers;
Now, alas, too late, I see
All I have gathered is vanity."

There was another who came "singing along the homeward way." "Glad one, where hast thou gleaned to-day?"

"Stay me not till day is done,
I've gathered handfuls one by one;
Here and there for me they fall:
Close by the reapers I found them all."

The good hand of our God hath been upon us throughout another year. The year's fruitage within our borders is blessed. Heavy appropriations up to a very narrow margin were assumed, but all our need has been supplied.

Our women have wrought with diligence. As the days have passed there have been the earnest efforts of our force of workers in the Auxiliaries, united with those of the missionaries on furlough, and of the District, Conference, and Branch officers, accompanied always by a real expectancy at the hand of God.

How could it be otherwise than that the year's returns should change our prayers to praise, and that the goodness of our God should have a new and precious manifestation to thankful hearts? Our forces are constantly inspired by the courageous faith of our loved Branch President, Miss Elizabeth Pearson, recently elected to her office for the nineteenth time. She is a member of our delegation in this meeting.

However, in the daily plodding toil of the seed-sower and the harvest-gatherer, there is to be found little of material for the making of brilliant reports. Common, every-day faithfulness is so common, yes, thank God, so common! So is the sunshine; so is the rain.

Yet the sweet consciousness of "something attempted, something done," is not the least of the toilers' rewards.

It is gratifying to report the completion of the two building enterprises upon which we have recently been engaged, viz.: the Emma Fuller Girls' School, at Yenping, China, and the Mary A. Knotts School, at Vikarabad, India. Both of these plants are admirably and advantageously situated and are a credit to the Church. It is good to know of the improved housing of these institutions.

Within the year a number of our missionaries have come home for necessary furlough: Misses Lawson, Wells, and Davis, of India; Miss Griffiths, of Japan, and Miss Stockwell, of Burma. A goodly number have gone out, returning in some cases for the third and fourth terms of service—Misses Ogborn, Wilson, Elicker, and Allen, together with two recruits, Misses Liers and Boddy. Soon after the close of this session Misses Griffiths and Bobenhouse will return to the field, and Misses Ankeny and Golisch will go out for the first time. Miss Trimble had the pleasure of attendance upon General Conference as one of the representatives of the Foochow Conference, and has since returned to China.

Some of our dear missionaries have suffered affliction, either personally or among those they love, and one of the delegates who represented our Branch in this meeting a year ago has ceased from her labors—Mrs. J. T. Miller, of Kansas City. She was the faithful and efficient Secretary of her District and an ardent lover of our great work.

Our Branch Quarterly Meetings have become significant occasions. We are too widely scattered over large States to meet in monthly executive sessions, but the one meeting of the quarter is a fine one, sometimes extending over a day and half, even in July.

The Annual Meeting is a great feast, "whither the tribes go up" with joy, returning with faith enlarged and strength renewed. Our recent session was one of our largest, and was the occasion of the sale of four hundred dollars' worth of literature, certainly a good indication of present interest in the work and, at the same time, a pledge of its increase. Each year our President prepares an excellent thank-offering leaflet. As this year celebrates the completion of twenty-five years as a Branch, since we were carved from the old Western Branch, our leaflet was made unusually attractive by its decoration of a string of happy bells.

Our statistics show encouraging increase in our membership and in subscriptions to the *Woman's* and *Children's Missionary Friends,* and our enthusiastic Children's Secretary was able to report one hundred and three little Life Members.

Our more than forty missionaries are our joy. What messages they send us! Through their eyes we see the pitiful, appealing needs of lands that need not the sun in the heavens as they need a Savior from sin. Through their eyes we also see the triumphs of the cross. We see One moving among men. He blesses and breaks the bread as of old; the blind are made to see, the deaf to hear; the lepers are cleansed, and the poor have the gospel preached unto them. And to-day, as of old, the throng by the wayside cry, saying: "Hosanna to the Son of David! Blessed is He that cometh in the name of the Lord! Hosanna in the highest!"

Mrs. Mary T. Thompson, *Corresponding Secretary.*

TREASURER'S REPORT.

Balance, October 1, 1907	$1,437 04
Annuities	1,000 00
Receipts	64,681 39
Total	$67,118 43
Disbursements	67,365 78
Deficit, October 1, 1908	$247 35

Mrs. W. H. Arnold, *Treasurer.*

MINNEAPOLIS BRANCH.

Twenty-five years ago the historic Western Branch, which for thirteen years had sought to keep the banner of the Woman's Foreign Missionary Society aloft in a vast region covering 871,000 square miles, with a population of six millions, died, and in dying gave birth to three beautiful daughters: Des Moines, Topeka, and Minneapolis, who like the fabled hero of old, from their birth sprang fully armed to the conflict.

These three Branches took up the work of the Woman's Foreign Missionary Society anxiously, but with unlimited faith in God, who never fails His children. What was before them of growth and attainment they could not fully see; but, repeating to themselves the divine exhortation,

"Be strong and of good courage; be not afraid, neither be thou dismayed: for the Lord thy God is with thee whithersoever thou goest," they determined to press forward.

"The index finger of time points ever toward progress." Each successive year since their organization has had its trials to record, its blessings and victories to enumerate. Increased resources and larger responsibilities have ever been theirs. The use which they have made of their opportunities tells the story of their faithfulness as stewards.

Minneapolis Branch began her twenty-fifth year encompassed by clouds and darkness. The hand of death had suddenly snatched from her the saintly woman who for six years had been her well-beloved leader. New and untried officers filled her posts of responsibility. A deficit in her treasury equal to one-fifth of her entire income confronted her. But leaning upon the God who delights in giving wisdom and strength to the weak, her faithful women have gone forward with the work entrusted to them.

We rejoice greatly in the fact that, notwithstanding all our losses and difficulties, notwithstanding destructive storms which have swept over our States, totally destroying the crops in many places, God has wonderfully blessed us, and our treasury shows a large increase in the regular receipts over last year. Nineteen hundred dollars has been laid aside as a trust fund toward the permanent endowment of a Carrie W. Joyce Memorial missionary. Nearly $2,000 more has been expended on last year's obligations, leaving us still, however, with a deficit to contend with. The completion and formal opening of the fine, new $12,000 "Mary J. Johnston Memorial Hospital" for the women and children in Manila has been one of the noteworthy events of the season. This investment and that of the purchase of the land site for the erection of the Anna Stone Medical Home in Kiukiang, China, represent our largest financial expenditures. The latter outlay being made possible by the bequest of Mrs. Joyce, who left the Branch $2,000 to be applied on this memorial.

One of the departments which has given us great cause for thankfulness has been that of the Children's Work. Here a splendid interest and growth has taken place. Forty-six new life members and forty-seven new Children's Bands have been added during the year, and next year the children hope to become responsible, alone, for the support of their own missionary.

Thank-offering services were held more generally this year than ever before, and a keener interest and a heartier co-operation on the part of the pastors was manifested.

Our representatives abroad have been kept in health and strength, and the amount and quality of the work accomplished has been most gratifying. Only one of the sixteen has been on furlough, Miss Ada Pugh, of Malacca. She has paid her first visit to America, greatly endearing herself to all who have met her. One new missionary has gone out during the past few weeks, Miss Luella Huelster, under appointment to Central China. Her departure was the result of the generous provision of Bishop and Mrs. Bashford, whom she accompanied. She will spend the year at Nanking acquiring the language. Miss Wilhelmina Erbst, our candidate for the Philippines, is doing acceptable work as an organizer at home.

Our Annual Meeting was in some respects the most notable in our history. For the first time the Conference and District Secretaries were called together for a business session, a day in advance of the regular meeting; many points of vital importance were touched upon. Sixty-seven Auxiliaries were represented by 122 delegates. An advance step was taken by the decision to create permanent headquarters, with a Secretary in charge, midway between the twin cities. We were most highly favored in having with us Bishops Oldham and Robinson. Bishop Oldham delighted and inspired his audiences, as always, with his splendid presentation of Malaysia and the Philippines. Bishop Robinson spoke to an appreciative people on Sunday morning. Much enthusiasm was created by the presence of the two Bishops, and our work will be easier for it throughout the entire year.   MRS. F. F. LINDSAY, *Corresponding Secretary.*

TREASURER'S REPORT.

Total receipts, October 1, 1907, to October 1, 1908.............. $38,967 48
Total disbursements 35,345 54

                                                                  $3,621 94
Deficit, October 1, 1907......................................   1,467 66

Cash on hand October 1, 1908.............................. $2,154 28

TOPEKA BRANCH.

In this year 1908, the twenty-fifth in the history of Topeka Branch, it is with gratitude we record the continued favor of God.

During this quarter of a century, the anniversary of which we have just been celebrating, we have raised $460,900, and sent to the field twenty-eight missionaries. For the success that has come to us we are glad, for the victories won we give thanks, humbly grateful to have had a part in so important a work. Our aim for the year has been $50,000 in the treasury, $25,000 thank-offering, and an increase of one hundred per cent in numbers.

While we have not realized our aim, we are all the stronger for the striving and ready for greater conquests.

The receipts are several thousand in advance, the thank-offering is more than twice the amount of any previous year, and there has been a healthy growth in membership.

As usual, we have been lacking in field workers, but tried to make the best use of those at hand.

Dr. Stevenson gave faithful service for a convention season. Miss McKnight worked to the limit of time and strength in Nebraska, Kansas, and Oklahoma. Mrs. S. P. Craver, of South America, spent two months in Nebraska, and Miss Spaulding gave a number of weeks to Oklahoma and Nebraska.

Mrs. R. S. Freeman, of Kansas City, Kansas, has since her return, in March, from a happy visit to our mission fields, responded to numerous calls for thank-offering services and anniversary addresses.

Under the enthusiastic leadership and fostering care of Mrs. S. A. Chappell, the Children's Work is making rapid progress, and the missionary workers of to-morrow are being trained.

There has been more than the usual number of changes among our missionaries.

Dr. Stevenson, who was with us in the last General Executive meeting, sailed July 11th, returning to China. The first letter tells of a pleasant voyage, a joyful welcome, and plenty of work awaiting in Tientsin.

Miss McKnight, who was also with us a year ago, has turned her face toward India, and expects to be in Muttra early in November.

In April, Miss Watson, after twenty-five years' service, returned from Japan and is with us to-day.

Miss Swaney, having given long years to South America, returned in June to receive a hearty welcome from the sisterhood of the Branch.

Miss Montgomery, who has given almost six years to India, reached the home land in July and is now in California ministering at the sick-bed of her father.

Mrs. Turner, after bravely trying to recover her health in India, by the advice of physicians sailed in September, landing only a few days ago and coming at once to Cincinnati to plead for needy Sironcha.

Miss Jennie Borg, our only recruit for the field last year, reached Chungking on Thanksgiving Day, which she pronounced a thanksgiving day with larger meaning than any hitherto. Her health has been good, and she reports having reached the place where the study of Chinese is really a pleasure.

The numbers on the field are shortly to be increased by three. Miss Gabrielsen sails November 4th, spending a month in Sweden organizing the work of the Society, and will reach Northwest India in time for Conference.

Miss Gardner and Miss Frazey sail in November; the former for Japan and the latter for China, where workers even now are awaiting with eagerness their coming.

Miss Roxanna Oldroyd, accepted at the semi-annual meeting of the Reference Committee and appointed to Lucknow, is spending the year in study for her master's degree and will then go to the chosen field.

The Annual Meeting, always a source of inspiration, was at its recent session characterized by unusual blessing. A spirit of hopefulness pervaded the gathering, causing the good women to pledge themselves to attempt even greater things for God.

The speakers were Bishop and Mrs. Oldham, Miss Stockwell, Miss Griffiths, and Miss Watson, and through their eyes we saw our work most clearly. At the close of a splendid address by Bishop Oldham on Sunday morning, very quickly and joyfully the people gave more than $700 to place Miss Gardner and Miss Frazey in the field. The literature sales amounted to $238, the largest at any Annual Meeting.

More than ever are we grateful to be numbered among the hosts who publish the tidings, and in the year to come, by prayer, money, and effort, we will seek more diligently to supply the need and enter the world-wide open door of opportunity.

ELLA M. WATSON, *Corresponding Secretary.*

TREASURER'S REPORT.

Balance, October 1, 1907	$1,418	13
Receipts	46,657	64
	$48,075	77
Disbursements	43,302	77
Balance, October 1, 1908	$4,773	00

MRS. L. E. McENTIRE, *Treasurer.*

PACIFIC BRANCH.

It is just twenty years since the Pacific Branch of our Society was organized in old Fort Street Church, Los Angeles. Our territory includes seven Conferences: Southern California, California, California German, Nevada, Arizona, Pacific Swedish, and Hawaii; four of which are Mission Conferences. The foundations were well laid by the strong leaders who took the initial steps and mastered the problems of the early days in our work, and thus the youngest of the then ten Branches has steadily grown larger and stronger. Every year except one has shown an increase in financial receipts, and there have been many other evidences of divine approval.

The phenomenal growth of last year enabled us to increase our appropriations for this year from $20,000 to $30,000, though several times since last October some of us feared that our promise was too large. When our Treasurer's books closed for this year we found that the total amount received is $37,240, an increase of $4,000 over last year, and from our hearts we say: "He is able to do exceeding abundantly above all that we ask or think." "The Lord of hosts is with us, and our Jehovah giveth us the battle."

The accomplishment of the work assigned to us in connection with our sisters of other lands depends so largely on our treasury that we naturally tell of its condition first. It indicates our strength and stimulates our love and loyalty in sacrifice and service.

Special gifts aggregating $7,000 have cheered us this year, also deeds for two valuable properties. Last month, when the death of one of God's noble women occurred— Mrs. Julius A. Brown, of Los Angeles—a bequest of $25,000 was announced, to be paid to our Society at the death of her husband. We are hoping that many others who can not give largely in any other way may use this method.

It is a great encouragement to find so large a part of our increase in regular receipts from Auxiliaries, Young People's and Children's Societies, and so we thankfully record forty-three new organizations. Growth marks the record in all departments, including subscriptions to the three *Friends*, the *Children's Missionary Friend* increasing from 1,400 to 2,200. Eight hundred dollars' worth of literature has been sold, which we think is very large for our Branch and is an increase of nine per cent.

Our local conditions are peculiar in that our two main centers of work are five hundred miles apart, a range of mountains forming a complete geographical separation of the two, and causing our officers to travel magnificent distances. In the Conference, which this year gave us over $25,000, there is one District which is as large as all New England except Maine, with New Jersey added and ten thousand square miles to spare. Still there are only four thousand members of the Methodist Episcopal Church in all of that District, so that the opportunity for the growth of our Society in that region, is quite limited.

We have one Conference which never fails to increase in every department every year. No matter what the rest of us do, the California German Conference marches straight on and up with an increase in Auxiliaries, Young People's and Children's organizations, as well as in financial receipts. Twenty-two of our German sisters were in attendance at our Branch annual meeting this year.

Our thank-offering services steadily increase in number and results, and in these we have been ably assisted by Mrs. Josephine Turnbull, Miss Elizabeth Parkes, Mr. W. E. Blackstone, Rev. J. W. Robinson, and Bishop Frank W. Warne, who came across the continent at our request, and gave us ten days of most valuable service. One of our leading officers said that never before had she heard the real work of the Woman's Foreign Missionary Society so forcefully presented to our people. Large audiences greeted him everywhere, and who that heard him will ever forget the story of the wonderful revival in India, as a result of which large numbers were added to the Church, of such as shall be saved.

All of our missionary representatives are at work in the various foreign fields, none are home on furlough, and, as far as we know, all are in good health.

A few months ago our Branch Secretary of Literature, Mrs. Wardwell Couch, passed from a life of exceptionally beautiful service to the life of broader opportunity and everlasting joy.

Another one, Mrs. William E. Blackstone, whose patient continuance in well-doing and large gifts during many years to our Society, greatly endeared her to all who knew her, passed to her home beyond after nearly three years in our sunny land. Her beautiful life is still a benediction to us.

Our annual meeting was held in San Francisco, that city which is giving to her people beauty for ashes, the oil of joy for mourning, the garment of praise for the spirit of heaviness. While the city is rising in its strength and beauty, our Methodism is still in great need of your help and mine, for we must remember that when the fire destroyed the business houses of our people it also destroyed their homes, and while these are being rebuilt, there is little money for church buildings.

The attendance during our whole meeting was much larger than ever before in that Conference, and a helpful enthusiasm pervaded every session. Twenty-four preachers and several returned missionaries were in attendance and greatly added to the enthusiasm of the meeting.

Among the special features may be noted the securing of six life members of the King's Heralds at one session, under the persuasive touch of Mrs. Lucie F. Harrison; the decision to begin the quarterly publication of the *Pacific Branch Messenger;* the securing of twenty-two new subscribers to the *Woman's Missionary Friend,* following an exercise on the Mystery Box, and the large Standard Bearer rally, Tuesday evening, when enthusiasm ran high as the young people sang and marched, and then listened to a most helpful address from Dr. Edna Beck Keislar.

Rev. Mr. and Mrs. G. A. Miller, Rev. J. W. Mell, and Rev. Mott Keislar brought much of information and inspiration from other lands.

Three Branch officers new to us were added to our list, and we rejoice in the character of the women chosen to fill these offices. They are: Secretary of Home Department, Mrs. Belle J. Anderson; Superintendent of Young People's Work, Mrs. J. L. Hooper, and Superintendent of Children's Work, Miss Lulu Heacock.

After much discussion and prayerful consideration it was unanimously voted to increase our appropriations for the coming year from $30,000 to $35,000, and an additional $5,000 will be appropriated for the Woman's College in Foochow, China.

We begin the new year with a courage strong and a sincere desire to follow closely the leading of the Holy Spirit.

MRS. S. F. JOHNSON, *Corresponding Secretary.*

TREASURER'S REPORT.

Balance in General Fund, October 1, 1907..................... $8,396 00
Receipts from Conferences........................$30,156 00
Receipts from Annuities 500 00
Bequests and gifts.................................. 6,584 00
                                                   ———— 37,240 00

Grand total $45,636 00

Disbursed in General Fund........................ $32,198 00
Transferred to Annuity Fund......................   500 00
Transferred to Trust Fund........................   6,584 00

    Total disbursed 39,282 00

    Balance on hand October 1, 1908....:............ $6,354 00

COLUMBIA RIVER BRANCH.

"Trust ye in Jehovah forever; for in Jehovah, even Jehovah, is an everlasting rock."

In common with our sister Branches, Columbia River experienced at the threshold of the past year that sudden fall in the national temperature which congealed its financial streams far and wide. The bank failures and business uncertainties of the first few months gave cause for questioning as to our ability to meet increased obligations without embarrassment, but through all we praise our Heavenly Father for complete deliverance from fear as to the final outcome. Thanks ever be to Him that, with the assurance of His direction in our undertakings, He grants faith for accomplishment.

Our increase in receipts has not been large, though perhaps all that could be expected under existing conditions, and the indications of quickened and spreading interest in our cause are encouraging prophecies for the future. Even in some isolated and small charges the work has been undertaken with eager and self-denying devotion.

The greatly increased sales in our Depot of Supplies, and the lengthening lists of subscribers to our missionary periodicals, are signs of substantial progress. The leaflet prepared by our Branch President on the duties of the Corresponding Secretary is being widely circulated.

No special outside help from speakers has been given us during the twelve months, save in a couple of instances when passing missionaries tarried a bit for a service or two, presenting the needs of their fields with such persuasiveness as to compel a vain wish to detain them for extended assistance.

Possibly if our missionaries who come and go by the North Pacific Coast were aware of the fact that our Seattle friends have prepared a thoroughly equipped missionary camping outfit to be at their disposal, they might be induced to arrange for tarrying through the delightful summers, where sea and lake, snow peaks and hills bear their message of peace and strength.

We are unable to report progress in our Young People's Work, owing to the serious illness of Mrs. Upmeyer, its Superintendent, who has lingered very near the border land of the other life. We are grateful for the prospect of her returning health and hope that ere long her skillful hand may be once again directing the forces that have so missed her care.

Mrs. Ryckman, the new Superintendent of Children's Work, is proving most admirably fitted for her department, and we are expecting that the coming year will show marked advance along these important lines.

A goodly number of Little Light Bearer life members have been added to our list. In this connection we have the distinction of reporting, that another lovely trio of sturdy baby boys have been recorded as the third set of Triplet Little Light Bearer life members, of Columbia River Branch.

This year for the first time in our history a bequest has been paid into our treasury, the loving remembrance of a widow of limited means.

As the years pass we miss here and there, those on whom we have depended, from Branch organization—some have been called to their heavenly home, others have removed from our territory. Among the latter we may not omit mention of the loss of our beloved Thoburn family. They were ours from the first by ties of fellowship in the struggle of establishing a new Branch in a new country, by the blessed helpfulness of Bishop Thoburn, by the sacred spot in our cemetery where the bodies of Mrs. Anna Thoburn and Chancellor Crawford Thoburn, wife and eldest son of the Bishop, await the resurrection day, and by the interest and love with which we have watched the development of the six children toward beautiful young manhood and womanhood. We hope to give them welcome home again after a few years. That their names might remain on our records, the Bishop has been constituted an Honorary Manager, and the others of the family life members of the Branch, and the guest chamber in the Mary E. Whitney Memorial Home in Nadiad, India, is to be known as the Thoburn room.

Our annual meeting was held in Spokane, farther from headquarters than any previous session. It was a joy to meet the faithful workers in that region and with them consider the claims of our cause and plan for its development. Arrangements were made by private contributions for bringing our Superintendent of Children's Work to this General Executive meeting, for the inspiration and help she may gain for her department.

The Sunday services were particularly inspiring, with an appropriate sermon in the morning by the pastor, the Rev. Dr. Rasmus, and addresses in the evening by Dr. Fulkerson, of Japan, and Dr. W. H. W. Rees, of Seattle, and closing words by Mrs. Wire, our President.

We enter upon the new year with renewed consecration and trust in our Divine Leader.   MRS. A. N. FISHER, *Corresponding Secretary.*

TREASURER'S REPORT.

Balance on hand, October. 1, 1907........................ $4,896 70
Receipts from October 1, 1907, to October 1, 1908......... 14,295 56

Total $19,192 26
Disbursements 13,886 20

Balance on hand, October 1, 1908.................... $5,306 06
MISS NETTIE M. WHITNEY, *Treasurer.*

GERMAN WORK.

With heartfelt gratitude we close another year. From the first we prayed and worked for an advance; progress was our watchword. As quarter by quarter advance could be noted, our hearts rejoiced, but the close of the year showed greater results than we had even dared to hope for.

Our receipts, $21,115.07, are larger than those of any previous year. In practically all lines there has been an increase. True, it has been but slight in the number of Auxiliaries and members, more in organizations and membership among Young People and Standard Bearers, while in the Children's Work there has been a very satisfactory advance. Fifty-one little life members were secured. In the Northern, Northwestern, and St. Louis Conferences especially, the Children's Work has been pushed.

Parents and others are recognizing more and more the benefits which come to the children themselves from this work. While it is not possible to report the exact sum gathered by the children, it is enough to be quite worth appreciation. May they never lose their interest in this great work. Besides the receipts from regular sources, we received about $1,000 in sums ranging from $100 to $500. The National Epworth League Convention at its meeting held in October, 1907, pledged itself to contribute $1,000 for the purpose of sending a missionary to Sieng-iu, China. Seven hundred dollars of this amount has been paid, and the remainder will be available as soon as needed. While the money came from the Leagues throughout the country, it was paid to Cincinnati Branch with the understanding that this Branch would send a missionary to Sieng-iu. Miss Paula Seidlmann, a native of Vienna, Germany, after having spent four years in this country in preparation, is now on her way to Sieng-iu.

We are sure that the interest of our Leaguers has been greatly increased by this offering from them.

The numerous inquiries that have come during the past year from young women and from pastors as to what are the necessary qualifications and preparation of a worker for the foreign field, evidence the fact that many are giving earnest thought to our work. A number are now fitting themselves, and we hope that at no distant time they may be our representatives in the service.

We have been able to do a little more than usual in the way of publications this year. Besides our Annual Report we have published a Study Booklet which met with a very good reception, four new leaflets, a thank-offering program, and one reprint. We are indebted to Northwestern Branch for help which helped us to do this. This is the only help in this line that we have asked for or have received during the last six or more years.

Our sales amounted to $298.30.

More and more interest is being shown in the prescribed study. Last year about 1,000 copies of the German study booklet were sold, besides a goodly number of the English book. Our young people are coming to understand the benefits of mission study more and more.

There has been quite a gain in the number of subscribers to the *Frauen Missions-Freund*, but the number still lacks a few of being as high as it was two years ago. There has been a fine increase of subscriptions to the *Children's Missionary Friend* reported, though we are confident that not nearly all are reported.

Our work in Europe does not show as good results this year as it has done in former years. This is no doubt due to peculiar conditions and difficulties which have made themselves especially felt during the past year or two. If ways and means of overcoming these can be found, there will without doubt be more rapid progress than heretofore.

The question of a German Branch has again commanded a great deal of attention. What it will be your pleasure to grant us remains to be seen. Our earnest prayer is that the Divine Will may be made manifest and put into execution, that only that which is pleasing to the Lord and which will help in advancing His work may be decided upon.

LOUISE C. ROTHWEILER, *Secretary of German Work.*

STATISTICS OF THE GERMAN WORK.

Conferences	Auxiliaries	Members	Standard Bearers	Members	King's Heralds	Members	Life Members	Mite-Boxes	Frauen Missions Freund	Woman's Missionary Friend	Children's Missionary Friend	Receipts in 1907-1908	Receipts in 1906-1907	Increase	Decrease	Contingent Fund
California	13	284	7	169	4	41	4	112	182	3	85	$1,424 20	$1,244 75	$179 45		$3 85
Central	35	1,088	6	110	2	34		627	419	24	216	3,653 09	3,004 17	649 52		74 85
Chicago	17	493	10	280				65	323	5	94	1,419 95	1,402 20	17 75		26 57
Northern	94	852	7	162	19	427	11	380	577	25	252	3,173 72	2,289 12	934 60		49 72
Northwestern	38	797	15	340	17	369	22	60	518	6	306	2,873 85	2,294 22	179 68		30 85
Eastern	21	752	1	54	3	96		82	386	8	167	1,954 00	1,720 25	183 75		50 97
Pacific	10	173						16	149			260 84	235 30	25 54		4 00
St. Louis	30	794	3	106	7	177	3		428	1	130	1,555 39	1,247 34	307 96		88 29
Southern	12	216	7	23	1				107			430 45	656 55		$226 10	4 07
Western	44	876	8	37		50	5	403	685	7	188	3,229 15	2,853 24	375 91		35 50
Scattering									452			700 00		700 00		
Total for United States	254	6,275	63	1,261	53	1194	45	1,745	4,176	79	1,488	$20,275 14	$16,947 14	$3131 45	$226 10	$378 17
North Germany	35	644	1	40					140			$200 71	$239 30		$88 59	
South Germany									160			175 05	287 91		112 86	
Switzerland	55	1,177							155			464 17	509 27		45 10	
Total for Europe	90	1,821	1	40					455			$839 93	$1,036 48		$196 55	
Grand Total	314	8,096	54	1,301	53	1194	45	1,745	4,631	79	1,488	$21,115 07	$17,983 62	$3131 45	$422 65	$378 17

SCANDINAVIAN WORK.

Our seventh year has been a year of unprecedented progress. Our Auxiliaries have had an increase of 22, our membership of 448, and our receipts are $1,071.51 more than last year's. In 1905, which has so far been our best year, the increase in Auxiliaries was 9, in members 304, and in receipts $400.

During the last year our beloved Miss Gabrielson, who stands now ready to go from this meeting to Meerut, India, has been traveling in all our Conferences except the Northern, strengthening the work that was already existing and organizing new Auxiliaries wherever this was possible. In every place she has visited she has tried to interest the children and young people in our work, and in some places she has succeeded in organizing Standard Bearers and King's Heralds bands, but our Epworth Leagues and Sunday-schools being largely organized Missionary Societies, they do not take kindly to the idea of more organizations. She has, however, been allowed to place mite-boxes in several places where she could not organize. Without a doubt the good results, over which we rejoice, are in a great measure due to her exertions. Our women are generally too busy to read much, and need somebody to keep the cause before their eyes constantly. But their interest is steadily growing and will continue to do so, the more workers we are able to send out. Miss Gabrielson is the ninth of our Swedish girls to go, and we rejoice greatly in hearing both from our Missionary Bishops and from returned missionaries that our girls are doing good and acceptable work. So far they have all been well and strong. Miss Judith Ericson had to move her school in Kolar out to a camp on account of the plague, but the dread disease reached them there, and one little girl died. The rest were mercifully spared.

Miss Norberg, who was with us at the Executive meeting last year and went from there to Asansol, feels very happy in her work; notwithstanding the fact that they have had a water famine several times and that provisions have been so high that her allowance has been insufficient, and she has had to take of her own money for the support of the little widows under her care.

Miss Swan is rejoicing in the expectation of soon welcoming her brother and his young bride to Pakur to help in the work there. They have just left New York on their way to India.

Our Church paper continues to give us a department for the missionary work twice a month. We give the Study there, together with letters from our missionaries, and such other information as we think will interest our readers. This year we have printed nothing except our Annual Report, but we are preparing a booklet with general information of the work of the Society, and especially with regard to our own work. We hope that this will prove a good help to us.

The buildings in Pakur have now been paid for in full, and Miss Swan is very desirous that we should be allowed to apply our contributions towards a hospital fund for Pakur. Eleven little girls have died in the school, and there is no provision for taking proper care of the sick. We who have been spared great afflictions during the year, long to do something towards alleviating the sufferings of those less fortunate. Leaving ourselves in His hands for strength and guidance, we are happy in the prospect of "one more year's work for Jesus."

MRS. HANNA HENSCHEN, *Secretary Swedish Work.*

STATISTICS OF THE SCANDINAVIAN WORK.

CONFERENCES.	AUXILIARIES	MEMBERS	MITE-BOX COLLECTIONS	SCHOLARSHIPS	BIBLE-WOMEN	WIDOWS	LIFE MEMBERS	SPECIAL GIFTS	THANK-OFFERING	COLLECTIONS	RECEIPTS	INCREASE	DECREASE	CONTINGENT FUND	STANDARD BEARERS	KING'S HERALDS	HONORARY MEMBERS
Central	21	706	$47 55	$230 00	2	1		$235 76		$74 00	$142 34	$383 14		$30 00			
Northern	81	774							$43 54	5 80	169 80		$12 42	49 94			
Western	39	852	484 64	140 50				87 96	60 70	158 15	192 18	408 38		31 44			
Eastern	19	553	10 79	20 00				21 20			?6 72	236 94		44 95	$4 10	$1 16	6
California District	5	190	5 20	20 00				30 00			$6 35	93 05		13 65	12 90		
Puget Sound District	4	61		40 00				8 80			11 73		3 94	8 50			
Total	119	3136	$548 20	$450 50	2	1		$383 72	$104 24	$288 54	57	$1071 51	$16 36	$173 48	$17 00	$1 16	6

YOUNG PEOPLE'S WORK.

Branch Superintendents.

New England—Mrs. C. H. Stackpole, Waltham, Mass.
New York—Mrs. Charles Spaeth, 11 Audubon St., Rochester, N. Y.
Philadelphia—Miss Ina Wilhelm, 1212 Buffalo St., Franklin, Pa.
Baltimore—Mrs. E. L. Harvey, 1314 Thirteenth St., N. W., Washington, D. C.
Cincinnati—Miss Mary I. Scott, Moundsville, W. Va.
Northwestern—Mrs. David C. Cook, 105 N. Gifford St., Elgin, Ill.
Des Moines—Mrs. R. S. Beall, Mount Ayr, Iowa.
Minneapolis—Mrs. C. F. Blume, 125 N. State St., New Ulm, Minn.
Topeka—Mrs. Jennie F. Rinker, 2636 N St., Lincoln, Neb.
Pacific—Mrs. J. L. Hooper, 2632 Pasadena Ave., Los Angeles, Cal.
Columbia River—Mrs. E. E. Upmeyer, Harrisburg, Ore.

REPORT OF YOUNG PEOPLE'S WORK.

The extreme youthfulness of the soldiers who fought the battles of the Civil War has been frequently remarked. Two million, one hundred and sixty thousand, or about three-fourths of the entire army, were between the ages of fourteen and twenty-one. Does this not suggest to us the hope that we may look to the young people of that age largely to carry on the conquests of the Cross?

A good general ought to be able to perfectly command his forces, but this great army of Standard Bearers, while fighting bravely all along the line, are not altogether concerted in action, and in some instances the chain of connections fails to carry the plans of the leaders to the individual companies and to bring back the necessary reports. It seems almost impossible to number the army and present to this body accurate statistics.

Treasurers' reports show that the young people's organizations are a source of large income to the Society, and this is only one of the results in which we should rejoice. The widening of the horizon, the helpful avenues of activity provided for youthful energy, the deepening of spiritual life through the increasing missionary interest, are results of chief importance.

We would be very sorry to have the strength or efficiency of our young people's work judged by the figures we are about to give, for they are only approximate, as some reports have failed to reach us, while others state that their own constituency has not been fully reported, hence the results are not numerically correct.

We have about 1,440 societies, including those designated as Young Woman's Societies and Standard Bearer Companies, with a membership of 36,500 (approximate). Nearly all of the merely contributing companies have gone out of existence or become fully organized companies. While this in some Branches has reduced the number of organizations, yet the reports show an increase of money raised, which proves that the results are better and more lasting, both to the work and to the worker, from the completely organized societies.

Fifty-one missionaries are supported on the field, in whole or in part, by the dues of these young people, in some cases with the help of the Epworth Leagues.

The thank-offering gifts of the young women this year were directed to the same objects as those of their Branches, so the results can not be given separately.

Perhaps we should not single out for special mention any one Branch, yet we can not forbear commending the completeness of organization followed in the New York and Pacific Branches, and to a large extent in the Northwestern Branch, which makes their work so effective.

We can not give complete figures for each Branch, but we must mention in the roll of honor our two largest Branches, Northwestern and New York. Northwestern stands at the head, with a membership of 8,740, a splendid increase this year of 816 members. Mrs. Cook, the Superintendent, personally sent to each of the eleven Conference Secretaries a $10 prize for the largest per cent gain in membership from May 20th to September 1st. This greatly stimulated effort in securing new members.

Mrs. Cook also did us an inestimable service in compiling and publishing the Standard Bearers' Handbook, which is being used quite generally as a guide for the work of our societies.

New York has made a healthful decrease, some societies which had a name to live and yet were dead having been buried (not too deeply for resurrection, we hope). They report a membership in Young People's societies of 7,628. Their contributions for special work amounted to $4,540, and total receipts to $8,966. One society, the largest in the Branch, has a membership of 255. The Branch reports two life members for this year.

Philadelphia Branch has made an unusually large contribution to special work. They also have made two new life members this year.

Baltimore Branch has loyally and enthusiastically followed the resolution of last year in regard to the dollar membership dues for the young women over twenty, and this membership of young people's societies is a large proportion of the total membership of the Branch.

Cincinnati Branch has made a good advance, having added thirty-three new organizations. The prize for the best exhibit, a foreign scholarship, to be placed where the Society might wish, offered by Mrs. Wm. A. Gamble, was won by the Salem (Ohio) Standard Bearers. This Branch has taken an advance step in employing a field organizer in the interests of the college and Young People's work.

Our newer Branches of the West are making a fine advance. Minneapolis and Pacific Branches have new Superintendents this year. The Superintendent of Columbia River Branch was incapacitated through illness and could not push her work. Nevertheless some societies that for membership and contributions will compare favorably with the largest in the East, are reported.

Three or more Branches have carried the work of the College Department, sending representatives to the summer Student Conferences, and connecting themselves helpfully with the Student Volunteers.

Our great needs are more motherly supervision on the part of the Woman's Foreign Missionary Society; field organizers who shall devote themselves more exclusively to the young people; free literature for the instruction of our new societies; uniform report blanks, which shall enable us to know just what our young people's work accomplishes; more and better leaders from among the young people themselves; and last, but not least, more spiritual and self-sacrificing methods of raising money, and less worldliness and more devotion to the Lord Jesus Christ on the part of our young people.

We hope much from the conferences of Young People's Superintendents held during the session of the General Executive.

Your Secretary wishes to express her gratitude for the cordial support of the officers of the Woman's Foreign Missionary Society in this her first year of service in this line of work, and for the hearty co-operation an sympathy of the Branch Superintendents of Young People's Work. d

With faith in God, love for each other, and renewed consecration to the missionary cause, our young people will undertake to do a better work the coming year.   WINIFRED SPAULDING.

CHILDREN'S WORK.

BRANCH SUPERINTENDENTS.

New England—Mrs. C. H. STOWELL, 99 Fairmount St., Lowell, Mass.
New York—Mrs. H. C. LEARN, 572 Lincoln Place, Brooklyn, N. Y.
Philadelphia—Miss INA WILHELM, 1212 Buffalo St., Franklin, Pa.
Baltimore—Mrs. WM. E. MOORE, 524 N. Caroline Ave., Baltimore, Md.
Cincinnati—Mrs. J. F. FISHER, 11427 Detroit Ave., N. W., Cleveland, Ohio.
Northwestern—Mrs. W. C. WHITCOMB, Rochelle, Ill.
Des Moines—Mrs. GEORGE IRMSCHER, 49 Arlington Ave., Dubuque, Iowa.
Minneapolis—Mrs. W. J. CLAPP, 824 Fifth Ave., Fargo, N. D.
Topeka—Mrs. S. A. CHAPPELL, Lincoln, Kansas.
Pacific—Miss LULU HEACOCK, Pacific Grove, Cal.
Columbia River—Mrs. J. H. RYCKMAN, 1410 Twelfth Ave., Seattle, Wash.

REPORT OF CHILDREN'S WORK.

The General Executive Committee meeting of one year ago gave a decided impetus to our Children's Work. This was occasioned by a majority of the Branches uniting in a plan to give the Branch Superintendents of Children's Work the privilege of uniting together at Springfield.

The frequent conferences of these Superintendents at that time gave splendid opportunity for exchange of methods and the evolving of new plans. The inspiration there gained has proved a potent factor in making this year in many respects the best in our history. Many of our Branch officers, as well as the Superintendents themselves, affirm this. Knowing that we should alternate with our Young People's Superintendents, there has been no similar arrangement among the Branches this year, yet the Cincinnati Branch has graciously extended the courtesy of entertainment to the Branch Superintendents and four have availed themselves of the privilege: Miss Wilhelm, of Philadelphia Branch; Mrs. Fisher, of Cincinnati Branch; Mrs. Ryckman, of Columbia River Branch; Miss Heacock, of Pacific Branch.

Miss Lulu Heacock, of Pacific Grove, Cal., our new Superintendent from the Pacific Branch, is a valuable acquisition to our corps of Branch Superintendents, as she has most successfully led the Children's Work for a number of years as Superintendent of Children's Work in the California Conference. We now for the first time have a Superintendent in every Branch, Pacific thus completing the list.

Our Branch Superintendents have sent out an unusual number of circular letters, leaflets, and novel devices to awaken interest. Samples of these may be seen in the folios on exhibition here. Each Branch has its children's work well represented in these folios. Some are very beautiful. It would be a good thing for the Branches to continue to exhibit these during the year at District and other public meetings. Some already do this.

Very many of the Branches have issued new report blanks, and the work in a number of ways is on a much firmer basis than ever before.

A most encouraging feature is the fact that the Presidents of local Auxiliaries are feeling an increase of responsibility in the Little Light Bearer Department. This should be universal. Every President should see to it that some one is found to care for the tiny lambs of the flock. This need not be difficult, since surely no woman is too young, and we find to our great advantage nòne are too old, to be successful in winning these youngest recruits.

Mrs. Burt, of San Francisco, seventy-six years old, is one of' our most successful and enthusiastic leaders. She is District Superintendent and also has charge of the Little Light Bearers in her local Church. The Branch meeting was held in her Church, and every time I met her she reported an advance. Her parting word as we said good-bye was, "I have two more—125 in all."

In Evanston and Chicago we have two just such workers nearing eighty years. This should encourage us all. Many of our women in every Branch right in the prime of life think it worth while to devote themselves to this work. Mrs. Bucklin, of Muncie, Ind., has three hundred Little Light Bearers.

Baby's First Letter and the Little Light Bearer's Pound Party have been prepared by your Secretary this year. The first-named is already gaining new members rapidly, and the post-card is being used in thank-offering gathering, when the mother, as a thank-offering, gives "a penny a pound for the baby." These are both very attractive, as everything ought to be pertaining to the Children's Work.

Secretaries' and Treasurers' books for the King's Heralds are in preparation and much needed.

During the Conference of Superintendents, last year, it was agreed to apportion among the Branches a certain number of new subscriptions to the *Children's Missionary Friend,* and then work hard to reach the amount. Circulars were printed later, which were to be sent to all the Auxiliaries, asking their co-operation in making up the apportionment. The folios will contain many of these circulars returned.

We stated that the Branch gaining the largest per cent above its apportionment would be the Publisher's Banner Branch. Pacific Branch was apportioned 150, and gained 697. Cincinnati was apportioned 500, and gained 979, and has won this distinction.

Next year we are going to ask the Publisher to present a banner to the Branch having the largest number of subscriptions in proportion to its membership of King's Heralds and Little Light Bearers, the winning Branch to keep the banner at their headquarters until another gains it. We hope this may be done. We place as our aim for next year a ten per cent increase in subscriptions.

We are encouraging the use of our study book in connection with the lesson in the *Children's Missionary Friend,* and also the Reading Course, which includes "Springs in the Desert," "Topsy Turvy Land," and the *Children's Missionary Friend.*

All of our Branches now have children's missionaries. This creates in the heart of the child a loving, prayerful interest in some missionary. She writes letters to the children of the Branch, thus keeping them in touch with her.

A few of our cities have held Children's Missionary Rallies. In Washington, D. C., twelve different societies sold tickets and gave a fine entertainment to an audience of five hundred, making a considerable sum of money and arousing an interest in missions.

Cincinnati also holds most successful rallies. May we not make a special point of these rallies this coming year, in centers where a number of Churches are near enough together to unite.

There should be one public missionary entertainment or King's Heralds anniversary each year, in every Church. These prove most valuable in interesting both children and grown people, and often good financial results are obtained either by a collection or sale of tickets.

We published circulars with the new aim for the Honor Roll at the beginning of last year and filled the orders as they came from the Branch Superintendents, each Branch paying for its own. It was intended to put one of these circulars in the hands of each Auxiliary.

Pacific Branch is again the banner Branch, having more Churches on the Honor Roll in proportion to the number of Auxiliaries.

We had 95 Churches reported on the Honor Roll: New England, 17; Philadelphia, 7; Baltimore, 4; Cincinnati, 14; Northwestern, 21; Minneapolis, 6; Des Moines, 8; Topeka, 3; Pacific, 12; Columbia River, 3.

Our aim for 1909 will be similar to that of 1908—not difficult to attain. It simply represents a normal condition. It is as follows—each Auxiliary to have: (1) A Supervisor; (2) Both King's Heralds and Little Light Bearers; (3) A combined membership of King's Heralds and Little Light Bearers equal to the membership of the Auxiliary, or, if preferred, at least three-fourths the membership of the Sunday-school, under fifteen years of age, including Cradle Roll; (4) As many copies of the *Children's Missionary Friend* as there are King's Heralds or Little Light Bearers, over two years old, unless there are two or more members in the same family; (5) A new Life Member.

Making life members of our King's Heralds and Little Light Bearers is still a favorite way to contribute to the missionary cause and also to interest and honor some little child.

The Branch Superintendents have been instrumental in gaining many new names at Branch Annuals and other public meetings. We have reported 490 Life Members this year. Mrs. Irmscher, Des Moines Superintendent, has gained in her own Church, which is itself a mission Church, eight Life Members each year for the past two years, and Des Moines Branch takes the lead with 103 Life Members.

Our Thank-offering object for the new year is a share in the school building in Rosario, South America. New Thank-offering letters, made attractive by pictures of former Thank-offering buildings, have been prepared by your Secretary for next year's work.

It is important to educate and train the child on the line of Thank-offerings. Fifteen hundred dollars—the amount asked for—apportioned to the different Branches can not prove a burden, while it promotes uniformity among the Branches, and a Thank-offering spirit among the children.

The primary room in the building will be named for the King's Heralds and Little Light Bearers.

It has been said, "Childhood is the battle ground of the Kingdom," and this is true. There is no period in human life when victories gained count for as much as in childhood.

LUCIE F. HARRISON.

STATISTICS OF CHILDREN'S WORK, OCTOBER, 1907, TO OCTOBER, 1908.

BRANCH	KING'S HERALDS BANDS	MEMBERS	LITTLE LIGHT BEARERS BANDS	MEMBERS
New England	75	2,848		1,463
New York	117	2,801	70	1,284
Philadelphia	110	8,157	57	1,605
Baltimore	29	877	38	808
Cincinnati	128	8,185	56	1,701
Northwestern	312	6.797	255	5,454
Des Moines	144	2,806	31	376
Minneapolis	86	2,443	52	1,048
Topeka	72	1,610	33	564
Pacific	63	1,151	46	939
Columbia River	22	481	40	839
Total	1,158	26,106	678	16,081

BEQUESTS

TO THE

Woman's Foreign Missionary Society, 1907-1908.

NEW ENGLAND BRANCH.

Names.	Residence.	Amount.
Anna W. Alvord,	Northampton, Mass.,	$200 00
Sophronia Carpenter,	Charlton, Mass.,	45 00
Cyrus Spaulding,	Webster, Mass.,	1,000 00
Francis E. H. Kingsbury,	Newton, Mass.,	500 00
Marcia S. Gilchrist,	Northfield, Vt., (Partial)	2,040 00
Almira H. Minard,	South Paris, Maine,	506 01
Mrs. Gilbert,	Portland, Maine,	300 00

NEW YORK BRANCH.

Mrs. Eva L. Harrison,	Syracuse, N. Y.,	500 00
Mrs. E. L. Hitchcock,	Putnam,	150 00
Mrs. Jones,	Westfield,	20 00
Dr. A. L. Gilbert,	North Cohocton,	1,900 00
Rev. J. C. Thomas,	New York City,	1,000 00
Mrs· Sarah J. Olmstead,	Hobert, (Net)	1,411 82
Mrs. K. C. Baker,	Great Neck,	1,000 00
Mrs. Salina Lewis,	Norwood,	100 00
Almon Baxter Merwin,		50 00
Mrs. Harriet T. Lane,	Bordentown,	500 00
Mrs. Hannah Gibson,	Poughkeepsie, (Net)	100 09

PHILADELPHIA BRANCH.

Miss Catherine C. Martz,		70 75

CINCINNATI BRANCH.

Miss Lilian F. Gamble,	Cincinnati, Ohio,	5,000 00
Mrs. Martha H. Brakefield,	Goodhope, Ohio,	210 00
Estate of Mrs. Stockton,	Carrollton, Ohio,	250 00

NORTHWESTERN BRANCH.

Mrs. B. C. Hinckle,	Mattoon, Ill.,	500 00
Lydia C. Kennedy,	Evanston, Ill.,	826 75
Mrs. Mary E. Way,	Geneseo, Ill.,	200 00
Lillian Hollister,	Mishawaka, Ind.,	25 00
Mrs. Irene Studley,	Detroit, Mich.,	100 00
Mrs. Eliza Ellen Lowe,	Grand Rapids, Mich.,	500 00
Miss Mary C. Robinson,	Chinkiang, China,	500 00

DES MOINES BRANCH.

		664 07

MINNEAPOLIS BRANCH.

Mrs. Carrie A. Joyce,	Minneapolis, Minn.,	2,000 00
Miss Betsey Galpin,	Minneapolis, Minn.,	500 00
A. Pfaff,	Waseca, Minn.,	20 00

TOPEKA BRANCH.

Mrs. Fannie Murrey, ...	Atchison, Kan., ...	$4,500 00
Benson C. Hinckle, ...	Shawnee, Oklahoma, ...	500 00
Mrs. John Sommerman, ...	Martel, Neb., ...	50 00

PACIFIC BRANCH.

Mrs. Avyette T. Richardson, ...	San Jose, Cal., ...	500 00

COLUMBIA RIVER BRANCH.

Mrs. Kenworthy, ...	Portland, Ore., ...	100 00

Total Bequests, ... $28,339 49

STATISTICS OF THE HOME WORK.

Branches	Receipts	Subscribers to The Study	Subscribers to Frauen Missions Freund	Subscribers to Children's Missionary Friend	Subscribers to Women's Missionary Friend	Members	Little Light Bearers' Bands	Members	King's Heralds Bands	Members	Young People's Societies	Members	Auxiliaries
New England	$51,487 00	2,215	56	8,689	1,961	1,463		2,848	75	2,882	111	11,089	451
New York	98,456 78	4,058	199	4,531	3,206	1,284	70	2,301	117	7,608	297	25,897	732
Philadelphia	62,049 56	4,617	49	3,087	3,233	1,605	57	3,157	110	4,059	142	18,168	511
Baltimore	21,751 41	963	65	1,298	706	808	38	877	29	1,204	42	4,943	149
Cincinnati	84,227 31	4,708	258	3,795	2,789	1,701	56	3,185	128	4,695	187	20,054	720
Northwestern	150,585 73	6,842	984	8,445	6,136	5,454	255	6,797	312	8,741	322	38,650	1,881
Des Moines	65,681 39	4,060	729	4,219	2,773	876	31	2,804	144	2,285	147	20,298	591
Minneapolis	38,967 48	1,221	655	1,241	843	1,048	52	2,443	86	955	51	6,621	304
Topeka	46,657 64	2,562	764	2,360	1,497	504	38	1,610	72	1,543	64	10,760	448
Pacific	87,240 00	984	182	2,325	959	939	46	1,151	63	3,121	101	5,090	169
Columbia River	14,295 56	997	149	973	641	839	40	431	22	845	28	3,022	125
Total	$673,400 04	33,244	4,631	36,415	25,535	16,021	678	26,106	1,158	37,978	1,392	164,591	5,581
*German	$21,115 07		4,681	1,498	79			1,194	58	801	54	8,096	844
*Scandinavian	5,528 57											3,136	119

Foreign and scattering subscriptions (†): The Study 17; Frauen Missions Freund 541; Children's Missionary Friend 502; Women's Missionary Friend 791.

* These figures are included in the above table.
† Foreign and scattering subscriptions.

FOREIGN WORK.

ASIA.

The Woman's Foreign Missionary Society commenced work by sending, in 1869, Miss Isabella Thoburn and Miss Clara M. Swain, M. D., to India.

November 29, 1859, the first Methodist Girls' Boarding School was opened by the Misses Sarah and Beulah Woolston, who had been sent to *China* by the Ladies' China Missionary Society. In 1871 the Woman's Foreign Missionary Society adopted them, and also sent Miss Maria Brown (Davis) and Miss Mary Q. Porter (Gamewell) to Peking.

The Woman's Foreign Missionary Society commenced work in *Japan* in 1874 by sending Miss Dora Schoonmaker (Soper) to Tokyo.

The Woman's Foreign Missionary Society commenced work in *Korea* in 1885 by sending Mrs. Mary B. Scranton to Seoul.

AFRICA.

The Woman's Foreign Missionary Society commenced work in *Africa* in 1874. In 1874 Miss Mary Sharp, who had been sent out by the Missionary Society that year, was adopted, and in 1879 Miss Emma Michener was sent to Monrovia.

SOUTH AMERICA.

The Woman's Foreign Missionary Society commenced work in 1874 in *South America* by sending Miss Lou B. Denning and Miss Jennie M. Chapin to Rosario.

MEXICO.

The Woman's Foreign Missionary Society commenced work in *Mexico* by sending, in 1874, Miss Mary Hastings and Miss Susan Warner (Densmore) to Mexico City.

BULGARIA.

The Woman's Foreign Missionary Society commenced work in *Bulgaria* in 1874. A Boarding School for girls was opened by Rev. D. C. Challis in November, 1880. In 1884 the Society sent Miss Linna Schenck to Lovetch.

ITALY.

The Woman's Foreign Missionary Society commenced work in *Italy* in 1874, and in 1885 sent Miss Emma Hall to Rome.

PHILIPPINE ISLANDS.

The Woman's Foreign Missionary Society commenced work in *Manila* in 1899 by sending Miss Julia Wisner, Mrs. Annie Norton, M. D., Miss Cody, and Mrs. Cornelia Moots.

Reports of Foreign Work.

OFFICIAL CORRESPONDENCE.

INDIA.

NORTH INDIA CONFERENCE.

Organized as a Conference in 1864.
Woman's Foreign Missionary Work commenced in 1869.
Official Correspondent, Mrs. R. L. Thomas.

The North India Conference embraces the Province of Oudh and 'the Northeast Provinces east of the Ganges.

MISSIONARIES AND THEIR STATIONS.

BAREILLY.—Esther Gimson, M. D., Alice Means, Celesta Easton, *Margaret D. Lewis, M. D.
BHOT.—Martha Sheldon, M. D., Miss Browne.
BUDAON.—Laura S. Wright, E. May Ruddick, Miss G. Peters.
CHANDAG.—Mary Reed.
GONDA.—*Florence L. Nichols, *Eva M. Hardie, Helen Ingram, *Lilavati Singh, Ruth E. Robinson, Alice M. Northrup, Ada Mudge, Katherine L. Hill, May C. Widney.
MORADABAD.—Isabella T. Blackstock, Nora Belle Waugh, Clara Organ.
NAINI TAL.—Sarah Easton, Rue E. Sellers.
PAURI.—Theresa J. Kyle, Mary E. Wilson.
PITHORAGARH.—Annie E. Budden, Lucy Sullivan, Mary Means.
SHAHJAHANPUR.—Fannie M. English.
SITAPUR.—Ida Grace Loper.
WIVES OF MISSIONARIES IN CHARGE OF WORK.—Mrs. Samuel Knowles, Mrs. L. S. Parker, Mrs. J. H. Messmore, Mrs. C. I. Bare, Mrs. F. L. Neeld, Mrs. John Blackstock, Mrs. L. A. Core, *Mrs. J. L. Robinson, Mrs. J. N. West, Mrs. N. L. Rockey, Mrs. G. W. Guthrie, Mrs. Florence Perrine Mansell, Mrs. G. C. Hewes, Mrs. P. S. Hyde, Mrs. B. T. Badley, Mrs. R. C. Thoburn, Mrs. Jennie Dart Dease, M. D., *Mrs. Flora Widdifield Chew, Mrs. C. M. Worthington, Mrs. Helen J. Wilson, Mrs. T. C. Badley, Mrs. Frey, Mrs. Alexander Corpron, Mrs. Robert I. Faucett, Mrs. Meek.

Because of the awful famine, and the sickness and suffering that always follow in its wake, our missionaries of North India have had a very difficult and trying year. Prices for food have been higher than was ever known in India and there has been much suffering among our Christians.

BAREILLY DISTRICT.—Mrs. West reports: "We are happy to say that it has been a most blessed year, and through it all we have been conscious of God's smile upon us. We have been able to visit all the circuits,

*Home on leave.

93

and some of them two or three times during the year. We have· done quite a good deal of itinerating, and have been rejoiced to see how eager the women are to hear. We had the wonderful· privilege of attending two great melas, where wonderful opportunities presented to sow seed in the hearts of the people. Since Conference Miss Alice Means has had charge of this work."

Mission Zenana Hospital.—Space forbids an adequate report of the work of Dr. Gimson. The work in all departments has been most successful and ever increasing. Neither day nor night has Dr. Gimson thought of self, never refusing a call. In addition to this heavy work, she has had to pass through another rainy season without a dry spot large enough to keep her instruments from being ruined. Is there not somewhere a handmaiden of the Lord who will build a new hospital in this, our oldest station? Dr. Gimson reports: "Throughout the year we have had large numbers in all departments. The early part of the year was like a nightmare. Plague was very bad, and we were called upon to treat many cases both at the dispensary and in the city. The outside practice has been large this year. Our work in obstetrics has been larger than it has ever been, having had more than seventy-five cases. The surgical work has been less, having performed only 120 operations in both the dispensary and hospital. The attendance in the hospital has been good. We have been called a number of times to the Orphanage this year, and the work among the women and children of the Theological Seminary has been entirely under our medical supervision, having had no special medical assistant for that work this year. Besides the regular work, we have been called a number of times to Budaon and Moradabad, and once to Aligarh.

"We take great pleasure in reporting the work of the training class for nurses; it has been a success in every way. We have seven nurses in training. Four seniors will complete their work in July, 1908, and return to their respective schools to take care of the sick there. We believe each girl able to take a position as trained nurse anywhere and do full work. Total number of patients treated, 27,691."

Orphanage.—More than two hundred girls, over fifty of whom are in the kindergarten department, have been in the Orphanage. The classes are large and the girls have done good work. Nine passed the first year's examination for Bible readers. The new roof on our dining and cook rooms has put our building in excellent condition. At a moment's notice specimens of writing and crochet lace were sent to a competitive bazaar; both got first prizes of Rs. 19. This money the girls voted for much-needed lights in the dormitory grounds. In their spare moments they have worked crochet lace, and from the profits of this paid their pastor's fund money and all "benevolences." Their Woman's Foreign Missionary Society Auxiliary collection for the year was Rs. 100.

Training-school.—Mrs. Mansell says: "The year has been one of unusual experiences. The kindergarten teacher, after weeks of triumphant suffering, was called Home. Near the end of March the seminary was closed, nearly seven weeks earlier than usual, to avoid the plague. Mrs. Mann, my assistant, was taken very seriously ill, and was obliged to be absent for several months. The Superintendent also was in poor health for some time. Despite these hindrances, the women did nearly as well as usual in their annual examination, held at District Conference time. The preparatory classes of village women did much better than usual. Fifty-one wives of students have been on our roll, five of whom have passed the four Bible-readers' examinations.

"Early in the year we had the joy of sending out our first family of foreign missionaries. Uday Singh, with his wife, Sarah, and their four bright children sailed for the Fiji Islands to work among the Hindustani colonists in connection with the Wesleyan Mission. Twelve women are now leaving us, with their graduate husbands, going out into life's work, not knowing what awaits them."

SHAHJAHANPUR.—Miss English says: "The year has been one of varied experiences and much blessing. In the spring we sent six girls for the Government middle examination, three of whom passed. The enrollment reached 132. The general health of the girls has been very good, though plague was very near us. Our School Missionary Society, and Senior and Junior Leagues have met regularly and have done very good work. In the spring we had some revival services and many of the girls were converted, while others were much helped and have taken a higher stand in the Christian life. Even some of the smaller girls have given very clear testimonies as to their conversion. Twenty-seven of the girls have been received into the Church in full membership, and others are on probation."

City and Village Work.—Mrs. Mozumdar has been set apart for Zenana work because of the increased calls. She reports encouraging work among the women. The city schools, three in number, report progress. We have about a hundred girls on the roll and an average attendance of seventy. The Catechism, Sunday-school lessons are taught, and Sabbath-school is held in each school. This work is very encouraging.

Home for Widows.—There are twelve women in the Home. They get religious instruction every day and are living up to the light they have.

Circuit Work.—In eleven circuits of East and West Shahjahanpur, consisting of about 150 villages, forty-six faithful Bible-women are carrying the gospel to hundreds of women and teaching as many more in the Sunday-school. There have been quite a number of converts, and the women are giving testimony in public as never before. Heathen customs are fleeing, and the light of Christ's gospel is spreading.

BIJNOUR DISTRICT.—The work in the district and in our Girls' Boarding School has suffered an irreparable loss in the death of Mrs. J. H. Gill. She was one of the most faithful missionaries in the foreign field and did as much for our Woman's Foreign Missionary Society work as any of our own missionaries. Two years ago she pleaded for money for new roofs and some additions, which was given to her by Mrs. Gamble in a personal gift. She was very happy in overseeing these additions. For several years she was a sick woman, yet never gave up her work, and at the very last she finished all scholarship letters and sent them to patrons. Faithful to the end, she has gone on to receive her crown and hear the "Well done" of the Master. In her last report, she says of the school: "At present we have the largest number of boarders we have yet had, and many were with us till April or May who have not yet returned. There have been ninety-one, all told, boarders and day scholars. We rejoice in the new roofs for schoolhouse and dormitories, and the permanent repairs, which make us so tidy and comfortable. A new addition to the assistants' quarters is nearly finished, which will make them much more comfortable. School has gone on without interruption. The girls are not only progressing in their studies, but in deportment, and are growing in Christian character. They are greatly helped by the precepts and examples of our good Christian teachers, who have so faithfully done their work. The larger part of the girls are real Christians, and all the larger ones are full members of the Church, while others are on probation. They are faithful and obedient in all their duties, and love the prayer-meetings and League, Missionary Society and Sunday-school. All this training is most important while in school. They live happily together and seldom require discipline.

"One boarder is in the normal class at Moradabad, training for a teacher. Another is in the training-school at Muttra, and the three who went last year we expect back in the summer for evangelistic work. So we are slowly preparing trained helpers for our work in all departments. We feel that we have had a good and fairly successful year."

Of the village and city work, Mrs. Gill says: "The work has gone on as usual, our faithful Bible-women carrying the gospel into the zenanas and mohullas. During the year all our women attended a Ganges mela, and talked to the women and sold or gave away Scripture portions. When there was plague in the city the latter part of the winter, the Bible-readers visited eleven villages near to Bijnour, and the women were so eager to hear that now we have arranged for them to give one day each week to village work. I was not well enough last cold season to go out in the district. In April I visited eight stations, and recently I have been to two others, about one-third of the whole number.

"One day some well-dressed, respectable Hindu women came into the crowd to listen to the preaching. Some male relatives tried to get them away, saying, 'These are Christians; you do not want to hear them.' But they refused to leave, saying 'They are good people and we do wish to hear what they are saying;' and before they left they bought some portions of Scripture and paid for them, and took them away to read. This could not have happened a few years ago. So we sow by all waters, and the truth is spreading in hearts and homes. 'In the morning sow thy seed, and in the evening withhold not thy hand.'"

BUDAON DISTRICT.—Miss Laura Wright, in charge of the Sigler Girls' Boarding School, reports an enrollment of 122, an increase of Government aid, and the best teaching staff they have ever had. She still pleads for new buildings. She says: "We are convinced of the advisability—yes, of the necessity—of new buildings on a new site, if we are to do justice to the girls, mentally, morally, and physically. We are overcrowded in the schoolroom, on the playground, and in the dormitories, to say nothing of the constant anxiety arising from the close proximity of the boys' school. We are grateful for the money which has been sent to help purchase the land, and we earnestly hope the land may be secured in a few months. We now earnestly beg of you to send money for the dormitories and other necessary buildings. Many of the girls understand spiritual teachings and are taught of the Holy Spirit as never before. May God help us to be faithful when there are no signs and wonders; may we learn to spell the word we can not read, and trust Him. The local Missionary Society collected about $10, which was sent to Dr. Sheldon for her work in Bhot."

City and Village Work.—Until Conference this was under the charge of Miss Waugh, and then passed into the hands of Miss Organ. Good work has been carried on in the zenanas, the day schools, and in the Bible class conducted by Mr. and Mrs. Childs.

BUDAON.—"Plague raged in the entire district during the winter. People left their homes in the city and went to live in groves and in the open country. Where possible, the preachers and Bible-readers carried on their work in these encampments. Heretofore the Christians have been spared, but this year many of them have died of this dread disease. On the Bilsi Circuit, though the work has been going on there for forty years, this year for the first time girls were sent to the Sigler Boarding School. The people look upon it as a sort of disgrace to send their daughters away from home. It is an extreme measure, to be resorted to only in famine times."

GARHWAL DISTRICT.—"Looking back upon the past year one can only say, 'Ebenezer, hitherto hath the Lord helped us.' How heavy the loss to this district is Miss Buck's death, only we know. Her mother, Mrs. Buck, visited Chopra a number of times during this year and occasionally taught a Sunday-school class and led the women's meetings. Since then the sisters have, except for occasional visits from the Gadoli missionary, looked after their work themselves, not having allowed it to slacken, but have been more earnest and energetic, working harmoniously as a Christian band of women, visiting distant villages, going to Srinagar, nine miles out, on foot, during the great bathing festival; holding night meetings, and helping in every good work."

PAURI.—Miss Wilson says: "The revival of last December was followed in the beginning of the year by another of more general influence and greater force. It affected every one here and better work has been done."

GONDA DISTRICT.—Mrs. Rockey, in charge of District work, says: "We have visited all but four remote places where we have work. Our workers have gone their rounds regularly, and our Heavenly Father knows the record. God has been with us, and we rejoice in Him and praise Him for the work accomplished."

Girls' Boarding School.—Miss Hoge, Superintendent, says: "The past year has been a good one in every way. The number has increased and the work has been faithfully done by both teachers and pupils. Bishop Warne came to Gonda for three days in August and held some blessed meetings with the girls. We are finding it difficult to make both ends meet on account of the famine prices of grain. The girls are doing without many things they should have, but are cheerful through it all. We need more buildings. If we had more room in which to store grain, we could have saved several hundred rupees by buying a supply for the whole season while the grain was cheap. As it is, we can only store enough for about two months. This necessitates buying all through the famine. Several girls sleep in the 'grinding room,' and also eat in the same place. It is so much more difficult to maintain good discipline in a crowded place, and it is hard to train the girls to tidy habits. All who have had charge of this school know how much new buildings are needed in the boarding department."

HARDOI DISTRICT.—Mrs. Tupper is Superintendent of the Girls' Boarding School, with sixty-two enrolled. They have been very happy in their studies and have made good progress.

Circuit Work.—The evangelistic work is under Mrs. Parker, who writes: "The prevalence of the plague in most of the circuits has prevented itineration, so that special evangelistic work has been largely confined to the time of the summer school in March and the District Conference in November. They have held revival services in a few of the circuits with blessed results."

KUMAON DISTRICT.—Mrs. Dease has charge of the circuit and village work and of the training-school. She says: "We have thirty-six girls in school and feel that real progress has been made. In the training-school the regular Conference Bible-readers' course is followed. The women have practical work in teaching in the village schools. The Bible-readers of this circuit have a wonderful opportunity for work, as pilgrims from all parts of India are constantly passing on their way to the plains after visiting the hill shrines."

NAINI TAL.—*Wellesley Girls' High School.*—Miss S. A. Easton and Rue Sellers, in charge of Wellesley High School, report the year ending November 22d as one of the best, whether considered from the standpoint of the health of the school, the attainment in scholarship, the enrollment, or the peace and harmony that have marked the year. Vacation time means no rest for these faithful missionaries, for it is full of work as is school time, with the moving down to Wellesley Lodge for the winter and the care of the children of the missionaries, who remain with them. Mrs. West, telling of the heartache that came as she sent her twin girls from her, said, "Thank God for Naini Tal."

Failing to secure recognition as a college, Miss Easton says: "We have decided to content ourselves by being a first-class high school, with a superior musical department. Looking to the good that may be done among girls devoid of technical home training, a new departure, in which we are seconded by the Government, of cooking and dressmaking classes, may prove a compensation. A teacher for these classes has been secured, quarters are being built, and a beginning will be made the coming year in that method of teaching the brain to think, the fingers to do." The new year opened March 6th with eighty-seven boarders and a few day pupils.

Hindustani Work.—Mrs. Worthington, who is in charge, reports that in the schools the work has been regular and the attendance increased. Some visiting has been done among the Christian families and in the hospital, but her one Bible-reader has had to fill up the gaps in the schools because of sick teachers, so that for the greater part of the time Mrs. Worthington has had the zenana work alone.

PITHORAGARH CIRCUIT.—In Pithoragarh there are many happy hearts, for Lucy Sullivan is among her people again and from all classes she received a demonstrative welcome. She writes: "In all departments of my work here I find progress and harmony, and am very grateful to Mary Means for the good manner in which she has handled everything." Miss Sullivan arrived in the midst of a wonderful revival, which has swept through the Girls' School and Women's Home, the manifestation of the Spirit's power being so wonderful that some prayer-meetings lasted six hours continuously. "God has surely been gracious to these uneducated village women, and the shine on their faces tells the story of the new life in the heart." The famine has brought into the Home many child widows between ten and fourteen years of age, so that a school has been organized in the Home with an enrollment of thirty-five. They will need more scholarships. To Miss Means was assigned the evangelistic and medical work. Miss Means and her Bible-women have made several long evangelistic trips on which she found much work to do and many interested listeners. During the summer she held a summer school for her Bible-women, which proved exceedingly helpful. The great burden has been the medical work. Without a medical education, the responsibility of dealing with human life is too great for any woman. In her serious cases, Dr. Corpron, of our General Society, has been most kind and helpful. A medical missionary here is an immediate necessity.

Miss Sullivan's new house is building slowly, but we hope before the close of another year this long-felt want will be a reality. Because of the drought the crops are less than usual, but Miss Means says that the faithful work of the women, "with God's blessing, has resulted in much better crops than the average Hindu farmers about have secured. Despite the lack of rain and the frequent visitations of locusts, when our hearts felt overburdened for the future, God has overshadowed us and taught us anew to put our confidence in Him alone."

Bhot.—Dr. Sheldon writes: "The door into Tibet, which had apparently swung open, seems now faster shut than ever to direct missionary effort—not this time by the hand within, but by the hand without. But we have an appeal to Him 'who hath the key of David—He that openeth and none shall shut.' Meanwhile we are not in the least discouraged. Right here on the borderland we can work among the Tibetans who come over, for the door opens outwards and inwards for them and the Bhootiyas. We are seeking to train more thoroughly those whom God has given us. It is our delight to teach the children. We have many friends among them, attending the sick, teaching their children in Sunday and day schools, etc. We need now the convincing power of the Holy Spirit in our midst, and for this, as never before, we have been waiting upon God. He will send it through whomsoever He pleaseth. I think there are several Christians in Bhot whose heart cry is, 'O, that He might use me!' He can not long withhold His hand; the break will come."

Moradabad District.—Mrs. Core, in charge of the evangelistic work of the district, writes: "The Jubilee broke into the work of the band during January. February was spent in Sambhal, using it as a center for the many villages in all directions. In March we were joined by Bishop Warne. We made an extended trip through three circuits. We took with us a large force of workers and a large meeting tent, in addition to all of the usual camping outfit. Instead of village to village visitation, as is our usual plan, we called the villagers to us for evangelistic services. Four years ago, in company with Miss Means, we tried the same plan. We had the meetings thoroughly announced and worked up, but the villagers did not come, so it was with some forebodings that we made this second attempt, but the results were very different. We had three camps, and the village Christians *came*—came in large numbers—from long distances. They came eagerly, and as if for a purpose. The meetings were spiritual and helpful. Many of our village Christians received a definite and special blessing. Some went back to their villages to kindle the revival flame there. When we think of our Christians scattered all over the district in 1,500 villages, when we think of the great mass of Chumár women who need to be taught and gently led into Christ's fold, when we think of those in zenanas whose hearts are being secretly given into Christ's keeping, when we think of the countless thousands that need Him—when we think of all these, and then of our feeble efforts and the little that we can do, we are troubled and perplexed. All we can do is to turn to Him and just let Him work through us.

Moradabad—*City Schools and Mohulla Work.*—The plague epidemic interfered with this work. Several girls, some of them the brightest in the school, died of this disease. The schools for the higher caste girls are more prosperous than those for the lower classes. Sunday-schools are held in all the schools. "In the Mohulla work large numbers of women and girls are reached., Most of the meetings are held in the open air, where many of the women go on with their work while they sit and listen, and often join in singing our hymns. They receive eagerly Scripture pictures, and from them many lessons are given. There are schools for Christian and non-Christian girls in most of the mohullas visited.

In some of them special meetings for Christian women are held. The Gospel leaven is working in all these mohullas, and the day will surely come when many now worshiping idols will worship the living God." She has a most faithful assistant in Miss Gantzer.

Training-school.—"This school was held most of the year on the veranda of the missionaries house, where the missionary could have supervision. Nineteen names have been enrolled, but the average attendance has been fifteen. One-half the women spend two or three hours a day in some work, having practice with their teaching. One of the most advanced women has acted as an assistant teacher in the school, teaching new women that have come in."

Girls' Boarding School.—Since January Miss Blackstock has been in charge. "The revival of which we spoke last year has proved itself genuine by the lasting effect it has had on the lives of the girls. Although the second year has nearly been completed, not an evening has passed without the girls gathering for at least two hours of prayer and praise. An epidemic of measles passed through the school in the early part of the year. Again, we have had to turn many girls away, and even now have five more than we have scholarships for, but this can not continue. These awful famine prices make it so hard to manage, and next year I do not know what is to be done. Through the kindness of Mrs. Gamble we were enabled to build some new rooms and a godown this year, and so have been able to vacate other quarters for kindergarten work. This department is flourishing now under Miss Maya Das, who is greatly interested in the little ones, and has made their room beautiful with pictures sent in boxes from America."

Miss Waugh, in charge of the Normal Department, deplores the fact that although the need of this department is so great, and although she has a class of nine promising teachers, yet money to meet the financial side has not been sent. It is so necessary to have better prepared teachers that she is hoping some one in the homeland will recognize the importance of this work and assist financially.

OUDH DISTRICT.—In the absence of his wife, appointed to superintend the district work, Dr. E. F. Robinson, the district superintendent, has kindly assumed district supervision of the women's work, because no woman was available. We are indebted to this busy man, already over-worked, for this kindness. "At District Conference time, when it is the custom to bring in all the Bible readers to instruct and indoctrinate, as well as to inspire and help them, our lack of funds compelled us to give up the usual plan and allow the women to stay at home. This is not good for the work.

"In spite of the handicaps, however, the year has been a fairly good one, and although the size of the district is almost a half smaller than last year, because of the setting off of the Gonda District, still there have been about 150 women and girls baptized from those taught by our Bible-readers. In addition to this it is to be remembered that those who had already were Christians have been taught, and the Gospel of Peace has been given to thousands of heavy-hearted and hungry-souled Hindu and Mohammedan women; so tied up in their awful caste system that they could not openly accept Christ, yet whose hearts have found peace in believing in Christ."

Isabella Thoburn College.—But three missionaries of the eight teaching in the college remain. Four others *must* be sent by January 1st. Miss Nichols writes: "When our school opened in July, fifteen girls entered who had passed the middle examination to district schools. For the first time we felt that the right relation was being started between our school and the other schools of the Mission. These girls will stay here four years, perhaps some will go to college and stay eight years. They will go back to their old schools with new ideas and new thoughts. Not only is the Isabella Thoburn High School the center of the Methodist school system, but it is acknowledged by the Government to be the best school in the Provinces. From far and wide the students are coming to the college, so that it seems to be representative, not only of North India, but of the whole Indian empire. Miss Singh has become preceptress of the school hostel, and a great change has come into the home life of the girls. Flowers and vines in the compound, pictures in the rooms, are but the outward signs of real change in the manners and lives of the girls. It has been a great surprise to find how many were ready to become God's children as soon as their confidence was gained.

"We were much disappointed that no appropriation was made for the nurse's salary, and how to repair all the buildings with $100 is a problem that is beyond solving. Besides these immediate needs, the college has many others. There are at present four vacant beds in the school hostel, and there are twelve applications for these beds. One of our missionaries who wants to send a girl in January, said, 'What are we to do if there is no room at Lal Bagh, for there is no other place for our girls to go for training.' If we could get money to pay the interest on the endowment fund, $350 a year, we could use the endowment fund bungalow, now rented, for the girls who want to come to school. There surely must be friends at home who will help to meet the needs of this school."

Deaconess Home and Home for Homeless Women.—Miss Ingram reports as follows: "This year has been a very unfortunate one for our work, for Miss Hardie, after spending the whole summer in Kashmir vainly trying to get well, was at last ordered home by the doctors. Only the Great Day will show how much she has done for our Home and work in Lucknow. During my own five months' furlough in England, Miss Hoge most nobly came to our help, and by frequent visits was able to superintend the work here as well as in Gonda. All our workers have done good, faithful service, and we are very thankful to God for them. During the year we have had fifty-eight women and babies in the Home, and have been obliged to refuse several cases."

SITAPUR CIRCUIT.—There was practically nothing done for the first three months on account of the plague, but work was resumed the first of April. In the villages the workers are gladly welcomed in the homes. In one village, a stronghold of Mohammedanism, there have been some accessions to the Church. We have opened new houses in all the mohullas, and the workers are called to the houses of the rich as well as those of the poor, for the weekly visit of the Bible-reader is a bright spot in the lives of these "shut-ins."

Girls' Boarding School.—Miss Loper writes: "Our new building has gone up without a hitch. In the school the good conditions of last year have continued. To the girls there has come 'a refreshment from the presence of the Lord.' The whole school was greatly blessed. Thirteen of the largest girls expressed a desire to devote themselves to special Christian work, and twenty-six came into the Church on probation. Even the little ones were awakened, and the good done is still evinced by a cheerful, obedient, helpful spirit in the whole school. Perhaps as a result of the above, our missionary collection was swelled to twice its usual size. We raised over fifteen rupees this year, and sent it to Dr. Sheldon for work in Bhot. Our numbers have steadily increased during the year, until now we have 104 on the roll, the largest number we have had in the eight years I have been here."

PHILIBHIT DISTRICT.—Mrs. Frey writes: "During the past year I itinerated in all the circuits, and saw many villages in which our Christians live. They were instructed and advised according to their needs. Our people had the privilege of attending the spiritual meetings held by Dr. H. Mansell, Dr. W. A. Mansell, and Mrs. Mansell last May for several days, where the workers from five circuits were present."

NORTHWEST INDIA CONFERENCE.

Organized as a Conference in 1892,
Official Correspondent, Miss Ella M. Watson.

The United Provinces of Agra and Oudh, south and west of the Ganges, the Punjab, and such parts of Rajputana and Central India as are north of the twenty-fifth parallel of latitude, are embraced in the Northwest India Conference.

MISSIONARIES AND THEIR STATIONS.

AGRA.—Charlotte T. Holman.
AJMERE.—*Anne E. Lawson, Lavinia Nelson, Sadie C. Holman.
ALIGARH.—*Laura G. Bobenhouse, Julia J. Kipp.
ALLAHABAD.—Bessie F. Crowell.
BRINDABAN.—Emma Scott, M. D.
CAWNPORE.—Lydia S. Pool, Lily D. Greene, Minnie Logeman.
MEERUT.—Melva A. Livermore, Lena Nelson, *Annie S. Winslow.
MUTTRA.—Mary Eva Gregg, *Isabel McKnight, Agnes E. Saxe, Mary A. Parkhurst.
PHALERA.—Carlotta E. Hoffman, Estella Forsyth.
WIVES OF MISSIONARIES AND DEACONESSES IN CHARGE OF WORK.—Mrs. P. M. Buck, Mrs. G. F. Matthews, Mrs. Rockwell Clancy, Mrs. W. W. Ashe, Mrs. D. C. Clancy, Mrs. H. R. Calkins, Mrs. Benson Baker, Mrs. J. B. Thomas, Mrs. G. W. Guthrie, Mrs. W. E. Tomlinson, Mrs. James Lyons, Mrs. J. T. Robertson.

AJMERE DISTRICT—AJMERE.—Another good year may be reported in the Boarding School. Since January, when Miss Lawson left on furlough, Miss Lavinia Nelson has been in charge, with Miss Sadie Holman, sister of our missionary at Agra, as her co-worker.

Including the Normal Department, there are one hundred and thirty girls in the school. There is an efficient staff of assistants and teachers. The "pupil teachers" in the Normal Department are "earnest workers and of great assistance, while they have been gaining for themselves a practical experience. They devote three hours daily to teaching in the kindergarten and the classes as high as the third standard; they also study principles of teaching, arithmetic, English, Persian, calisthenics, writing, and drawing."

Five girls have recently passed the Government middle examination creditably. One who passed the year before, is taking advanced studies at Lucknow. Several have been in the Training-school at Muttra, and

* Home on leave.

others have gone out as wives of workers in Rajputana and the Punjab, winning favor for themselves and the school by the evidences of good training. Early in the year twenty-six girls were received into full membership in the Church.

In the city and villages the Bible-readers have done faithful and able work. Several families in particular seem near the kingdom, but still hold back from baptism. The floods have caused great damage even in dry Rajputana this year, and there has been more or less sickness.

PHALERA.—Here Miss Hoffman and Miss Forsyth are holding the fort, Miss Greene having been transferred to Cawnpore at Conference time. Miss Hoffman writes: "Although all the progress that was desired has not been made, yet there has been a real advance, and the prospect is encouraging for the coming year. That which is most gratifying to me is the spiritual advancement of the girls. They are really trying to do right, and in many ways we can see the results of their trying. It is a happy privilege to work among them, and nothing counts as hard in our lives here, if we are helping them to know the Master a little better as the days go by."

Mrs. Ashe writes of the village work: "Failures we have had, but thanks be to our heavenly Father, we have also had some success. We have been able to open up work in three new villages, with a Bible-reader in each place." Of the medical work: "While we have not a large dispensary practice here, yet it is very important. There are great opportunities for medical work in the surrounding villages, where they never see a doctor unless they are able to come to us for treatment. Very often they do come ten or twelve miles or more on foot or carried by their friends, but there are scores of them who are too sick to come, and who must die for the want of a little medical attention."

The Sanitarium at Tilaunia is meeting a great need. The services of an experienced medical assistant have been secured, and the matron is "untiring in her efforts to make the patients comfortable and happy, and is like a real mother to them. The nurses also have given valuable help. Twenty-four patients from seven different schools have been admitted during the year, of whom five have died, five have been sent back as well, and the remainder are improving."

ALLAHABAD DISTRICT.—Miss Crowell writes: "I am very happy and greatly interested in my work here. Already things look in a better condition. When I get the language a little better, I hope to do some evangelistic work on the district, and thus come in close touch with India's women." Throughout the district the Bible-readers show real growth in their spiritual lives, and a greater desire than ever to teach the people.

CAWNPORE DISTRICT.—Miss Pool reports for the Girls' High School (English): "This is the most successful of the four years I have been here. Our present enrollment fixes the high-water mark for the school. We have a total of one hundred and forty-seven names, an increase of twenty-six over last year. The report of the Government inspector was more encouraging than it has been for years. The kindergarten and the music departments have been kept up with interest. A more efficient and helpful staff of teachers would be hard to find. The work of this school is not merely the education of the domiciled community, but for the development of assistants for our work. We have furnished our proportion of these. Were our hopes only realized this school would be a power for the uplifting of man and for the glory of God. Our part is to do the utmost toward training the young lives that come ·to· us, and leave the rest to Him."

In the Hindustani Girls' School since January Miss Greene has been in charge. This is the school of which the Government inspectress has said: "It would be difficult to find a happier and more helpful lot of girls anywhere in this Province. I trust the school will ever keep up its reputation for integrity, simplicity, domestic usefulness, and training." Miss Greene is praying that during the special evangelistic campaign planned for November the revival power may be felt in this school.

"The work throughout the district is being more and more established. The very best people, especially among the officials, recognize the blessed influence of Christianity and gladly welcome our Church." Of the work in one new circuit the Bible-reader said: "At first they would not listen, and hated us. But we all stopped eating and prayed all night, and would not let go—and now they love us."

KASGANJ DISTRICT.—Faithfully the work has been carried on throughout the year by the Bible-readers of this district, under Miss Holman's lead. Again the District Conference proved to be a time of great spiritual blessing. "Twice, during these days, special night meetings were called after days of heavy work. One night the meeting lasted about three hours, the time being spent in pleading with God for an outpouring of the Spirit."

MEERUT DISTRICT.—In the school Miss Livermore reports a larger enrollment than ever before, and girls being turned away for lack of dormitory room. "Throughout the school the tuitional results have exceeded any other year of the school's history. Weekly teachers' meetings and a teachers' normal class have helped to bring about these results. Spiritually the school was never on so high a plane as it is now. We have been noting with joy these advance steps. A room is set apart for quiet prayer, and a band of faithful girls meet daily at an early hour for prayer." An outbreak of cholera in August made it necessary to close the school for a short time. But God heard and answered prayer! With twenty-two cases there were but two deaths, and the work of the school was not long interrupted.

Of the district work we are glad to learn that "the revival, coming with power in our Jubilee year, abides. Many of the village converts are realizing in a new way God's power to save. There have been more inquirers and baptisms from higher castes this year than during any previous one."

MUTTRA DISTRICT—AGRA.—Here Miss Holman is in charge of the city work, and was in charge of the Medical Home until it was closed. She writes as follows: "The Principal of the Medical School of Agra sent us a notice to the effect that after November 10th all students in our Home who were drawing scholarships from the Dufferin Fund would be required to live in the Government Boarding House, new buildings having been erected which enabled them to accommodate all the female medical students. This left our Home with only five girls, and the Board of Trustees decided that the Home should not be kept up for such a small number. So on November 11th, after a farewell breakfast and a devotional service, all the students of the Agra Medical Home were transferred to the Government Boarding House." Of the city work she writes: "The year has been one crowded with opportunities—so many open doors which we were unable to enter." One of the interesting incidents of her work is the case of a high caste Hindu woman who asked to be taught to read.

"Carrie (the Bible-reader) began visiting her once a week, and we were pleased to note the progress she made in a few weeks. It was not long until she had mastered the first and second Hindi books, and now, after having received instruction once a week for about seven months, she is reading the book, 'Dharm Tula' (Religion Weighed), which shows the fallacy of the Hindu religion and the efficacy of the Christian religion. We heard her say one day while reading, 'By the time I have finished this book I shall have become a Christian.'"

ALIGARH.—Another year of progress can be reported in the Orphanage, now, in charge of Miss Kipp. The educational work has been especially good this year, the industrial work as well, while the spiritual growth of the girls is a cause of great gratitude.

Mrs. Matthews finds the responsibility of the Woman's Industrial Home, with two hundred and sixty-six inmates, to be "no light burden." "We are thankful not so much for increased numbers and efficient work done as for the Christian experience which has become a personal reality to so many. Hand-to-hand work has helped many unto a knowledge of Jesus as a personal Savior."

BRINDABAN.—Dr. Emma Scott reports progress in nearly all departments of the work. "Since this time last year we have had over ninety in-door patients. This is more than we have ever had during one year before, but we will expect the number to increase now that we are to have more room. If the hospital were finished we would have more patients now. The yearly attendance (at this dispensary) has varied very little from former years—about four thousand new patients, and total attendance between seventeen and eighteen thousand. The zenana work, too, is very much the same. We have two widows here, one a Hindu and one a Bengali, waiting to be baptized."

MUTTRA.—The long illness of Miss Saxe, now well on her way toward recovery, has left the work here somewhat short-handed. Miss Gregg writes: "We have ninety girls in the Boarding School, and I am overseeing the work of that as well as I can in Miss Saxe's absence. We have ten in the English Department of the Training-school this year. Two of them are very interesting in that they have just come from Roman Catholic convents. One has been converted but a few months. There is an enrollment in the Hindustani Department of the Training-school of forty-eight girls. I am glad to say that they are better educated than any we have ever had before. But they should have more personal attention for their development than it is possible to give them unless we have a missionary specially for them. When this is by far the largest and best equipped training-school of any mission in India, is it not worth while to have one missionary set apart for the Hindustani department? My heart aches these days to be with the girls more personally and help them spiritually, and lead them individually, but at present it is an impossibility." Of the district work Mrs. Clancy writes: "During the winter months a great deal of itinerating was done. Miss McLeavy, my assistant, with her band of workers, was out for nearly four months, and Miss Gregg, with her Training-school students, gave ten days to the village work. More than three hundred villages must have been visited, nearly eight thousand Christians were seen and taught, and more than thirty-two thousand non-Christians were preached to; all this in addition to the regular work carried on in the villages by the workers living there already."

PUNJAB DISTRICT.—"We have only praise and thanksgiving for the wonderful way in which our heavenly Father has led in the work of this large district. The work in this district has grown, and though we were short of funds, it seemed impossible to restrain the growth. But we are still without the girls' school, which is needed so much, and without which our work can never be what it should be."

ROORKEE DISTRICT.—Cheering progress is reported in this district. Mrs. Lyon writes: "In our visits after our regular work in Quarterly Conferences and examining schools, we have studied always to have evangelistic services, and have had many blessed meetings. Our District Conference was a remarkable one and the best we have ever had: So many received and rejoiced in being restored to the joys of salvation, and prayers went up and continue that Roorkee would be a spiritual district always."

SOUTH INDIA CONFERENCE.

Official Correspondent, Mrs. E. D. Huntley.
Organized as a Conference in 1876; reorganized in 1886.

The South India Conference includes all that part of India lying south of the Bombay and Bengal Conferences and the Central Provinces Mission Conference.

MISSIONARIES AND THEIR STATIONS.

BANGALORE.—Elizabeth M. Benthien, *Urdell Montgomery.
BIDAR.—Norma H. Fenderich.
HYDERABAD.—Catherine A. Wood and Alice A. Evans.
KOLAR.—Harriet A. Holland, Florence W. Maskell, *Fannie F. Fisher.
MADRAS.—Grace Stephens.
BELGAUM.—Mrs. C. W. Scharer, Judith Ericson, *Grace M. Woods.
VIKARABAD.—Mildred Simonds, *Elizabeth J. Wells.
RAICHUR.—Mrs. Cook.
WIVES OF MISSIONARIES.—Mrs. Roberts, Mrs. Lipp, Mrs. Butrick, Mrs. Toll, Mrs. Hollister, Mrs. Schermerhorn, Mrs. Ross de Sonza, Mrs. King, Mrs. Ogg, Mrs. Tindale, Mrs. Grose, Mrs. Ernsberger, Mrs. Scharer, Mrs. Cook, Mrs. Gardner.

BANGALORE.—Miss Benthien is alone at Bangalore, carrying the work that formerly has been cared for by two. The school is larger than it ever has been. Here they have a Student Volunteer Band and a Study Class. The purpose of this Student Volunteer Band is to pledge the girls to definite missionary work. Twelve are enrolled. There is a call for a large number of scholarships to be taken for the needy Eurasian girls. The school gives one free scholarship for every ten boarders. The debt on the building is still crowding them, and the school is taxed to its utmost capacity. Here pupils are prepared for the Madras University matriculation. Everything that you have in a first-class High School is taught here, kindergarten training all through the course. The children of the Kindergarten have made this last year a fine bead curtain which is to be given to the school. The work that was done by them last year was sold, and with the money the beads were purchased for the curtain, which is being woven. A Young Woman's Christian Temperance Union organization was formed last February, the officers for the year elected, and very fine programs

* Home on leave.

have been given at the monthly meetings. It is surprising to notice how up-to-date everything pertaining to this school seems to be.

BIDAR.—The last news from Miss Fenderich announces the fact that the Government has sanctioned the purchase of the land already bought, and has given us land adjoining which will give us a fine building site and agricultural land. In all we will have ten acres, on which is a good well. In the near future we hope the friends interested in this field will give sufficient money to put up the buildings needed. After paying for the land, she has in hand about $500 toward this building fund. Her plan is to begin immediately the erection of one or two rooms. While it is not our aim to greatly enlarge this work, we do feel that we must hold work already started. In order that we may do this, it will be necessary to leave Miss Hudson in charge of the work and a new assistant to look after the evangelistic and Bible work which has formerly been cared for by Mrs. Batstone. During the absence of Dr. Batstone and his wife, Miss Fenderich had the care of all the work of the General Society. The strain of this has told materially on her physically and she hopes to take a six weeks' rest, thereby enabling her to stay until the close of the Conference year.

HYDERABAD.—Miss Wood and her Bible-women are visiting in four hundred zenanas of Hyderabad District, where five different languages are spoken. This work is in seventy-five different villages. The day schools and the twenty Sunday-schools, together with the industrial work, the training-school, the oversight of the ten Bible-women, and the Treasurer's work, does not leave much spare time for her. *It is eight years since Miss Wood was home on furlough.* In one village where Mr. Baker, the missionary of the General Society, and we are at work, there have been five hundred baptisms and more would join the ranks if there were Bible-women and teachers to give them instruction. The great need in this section is a training-school. Twenty-five dollars will keep a woman in school for a year. The day schools are held from nine in the morning until four in the afternoon, with a half hour at noon. The ages of these girls are from four and a half to fourteen years. From these day schools come our girls for the boarding schools.

In the industrial school the women come very early and stay very late, as they are paid by the piece and are anxious to do all that is possible. During the noon hour these women commit to memory Scripture and hymns and listen to explanation of portions of the Bible given by a native assistant. The seed sown at this noon hour is bringing an abundant harvest. Seven day schools and twenty-four Sunday-schools are held. At one place between forty and fifty are present regularly. Some of these girls can recite both questions and answers of nearly the whole Catechism and the Golden Texts for the Sundays of the year. Oftentimes these day schools and the Sunday-schools are held on the shady side of a little hut or under a tree. The only expense will be the support of a native teacher or Bible-woman. These day schools are supervised by Miss Smith. She pays a visit to each in turn during the week. Miss Wood has given us many a glimpse of the power of God and the comfort which these poor people have found in believing in Christ.

KOLAR.—Last year the bubonic plague swept over the town of Kolar and the surrounding villages, causing many deaths and leading to the evacuation of the city. Not one of our school girls died from this dread disease. On account of the plague the schools and zenana work had to be closed for some time; but now everything is fully established and 417 homes. are being visited. One encouraging feature is that the officials are eager to have us teach their wives and daughters. One of the pupils belongs to the royal family of Mysore. She is interesting and very anxious to learn. Miss Maskell writes: "The cloud in connection with the Mohammedans which so darkened our horizon last year is slowly passing away. Our girls are now allowed in all the homes we formerly visited." Kindergarten work has been introduced into the Brahman Girls' School, and an effort will be made to introduce it in all of the day schools. Miss Holland writes: "In the boarding school we have had 168 pupils. Fine work is being done. Our girls are standing well in their Government examinations. Twelve new pupils came at the beginning of the year; some are day scholars. High school work has been added to the course in the boarding school. The married women in this community can go to the villages and work, while the unmarried ones can not; hence we give the preference to the unmarried women for teachers in our orphanage."

MADRAS.—Madras with its varied kinds of work is supervised by Miss Grace Stephens. High caste and low, city and village people alike receive the loving care of this eminently successful woman. Her ten assistants are factors in the upbuilding of what is a most remarkable work in this colony at Madras. The pioneer in village work is "Joseph." His experience of one month would occupy all the time given for this report. In one of his villages the head man was converted and in every way is assisting in our work. He has transformed his cow shed into a tidy schoolroom and given a piece of land for the burial ground of poor village Christians. Conversions follow in the wake of this good man. In the early part of the year the high caste girl's school was greatly interfered with by the natives. The number has greatly increased until now we have 120 girls. The Government examination last week was held and was successful. The girls have been faithful notwithstanding the persecution. In many of the zenanas we find the child widow abused, mistreated by all the family circle. The only happy moments in their lives will be when the Bible-woman or missionary comes with a word of comfort and cheer. They are happy when they have learned to sing our hymns and to read our Church Catechism. Not always are the shut-in women allowed to receive the attention of the missionary. In the poor girls' school there have been many conversions this year. All the village schools are in good condition. The night school in one of our villages is largely attended by men and women of the sweeper class, who work all day, coming for instruction in the evening. This school has caused quite a commotion in the villages. Miss Stephens writes: "We get a little nervous at times to be there, but the men and women in the school protect us most loyally and walk with us until we are quite safe out of the village. The schoolroom was once a heathen temple; now Christian songs are heard. One of the little girls in the poor girls' school, whose father was a devil dancer, was taught from babyhood to worship the family goddess and had been dedicated to the worship of this goddess and at the death of her father was to take his place as the devil dancer in the temple. At one of the meetings in this school this child gave her heart to Jesus, and since that time would not visit the temple and worship any idols. Her parents refused to feed her and she comes hungry to school. She is trying to persuade them to allow her to be baptized and become a member of the Church." Many conversions are reported in the school this year. Evangelistic work is bearing much fruit. On last Easter Sunday there were seventeen baptisms. In the orphanage the regular school work receives attention. Added to this is the industrial feature. Many of our girls are not able to do much intellectual work, and here is a field in which many of them excel. I must give you some figures. Miss Stephens writes: "In the zenana work for the past year we have had five hundred pupils. The total number of visits and lessons in the zenanas have been 16,228. The listeners alone in the homes, beside the pupils, were 7,045. Direct conversions for the year among the women were seventeen. This does not include all the other secret disciples that we have. Twenty-three idols were surrendered by the women. Besides all this they have given freely toward our mite-boxes; they have done needle-work for us and have passed Scripture examinations, etc. I told you in my last letter how over fifty women came forward publicly in the midst of a vast assembly and received prizes for having passed their Scripture examinations. In the school department we have taught daily over one thousand children from every grade, and from the lowest to the highest caste. We have had among the children for the past year 250 conversions. Fourteen idols were given by them and we have had thirty-seven baptisms."

VIKARABAD.—Miss Wells is at home on furlough. Her place has been supplied by Miss Simonds and heroically she has faced the problems confronting her. It is never an easy task to superintend the erection of buildings. While the work was well under way when Miss Wells left for America, it was not completed. Some perplexing questions presented themselves. The most difficult was the digging of a new well. Present results are satisfactory except the large expenditure of money necessary because of the treacherous soil and the caving in of the well.

Our boarding school and orphanage have been doing good work. Our new quarters when completed will be none too large for the numbers applying.

Early in the year revival services were held. It is gratifying to notice that the study of the Bible is the most popular branch which we have. Several Scripture classes have been organized aside from the regular study of the Bible. The burden of souls has been laid on the hearts of Christian girls, and reaching out for those who are unacquainted with our Father seems to be the aim of our Christian girls. A woman's class was organized to teach the village women. There are many instances which could be mentioned' of the rescuing of girls from lives of shame. Miss Simonds writes: "The evangelistic work is doing well. There have been many baptisms in the villages. In Kosgi, one of our villages twenty-five miles from here, there is an especially good work among the high caste people. One man came to Vikarabad with the native worker from that village and was baptized here. He seemed so interested in everything in our bungalow and asked for some books to read. We gave him the Gospel of Matthew and some other Telugu books which we had. We showed him a Sunday-school roll which some one sent from home. He was perfectly fascinated with the pictures and stories. He said he couldn't see why we didn't have these pictures up on our walls. We gave him two or three to take home with him and he was very much delighted. He invited us whenever we went to his village to come and eat with him. We have heard since he has gone back to his village that he is being very bitterly persecuted by his relatives and neighbors."

BELGAUM.—Miss Wood is at home on furlough. At the last Conference, Miss Urdell Montgomery was given charge of the work. In less than a year she has been obliged to return to the homeland, and again a change has been necessary. At present Miss Ericson has charge of the school. They are still in very poor quarters and not at all safe because of the lack of a wall around the Compound. In moving our boarding school from Raichur to Belgaum we have secured for our missionaries a desirable location and one far removed from any other station where we have a boarding school. Now we are in a good-sized Christian community. The needed buildings must be given for the best interest of the work and the comfort of the missionary sent there. In October the plague broke out and interfered with our work. During the last year there has been an average of thirty-seven orphans and boarders.

Evangelistic Work.—Mrs. Scharer writes: "Eight Bible-women are at work within a radius of thirty miles. These women have worked faithfully during the year. Oftentimes the meetings are held on the veranda of a house, and the men gather around to listen." There are two day schools at this place needing support. Good work is being done. Shall they be closed?

RAICHUR.—The work here is under the supervision of Mrs. A. E. Cook. Here we have a small school sufficient to take care of our primary department. The evangelistic work and the Bible-women have been looked after by Mrs. Cook. The reports are encouraging.

CENTRAL PROVINCES CONFERENCE.

Organized as a Mission Conference in 1905.
Official Correspondent, Mrs. A. N. Fisher.

The Central Provinces, with their feudatory States, Berar, a section of the southern part of Central India, and a section of the northern part of the Nizam's dominions, are included in the Central Provinces Conference.

MISSIONARIES AND THEIR STATIONS.

JABALPUR.—Mrs. A. H. Holland, Elsie Reynolds.
KHANDWA.—Anna R. Elicker, Mabel Lossing, Josephine Liers.
RAIPUR.—Emily L. Harvey.
SIRONCHA.—*Mrs. Maud A. Turner, Ada J. Lauck.
WIVES OF MISSIONARIES IN CHARGE OF WORK.—Mrs. Louise Blackmar Gilder, Mrs. W. D. Waller, Mrs. Martha Day Abbott, Mrs. V. G. McMurry, Mrs. F. C. Aldrich, Mrs. H. A. Musser, Mrs Nettie Hyde Felt.

MARATHI DISTRICT.—The Marathi people are acknowledged to be a bright, intelligent, sturdy class. Among the six millions of these in this District there is no representative of the Woman's Foreign Missionary Society. Mrs. McMurry, Mrs. Waller, and Mrs. Musser are in charge of all the work that has been undertaken for women and girls.

BASIM.—Mrs. McMurry reports that the girls' school, under the care of Miss Sprague, has maintained its good record. Thirty-two girls passed the final government examination. There is great need of more Bible women for the evangelistic work. Most encouraging reports have come

*Home on leave.

from those in the field. Mrs. McMurry writes: "Much has been said about the down-trodden condition of India's women, which is all too true; but, after all, she is in a sense the moving factor among her boys, and we believe much of the seditious spirit found among the school boys in India to-day can be traced to the education they receive from their poor, deluded mothers."

KAMPTEE.—Mrs. Waller writes: "We have been patiently and hopefully prosecuting the work, and despite many drawbacks and difficulties we are able to look around at the prospects and take courage.

"The day school at Kamptee has made great improvement during the past four years. Our government grant now amounts to one hundred rupees a year. Mrs. Butterfield visits the homes of the zenana women regularly once a week. They have asked for our gospel hymn-books, and they sing our hymns in their Marathi language. Even their husbands read and sing our hymns.

"Our five Bible-women still continue their very needful work. We have been endeavoring to reach more of the village population and have succeeded to some extent. Had we the means we should like to open girls' schools in the villages. There is such a call for them! Government is doing little or nothing for girls, although there are schools for boys in every considerable village. The cost would be from seven to nine dollars a month.

"Then we shall soon have to meet a very pressing need here in Kamptee—we have a good boarding-school for boys, but there is nothing for their poor sisters. The people are very destitute in the matter of education, only one-tenth have a smattering of what we call education. Their lives are terrorized by most appalling superstitions. They believe in witches, and nearly every village has its witch. Their religious knowledge is too woeful for words to describe, especially among the women. God is giving us many gracious opportunities."

NAGPUR.—The work at Nagpur is very interesting. There are several small primary schools and some interesting zenana workers. The District Superintendent, Rev. H. A. Musser, has recently purchased a beautiful property in Kamptee, twelve miles off on the railroad, where it is his earnest desire to have a missionary of our Society stationed, from which point she could also superintend woman's work at Nagpur.

One interesting feature of the work here is the recent baptism of a young woman who gives promise of becoming a fine helper. Daily she gathers a large crowd on her veranda and reads to them from the Bible, sings, and tells them of Jesus. On Sunday she has a class of twenty little girls.

GODAVERY DISTRICT—SIRONCHA.—In reporting the evangelistic work, Mrs. Turner says: "There have been failures and disappointments, but the victories, the pleasures, and joys of service far outweigh the discouragements. Souls have been reached by this blessed gospel of Jesus and hearts have been touched by the love of God and quickened into new life. Much time has been given to zenana work, and many calls to enter into new homes have come to us. The Bible-women in the out-stations have been doing faithful work. These have known the burdens of Hindu life, and they now know the joys of redeeming love. They know how to sympathize with their sisters and can also tell of the Comforter, Jesus Christ our Lord.

"Twelve Sunday-schools have an average attendance of 329 non-Christian children. The older people, both men and women, often attend. They seldom ever object to anything we teach the children."

There has been an encouraging growth in the school and the orphanage, a considerable number of children coming from distant jungle villages.

Sironcha also stands for a home for homeless women. There is need of a new building for these, the temporary huts having been destroyed by fire.

Another change has been necessary in the missionary force, owing to the serious illness of Mrs. Turner and the return of Miss Galbreath to America; but with Miss Ada Lauck in charge the work will still go graciously forward.

JABALPUR DISTRICT.—JABALPUR.—Mrs. Holland writes: "Jabalpur is an increasingly important center, and we feel that we must have a strong work here. We are glad to report progress in the school work. Miss Reynolds is supported by a fine staff of teachers, of whom six in the lower grades are of our own orphanage girls. All are Hindustani young women and all except our orphanage girls have finished the high-school work, while several have taken some college work. A class of seven was sent for the teachers' examination this year, and five girls passed the Anglo-vernacular middle school. We now have two classes in the high-school work. The director of public instruction paid us a recent visit and reported 'everything in excellent order.' There are about 210 girls in the orphanage. They are a happy family, and, while there are many problems and anxieties, yet it is a joy to work among them and we thank God that He has put us here. We are praying that their souls may develop along with the development of body and mind, that these girls may be truly converted and be faithful workers for the Master."

The removal of Mrs. Felt to Jagdalpur left the evangelistic work without full supervision. "In the city and immediate vicinity there are seven Bible-women and one assistant at work, but it is a force entirely inadequate to meet the needs. A dozen older girls from the Bible training-class of the orphanage, who have had some training, are anxious to do zenana work; as far as possible we are planning for them to go out with the older women. The older Bible-women are glad to take these girls under their protection and give them the help and training they can, in the actual work.

"In the District there are six Bible women. There are a number of fine villages for work which we are unable to supply. Much good could be done if a missionary could give her entire time to itinerating." Mrs. Holland is looking after this work as best she can with other duties devolving on her.

KHANDWA.—The Central Provinces Conference, which met in Khandwa in January, was a source of great spiritual blessing to all. Miss Liers writes: "I realize as I never could at home, what a feast such an annual gathering proves to those, who have been giving all the year of their spiritual store without receiving the inspiration that comes by contact with others.

"The educational work has been making steady progress with Miss Lossing to superintend and do much of the teaching. At present there is a teachers' training-class of sixteen girls, from which she will be able to fill the vacancies when the present teachers leave for the Bible-women's work, which they are to do under Miss Elicker. They are well equipped for evangelistic service.

"Miss Lossing's specialty is the kindergarten. Not long ago the inspector-general visited the school, and he was so pleased with the work in general, and the kindergarten in particular, that he gave them some prize

NAMES OF STATIONS.	Basim	Kamptī	Nagpur	Godavery District—Sironcha	Chindwara Cir't	Gadawara Circ't	Jabalpur	Khandwa	Burhampur	Narsinghpur	Raipur	Raipur District	Total
. F. M. S. Missionaries				2			2	2			1	1	7
ives of Missionaries in Active Work	1	1	1				1	1		1			7
oreign or Eurasian Assistants		1		2			3				4		10
ative Workers		1					12	9					22
OMEN IN THE CHURCH—Full Members	25	25	28	30	2	4	156	40		33	‡		343
Probationers				32			52	260					344
Adherents				33			10						44
omen and Girls Baptized During Year		3	3	23			18			1			43
o. Christian Women Under Instruction			18	14			14	30					76
on-Christian Women Under Instruction			100		43	60	400	125					725
o. Bible-women Employed	8	4	5	21	2	4	21	8		18	11	11	108
IBLE INSTITUTES OR TRAINING CLASSES													
No. of Institutes							1						1
No. Missionaries Teaching							1						1
No. Native Teachers							1						
Enrollment							12						12
RPHANAGES—No. Orphanages	1			1			1	1			1		5
No. Foreign Missionaries				2			2	2			1		7
Foreign or Eurasian Teachers				2							1		3
No. Native Teachers	5			3			12	5			4		29
Total No. Orphans	65			33			228	125			65		516
Receipts for Board and Tuition							$134						$134 00
Government Grants and Donations	$200			$24			G$460	G $80			$66 66		$830 66
OMES FOR WIDOWS AND HOMELESS WOMEN—No. Homes				1							1		2
No. Foreign Missionaries													
Foreign or Eurasian Teachers													
No. Native Teachers				1									1
No. Women				14							6		. 20
Receipts for Board and Tuition													
Government Grants and Donations													
AY SCHOOLS—No. Schools	1	1			1		2						5
No. Teachers	1	2			1		2						6
Total Enrollment	30	47			10		18						105
Average Daily Attendance		17											17
Receipts for Tuition													
Government Grants and Donations		$ 33.33											$33 33
INDERGARTENS—No. Kindergartens							*1	*1					2
No. Foreign Kindergartners													
No. Native Kindergartners							1	1					2
Native Kintergartners in Training													
Total Enrollment							9	8					17
Average Attendance							7	8					15
Receipts for Tuition													
Government Grants and Donations													
NDUSTRIAL SCHOOLS—No. Schools							*1	*1					2
No. Ind. Depts. in Other Schools													
No. Foreign Missionaries													
Foreign or Eurasian Teachers													
No. Native Teachers													
No. Pupils							†	†				†	
Receipts for Tuition													
From Sale of Products							$25	$20				$29	$74
Government Grants and Donations													

* Part of Orphanage.
† All capable of work are enrolled.
‡ No report.

money, asking what they would do with it. They promptly replied that they would like new books for supplementary reading, and this pleased him more than ever. He also granted the school some very desirable printed matter, ordinarily used only in the Government schools for boys. The girls meet once a month in joint Epworth League with the boys of the orphanage to render a literary program, which is always full of interest."

NARSINGHPUR.—The evangelistic work is carried on by a promising band of Bible-women, who go out two by two. The weekly Saturday meetings continue to be a blessing to all. These are times when any difficulty in the work or any special victory is reported, and when together they pray for needed guidance and success.

RAIPUR DISTRICT.—RAIPUR.—Miss Harvey pleads for a co-laborer in her work. She says: "There is much to encourage. We have never had as good interest among the women about us. Especially is this true of the zenana work. The gentlemen of these homes bid us welcome. Several native judges and other officials have come to us in person, asking us to visit the women of their households. There is an increasing demand for the city school. This affords a wonderful opportunity for work among the Mohammedans. They have pressed this school upon us. They have come to the point where they are determined to have their girls educated. In giving them some education, we have an opportunity to give them the gospel. Wide-open doors are before us.

"The girls in the orphanage are making satisfactory advance in school work and in Christian character."

Mrs. Gilder reports greater regularity in the district evangelistic work than heretofore: "As yet it is only seed-sowing throughout the district. My sixteen Bible-readers, however diligent, can reach but a very small proportion of the 500,000 heathen women within our borders, and sometimes it seems a hopeless task to bring all these into the light and knowledge of God. They are so densely ignorant, inheriters of ages of heathen darkness and superstition, that we cry daily, 'Who is sufficient to penetrate and dispel this terrible darkness?' Our sufficiency is of God."

BOMBAY CONFERENCE.

Organized as a Conference in 1892.
Official Correspondent, Mrs. Wm. B. Thompson.

MISSIONARIES AND THEIR STATIONS.

BARODA.—Mary E. Williams, Margaret D. Crouse, Belle J. Allen, M. D.

BOMBAY.—Elizabeth W. Nichols, Helen E. Robinson, *Joan Davis, Anna Agnes Abbott.

NAIDAD.—*Ada Holmes, Cora Morgan.

GODHRA.—Laura F. Austin.

POONA.—*Mrs. S. W. Eddy, Harriet L. R. Grove.

TELEGAON.—*Christina H. Lawson.

WIVES OF MISSIONARIES IN CHARGE OF WORK.—Mrs. Bancroft, Mrs. Butterfield, Mrs. Clark, Mrs. Fisher, Mrs. Hill, Mrs. Parker, Mrs. Stephens, Mrs. Fox.

*On home leave.

The political unrest prevalent in India has been acute in the city of Bombay, it being for a time under police and military control. The situation was such as to cause much solicitude among the missionaries of that region. The Conference has had occasion to rejoice for various material improvements. A goodly number of new buildings in various stages of progress, from corner-stone laying to final completion, promise better housing of both work and workers. The year has also been marked to an unusual degree by vicissitudes. There were the losses to the always slender force of missionaries through the departure of a number for health reasons. Sadder still were the bereavements that came to the missionaries in the death of two of their number—our Miss Curts and the Rev. A. C. Parker, of the Board of Foreign Missions.

Miss Curts' health had been declining and the good rest in Ceylon during the hot months proved to be only a temporary benefit. In early December she wrote pleading for some one to be sent out to make ready to take her place, as it was thought she should not attempt another hot season in India. Yet she hoped to continue longer. However, typhoid fever set in and in a brief time all her work was done; and now she rests indeed.

The serious illness of Miss Morgan more recently, was the occasion of much anxiety, but good improvement is now happily taking place.

POONA.—The Taylor High School for Girls is enjoying its improved outlook and everything is encouraging. It recently registered its highest mark in attendance in the history of the school. It is hoped that the boarding department will soon be fully able to meet its expenses. Minor improvements have added to the comfort of all. The buildings are now in first-class condition and are a credit to the Society. The work of the teaching staff is of high order and the Government examinations have been successful.

Mrs. Fox, who is in charge in the absence of Mrs. Eddy, says there has been an encouraging spirit of inquiry among the students regarding spiritual things. At a meeting recently held in the school nearly every one not only spoke, but also led in prayer, and it was with difficulty that we brought the meeting to a close, so earnest and intense was the interest pervading the meeting. The Holy Spirit was manifestly present in great power.

BARODA.—This has become a notable center in the vernacular work. Here are the Girls' Orphanage, the Florence Nicholson School of Theology, with its woman's department, and the Mrs. William Butler Memorial Hospital, under construction. Who can say which of these institutions in its own sphere of work is most full of significance for the future? The orphanage has industrial line of activity which is promising, weaving being a principal feature. The educational work is excellent.

The woman's department of the theological school is going on well, with an improvement in this regard, that more of the women than formerly have once been students in the mission schools, and the advantage accruing is easily perceived. Altogether 107 have been enrolled. Last year it was noted with pride that two of the women were in not only the woman's department, but the theological school proper, taking the same course as their husbands. They passed with credit and are now in the second year's studies, while seven others formerly in the Baroda and Godhra orphanages are venturing to follow their courageous example.

The Evangelistic Department hopes to send out several good helpers this year.

Medical work greatly needs the early completion of the hospital building that all the varied ministries appropriate to this line of work may proceed, such as the care of the suffering, healing of the sick, and the training of helpers. Dr. Allen says: "The assistants have rendered faithful and efficient service, making many visits besides doing the dispensary work and having the care of many cases. The difficulties attendant upon this work baffles description." The doctor has not only the heavy burden of medical work among the suffering natives, but she has been most faithful in her care of the sick among the missionaries, and her services are deeply appreciated.

GODHRA.—A great sorrow shadowed this household in the death of their faithful and efficient missionary, Miss Curts; but God has been very good to the school, and in spite of all the changes and hindrances the work has been going on well. One of the triumphs of the year is the new school building which they only recently began to use for class work. It is a great delight to have a real schoolhouse to work in instead of the old place on the verandas of the dormitories, exposed to the dust and heat in the hot weather and to wind and rain in the other seasons. It will be a great help not only to the teachers and pupils, but to the missionary as well, making it possible to superintend the work to a much better advantage.

The general health of the school has been good. Two hundred and seventeen girls constitute a good-sized family, but they are very lovable and give no more trouble than any such number of girls would give. There is a class of twelve in the sixth standard this year. It is the first time that this standard has been carried through the year, partly for lack of teachers and partly for lack of girls enough to make a good class. Three of the girls brought up in this school are now in the Government Teachers' Training College in Ahmedabad. They are making good progress and give promise of becoming good teachers. We are anxious that other girls may have the same privilege. Of the girls who have married this year some are wives of Christian workers; one teaches in the training-school of Baroda; some are studying with their husbands.

The evangelistic work about Godhra was left so short of workers, by the shifting necessary to supply vacancies elsewhere, that the missionaries wives have had to take a large part of its supervision. Many attentive hearers are found as the workers go from village to village. Many have been led to give up idol worship and are now serving the true God.

KATHIAWAR.—This region is having its best year in woman's work, notwithstanding persecution. One village where there had been no baptisms previously has been so stirred, by the voluntary efforts of a Christian widow, that there has been quite a break up and thirty-five have now been baptized, so that there is here a good field for Christian instruction. In another region recent breaks have given ample field for the three workers employed, to say nothing of the numbers of candidates not yet baptized and at other villages calling for help. But they are too far away for the workers to visit them with their present equipment. These scattered circuits and villages demand the presence of a missionary free to the work, furnished with the needed equipment. This has been asked for repeatedly, but not yet granted.

Marathi Work, Bombay City Schools.—In this work Miss Robinson has twelve teachers, some of whom are still in training. That really good, substantial work is being done is evidenced by the fact that girls are securing preparation for middle school work. One of these girls is trying for the Government scholarship, which will enable her to stay on in the school as pupil-teacher.

An interesting incident is reported from Colaba School. "A Parsee matriculate was employed last year, but she left us at the beginning of the year to enter college. However, she had learned a good deal of Christianity while with us and even attended the Y. W. C. A. camp in Lanauli, and was really stirred to do some spiritual work for her Parsee sisters, so that they might enjoy their religion as we do ours. But her efforts failed, and we hope she saw how much more there is in Christ to enjoy than in Zoroaster. We see little of her now, but when we meet she likes us to explain to her such things as Jesus the Good Shepherd, the Bread of Life, etc.—it is all so different from her own religion."

"The Inspector told me he had recently sent in a report to the Government giving a list of five hundred places where schools are urgently needed in this city. He has told us over and over that we can not have a good school until we have our own building, and I am promising some of my teachers who are working in the slums a short distance apart, that we are really going to have a school near them, where we can be clean and comfortable, just as soon as the City Improvement Trust listens to our repeated requests and grants us land. They have been waiting a year and a half and we seem no nearer the realization of our hopes than at first, but we are doing our best, writing and interviewing them frequently, and I am confident something will soon be done."

There is a very great need for schools among the girls in the Gujerati community. A very needy class is in danger of going back to heathenism for lack of instruction and help. In one place the only Christian woman gathers her neighbors about her every day to talk and pray with them. Two young women, the daughters of ignorant Christians, received the little education they have in Miss Lawson's school while it was in Bombay. One is now studying the Bible-woman's course and wishes to go to Government Training-school. The other is now the wife of a Gujerati preacher in Karachi and is to continue her Bible-woman's study.

The Marathi *Woman's Friend,* gotten out with much difficulty, meets with encouraging appreciation. One of Ian Maclaren's characters is being dressed in India costume and now speaks in Marathi to the women who read the paper.

Evangelistic Work.—Although the year began with such scarcity of helpers as to cause a sinking of the heart of the missionary in charge, yet it has gone on in a wonderful way, no houses being neglected and new ones constantly being added.

"In April we had the great privilege of receiving into the Christian faith a Parsee family consisting of the mother and two children, the father having died some time ago. Mrs. Sorabjee comes of a good family. She was first visited by us about four years ago. From that time she has always evinced a deep interest in the Word of God. Lately she has been coming to the bungalow every week to study English, and this always ended in an earnest talk and prayer. She often said, 'I believe Jesus is the Son of God, but I can not confess Him.' However, last April she went with Mrs. Bhimjibhoy, our Parsee Christian worker, to our camp-meeting in Lalauli, and there on Easter Sunday in our little tent on the hillside the battle was fought and won—Christ was revealed in the Word. This resulted in prayer and praise, and she exclaimed, 'I have life now; Zoroastrianism is a dead religion.' She then gave up her sacred cord and in the evening was publicly baptized with her little daughter. She immediately came to Bombay, made known her change of faith to her Parsee friends. removed her little boy from the school, had him baptized, and now both the children are being educated in the Taylor School in Poona. This has meant literally loss of friends and income. She said, 'When I became a Christian I gave up everything; but I know God will take care of me' Her family are very angry, and have entirely discarded her. She is going on nicely and really learning to know her God. The other day she wrote a letter to her friends, saying, 'Although you are angry with me, I never can give up Christ, for He has given me life, and joy, and peace, and even if you can never forgive me I shall always pray for you.'

"We have on our roll two hundred high-class homes, and some of them are seriously considering Christianity. We believe this family is only the first of many which we are to see in Bombay. Among the lower classes also the work is growing, and some are continually coming into the Christian faith."

TELEGAON.—This school felicitates itself upon the possession of its new and comfortable building, the Ordella Hillman Memorial.

The year has wrought the usual changes in the release from suffering of some of the frail little lives and in the marriage of some of the older girls. Some have gone out into active Christian work and some to the quiet, congenial task of making a happy Christian home. Some of the schoolgirls have been going out to teach in the Hindu Sunday-schools. Most of the seniors passed the first year of the Bible-woman's course, Miss Durant having prepared them. Fifty-four passed the vast all-India Sunday-school examination. Much interest is manifested throughout the school in Bible study, which is systematically carried on from youngest to oldest.

The village work under Miss Durant has gone steadily forward and new doors are opening. The high caste who at first showed opposition are becoming more friendly. Recently a gentleman connected with the Swadesi School has invited her to teach his wife English and permits the Bible to be taught. Another Brahman gentleman, after listening to the message, said, "I am sure Christ is the only true Savior and that through Him alone is salvation." When asked why he did not make a public confession, he replied, "I dare not; I am afraid of the consequences." He says he often reads parts of the New Testament given him long ago. An old woman said she wished she knew Jesus, and upon being told how she might know Him, she said, "But I do n't understand how He who is so great can love an old woman like me." She was taught to pray, and when they left she was still standing outside her door with her hands folded, repeating the words she had been taught. A girl of nineteen expressed a desire to become a Christian, but her relatives said: "If you become a Christian you must leave us for good; we will never allow you to come back here. Go now, but never return." The sacrifice was too great; she felt she could not then leave her people. Doubtless there are many like these—just ready to accept Christ—but fear keeps them back.

Within the year twenty-eight villages have been visited, ten of them regularly, and nearly two thousand have listened to the gospel. Of course this number includes men, for in the villages the preaching must be done out of doors and a mixed crowd is inevitable.

Our Poona and Circuit work are ever on the increase and we find it hard to keep up with it, as the money does not increase with the work. New villages have been added to the list, also new schools in Poona. The help our women get in their department of the theological school is making quite a difference in our workers. We must have trained workers who will keep up with the India of to-day.

The Frederick Rice Memorial Dispensary is flourishing and reaches many with the Word, both in the city and the villages.

SUMMARY OF WORK IN THE BOMBAY CONFERENCE.

District groupings — **Bombay District:** Bowen Church, Igatpuri, Taylor Memorial Ch., Poona · **Gujerat District:** Godhra, Baroda Station, "Nadiad, Ahmedabad, Degan, Mahnda, Kathlal & Kapadvanj Circuits", "Baroda, Kalol, Jambusar, Palej and Savali Circuits" · **Kathiawad District—Vaso Circuit** · **Marathi District:** Bombay, Colaba; Bombay; Poona; Talegaon · **Totals**

NAMES OF STATIONS.	Bowen Church	Igatpuri	Taylor Memorial Ch.	Poona	Godhra	Baroda Station	Nadiad, Ahmedabad, Degan, Mahnda, Kathlal & Kapadvanj Circuits	Baroda, Kalol, Jambusar, Palej and Savali Circuits	Kathiawad—Vaso Circuit	Bombay, Colaba	Bombay	Poona	Talegaon	Totals
W. F. M. S. Missionaries	1			1	3	2					2		1	11
Wives of Mis'aries in Active Work	1				3	1						1		7
Foreign or Eurasian Assistants					5	2					2		1	10
Wives of Ordained Native Preachers					1	1							1	3
WOMEN IN THE CHURCH—														
Full Members														......
Probationers														
Adherents														
Women and Girls Baptized dur'g Yr,							118	125	35	8				281
Christian Women under Instruction							1009	1075	556			2		2,642
Non-Christian Women under Inst'n,						3	85		2					90
No. Bible-women Employed							27	30	7		12	10	1	87
BIBLE INSTITUTES OR TRAINING CLASSES—No. of Institutes														
No. Missionaries Teaching														
No. Native Teachers														
Enrollment														
SCHOOLS FOR TRAINING BIBLE-WOMEN—No. Schools					1									1
No. Missionaries					1									1
No. Native Teachers					4									4
Enrollment					85									85
Receipts for Board and Tuition														......
ENGLISH BOARDING SCHOOLS—No. Schools				1										1
No. Foreign Missionaries				1										1
Foreign or Eurasian Teachers				9										9
No. Native Teachers														
Self-Supporting Students														
Wholly-Supported Students														
Boarder Students				35										35
No. Day Students				21										21
Total Enrollment				56										56
Receipts for Board and Tuition				*										
Govern't Grants and Donations				*										
ORPHANAGES—No. Orphanages					1	1								2
No. Foreign Missionaries					1	1								2
Foreign or Eurasian Teachers														
No. Native Teachers					12	15								27
Total No. Orphans					215	230								445
Receipts for Board and Tuition					*	*								
Govern't Grants and Donations					*	*								
DAY SCHOOLS—No. Schools							15	13	3		6	5		42
No. Teachers							15	13	3		9	5		45
Total Enrollment							209	107	47		164	122		649
Average Daily Attendance							*	*	*		*	*		......
Receipts for Tuition														
Govern't Grants and Donations														
MEDICAL WORK—No. Hospitals							1							1
No. Foreign Physicians							1							1
Eurasian or Native Physicians														
No. Medical Students														
No. Foreign Nurses							1							1
Eurasian or Native Nurses							1							1
No. Nurse Students														
No. Hospital Beds														
No. Hospital Patients							57							57
No. Hospital Clinic Patients														
No. Out-Patients							307							307
No. Out-Dispensaries														
No. Dispensary Patients							2268					3234		5502

* Not reported.

The dispensary in Aloni is now in the new building and is a great blessing to about forty villages. Who can measure the good done in this way where thousands of people are reached in a year?

The Wagoli Circuit is being worked by a man and his wife who live in the village. Workers are also sent out from Poona from time to time, and the Poona compounder visits this village and takes medicine along for the people.

You may be sure we have our disappointments. One day I visited one of my city schools and found a dear little girl of about eight who had been taken to the temple and married to one of the gods, thus dedicated to a life of sin. I gave her name to the City Inspector that he might report the case to the Government and save the child, but she was not to be found. Another day I found that a little girl of ten, who was in the second standard, had been married to a man fifty years old. He has a wife, but no children; so he was marrying this child that he might have children to help him to a high place in Heaven. In another school I had a beautiful Mohammedan girl who wanted to be baptized, but the father was frightened and afraid of his people and took the girl out of school.

But we have bright days, too, and we know that the work is not in vain. We have had several baptisms from our city schools and saved one little girl from a Hindu marriage, and she is now in our girls' school and will be sent to the boarding school at Telegaon as soon as her people consent. Our Bible-women bring many encouraging reports of their work.

From many parts of this Conference come urgent appeals for more missionaries to be sent to the needy, promising fields.

BENGAL CONFERENCE.

Organized in 1886. Reorganized in 1893.
Woman's Foreign Missionary Work opened in 1882.
Official Correspondent, Mrs. S. F. Johnson.
Bengal Conference includes all of the Province of Bengal. ·

Missionaries and Their Stations.

ASANSOL.—Eugenia Norberg.
CALCUTTA.—Elizabeth Maxey, Nainette Henkle, Hilma Aaronson, Fannie A. Bennett.
DARJEELING.—Bertha Creek, *Emma L. Knowles, *Julie E. Wisner.
MAZAFFARPUR.—Jessie I. Peters, Grace I. Bills.
PAKUR.—Pauline Grandstrand, Hilda Swan.
TAMLUK.—*Katherine A. Blair, *Jennie E. Moyer.
WIVES OF MISSIONARIES IN CHARGE OF WORK.—Mrs. Ruth Culshaw, Mrs. Ada Lee, Mrs. J. P. Meik, Mrs. F. P. Price, Mrs. M. B. Denning, Mrs. E. G. Saunderson, Mrs. Byork.

ASANSOL.—Miss Norberg, who is in charge of the evangelistic work and the Widows' Home, writes encouragingly of her work. She has spent much of her time in the villages, four of the workers accompanying her to do the teaching and singing. One of ther Bible-women brought in a whole family from her village to be baptized. There has been a good

---

* Home on leave.

deal of sickness among the widows and in the Hindu day schools. Miss Norberg is working hard on the Bengali language and is very happy in her work.

The boarding school having suffered the loss of Mrs. W. P. Byers, now on furlough, is still happy in the enjoyment of its new dormitories, class-rooms, and kindergarten hall. Miss Hosking, now in charge of the school, writes as follows:

"Quite a number of new girls have come in since the beginning of the year, driven to seek shelter and food because everything in the market is so expensive, and owing to cholera and small-pox, which has been raging in Asansol. Three of our dear girls were taken by this dread disease, cholera. Others had it, but by God's blessing and careful nursing they recovered. Some of our widows had small-pox, but were spared, thank God! During this trying time we were not surprised when we found a family of four children on the back veranda of our ladies' home. Three were girls and a dear baby boy of about a year old. They were so dirty and miserable! Their parents had died of cholera, and they were without friends, wandering about, begging, when some one told them of our school home. We took them in, bathed and cleaned them, cut off their hair, which could not be combed or cleaned. They are happy now in school. When the baby first came, we thought he would die, he was so sick. We had an anxious time nursing him, but he is well now, and a fine boy. One of the older girls cares for him, and he is very fond of her. How glad we are that God gives us the opportunity of taking in these dear children to train in ways of usefulness and teach them to know Him who loved us and gave His life for us.

"Before the rains broke we had great scarcity of water and were concerned when our tank dried out; but were more so when we found our well, the only means of water supply, had no water in it. But God did not allow us to suffer. We appealed to a coal mine manager for permission to draw water from a pit which had been recently made and which had beautiful, clear water in it. Our request was granted. Then we all went down to the pit, some to help draw and some to carry. We took our bullock-cart, with two large barrels on it, and, though the buckets were very heavy to draw up, a number of the larger girls and some of the widows took hold and we succeeded in getting sufficient water. Every vessel was filled, as we are a large company here. The rains have broken now, and we have all the water we need. The season has been extremely hot, so we hail the cool, rainy season with delight."

CALCUTTA.—With the addition to the high school building and the complete renovating of the whole building, Miss Henkle and Miss Aaronson feel as if they had an entirely new structure and are greatly enjoying the improved accommodations. With the help of a "fresh air fund" raised in Calcutta, these faithful workers took twenty-two of the girls who had no homes to the hills with them on their summer vacation. Miss Bennett, of the orphanage, did the same thing with ten of her school. Just where the word "vacation" can be applied to such self-sacrificing labor it is difficult to see. The majority of the children were small, and therefore required much care. One writes that when they got through they wondered how Susannah Wesley ever got along with her family, and decided that she deserved to be called the mother of Methodism. At the Deaconess Home Miss Maxey still holds sway, and extends her helpful ministrations to very many people. She has given twenty years of her life to missionary work in India and now urges us to send a deaconess who can take her place, and we would like to grant this most reasonable request. That Deaconess Home under Miss Maxey's care has done much for the Methodism of all Bengal.

The Hindustani work of Calcutta and Kidderpore is in the care of Mrs. Saunderson and Mrs. Byork, and the latter is greatly in need of money for medical work which was begun by Mrs. Price, who still pleads for it. Large numbers of Eurasians, Hindus and Mohammedans come for treatment.

Here, too, is a great opportunity for work among sailors and all sea-faring people. Mrs. Byork speaks to large audiences on the coal docks.

The Bengali work of Calcutta is still under the capable management of Mrs. Ada Lee. She rejoices in the progress of her new building as well as in the added reinforcement of missionaries who went out to help her about a year ago.

At Beg Bagan, where Mrs. Meik is in charge, there are more than a hundred pupils in the day schools. The smaller children need a larger room than they now have, also kindergarten materials. Four Bible-women are doing good work on this circuit.

TAMLUK.—After working so long alone at Tamluk, Miss Blair is now home on furlough. The schools and Bible-women there are in charge of Mrs. Price, but it is impossible for her to be there all the time; so we are still looking for the best way to permanently care for Tamluk, where Miss Blair has been so bravely holding the fort, far from other than native workers.

DARJEELING.—Here Miss Creek is in full charge of our large school, as Miss Knowles and Miss Wisner are home on furlough. This leaves heavy work for Miss Creek, but none but encouraging reports come from her or from those who know of her work. A new missionary is greatly needed here in beautiful Darjeeling, where every prospect pleases, including the opportunities before our Queen's Hill School.

MUZAFFARPUR.—With a splendid corps of teachers, Miss Bills reports encouragingly concerning the school work. Fifty-four children are in attendance, the general health excellent, progress in class work good, and a real spiritual uplift evident.

In the District evangelistic work Mrs. Denning has had an assistant and the efficient help of five Bible-women. Two of the day schools have had to be closed for a time because of the prevalence of cholera.

Miss Peters, in charge of the zenana work, writes: "From month to month the interest is maintained and increased. Books of a religious nature and good stories are eagerly read by the Bengalees, and frequently the Bible is asked for. The New Testament in story form is read, we know, because when we read and explain it the women say, 'Yes, we read it in the Book you gave us,' and then they frequently go on with the narrative themselves. Thus we feel as if the leaven is working."

PAKUR.—One piece of good news from Pakur this year is that by the aid of a Government grant the last of the debt on our fine new school building has been removed. This gift was made on condition that not more than eighty-five girls occupy the building and that some exterior sanitary conditions be improved. The first-named condition compelled the removal of the widows to another home, and to secure such, all money appropriated for this year will be needed. It is a great advantage to have the widows' home separate from the girls' school. Miss Grandstrand is in charge of the former and Miss Swan of the latter. Miss Grandstrand also has charge of the evangelistic work among the Santali people, which she finds intensely interesting because of their ambition to learn of the

SUMMARY OF WORK IN THE BENGAL CONFERENCE.

NAMES OF STATIONS.	Asansol District— (Including 3 Stations.)	Calcutta District.	Diamond Harbor District.	Tirhoot District.	Total.
W. F. M. S. Missionaries	3	5		2	10
Wives of Mis'aries in Active Work.	3	5		2	10
Foreign or Eurasian Assistants	2	18		2	22
Native Workers	21	19	1	6	47
WOMEN IN THE CHURCH—					
Full Members	195	20	175		390
Probationers	232	15		405	652
Adherents	35	11			46
Women and Girls B'zed during Year.	53	4	3	175	235
No. Christian Women under Inst'n.	375	35		50	460
Non-Christian Women under Inst'n,	50			200	250
No. Bible-women Employed	20			5	25
BIBLE INSTITUTES OR TRAINING					
CLASSES—No. of Institutes	1				1
No. Missionaries Teaching	1				1
No. Native Teachers	2				2
Enrollment	3				3
ENGLISH BOARDING SCHOOLS—					
No. Schools		2			2
No. Foreign Missionaries		3			3
Foreign or Eurasian Teachers		28			28
Self-Supporting Students		168			168
Wholly-Supported Students		13			13
Partly-Supported Students		8			8
No. Day Students		126			126
Total Enrollment		388			388
Receipts for Board and Tuition.		$14,509 00			$14,509 00
Govern't Grants and Donations.		{ $2,914 00 G } { 545 00 D }			{ $2,914 00 G } { 545 00 D }
VERNACULAR AND ANGLO-VER-NACULAR BOARDING SCHOOLS—					
No. Schools	2	1		1	4
No. Foreign Missionaries	1			1	2
Foreign or Eurasian Teachers.	3				3
No. Native Teachers	9	11		4	24
Wholly-Supported Students				66	66
Partly-Supported Students				2	2
No. Day Students	2				2
Total Enrollment	175	208		68	451
Receipts for Board and Tuition.				$8 00	$8 00
Govern't Grants and Donations.	$340 00			$558 00	$898 00
HOMES FOR WIDOWS AND HOME-LESS WOMEN—No. Homes	2				2
No. Women	38				38
DAY SCHOOLS—					
No. Schools	5	5	1		11
No. Teachers	5	6	3		14
Total Enrollment	118	144	92		354
Average Daily Attendance	80	122	88		290
Govern't Grants and Donations.		{ $40 00 G } { 3 00 D }	60		
KINDERGARTENS—					
No. Kindergartens				1	1
No. Native Kindergartners	1			1	1
Nat. Kindergartners in Training				1	1
Total Enrollment	25			21	21
MEDICAL WORK—					
Eurasian or Native Physicians.				1	1
No. Out-Patients				50	50
No. Dispensary Patients	3.082				3,082
Dispensary Receipts	$150 00				$150 00

Christian religion and the wonderful gift of memory which they possess. She writes: "Can you really believe that these grown-up women are exactly like small children, who must be taught every little thing? O, if you could realize the darkness that is found on this side of the earth! I never pass through a village without the thought, Lord, how is it possible? What terrible influences could have dragged Thy creatures, made in Thy image, so far from Thee? It is only the gospel of Christ that can change them. During the last year seventy of these Santals have been baptized. The Sunday-school and day schools are most hopeful."

The medical and Bengali evangelistic work is in charge of Mrs. Culshaw. Including Bolpur, where more money is greatly needed, she has ten Bible-women, two teachers, and several village schools under her care. Sickness has hampered the work somewhat, but the Bible-women are faithfully telling the gospel story in the zenanas and villages, and thus the good news of salvation from sin is told over and over till all shall hear, from the least to the greatest.

Surely no stronger appeal comes to us for help physical and help financial than comes from Bengal Conference with its four Districts, including twenty-six stations. The question is, Will we rise to our opportunity and send the necessary help to our noble band of workers in this needy field?

BURMA.

Started in 1879.
Organized as a Mission Conference in 1907.
Official Correspondent, Mrs. Wm. B. Thompson.

MISSIONARIES AND THEIR STATIONS.

RANGOON.—Methodist Girls' High School (Charlotte O'Neal Hall), Alvina Robinson, *Grace Stockwell, *Josephine Stahl; Methodist Burmese Girls' School (Shattuck Hall), M. L. Whittaker; Burmese Evangelistic Work, Luella Rigby, Phoebe James.

THANDAUNG.—Methodist Girls' School (Elizabeth Pearson Hall), Fannie Perkins, Charlotte M. Illingworth.

This small force in Burma is as engrossed and enthusiastic in their work as are our missionaries in all lands.

The Methodist Girls' High School has enjoyed a year of great prosperity. One of the banner days of the year was when in the *Government Gazette* of Burma appeared the list of names of those who had succeeded in passing the Government high school examination (held annually for the whole Province), and the three highest on the list were girls from the Methodist Girls' High School, Rangoon. It was especially gratifying because their teacher, Miss Clara Garate, is one of our own Methodist girls, having taken her high school course in our Calcutta Girls' High School, Calcutta, India. After teaching four years in Queen Hill, Darjeeling, she spent two years in a teachers' training college. The high quality of her work this year emphasizes again the great value of normal training in our mission schools. We are fortunate in having a staff of earnest, conscientious young women in this school who continue year after year with untiring faithfulness, giving their best in effort and influence to their pupils.

*Home on leave.

Miss Robinson reached Rangoon in November, 1907, and began work in the Methodist Girls' High School. In March, when Miss Stahl left for her furlough, Miss Robinson took charge of the school—a heavy responsibility for one so new to the field, especially as in the English-speaking schools the support of the school does not come from America, but must be secured on the field. It comes from two sources, viz.: Tuition fees and Government aid. This implies on the part of the principal of the school most careful business management and a large amount of routine work. Frequent news from the school tells of the satisfactory way in which every department is progressing under Miss Robinson's supervision. Along with this is the statement, in almost every letter, that she is working too hard and can not stand the strain alone very long. A recent letter from Miss Robinson gives us a fine glimpse of the school at work:

"The children's dormitory of the Charlotte O'Neal Hall, the boarding department of the high school, has been undergoing quite extensive and greatly needed repairs, which are now practically completed. The building has a new corrugated iron roof, with an excellent ventilator extending the full length. Since this dormitory is, like a great many other buildings in Burma, raised about ten feet from the ground, nearly fifteen hundred square feet of this space below the sleeping-rooms has been inclosed for dressing-rooms and bath-rooms. There are three large dressing-rooms, one large and eight small bath-rooms. By this new arrangement everything is removed from the sleeping-rooms except the beds, thus giving much more floor space, so that now a larger number of children can be accommodated and still the Government requirement of four hundred cubic feet per child be complied with. The highest number of boarding pupils at any one time this year is forty-three. Interest along the different lines of school work is good.

At present a great deal of interest is taken in the library. The stock of books is being constantly replenished from funds earned by the school last year, and the children eagerly look forward to Friday, when they may have a new book to read.

An attractive feature has also been recently added to the day school in the form of a reading-room, where teachers and pupils are at liberty to spend their leisure moments. Owing to the suggestion of our energetic high school teacher about fifty rupees were collected by the school children during the holidays. This money has been partially invested in periodicals, and in addition to this kind friends have made donations, until now our reading-room contains the following: The *Northwestern Christian Advocate,* the *Epworth Herald, Pathfinder, Outlook, Sphere, Illustrated Times of India, Review of Reviews, Teacher's Magazine,* and *School Century.* It might be added that our tables are large enough for still more magazines, if any kind friend of missions wishes to dispose of his as soon as he has finished with them. If addressed to the Methodist Girls' High School, Lewis Street, Rangoon, Burma, they will reach their destination.

The boarding pupils take great interest in the Band of Hope, which meets twice during the month, and in the Junior League, which meets at the boarding-hall every Sunday afternoon from 4.30 to 5.30. The big girls are very helpful and spend much of their recreation time in practicing for the different programs and in training the little ones in their songs and recitations. The Junior League gives a missionary program once each month and takes up a collection for the support of a scholarship in the Burmese Girls' School. Just now the members are trying to get up a program to give in public, hoping to raise some money to apply on the scholarship, since the monthly collection is not quite sufficient. One would have to search a long time to find a Junior League whose members are more willing to lead in prayer, quote Scripture, tell Bible stories and sing songs than this one in Rangoon."

Miss Perkins and Miss Illingworth, at Thandaung, have not ceased to express their joy in the splendid Elizabeth Pearson Hall, so well adapted to their needs. This school continues its policy, in which it is unique among English-speaking schools, of having the ordinary work of the household done by the pupils. Like all new departures, the idea must have time to grow. The children enjoy their work, and the teachers are untiring in their willing devotion to the interests of the home. The Sunday preaching service and the Sunday-school, also the Epworth League and midweek prayer-service, are kept up.

Evangelistic Work.—In Burma the city and village or District work has not been divided, but this work is carried on both in and out of the city, on the boats and trains, in the fields and bazaars, everywhere where Burmese people are found these workers with their faithful Bible-women are welcome, and their message is listened to by large numbers of men, women, and children. Wherever they go the parting word is, "Come again soon," or, "Come often."

Regular Sunday-school work is carried on in six different parts of the city, and in these same sections the visiting work is done during the week, except when the workers are obliged to be out of the city for work in the numerous villages where there are already some Christians who need teaching and shepherding. Another missionary for this work is much needed.

During the rains a Bible training-school was held for the workers and any other women who wished to come in, and it was a great joy to the missionaries to see the growth and development in spiritual things during these weeks. Some of these who are now too young and inexperienced for work would be glad to continue the training regularly until prepared, if there were but some one who could give her time and attention to this work, and native workers are so much needed it is hard to refuse them this privilege; but again comes the cry, "Lack of workers."

Results of the Sunday-school and visiting work could furnish the material for many an interesting incident. One missionary writes of a poor, blind woman who had come to the Sunday-schools and there learned a number of songs and Bible verses, and later, in the Government hospital, where she was being treated, she sang and talked so much with the women that they all called her Christian. She was even known to pray with some of her Burmese sisters. When she came out of the hospital, who could refuse her and her two little ones baptism? The missionary says of her, "She has such a beautiful, child-like trust." Another writes of the wonderful growth and consecration of one who came to us under trying and questionable circumstances. We feared her motives were not the best for desiring to be a Christian, but the result of teaching has brought her in touch with the Christ, and she has given up things in her life that were most difficult, saying, "I think not how hard this is for me to do, but how good God has been to me."

Burmese Girls' School, Shattuck Hall, Rangoon, Burma. Missionary, Miss M. Loth Whittaker. The history of the school has been, from the first, a story of wonderful growth, especially since having their own home for the school "Shattuck Hall." Heavy has been the work resting upon Miss Whittaker during the past year, and at times there have been serious fears of a break in health, but now she seems to be improving. The boarding-school now numbers sixty, and the large number of day pupils makes the entire enrollment more than two hundred and twenty-five. This last year the seventh standard has been added, and the girls who pass that examination at the end of the year are ready for training as teachers,

SUMMARY OF WORK IN THE BURMA CONFERENCE.

NAMES OF STATIONS.	Pegu Sittang Circuit.	Rangoon and Vicinity.			Thandaung.	Thongwa Circuit.	Total.
		Burmese.	English.	Tamil.			
W, F. M. S. Missionaries		3	1		2		6
Wives of Mis'aries in Active work			1			1	2
Foreign or Eurasian Assistants							
Native Workers							
WOMEN IN THE CHURCH—							
Full Members	1	22	120	28			171
Probationers	*40	18	25	12			95
Adherents			25				25
Women and Girls B'zed during Year,		13		†6			19
No. Christian Women under Instr'n,		17					17
Non-Christian Women under Inst'n,		35					35
No. Bible-women Employed		3					3
BIBLE INSTITUTES OR TRAINING CLASSES—No. of Institutes		1					1
No. Missionaries Teaching		2					2
No. Native Teachers							
Enrollment		7					7
ENGLISH BOARDING SCHOOLS—							
No. Schools			1		1		2
No. Foreign Missionaries			1		2		3
Foreign or Eurasian Teachers			16		3		19
No. Native Teachers							
Self-Supporting Students			30		28		58
Wholly-Supported Students			2		9		11
Partly-Supported Students			3		7		10
No. Day Students			200		4		204
Total Enrollment			285		48		283
Receipts for Board and Tuition			$9,014.		$2,622.		$11,636.
Govern't Grants and Donations			{ G$3,193. { D-Nil		{ G$1,183. { D $300.		{ G$4,376 { D $300.
VERNACULAR AND ANGLO-VERNACULAR BOARDING SCHOOLS—							
No. Schools		1					1
No. Foreign Missionaries		1					1
Foreign or Eurasian Teachers		4					4
No. Native Teachers		5					5
Self-Supporting Students							
Wholly-Supported Students		27					27
Partly-Supported Students		8					8
No. Day Students		151					151
Total Enrollment		210					210
Receipts for Board and Tuition		$1,705.					$1,710.
Govern't Grants and Donations		{ G$1,572. { D $41.					{ G$1,572. { D $41.
DAY SCHOOLS—No. Schools					1		1
No. Teachers					2		2
Total Enrollment					42		42
Average Daily Attendance					38		38
Receipts for Tuition					$79.		$79.
Govern't Grants and Donations					{ G$92. { D-Nil		{ G$92. { D-Nil
KINDERGARTENS—							
No. Kindergartens			‡1				1
No. Foreign Kindergartners			3				3
No. Native Kindergartners							
Nat. Kindergartners in Training,							
Total Enrollment			71				71
Average Attendance			40				40
Receipts for Tuition			$636.				$636.
Govern't Grants and Donations			G $160.				G$160.

List Government Grants and Donations separately, one above the other, marking Grants (G) and Donations (D)

* Baptized women.

† Infants baptized.

‡ Figures included in English Boarding School, Rangoon.

and if they are held for our own work this should be provided in our own school, else they will go elsewhere, and that will mean a great loss to our work, and just when and where it will bring most difficulty, as teachers especially are exceedingly difficult to get. The opening of this training department can not be undertaken by Miss Whittaker because of her being already overburdened. Where can we find the normal-trained young woman who will go and help out in this emergency? She is needed *now*.

The Sunday-school and Junior League Work have been most helpful in bringing the girls to Christ, and class-meetings and prayer circles have also been a large factor in developing the spiritual life of the school.

MALAYSIA.

Organized as a Mission in 1887, as a Mission Conference in 1893; reorganized as a Conference in 1904.

Official Correspondent, Mrs. F. F. Lindsay.

The Malaysia Conference includes the Straits Settlements, the Malay Peninsula, French Indo-China, Borneo, Celebes, Java, Sumatra, and the adjacent islands inhabited by the Malay race.

MISSIONARIES AND THEIR STATIONS.

KUALA LUMPUR.—Miss Ary J. Holland, Edith Hemingway.
MALACCA.—*Ada Pugh, Jessie Brooks.
PENANG.—Clara Martin, May B. Lilly.
SINGAPORE.—Sophia Blackmore, Mary Olson, Minnie Rank.
TAIPENG.—*C. Ethel Jackson, Marianne Sutton, Thirza E. Bunce.
WIVES OF MISSIONARIES IN CHARGE OF WORK.—*Mrs. W. F. Oldham, Mrs. H. L. E. Luering, Mrs. J. R. Denyes, *Mrs. B. F. West, Mrs. G. F. Pykett, Mrs. W. E. Cherry, Mrs. Emma Ferris Shellabear, Mrs. Emily E. Buchanan, Mrs. W. E. Horley, Mrs. Mary Hoover, *Mrs. Florence Pease, Mrs. A. J. Amery, Mrs. B. F. Van Dyke.

Our hearts have been stirred for Malaysia this year as we have listened to the telling enumeration of the growth and needs of this magnificent field, as they have been presented to us by Bishop and Mrs. Oldham and other devoted workers.

With a growing population of seventy millions of people, among which no other American Church is laboring, the call to the women of Methodism is clear and persistent. Our schools there must be increased in number and efficiency and a strong spiritual atmosphere must be maintained. Owing to the fact that the Government is continually raising the standard of our schools, it is becoming imperative that more thoroughly trained American teachers be sent to the assistance of those already in the field.

The Deaconess Home in *Singapore* has been in charge during the year of Miss Minnie Rank, Miss Blackmore, its former Superintendent and our first representative to Malaysia, having spent the year in Australia. The Home has been filled to overflowing, and a dormitory, long needed to house the girls, has become an absolute necessity. The three girls who were sent to Lucknow College for further training have returned and give

*Home on furlough.

promise of being good teachers; one is to be sent to Kuala Lumpur, and the other two remain in Singapore.

The Methodist Girls' School, situated a half mile from the Deaconess Home, and the school at Telok Ayer, a wealthy Chinese suburb, have both been in charge of Miss Mary Olson, who has cheerfully and efficiently carried the work done in former years by two and sometimes three ladies. More than 200 girls have been in the two schools, many of them from homes where Christ is unknown. The parents, at best, have but little appreciation of female education, but they are sending their girls younger and allowing them to remain longer in the schools.

One of the most encouraging aspects of the work in Singapore during the past year has been the fact that girls from non-Christian homes have been permitted to attend Church when they were called for by the missionaries. The old barriers of superstition and ignorance are breaking and better days are dawning.

Miss Olson's furlough is due this fall, and if sufficient help can be sent to Singapore to relieve her, she will return home the coming winter. A teacher trained in primary methods, is a crying need in the Methodist Girls' School in addition to the principal, and Miss Olson pleads that both shall be sent. Of their difficulties there she says: "The problem in the girls' school is a much harder one than in the boys' school, in some ways, for the people think the boys must have an education, and the girls—well, it does n't matter so much, they are only girls. So if, for any reason, all in a family can not go to school, it is the girl who stays at home. The time is coming, however, when the girls will have a better chance. It is already being agitated and the girls are eager to go on as far as possible with their studies. A non-Christian Chinaman said to me the other day: 'In ten or twenty years the Chinese girls and young women are going to be able to talk English more generally; they will all want an education, and then they will all turn Christian. It 's bound to be so.' "

PENANG.—Work in the Anglo-Chinese Girls' Boarding and Day School has much of encouragement in it. Though limited by lack of dormitory space, their surroundings since moving, in May of 1907, into the new Charlotte S. Winchell Home, have been so much more hygienic that more and better work has been accomplished. Miss May Lilly, who has been in charge of this school, should come home this fall, and an efficient teacher is required to relieve her.

The Tamil work, Rescue Home and Orphanage, under Mrs. Pykett's wise and devoted care, continue successful. One of the heathen girls has been converted and baptized. Several of the younger girls of the orphanage have united with the Church, and the spiritual growth of the older girls has been marked.

Of the Deaconess Home and the evangelistic work at Penang, Miss Martin writes: "We have to report much the same as in years past: many heathen homes visited; a few women and girls being taught to read; the bringing into the Church of two or three Christian women recently come from China, who might otherwise have drifted back into heathenism; lukewarm members kept from backsliding by constant visit; a full attendance at the morning services, and meetings held with the Christian women for prayer and Bible study."

At TAIPENG the girls' boarding-school and day school, presided over by Miss Jackson and Miss Sutton respectively, have had a prosperous year. Under trying conditions the work has advanced, the indebtedness has been cleared up, and the school is on a firmer foundation than before. Miss Jackson, who will return home after Conference for a well-earned rest, has been relieved by Miss Thirza E. Bunce, who was sent out by the Northwestern Branch and sailed on September 2d.

9

At KUALA LUMPUR, where the girls day and boarding-schools are in charge of Miss Amy Holland and Miss Edith Hemingway, the work is much handicapped for want of room and the ordinary conveniences of every-day life.

At MALACCA the growth of the work has been phenomenal. The Bible-woman's training-school, which was moved to Malacca from Singapore last year, is in charge of Mrs. Shellabear. It has eight women in attendance who are earnest in their study and have made marked advance in their grasp of spiritual things. Five dialects are spoken in this little school. A Chinese teacher has been secured, who will be a great relief to Mrs. Shellabear.

The girls' school, so wonderfully developed by the efficient efforts of Miss Ada Pugh, has an enrollment of about ninety girls at the close of its third year's work. The story of the opening of this school reads like a romance and verifies the truth of the proverb, "Cast thy bread upon the waters." The school received its first impetus and has been constantly aided by a Chinese who twenty-five years ago was kindly treated during his sojourn in America, and hence came to believe in the reality of Christianity. There are 16,700 girls in the city of Malacca under fifteen years of age, whose only chance for a Christian education is in this school. If we can make them Christian in life and character we can have Christian homes and a Christian civilization. The rent of the building now used for the girls' school is paid from a Protestant fund left by early missionaries of another denomination. Neither Miss Pugh nor Miss Jessie Brooks, who has been in charge of the work this year during Miss Pugh's furlough, keep any servants. All the work of the entire school is done by the missionary, with the children's help, and the house is a model of cleanliness and order. Although the work has been carried on so far at a minimum expenditure financially, the time has come when the rented building will no longer house the school; we must either invest money enough to buy land, build and properly maintain the institution, or we must close this work upon which God's approval seems so signally to rest.

The erection of a Church in Malacca during the past year has added greatly to the strength of our enterprise there.

IPOH, with its large grounds, its church, mission house, and residence for a Woman's Foreign Missionary Society representative, still pleads unavailingly for a missionary.

JAVA, too, urges through our faithful Mrs. Denyes, that a lady missionary, free from family cares, be sent to spend her time among the Japanese women. During the past summer Miss Sophia Blackmore, en route from Australia, stopped off to spend a few weeks in evangelistic work in Java. She reports a very interesting trip, weak Christians strengthened, and disheartened ones encouraged.

BORNEO at last has seen the beginnings of active missionary work. Mrs. Hoover has a girls' school in Sibu numbering sixteen, teaches in the boys' school every day, conducts a boys' class of ten, who are learning the Lord's Prayer, the Chatechism, etc. She has a class in singing and assists Mr. Hoover on the District. Verily she is in labors abundant.

Malaysia's present needs are: two teachers for Singapore and a dormitory for the Methodist Girls' School; land, a building, and a missionary assistant for Malacca; a deaconess for Ipoh, and a missionary for Java.

PHILIPPINE ISLANDS.

Organized as a Mission in 1904; reorganized as a Conference in March, 1908.
Official Correspondent, Mrs. F. F. Lindsay.

MISSIONARIES AND THEIR STATIONS.

DAGUPAN.—Elizabeth Parkes.
LINGAYEN.—Louise Stixrud, Mabel Crawford.
MANILA.—Marguerite Decker, M. M. Crabtree, Rebecca Parish, M. D., Gertrude l. Driesbach, Rose Dudley.
WIVES OF MISSIONARIES IN CHARGE OF WORK.—*Mrs. M. A. Rader, *Mrs. A. E. Chenoweth, Mrs. Harry Farmer, Mrs. C. W. Koehler, Mrs. I. B. Harper, Mrs. W. H. Teeter, Mrs. D. H. Klinefelter, Mrs Edwin L. Housley, *Mrs. W. A. Goodell, Mrs. E. S. Lyons, Mrs. E. A. Rayner, Mrs. B. O. Peterson, Mrs. O. Huddleston.

The marvelous growth and development of the Phippine Conference and the unprecedented opportunities which it offers demand the most thoughtful consideration. Within the past quadrennium 27,800 Filipinos have entered our Church on probation. Of this number 7,000 have been added within the past year. In March, 1908, the Philippine Conference was organized. This is the first Methodist Episcopal Conference regularly organized under the "Stars and Stripes" outside of the geographical lines of the United States.

In Manila, where the woman's work was opened in 1896, it has become a well-established and powerful factor in the spread of Christianity. Both arms of the work, evangelistic and medical, are now well equipped.

The "Harris Memorial Deaconess Training-school," housed in its commodious, airy quarters, has had a successful year under Miss Decker's consecrated management. At the May meeting of the Secretaries, held in Baltimore, Bishops Oldham and Robinson both unqualifiedly commended the work of the Deaconess Home, mentioning in particular the quiet spirituality and deep consecration of its girl deaconesses, fourteen of whom are now actively engaged in evangelistic work in different Districts of the Mission.

A family of thirty-eight has been in Miss Decker's care during the past year, of which number all but ten are taking the regular Bible Study course, fitting themselves for active evangelistic effort. Thirty-one classes have been conducted weekly by the students, fifteen of which are Sunday-school classes, six for children and nine for women, two of the latter being among the women in Bilibid prison.

Within the Home itself, besides its regular work, a new experiment has been tried. This has been the adoption of a laundry day, making it compulsory for each pupil to attend to her own laundering. In every way possible the gospel of the dignity of labor is inculcated. The pupils do all their own work, cleaning the floors, and taking entire charge of the dormitories and the dining-room. Although labor is not especially popular in that tropical climate, yet now and then gratifying commendation of the methods employed in the Home is expressed by the people. A well-educated Filipino brought his daughter, who spoke English fluently, to the institution. "I would like to leave her here," he said, "and will

---

*Home on furlough.

gladly meet all expenses." They live quite near the school, and it was suggested that he send her as a day pupil, in which event there would be no charges. "But," he objected, "the custom of my people is very bad; they are irregular in their habits. I wish my daughter to be punctual as well as proficient in the knowledge contained in books."

The Mary J. Johnston Memorial Hospital, completed in May, is a fine, substantial structure, erected at a cost of $12,000, in the heart of the Filipino district of Manila. It has a frontage on Manila Bay, from the encroachment of which it is protected by a strong sea wall. The location, giving it the benefit of the sea breezes, is a most favorable one. The first floor of the building is of stone, the upper one of cement. Thoroughly modern and up to date in every respect, it has room for forty beds, surgical and sterilizing-rooms, diet kitchen, dispensary, etc.

Dr. Parish, whose skill and ability are recognized by the leading American and English physicians of the city, has spared no effort to have the building the best that the amount of money invested would build. She expresses grateful thanks, not only to the kind friend at home whose loving provision has made this building possible, but to the good brothers of the mission, whose helpful advice and constant supervision have done so much toward securing satisfactory results. Dr. Parish's work has been signally successful from the beginning; at the close of the first year's work she reported more than 2,500 dispensary patients, about 300 out-calls, more than 80 hospital cases, and 3 Filipino girls taking nurses' training. Given larger opportunities and more favorable surroundings in the new hospital building, this feature of our work in the Philippines is destined to be far-reaching in its results. Already the new institution is not only taking care of the sick in Manila, but also those from the provinces, as far as one hundred miles distant.

At LINGAYEN, Pangasinan Province, our Woman's Training-school has become an accomplished fact. Lingayen is considered one of the most beautiful as well as one of the most healthful cities in the islands. It is the seat of the only high school in the province. The trade school, and probably the agricultural school, of the province will be located here. This will bring into the city every year from one thousand to two thousand of the brightest and best young men and women of the ten intermediate schools located in Pangasinan Province. Here, at a cost of $2,500, our Society has acquired a fine property, which, at an expenditure of $500, has been repaired and adapted to the twofold purpose of a Bible-woman's training-school and a dormitory for girls and women. By means of the latter, which is under the management of Miss Mabel Crawford, it is hoped that very many of the out-of-town girls in attendance upon the Government schools, will be brought under strong Christian influence and training.

Of the Lingayen Training-school, in charge of Miss Louise Stixrud, much might be said. Opened because of the dire need of more women workers and because of the very real difficulty in getting the women of the north to go to Manila, where, to them, strange customs and a strange dialect prevail, it is designed to minister to the needs of an older class of women, who will be taught the Bible in their own dialects in the morning, and in the afternoon they will be able to go out, unattended, to visit among the women and children of the city. After a year or more spent in the school they will return to their own homes, prepared to work in the native Churches. Since the opening of the school, May 1st, eighteen strong characters have been enrolled for study and Miss Stixrud is already embarrassed by her success. As an illustration of the class of women applying for admittance, the wife of Eduardo Benitez might be cited. "This young Filipino pastor speaks English, Spanish, Ilocano, and Pangasinan fluently, and has been of invaluable assistance to our mission in its work of translating and revising the Scriptures. Now, besides doing the work of a pastor on his circuit, he proposes to assume the care of his four little children in order that his wife may enter the woman's training-school in Lingayen, and learn more perfectly the duties of a pastor's wife." The woman who has been sent to the Lingayan school from Aparri, our most northern station, is enthusiastic over the work and in love with her teachers, while where girls have been sent to Manila from Aparri, homesickness and discouragement followed. These experiences seem to justify the Mission in feeling that the difference between the customs, traditions, and dialects· of the northern Ilocanos and the southern Tagalogs made a second training-school an absolute necessity.

DAGUPAN, eight miles from Lingayen, is the headquarters of Miss Elizabeth Parkes, who spends almost her entire time in evangelistic work

SUMMARY OF WORK IN THE PHILIPPINES.

NAMES OF STATIONS OR DISTRICTS.	Manila District.	Central District.	Northern District.	Totals.
W. F. M. S. Missionaries	5		3	8
Wives of Missionaries in Active Work	4	3	4	11
Foreign or Eurasian Assistants				
Native Workers	3	2	8	13
*WOMEN IN THE CHURCH—Full Members				
*Probationers				
*Adherents				
*Women and Girls Baptized During Year				
*No. Christian Women Under Instruction				
*Non-Christian Women Under Instruction				
No. Bible-women Employed	3	7	1	11
BIBLE INSTITUTES OR TRAINING CLASSES—				
No. of Institutes	1	3	6	10
No. Missionaries Teaching	2	3	5	10
No. Native Teachers	2	3	1	6
Enrollment	30	80	100	210
SCHOOLS FOR TRAINING BIBLE-WOMEN—				
No. Schools	1		1	2
No. Missionaries	2		2	4
No. Native Teachers	2		1	3
Enrollment	32		17	49
Receipts for Board and Tuition	$157 50			$157 50
MEDICAL WORK—No. Hospitals	1			1
No. Foreign Physicians	1			1
Eurasian or Native Physicians				
No. Medical Students				
No. Foreign Nurses	2			2
Eurasian or Native Nurses				
No. Nurse Students	4			4
No. Hospital Beds	40			40
No. Hospital Patients	109			109
No. Hospital Clinic Patients				
No. Out-Patients	360			360
No. Out-Dispensaries				
No. Dispensary Patients	3260			3260
Dispensary Receipts	$25 00			$25 00
Hospital Receipts	50 00			50 00
Fees and Donations from Foreigners	455 00			455 00
Government Grants				

* Conference Minutes do not indicate.

upon the northern District. Miss Parkes, familiar with every phase of the work in the Philippines, pleads most earnestly that a Woman's Foreign Missionary worker be sent to Tuguegarao, in the Cagayan Valley.

TUGUEGARAO is situated in the center of the Cagayan Valley and is the capital of this northern province. It has the only high school in the entire valley. The mountains and the distance make this province entirely separate from our southern work. and one must needs travel farther than from Manila to Hong Kong when one goes from Tuguegarao to Manila. In addition to the Woman's Foreign Missionary Society representative, a dormitory for girls is needed at Tuguegarao, as the parents dare not send their daughters to school unless a suitable place is provided for them to board. A dormitory and a missionary at this station, with the United States Government furnishing the schools, could accomplish as much as in our older missions is effected by a large teaching force and the endowment of many scholarships.

In summarizing the special needs of the woman's work in the Philippines, a new worker for the training-school in Manila should not be forgotten, nor the dormitory for non-resident girls, so much desired, at the rear of the Deaconess Home. The many requirements of the new training-school at Lingayen should be remembered, as well as the great need of properly taking possession, with a missionary and equipment, of the strategic point, Tuguegarao.

CHINA.

NORTH CHINA CONFERENCE.

Woman's work commenced in 1871; organized as a Conference in 1893. The North China Conference includes the Provinces of Shantung and Honan, and all north of these.
Official Correspondent, Mary E. Holt.

MISSIONARIES AND THEIR STATIONS.

PEKING.—Mrs. Charlotte M. Jewell, Anna D. Gloss, M. D., Melissa Manderson, M. D., Effie G. Young, Gertrude Gilman, L. Maude Wheeler, Alice M. Powell, V. Evelyn B. Baugh, Estie Boddy.
TIENTSIN.—Emma E. Martin, M. D., M. Ida Stevenson, M. D., Frances O. Wilson, Emma M. Knox.
CH'ANG-LI.—Ella E. Glover, Clara P. Dyer.
SHANTUNG.—Edna G. Terry, M. D., Sue L. Koons, M. D., *Rachel Benn, M. D., *Lizzie E. Martin.
WIVES OF MISSIONARIES IN CHARGE OF WORK.—Mrs. Maria B. Davis, Mrs. M. G. Headland, M. D., Mrs. Agnes Brown, Mrs. Irma R. Davis, Mrs. Elma E. Keeler, Mrs. Emily H. Hobart.

PEKING.—*Mary Porter Gamewell and Lucy G. Alderman Schools.*—The girls who have gone from these schools are making good records, as shown by the following taken from Mrs. Jewell's full report: "There were seven girls whose desks were in a row in the old schoolhouse. That was when the now gray-haired teacher was a newcomer—when Miss Cushman and Miss Sears were at the helm. These teachers are gone—one to

---

*Home on leave.

America, the other to the Better Land. What about these girls of a quarter of a century ago? One is a Methodist pastor's wife; a wise and loving mother; a blessing to every parish where they are sent. Another, recently widowed, is at the head of a mission school in Shanghai. She has four beautiful children, brought up as carefully as your own children, Christian mother. The eldest son is soon to finish college; the eldest daughter, a rare and gifted girl, is teaching near Shanghai. The third in the row is also widowed, her husband being one of our preachers who, in 1900, sealed his faith with his blood. She is one of our Bible-women now, her life growing stronger and richer as the years go by. 'Her children rise up to call her blessed.' The fourth is the respected wife of a Congregationalist deacon. The remaining three were long since called to higher seats above. One of the two left a beautiful testimony to Jesus' sustaining presence in her extreme hour. The other left her testimony in the solidifying influence she had upon her husband's rather vacillating purpose. The preaching of the gospel, which doubtless she held him to during her life, he has never since left." Who can estimate the value of this school in its influence upon the lives of these girls who have come under its teaching?

The school opened September 11th. The summer had been an unusually bad cholera season, but through the exercise of great vigilance and by taking careful precaution the girls reached the school after vacation in good health. Two hundred and forty-four pupils have been registered during the year. It is thought by the teachers not desirable to bring too large numbers of small children into the school, believing it to be more advantageous, as well as economical, of our force of foreign teachers, to have larger classes of advanced pupils. More schools of a lower grade are therefore desired, which shall send their pupils to this high school now so well established. Our Society has consummated a union with the North China Educational Union, and now has a clear path for the girls in North China to a college and also to a medical course. As yet there is no candidate for the Woman's College. Mrs. Bashford's mother, Mrs. Field, has given a generous centennial gift of $3,000 for the benefit of the college, $1,000 going to each of the three missions interested in the Union. Our share will support a perpetual scholarship. Dr. Edward S. Ninde and his sister, Miss Mary L. Ninde, have given $500 for the support of a perpetual scholarship in the Mary Porter Gamewell School. Gifts have come towards a second scholarship. This is a step in the right direction to provide for the permanent maintenance of the school.

The Standard Bearers keep up their contributions, which this year amounted to $36.97 gold.

Christmas, as usual, was celebrated with an entertainment arranged by the girls, helped out by the contents of boxes from America—always a welcome adjunct.

The scholarship letters have been interesting as always. Each contained a photograph of the girl for her patron. Wedding bells sounded in the school at the close of the term, and one girl went out to assist her husband in keeping up his courage in the management of unruly pupils in his school. Another who married, was a girl who had been in the school twenty years—fourteen as pupil and six as teacher. She is greatly missed.

Among the pupils at present may be found representatives from various classes. Two daughters of one of the men sent to the United States years ago for an education, have been in the school taking work preparatory for entrance to the medical school.

Miss Wheeler has been giving piano lessons to two little tots, the great-great-nieces of Li Hung Chang.

A month of special meetings following Easter, and led by Dr. Pyke, were most helpful. Many of the girls were led to see that they were living below their blood-bought privilege and, by a real faith, stepped on higher ground.

Three girls graduated in June. One was too ill to be present at the Commencement exercises. The other two girls are pledged to teach in some of our schools.

Miss Gilman, as formerly, has looked after the day schools, which she reports as well attended and faithfully taught. There is great need for evangelistic workers on the District, and for such help most earnest appeals are sent.

Medical Work.—"I have never been so driven as this year," writes Dr. Gloss. "The medical work here is quite large enough for two persons, and I have had to do it alone. Miss Powell and Dr. Manderson have both come to help me, but so far they have had to give their time to the study of the language. The Medical School is at last a fact, opening in February last with two pupils, one a graduate of our Mary Porter Gamewell School and the other of our Nanking Girls' School. This is a union school. We have some fine teachers, and in such a small class these girls will have the advantage almost of private instruction. We have the same course and some of the same teachers as in the Men's Union Medical College. For the present the school is housed in the Sleeper Davis Memorial Hospital.

"The Training-school for Nurses is growing in popularity. Several girls from the boarding school have asked to come into it, and two young women from Hing Hua are ready to enter at the beginning of the term. They are wives of two men who are in the Peking Medical School. One girl left before she had quite finished to enter the medical; another has done splendid work. We hope to have five girls in the class next year. Miss Powell's coming—she is a trained nurse—will mean much to the school. This school is also accommodated in the hospital.

"The progress of the medical work during the year has been wonderful and never was so full of interest. Foreign medicines are growing in popularity. Notwithstanding the terribly neglected cases that come to us too late for help, there is an encouraging increase of intelligence among the people in medical matters. The people are beginning to understand the necessity for precaution in the presence of epidemics, and are more willing to call in the aid of the foreign physician.

"The boarding school adds always a great deal of work. It takes from half an hour to an hour every day in the clinic to see these girls, and they furnish at least a third of the patients. The reward for this labor is the opportunity afforded for students and nurses to study acute diseases. The clinic has been fine this year—from fifty to a hundred in daily attendance—a large proportion being from the so-called 'upper classes.' Many buy first-class tickets and pay for their medicines.

"We have but one Bible-woman for Church work and the hospital. As she is an unusually strong worker, she makes the most of her opportunity at these clinics, and afterwards follows up these women at the Church and in their homes. We could easily use another Bible-woman, but, alas! there is none to spare for this work.

"We have more house patients than ever before, and these include more people from other towns and villages. We have been very glad to see this, for it extends the influence of the work in many directions. One dear old lady came to us blind. The cataract was removed and she went out seeing. Several people have been released from the opium habit. Another's life was saved by the amputation of an arm. All these return to their homes to 'publish the tidings' of the good things that have come to them in the hospital.

"The out-calls have been numerous. There is seldom a day when I do not go somewhere, and often I make several calls a day. About two-thirds of these pay. We have been called to the palaces of princes and homes of officials of every class. God is blessing this work."

Number of house patients, 260; number of obstetrical cases, 51; number of out-calls, 560; number of dispensary patients, 4,680; number of prescriptions, 14,800; received from fees, donations, and sale of drugs, $1,052.66.

TIENTSIN.—We regret that the Sarah L. Keen School is still closed, no teacher having yet been found to re-open this work, but there is a probability that some one will be appointed to this school at the Conference this fall. Dr. Stevenson and Miss Wilson have returned to take up their work again in hospital, and city, and District. Dr. Martin, with Miss Knox, has done faithful work in the past year.

CH'ANG-LI.—The first event of importance in the year was the welcoming to this field of the new missionary, Miss Clara P. Dyer. She has been an earnest and untiring student of the language since her arrival and passed the year's examinations after ten months' study with a high average. She has assisted in the Home, in industrial work, in the training-school, in teaching the children exercises, and helping in various other ways, thus showing her fitness to be a missionary. With it all she is happy and glad to be in China.

Catherine E. Thompson Memorial School.—Miss Glover reports that the year has been filled with blessings. Thirty women have been enrolled, but all could not stay through the entire term. The younger of the two teachers, Mrs. Ti, is a graduate of the school and has done faithful work. The older woman, Mrs. Chou, is an inspiration both to the foreigners and to the women through her cheerfulness, tact, and devotion to God, and to her work is due much of the success of the school. During the year an offer came of a position with three or four times her present salary, with liberty to carry on Christian work and with less arduous toil. It was a temptation, but after much prayer she decided to remain in our school, saying, "My heart was not peaceful until I decided to stay."

At times the presence of God has been consciously felt. The usual Sunday class meetings were discontinued the latter part of the term and the women visited in heathen homes, each group in charge of an experienced worker. One Saturday evening four of the women came in to report their day's work. Their faces beamed with joy as they told of the good time they had had in witnessing for Christ.

A very important part of the school is the industrial department, carried on most ably by Mrs. Irma R. Davis, and after she had gone to Japan, taken up by Miss Dyer, who is planning large things in the coming year. The general health of the women has been good, and when medical help has been needed Dr. and Mrs. Keeler have kindly attended to the sick ones.

The Faith Butler's Day School has had the most prosperous year of its history. At one time the daily attendance reached twenty-five and it looked as if larger quarters would soon be needed. The teacher, Miss Mu, loves her little pupils dearly. She will remain in charge another year. Two big swings in the yard have helped to attract the outside children and it is hoped that the school will continue to increase in numbers, which will indicate that the walls of opposition are falling down.

Three country day schools are reported at Pai Tao Tsu, Ti Chuang, and Laot'ing, while others are asked for, but funds and teachers are lacking. In one place the pastor reported that a woman had come into the Church through the influence of the day school started there.

Miss Glover regrets that the force of foreign workers is so inadequate, and consequently evangelistic work on the District can not be carried on to any great extent. Last fall she, with Miss Dyer, made one short trip, and during the winter only short trips to the nearby villages could be made. Mrs. Chou went out twice in the spring, returning each time very tired, as she had talked nearly all the waking hours of several days. Later Miss Glover and Mrs. Chou were away eleven days, sleeping in six different places and visiting sixteen villages where are Christians. Mrs. Taft has been out with her husband a few times and hopes in another year to do more of this work that lies so near her heart. The local work is in a more encouraging condition than in the past.

In closing her report, Miss Glover speaks of the Missionary Auxiliary which holds its meetings regularly each month. She says: "A missionary meeting is no drug in the market here, but is the most largely attended gathering in the month. An ideal Auxiliary, with raw heathen present to work on; with Christian women all anxious to answer to the roll call; with dues promptly paid, and paid from poverty's purse. If the women of the home land want to be inspired, just let them drop into one of our meetings some day."

Dr. and Mrs. Keeler report the medical work, and make a most urgent appeal for a woman physician to be sent to this District in which are ten thousand sick and suffering children and women crying, "Come over and help us."

Until March it was found necessary to give all surgical treatments in the men's hospital, after which time the woman's hospital was opened for daily clinics. These were well attended, the number often reaching twenty-five, with as many as sixteen in-patients at one time. Many interesting cases are mentioned, among them that of a little girl from the Saman who was suffering with a badly infected hand. After she recovered her father was so grateful that he sent a feast, already prepared, of more than twenty courses—all that four men could carry, and more than twenty people could eat. This opened the way, and later invitations came to visit several official homes in the city socially and professionally. These people also visited our homes, hospital, and school. The seclusion of the Chinese women makes it almost impossible for a man doctor to attend the sick in their homes. A woman doctor with a few trained assistants could do much to relieve the untellable suffering among Chinese mothers, and thus break down the walls of conservatism and reach the homes and hearts of the most influential families. Notwithstanding the lack of such help, more than twelve hundred women have come under the treatment of Dr. and Mrs. Keeler during the year.

SHANGTUNG, T'AI AN FU.—Dr. Terry reports for the Woman's Training-school: "The school opened November 20th. Twenty-three women were enrolled during the term, nine of whom were in the school last year. Many applicants for admission had to be refused for two reasons: lack of funds and lack of room. Seven small rooms comprise the training-school accommodations, and one of these has to be used for a storeroom. There is no schoolroom and, to overcome the difficulty, the partition between two rooms was taken out. The selection of women, in many cases, was irrespective of age or intelligence, but because of the fact that they were wives of preachers, colporteurs, or students preparing for Christian work. More than one-third of the women were of this class and most of them were remarkably bright. One especially has been very helpful in the school. She was a catechist in the Church of England Mission. She was anxious to be admitted, but was told that she must have a recommendation from her mission. Greatly to our surprise she returned the next day with a letter from the wife of the Bishop of the Province, and so she was allowed to enter our school.

"On Christmas Day ten women unbound their feet. Through the generosity of Mrs. Hanson, they were all provided with material for shoes and stockings. It was a happy day for all to see so many emancipated women. At the close of the term there were but four women with bound feet; but as soon as husbands and mothers-in-law consent they, too, will be free. The women all studied diligently and there has been marked improvement in many ways. Gradually their manners have softened; new garments and more frequent use of brushes and combs have effected changes in appearance; and the grace of God working in their hearts has been shown in their efforts to control temper and tongues. The women of the neighborhood sometimes gather about our gate, and passing pilgrims often stop to rest awhile, thus affording opportunities to tell the gospel story. One who overheard them said, 'These women know how to explain the doctrine.'

"After the training-school had closed and before the women had left for their homes, the Bible-women, day school teachers, and pastors' wives on the District were invited to T'ai an for a week of special meetings, study, and conference together. This meeting was the first of the kind in our mission in Shantung and was much enjoyed by all."

Dr. Terry gratefully mentions the assistance of Mrs. Lin and Mrs. Ch'en, whose influence in the school has been a large factor for good.

In the Lettie Mason Quine Day School, which is taught by a granddaughter of old Mrs. Wang, there have been twelve girls enrolled during the year. The children from Christian families are the ones upon whom we have special claim, and these will, sooner or later, enter the boarding school; yet those from heathen homes deserve special attention. This is their only chance to learn a few characters and to be impressed with religious truth. We regret that these are not allowed to remain long in the school, but even the little that they can be taught may bear fruit in after days and years.

The health of Miss Martin, who was appointed to the boarding school, has seriously failed during the year, making necessary her return home, leaving no one in charge for a time. The building has been far too small to accommodate the pupils, but a recent gift of $7,000 from a friend in New England Branch will help largely in the erection of more suitable quarters. Plans are being considered and work is already begun.

Dr. Koons has been very ill for some time and, as soon as she is able, will return home. Dr. Benn, who remained at work long after she should have taken her furlough, is now resting in the home land. We hope soon to hear that another physician is ready to go to this destitute field, where other workers are needed as well.

SUMMARY OF WORK IN THE NORTH CHINA CONFERENCE.

NAMES OF STATIONS OR DISTRICTS.	Peking District	Tientsin District	CH'ANG LI.			Shantung District	To....
			Tsun Hua Dist.	Lanchou District	Shan Hai Kuan District		
W. F. M. S. Missionaries	6	2			1	3	12
Wives of Missionaries in Active Work	1	2			2	2	7
Foreign or Eurasian Assistants							
Native Workers	9	7	6	2	4	11	39
BIBLE INSTITUTES OR TRAINING CLASSES—No. of Institutes	1				1		2
No. Missionaries Teaching	1				1		2
No. Native Teachers	1				2		3
Enrollment	15				16		31
SCHOOLS FOR TRAINING BIBLE-WOMEN—No. Schools		†			1	1	2
No. Missionaries		†			1	1	2
No. Native Teachers		†			2	1	3
Enrollment		†			23	20	43
Receipts for Board and Tuition		†			$3 00		$3 00
VERNACULAR AND ANGLO-VERNACULAR BOARDING-SCHOOLS—No. Schools	1					1	2
No. Foreign Missionaries	4					1	5
Foreign or Eurasian Teachers							
No. Native Teachers	8					4	12
Self-supporting Students							
Wholly-supported Students	97					83	180
Partly-supported Students	134					4	138
No. Day Students	6						6
Total Enrollment	237					87	324
Receipts for Board and Tuition	$410					$16	$426
DAY SCHOOLS—No. Schools		3	5	1	1	6	16
No. Teachers		3	5	1	1	6	16
Total Enrollment		75	28	10	16	51	180
Average Daily Attendance		55	20	8	12	37	132
INDUSTRIAL SCHOOLS—No. Schools							
No. Ind. Depts. in Other Schools					1	1	2
No. Foreign Missionaries					1	1	2
Foreign or Eurasian Teachers							
No. Native Teachers					1		1
No. Pupils					23	20	43
From Sale of Products					$40 00		$40 00
MEDICAL WORK—No. Hospitals	1	‡			1	1	3
No. Foreign Physicians	1	‡			1	2	4
Eurasian or Native Physicians		‡					
No. Medical Students		‡					
No. Foreign Nurses		‡					
Eurasian or Native Nurses		‡				1	1
No. Nurse Students	3	‡					3
No. Hospital Beds	50	‡			20	30	100
No. Hospital Patients	150	‡			25	37	212
No. Hospital Clinic Patients	10525	‡			280	2600	13405
No. Out-Patients	360	‡				111	471
Dispensary Receipts	*$860	‡					*933 48
Hospital Receipts		‡			$5 68	$67 80	*
Fees and Donations from Foreigners	$20	‡					*$20 00

* Dispensary and Hospital Receipts included.
† Work closed.
‡ Work closed for the year.

CENTRAL CHINA.

Central China Mission was opened in December, 1867, by missionaries belonging to Foochow, and was set apart as a separate mission in 1869.

Woman's work organized in Kiukiang, 1874; in Chinkiang, 1884; in Nanking, 1887; in Wuhu, 1897; in Nanchang, 1903.

Official Correspondent, Mrs. J. M. Cornell.

MISSIONARIES AND THEIR STATIONS.

CHINKIANG.—Girls' Boarding School—Miss Grace A Crooks (N. W. 1904). Medical and Evangelistic Work—Dr. Lucy A. Hoag (N. W. 1872). Dr. Gertrude Taft (Pac. 1895).

NANKING.—Girls' Boarding School—Miss Laura M. White (Phila. 1891). *Miss Ella C. Shaw (N. W. 1887). Miss Alice Peters (N. W. 1904). Bible Training-school and Evangelistic Work—*Miss Sarah Peters (N. W. 1888).

WUHU.—City and District Evangelistic Work—Miss Edith M. Crane (N. W. 1904). Miss Kate L. Ogborn (Des M. 1891).

KIUKIANG.—"Mrs. S. A. Rulison Fish" Girls' Boarding School—Miss Clara E. Merrill (N. W. 1896). Miss Adaline N. Smith (N. W. 1907). "Ellin J. Knowles Bible Training-school" and Evangelistic Work— Miss Jennie V. Hughes (N. Y. 1905). "Elizabeth Skelton Danforth" Hospital and Dispensary—Dr. Mary Stone (Des M. 1896).

NANCHANG.—"Stephen L. Baldwin Memorial School"—*Miss Alta L. Newby (Des M. 1905). Miss Welthy B. Honsinger (N. Y. 1906). Assistant—Miss Ilien Tang (Minn. 1906). Medical work—*Dr. Ida Kahn (N. W. 1896). City Evangelistic Work—*Miss Gertrude Howe (N. W. 1872).

NEW BUILDINGS COMPLETED AND OCCUPIED IN 1907 AND 1908:

WUHU.—Second Street Day School and Temporary Home, January, 1908; New England, $1,000.

KIUKIANG.—S. A. Rulison Fish High School, September, 1907; Northwestern, $7,500.

SZ-TZ-GNAN.—Cora Bell Rawlings, Cripples Bungalow, June, 1908; New York, $1,200.

NANCHANG.—Mary P. Read Home, February, 1908; Topeka, $3,500.

Chinkiang School.—After years of waiting and hoping several· "patches" of land have been secured, altogether making a good sized strip as an addition to our school property. Famine relief funds have been used in employing some of the thousands of refugees to fill and grade a portion of this. The new building so urgently needed will be on solid foundation, while the filled-in portion will give the space for playground, and the longed-for trees and flowers. Semi-yearly reports to the parents are not only sent, but are eagerly received, which is a marked indication of advance. In common with other schools this one is receiving a better class of scholars. Music is in such demand that even with an extra charge the department is full. Vocal music and English are given to all alike. The graduates are fitted to enter the Freshmen's year in American colleges. The course of normal training is highly popular, requests coming from other Missions, not only to receive advanced students, but within two years from thirteen different schools, both Government and Mission, have come urgent requests for teachers. Perhaps the very best news

---

* Home on furlough.

from this school is of the interest in Bible study. Many of the pupils from babyhood have had an hour's instruction daily in this Book of books, and almost know it by heart. They will turn to any verse mentioned with a quickness which puts our concordance-hunting habits to shame. Miss Crooks assures us that "few Sunday-school classes in America, none which we have known—with all due apologies to the sixteen young ladies of High School age whom we loved and taught in Michigan—will keep pace with them." One beautiful girl, much tempted to marry into a·wealthy heathen family, who had been but two years in the school and seemed a mere child, used this Sword of the Spirit with a power which astonished her teachers to refute the arguments of her so-called Christian advisers. Miss Crooks writes enthusiastically of her loyal, efficient native teachers, but longs for another foreigner in the pressing work.

The Hospital and Medical Work, in charge of Dr. Lucy Hoag and Dr. Taft, reports 5,770 patients, and an income from outside sources of $666 Mex. Dr. Taft has had many operations this year and much work with her training class for nurses, finding it necessary to translate books on training and Materia Medica for the use of the students. The first nurse graduated at New Year, 1907; the second, 1908 New Year, Miss Tang, who is giving valuable help in the hospital. The present class of four students in their second year hope to graduate in 1910. They enter as graduates of our High Schools in Chinkiang and Nanking. Northwestern Branch has promised money for the new hospital, and much time has been spent in the effort to secure needed land and in the grading and filling the gullies in preparation for this building. Thirty thousand famine refugees gathered in Chinkiang in 1907, and crops being poor this year many are still there. Some of the men were quite desperate, and it needed careful personal oversight in the beginning when three hundred men were given employment. Dr. Taft began in faith and soon the money came. One thousand nine hundred and seventy-three dollars was sent from the Woman's Foreign Missionary Society for famine relief; hundreds of lives have been saved, and the hospital site is ready for the new building. Dr. Taft, closing the seventh year of her second term of service, comes home this October. Dr. Hoag has had a good vacation in the mountains at Kuling, and reports herself as very well and ready to carry the work alone for the coming year.

NANKING—*School.*—On receiving her appointment as Principal of the Girls School, Miss White was instructed by Bishop Bashford to develop it as rapidly as possible into a woman's college. Very wisely, we think, Miss White has obeyed his wish by emphasizing normal work. At China New Year, normal classes were begun, the classes ranging from ten to twenty students in each. This department had already become a necessity, as the graduates of High School grade are needed to teach in the lower classes. So ten of the normal students have given one and a half hours daily in teaching. In addition the course includes about all the studies of an ordinary Normal School at home. In this Normal work several other Missions join by sending their advanced students. Once a month, in addition, a lecture on some popular subject is given at our Methodist Chapel. On the opening of the new railroad between Nanking and Shanghai one hundred Normal and High School students united in an excursion to Chinkiang, where they were most hospitably entertained by our Girls' School. This was memorable, as it was their first railroad trip. College freshman work is pursued by a few, and any work beyond High School grade in the Normal School is to be accredited toward a college degree. The students who do daily teaching are given their board and a small monthly stipend, while Government schools, for the same amount of work, offer $30 or $40. One of Miss White's former music pupils, for a few hours daily instruction, is now receiving from the Government a larger salary than that of her old teacher,

Twenty-five of the girls were received into the Church either as full members or by baptism in June last. "Nowhere in history," Miss White writes, "can one discover such a wonderful renaissance as we have here in China. Our Consul General in Shanghai has stated to the department in Washington that the intellectual awakening of the women of China is the most remarkable feature of the whole movement. One rarely sees a child with bound feet to-day, even earrings are being discarded as unnatural, but gold eyeglasses are fashionable."

Miss Alice Peters has charge of the music and teaches some of the English classes. She is also preceptress of the school and bookkeeper of the institution. Miss Adaline Smith served for a few months in the Nanking School, but in the spring was transferred to Kiukiang, where Miss Merrill, being quite alone after Miss Pierce's home coming, was greatly in need of help.

Miss Sarah Peters is now at home recruiting her health, much impaired by long years of service in Nanking. Her work has been the superintendence of the Bible Training-school, supervision of the day schools, and country evangelistic work. She writes that because of overcrowding in the Training-school she must ask for an addition to the present building. She has done much in preparation for the new building, old houses have been torn down, the land graded and made ready for the work. Her appeal, seconded by Miss Shaw, is a very strong one and worthy of attention. They need three thousand dollars for this enlargement.

WUHU.—The new day school building near the Second Street Church, completed and moved into in January, is used also as a temporary home for the missionaries. The school accommodations, with desks for twenty and twenty-two enrolled, have to be rather restricted. The school at the West Gate, under a change of teachers, is also very successful, and with thirty-eight pupils is filled to the fullest point. The force of Bible-women has been strengthened, and in consequence there is a decided increase in the number of inquirers. Miss Crane feels it a great advantage to be in her new quarters, where she can receive socially the curious who become friends on better acquaintance. Never has there been so good a class of evangelists as at present. Miss Ogborn, after her visit at home, reached her new station of Wuhu in May. In late August she writes that the site for the Mrs. Charles Green Memorial Home is likely to be on the Han Chia San (hill), and they are preparing to remove the graves, fence the land, level the hill, and build the foundation immediately. They must then wait the promise of $3,500 more for completion and furnishing of the Home. The temporary Home over the new day school is in the midst of the most unhealthy old city, and an outbreak of cholera this summer made it necessary for them to flee the city for a time, and strengthens our recognition of their need of the new building outside the city walls.

KIUKIANG.—*The S. A. Rulison Fish School.*—The excellent health of the 125 girls enrolled in the new building is to be laid directly to their airy rooms and better sanitation. A class of six most promising young women is to be graduated in January. Miss Merrill believes they will compare favorably with American High School girls, and we venture to add that probably they know the Bible very much better than the majority of their Western sisters. Two last year's graduates have proven capable helpers this year. Miss Smith's first year of study has been diversified and Miss Merrill has been much helped by her taking two classes in English. All the workers had united in arranging for ten days of special meetings under the well known Dr. Li, of Soochow. When, at the very last, he was detained from attending, they determined to carry out their intention, even though deprived of the evangelist's presence, and a season of great refreshing followed. Of the fifty girls in the new building only one remained unmoved, and she later gave her heart to the Lord Jesus. In the primary department, too, many of the girls are Christians. Their delight is to hold little prayer-meetings among themselves. One hundred and fifteen girls are in regular attendance. Six are in the graduating class who will compare favorably with American High School graduates.

The gift in memory of Mrs. Rawlings, mentioned in our last report, is bringing great comfort, not alone to the poor waifs and cripples who find a healthful, happy home, but to the missionaries who there are privileged to reduce the sum of misery by which they are surrounded. The bungalow is built at Sz-tz-gnan, a few miles out of the city and on the mountain side, where it is much cooler than in the crowded, narrow streets. The name has been put up in great Chinese characters, reading "Rah-Lin," and meaning most truly, "Joyous Grove."

The Ellin J. Knowles Memorial Bible Training-school with the evangelistic work and the city day schools have all been in Miss Hughes' care since her return with Dr. Stone. The Bible Training-school has had sixty-two women studying, eighteen of whom are old students. Excellent native teachers have been of inestimable value, showing a rare consecration to the work. While the main building is still in the future, the beautiful and spacious site, inclosed with a fine ten-foot wall and a well-built gate-house surmounted by the name of the school in large characters, is an accomplished fact. A small house already on the property is being used to its limit, and a neat schoolhouse, intended to hold a day school, has been built from material left from the old building, but is used at present for the Bible Training-school. In the beginning of the year many of the students were not Christians; at its close all but two of the sixty-two were confessed followers of the Lord Jesus.

The evangelistic work in Kiukiang has been directed by Miss Hughes, but carried on chiefly by the excellent Bible-women, who have increased in number to eight. Mrs. Stone, herself the first fruits of Christianity in the city, has preached the Gospel to more than ten thousand visitors in her daughter's dispensary. One valuable result of the work of the Bible-women has been shown in the increased attendance of women at the Street Chapel, whose congregations formerly were chiefly men. The Day Schools, too, have prospered. A year ago there were two in the city and one across the Yangste. These have doubled in number and more than doubled in attendance. Two of them are supplied with satisfactory buildings. A revised course of study, by which the day school pupils can go directly into the Boarding School, has much increased the efficiency of this valuable form of mission work. We now have to compete with Government schools, a matter to which we have already referred. Mrs. Mei, the village evangelist, has preached to thousands, and eager hearers have remained until after midnight to ask questions and listen to her replies. She is a widow, only twenty-five years old, has one little child, whom she must trust in kind hands at home during her extended trips; this year she has made three with Miss Hughes and two long trips alone. In one place on the district she preached in four days to eight thousand people. The district superintendent testified that the city and surrounding villages were stirred as no foreigner had ever been able to stir them.

The Elizabeth Skelton Danforth Memorial Hospital has been spreading its beneficence far and near. On Dr. Stone's return it was reopened, and in the nine months of this year has had more patients than formerly visited it in twelve. Vaccinating babies is an important department of the work, and Dr. Stone hopes the nurses now in training will be able to go out to do this in another year, thus saving many from a scourge whose dreadfulness we have almost forgotten, because of the universality of its prevention by vaccination. This promising class of nurses numbers thirteen already, and gives the brightest promise of high usefulness. The new wing of the hospital will be ready for occupancy very soon, and it is hoped that Dr. Danforth may be present at its dedication, when also the first class of nurses will graduate. Both Miss Merrill and Dr. Stone relate at length the story of an interesting pupil in the school, who was ill with diphtheria. Some of us may remember her as the daughter of the friendly official in Nanchang during the riot of 1906, who saved the life of a fleeing French priest. From the beginning of the attack the case seemed serious, and in response to a telegram to the father, the answer was flashed back, "Save life, spare no expense." After despairing of her life she began to show signs of recovery, and very earnest prayer was offered for her. Just after the crisis her father came from Nanchang on his private launch. Before seeing his daughter he thanked Dr. Stone for her care, and the Doctor thought it wise to tell him that the Lord had spared his daughter's life for a purpose, and that she had decided to confess Christ, adding, "You will do nothing to hinder her, will you?" With emotion he replied, "O no, I will not hinder; she may serve Him all her life!" True to the promise she had made on her sick bed, she was baptized the first week she left the isolation ward. She is a character of force and beauty, and her friends have high hopes that she will prove a leader in the regeneration of her people.

NAN CHANG.—Baldwin Memorial School has had throughout the year an average attendance of fifty pupils. Miss Ilien Tang has begun her kindergarten with seven little Celestials, the nucleus of what is bound to become a work of influence. Early in the year Miss Tang invited the older girls to her study on Saturdays for an evening of story-telling and chat. By imperceptible steps this grew until it became a prayer band, and on the Sunday before Easter nine of the most promising girls in the school, daughters of merchants and officials, were received into the Church.

Miss Honsinger's report for the year is largely the story in detail of two or three of the girls and their persecutions and temptations. Evidently they are of the stuff of which martyrs are made, and know Him whom they have believed. The health of the girls is a serious question. Some of them are showing tubercular tendencies. Swedish movements, a tennis court, and basket ball have all been introduced to the great advantage of their physical wellbeing. In spite of her heavy work, Miss Honsinger is allowing nothing to interfere with her daily study of the language. She finds "the girls take to music like ducks to water," and writes of extensive preparations for Easter music. Miss Ilien Tang's health is far from satisfactory, and although at latest accounts she was reported as improving, it is only by taking light work that she will be able to continue in the school.

In March of this year Miss Howe and Dr. Kahn went to Shanghai, expecting to come at once to America, but were surprised by the refusal of the authorities to take Dr. Kahn as a passenger, owing to some trouble of the eyelids. Being obliged to retrace their steps they made opportunity to visit some of the interior towns of the great Kiang-Si Province, with its population of thirty millions. They found white harvest fields and no workers, and urgently ask for more laborers. In July they resumed their

10

SUMMARY OF WORK IN THE CENTRAL CHINA CONFERENCE.

NAMES OF STATIONS.	Chinkiang	Kiukiang	Nanchang	Nanking	Wuhu	Total.
W. F. M. S. Missionaries	3	4	3	5	2	17
Wives of Mis'aries in Active Work			1			1
Foreign or Eurasian Assistants			1			1
Native Workers	14	28	6	23	6	77
WOMEN IN THE CHURCH						
Full Members		93	15	70	25	203
Probationers		20	35	25	18	98
Adherents		(?)	150		100	250
Women and Girls Baptized dur'g Yr,		72	2	25	2	101
Christian Women under Instruction		(?)		18	118	136
Non-Christian Women under Inst'n,			185	6		191
No. Bible-women Employed	2	7	1	5	2	17
SCHOOLS FOR TRAINING BIBLE WO-						
MEN—No. Schools		1		1		2
No. Missionaries		1		1		2
No. Native Teachers		4		3		7
Enrollment		72		24		96
Receipts for Board and Tuition		¶$139.		*¶$128.		¶$267.
SCHOOLS OF COLLEGE GRADE,						
NORMAL—No. Schools				1		1
No. Foreign Missionaries				4		4
No. Native Teachers				1		1
Self-supporting Students				13		13
Total Enrollment				†23		23
Receipts for Board and Tuition				¶$160.		¶$160.
VERNACUL'R AND ANGLO-VERNAC-						
ULAR BOARDING SCHOOLS—						
No. Schools	1	1	1	1		4
No. Foreign Missionaries	1	†2	2	4		9
No. Native Teachers	8	8	4			20
Self-Supporting Students	14	3		18		35
Wholly-Supported Students	§27	‖22	4	2		55
Partly-Supported Students	39	100	56	64		259
No. Day Students	2	2	1			5
Total Enrollment	80	125	60	84		349
Receipts for Board and Tuition	¶$610.	¶$938.50	¶$357.76	¶$556.		¶$2,462.26
Govern't Grants and Donations				¶$25.		¶$25.
ORPHANAGES						
Total No. Orphans	21	22	2			45
DAY SCHOOLS—No. Schools		6	1	2	2	11
No. Teachers		6	3	5	2	16
Total Enrollment		175	20	105	60	360
Average Daily Attendance		128(?)	18	80	47	273
Receipts for Tuition		¶$20.	¶$36.	¶$43.26	¶$19.	¶$118.26
KINDERGARTENS						
No. Kindergartens			1	1		2
No Foreign Kindergartners			1	1		2
No. Native Kindergartners				2		2
Total Enrollment			8	10		18
Average Attendance			8	10		18
Receipts for Tuition				¶$6.25		¶$6.25
MEDICAL WORK—No. Hospitals	1	1	1			3
No. Foreign Physicians	2					2
Eurasian or Native Physicians		1,	1			2
Eurasian or Native Nurses	1	4	2			7
No. Nurse Students	4	6	1			11
No. Hospital Beds	14	75				89
No. Hospital Patients	188	410				598
No. Hospital Clinic Patients	5492	12709				18201
No. Out-Patients	85	314	300			699
No. Dispensary Patients			7529			7529
Dispensary Receipts			¶$705.24			¶$705.24
Hospital Receipts	¶$609.11	¶$1,556.67				¶$2,165.78
Fees and Donations from Fo'ners,	¶$54.55					¶$54.55

* Including donations from foreigners. † Including other missions. ‡ One, a student of the language. § 21 orphans. ‖ Orphans. ¶ U. S. G.

homeward journey, this time coming through Siberia. Now that they are again with us, we welcome them heartily. Miss Howe, after an absence of fifteen years, and Dr. Kahn, who has worked steadily for twelve years. A pleasant feature of their journey was their stay in London as guests of Mr. Hwang, one of the Secretaries of the Chinese Legation to England, whose wife is one of Miss Howe's own girls.

The Yonkers J. V. Hughes Day School in Nan Chang has had about twenty-five pupils this year. It suffers somewhat because of the proximity of Government schools giving tuition free; however, we get a very desirable class of scholars because we teach English and send on our pupils to the boarding-schools.

Dr. Kahn's dispensary work showed increase, not only in number of patients, but what perhaps is even better, in the readiness of both patients and visitors to listen to the gospel story. The Doctor hopes to spend two years in the United States in study that will better enable her to carry· the responsibility of the lives entrusted to her care. The gentry of Nan Chang have given ground inside the city for a hospital for women, and we are anxious that Miss Howe may take back with her next summer money and pledges that will warrant the immediate beginning of the building, that the hospital may be ready for Dr. Kahn on her return to the field.

For the rapid growth in Central China there is need of more new buildings to healthfully house our workers and the many women and girls now eagerly seeking instructions, but all agree that the paramount need is of more missionaries, well equipped for training teachers and leaders to go out among their own people as Christian teachers in Government schools as well as in our own Mission schools, and as evangelists to reach the scattered villages, where women seem now ready to hear of the Christian's God and to follow Him.

WEST CHINA.

The official correspondent of West China was unable, through severe illness, to prepare the report.

FOOCHOW CONFERENCE.

Organized as a Conference in 1877.
Woman's work commenced by Baltimore Ladies' China Missionary Society in 1848.
Woman's Foreign Missionary Society commenced work in 1871.
Official Correspondent, Mrs. E. D. Huntley.

The Foochow Conference includes the Fuhkien Province, except what is now the Hing Hua Conference.

MISSIONARIES AND THEIR STATIONS.

FOOCHOW.—Lydia A. Trimble, Carrie I. Jewell, *Florence J. Plumb, *Mrs. S. A. Tippett, *Julia A. Bonafield, Ellen Lyon, M. D., *Hu King Eng, M. D., *Phoebe C. Wells, *Phoebe A. Parkinson, Elizabeth M. Strow, *Ruby Sia, May Hu, L. Ethel Wallace, Jean Adams, Cora E. Simpson, Lena Hatfield, M. D., Edna Jones, Elsie M. Sites, Mrs. S. Moore Sites.
MING CHIANG.—Isabelle D. Longstreet, *Mary E. Carleton, M. D.

* Home on leave.

NGU CHENG AND HOKCHIANG.—Carrie M. Bartlett, Li Bi Cu, M. D., *Mabel Allen.
HAI TANG.—Mamie F. Glassburner.
KU CHENG AND KU-DE.—Frieda V. Lorenz, Mary Peters, *Grace B. Travis.
YEN PING.—Mable C. Hartford, Alice Linam.

FOOCHOW REPORT.—It is a difficult task in the twenty minutes allowed to properly state the conditions in a territory covering 29,000 square miles, larger than Vermont, New Hampshire, Connecticut, and Rhode Island, with a population of 18,000,000 people. We have here seven centers of activity, with hospitals, boarding and day schools, women's training-school, industrial work, and crowded beyond the capacity of buildings and equipments.

At the last Conference Miss Florence Plumb and Miss Ethel Wallace were jointly given charge of the boarding-school. Early in the year Miss Plumb was obliged to return to the home-land on account of ill-health. A readjustment of the work brought Miss Strow and Miss Sites to her help. Miss Wallace writes: "Miss May Hu has been in the school for many years, and had it not been for her I do not know what we would have done." Miss Strow writes: "A gracious revival has been in progress. Personal work has been done by the teachers, and every day for a number of weeks before meetings opened little girls were meeting all over the buildings. After the dinner hour in the bed-rooms, class-rooms; even in the study, girls were talking with those who had not accepted Christ or had grown cold. Many instances might be given of the effect of the revival on the lives of the girls. One of them who is from a village in which there is not a single Christian, said, 'O, I do want to become a Christian, but I dare not.' Before the meetings closed she had given her heart to Christ, and when testimonials were called for she was most always the first to testify. She came to Miss Wallace and asked for a Chinese calendar which gave the dates of the moons. In her village they know nothing about Sunday and reckon it as the first, second, and third of the moon. She desired the dates marked which were Sundays, wishing to observe them as a Christian child should. She will be the first Christian to tell the story of Christ in her home. On the third Sunday of May twenty-three of the girls received baptism." Miss Wallace says: "As I stood at the altar with them there was a song of praise in my heart." This year eleven girls will graduate. One hundred and seventy-five are enrolled. Step by step the standard has been raised, and now that the normal training class is a part of the plan, and the long-wished-for college seems an actuality, we hope to see our girls step from primary to middle, normal, and college grades.

The day schools and the musical department of the boarding-school at Foochow have been under the care of Miss Ruby Sia. During the year she has visited many homes and taken trips in the country inspecting the schools, taking with her native teachers to the villages, going from seven to eight miles. Fifteen of these schools are located in the Foochow District. The largest number in any one school is thirty, while the smallest is ten, making the total attendance about 250. Five girls have completed a three years' course in these day schools, and have been admitted to the boarding-school. The greatest lack is a normal training-school for our teachers. This has been overcome in a measure by what is called a teachers' institute. It is difficult to give the necessary training in a month or six weeks. In former years books and furniture necessary

*Home on leave.

for these day schools were furnished free, but this last year the pupils, as far as they were able, were asked to furnish their books, desks, and chairs—a step toward self-support. Added to the duty of caring for these schools, Miss Ruby Sia has had charge of the musical department. Forty-five girls have been taking lessons in vocal culture. The two higher classes are now able to read readily. A choir of nine girls meet semi-weekly for drill in different choruses and quartets which are well learned, and furnish our music at Christmas times and at the graduating exercises. Nineteen girls have had lessons on the organ.

On the hill overlooking our group of buildings occupied by our boarding-school we find the Industrial Home, cared for by Miss Jean Adams. This work is a beautiful, helpful charity. At her own expense she plans and carries out an industry which enables 150 women to earn their living. During the eight years given to this work she has made it possible for hundreds to have some bodily comforts as well as rest of soul. Associated with her the past year has been Mrs. S. Moore Sites. Her knowledge of the Chinese language has enabled her to reach the hearts of the unconverted. In every way God has blessed this work. The past year has been the best in its history. Eight women have accepted Christ.

Mary E. Crook Memorial.—On your way down the hill stop at the Mary E. Crook Memorial. Here we find forty-five little waifs, every one demanding our loving care. This year they have had their first graduate. Her home has been in the orphanage; her education for four years has been in the boarding-school. If it were possible, would like to have her continue her education and be one of the first class to graduate from our Woman's College of South China. These little ones have been cared for by Miss Elsie Sites. Her work for 1908 will be gratefully remembered.

Leper Village,—About five miles from Foochow City we have a day school, with forty children and a Bible-woman at work. Miss Simpson writes: "The sufferings of these people and the utter darkness of their lives can not be imagined. They are outcasts on earth, and have no hope in the life beyond, only as the story of Jesus Christ cheers and changes the outlook for them."

Woolston Memorial Hospital.—If there is a physician in the homeland sitting with folded hands because there are no calls requiring her services, listen to the report that comes from Dr. Hu Senk Eng, sister of Dr. Hu King Eng. She says: "The patients have been more in number this year than ever before; in fact, so many have thronged the hospital begging for healing that my sister, the physician in charge, has been overwhelmed with work and has broken down in health. During the months of sickness many people came asking to see the great 'Dr. Hu.' They did not want the 'little doctor,' as they call me. When the plague was raging in our hospital, and while other difficult problems were beyond solution, we called on Dr. Kinnear. Because of his kindness many a heavy burden was lifted and new enthusiasm and inspiration given to carry on to completion this important work." For nearly a year Dr. Hu King Eng has been laid aside, but is now regaining her strength. May the dear Master save her for this needy field in Foochow. For nine years she has served her people with loving care and with skill that seemed to the suffering ones almost miraculous. Too much can not be said of the work of the Bible-women and students of the hospital during these trying times. Their co-operation made the work possible. One of the native physicians, Dr. Dang, has done helpful work during the past year. While the high class people are difficult to reach with the gospel, still they are fast losing faith in their idols, and are understanding better than ever before that the religion of the Lord Jesus Christ is the need of the Chinese people.

The statistical report of the Woolston Memorial Hospital:

Receipts	$1,133 96
Christmas gift (Miss Jean Adams)................	$10 00
Total receipts	$1,143 96
Dispensary patients	13,557
Patients seen at visits..........................	446
Total patients seen...........................	14,003
Total prescriptions written and filled..............	14,779
Hearers at Dispensary...........................	21,695
Total number of hearers at all services..........	44,612
Number who have unbound their feet.............	87
Number probationers received	28
Number baptized	15
Number who have joined the Church in full connection	12

I am yours in His happy service,

HU SENK ENG, M. D.

YEN PING.—From Foochow let us take a trip up the Min River 150 miles. Here we will find the walled city of Yen Ping. Our beautiful buildings of gray brick with white trimmings make an attractive picture on the hills overlooking the city and river. The work here is under the care of Miss Mable Hartford. The building is less than a year old, and pronounced most artistic. Within its walls are housed the children of our native Christians. During the last year three of the students have been married; four detained at home because of sickness, leaving only seventy-six at the close of the year. Eight new girls have been enrolled, and the outlook for the future is bright. *Wanted,* five scholarships at $25 each. During the past year two events are worthy of especial notice. The dedication of the building and the first graduating exercises. The building was the gift of friends living in Kansas City, Missouri, a memorial to Mrs. Emma Fuller. Step within its walls and you find a large chapel, two large school rooms, four recitation rooms, a dining-room, and kitchen on the first floor; all the conveniences necessary for a well-equipped house. In the second story are sleeping accommodations for seventy girls. The morning watch from eight to eight-thirty is kept by all.

IU-KA DISTRICT.—Eight Bible-women are working here. At one place last winter not one single Christian was to be found, now we have meetings largely attended; oftentimes a hundred women are present at Church; some out of curiosity, but the gospel will find lodgment in their hearts.

There are five day schools in the district. These schools are the feeders for our boarding-schools. Provide for these schools at $30 each and you will be preparing many girls and boys for the higher education found in the boarding-schools. Miss Hartford has spent many weeks visiting the schools and the Bible-women on the district.

YEN PING CITY.—Closely allied to this work is that supervised by Miss Alice Linam. She has a fine building for the Woman's Training-school, pronounced by many as the most beautiful in China. Here we have a chance to educate Bible-women. Twenty dollars will keep a woman for a year in this school. This work is most encouraging. A year of study in many cases will fit a woman to go out in her village and work among the unconverted. Twenty-three women have been enrolled during the year. Many of them live in distant villages, where there is not a single Christian woman. At vacation time they return to their homes and are the bearers of the good news of a Savior for all. Ten of these women are still unprovided for. Lend a hand! Industrial work is carried on one afternoon in the week. A Woman's Foreign Missionary Society has been organized. The subject at one of the meetings was, "The Origin of our Society." The motto adopted was, "two cents a week and a prayer," a very familiar one to all missionary workers. The kindergarten is a new feature. Fifteen children are under instruction, and good results are apparent. Money is needed for the development of this department.

NORTH IONG BING.—Six day schools are the lights which we trust will guide many little ones to the feet of our Master. Very little opposition is met. Sometimes a child will steal away from home and come to school out of curiosity. Curiosity brings them, interest keeps them, conversion holds them. With this outline of work you would think there was enough to occupy all the time of one woman, but she has added to this the supervision of eleven Bible-women, and like Oliver Twist is still asking for more. Twenty-five dollars will keep a woman at work a year.

MING CHIANG.—At Conference Miss Longstreet and Miss Strow were appointed in charge of the boarding-schools, day schools, Bible-women, and training-school; a big work and only two missionaries, and one new to the conditions. But alas! before the year was half over Miss Strow was necessitated to return to Foochow and assist in the boarding-school. Miss Longstreet writes: "Two new girls have been admitted into our school. Fifty-eight pupils have been enrolled during the year. Two new ones were admitted in March. Five days prior to the opening of school a 'district woman's revival meeting' was held, from 100 to 120 sleeping and eating within the hospitable walls of the boarding-school, many others coming just for a day at a time." She says: "Truly God was in our midst, and our hearts were warmed as we felt the Spirit's presence wonderfully manifested as the dear women testified. Five of our boarding-school girls have entered the Church in full connection. Their changed lives are proof that they, too, have talked with God and are following the Master." The ten Bible-women and the thirteen day schools need the supervision of another competent, well-equipped missionary. Who will go and who will send? For years the need of new buildings has been presented by the Estimating Committee, and thus far only the one school building has been given. Now the best interest of the work demands that some provision be made for the woman's training class. At present they are occupying the missionaries' home.

HAITANG.—A trip down the Min River brings you to the Hai Tang archipelago, thirty miles from the mainland, consisting of the island of Hai Tang and ten smaller ones, with a population of 75,000. It has been over thirty years since the first message of a risen Savior was told them by Captain Ding. Now more than one thousand are followers of the risen Savior, and have turned from idol worship to serve the living God. Our boarding-school, with twenty students, the Woman's Training-school, day schools, and Bible-women are receiving the loving care of Miss Glassburner. Her helpers are all native workers, and most of them are graduates from the Ngu Cheng School. A mandarin teacher has been secured, and an industrial department has been added. This, together with the regular school work, has fully occupied the time of the girls. The girls are giving their Saturday holiday for work in order to increase their subscriptions to the pastor's salary. They are good Bible students, and give promise of being stalwart Christians. A kindergarten department on a small scale, with a class of twenty, has been organized under the leadership of one of our Chinese girls, whose English name is Bertha Lee. While in America a year ago she received some instruction in kindergarten training. The Woman's School has been greatly interrupted by many severe cases of illness. The plague has been of such a malignant type that it was thought best to close school earlier than usual. It is hard to tell what work is accomplished in the lives of these women. Occasionally a report reaches us of one of these students at work in her own village; oftentimes the only Christian in the community. Not long since one of these girls visited Miss Glassburner and told her of the work. She goes from house to house talking with her neighbors of Christ. Another woman came to the Romanized school, a refugee from her husband, who was cruel and threatened to sell her. She was in the school three terms. During that time she learned to read her Bible and hymn book, and to talk to her Heavenly Father. Then the heathen family into which she had been married concluded that since she would not live with her husband they would not be burdened with her support, and made an effort to have her married to another man, and her own husband was perfectly willing as he would get part of the bethrothal money. Later her husband came for her. She went away with a heavy heart.

Two women have graduated from the Training-school. Each of them is teaching a day school. Nine of the girls who entered the boarding-school were from our little day schools on the island. Miss Glassburner writes: "I have in mind a little school among the hills, housed in a miserable little hovel and taught by a weary little woman, mostly with a fretful baby in her arms. The number of pupils were small, and we wondered whether it would not be better to close it. Five of our brightest and dearest girls came from this discouraging little school, and three more will be ready to come next year. Here is one of another kind. It is in a village where the people have long asked for a school. Here is a nice, clean room for a school; there is no fretful baby to hinder the work, and eighteen pupils presented themselves for examination." Twenty Bible-women are doing good work. The medical work has had very little financial support. Des Moines and Pacific Branch each gave $25. This is hardly sufficient for the support of Dr. Hung, leaving nothing for medicines and supplies for the dispensary. Dr. Hung is a graduate of the Foochow Hospital, under Dr. Lyon, and is a capable, experienced woman, and if the opportunity is her would be a great power in this community. Is there not some one who would advance the money for medicines, thereby enabling them to have capital sufficient to lay in a stock that might be sold at prices within the reach of the poor and the sick?

Hok Chiang and Ngu Cheng.—There is an effort all through our boarding-schools to introduce up-to-date text-books, illustrated readers, Chinese histories and mandarin, and put in much time for mathematics, geography, and physiology, and very little time on Chinese classics. Miss Bartlett describes their Christmas entertainment. She says: "It was somewhat out of the beaten track. A fine program was prepared which occupied the morning and afternoon, and the women and children from the surrounding villages were invited. They came eight hundred strong, staying with us from early morn till night, hearing all day long of the 'Christ born and Savior given.' We were able to give them a mid-day luncheon, because the girls gladly gave up what would have secured for them Christmas gifts." In June three of the girls graduated. Seventeen Bible-women are at work on these two districts. The increasing calls for Bible-women have been met by the answer, "No, we have no one to send."

The hospital at Ngu Cheng has been completed. The Dispensary has had from thirty to forty cases daily. The beautiful building and the comfort that these poor people find make them feel that it is a veritable heaven. This work is under the care of Dr. Li Bi Cu. Now with the new building and equipment we expect great things. During Miss Trimble's stay in America, Doctor Li Bi Cu has had added to the care of her hospital work the supervision of the day schools. With the help of a student as an assistant while on her trip she saw seven hundred patients. Since November she has treated 5,500 patients, and by Conference time will have added another thousand to the number. The hospital is a beautiful building, accommodating about sixty patients. The largest number cared for at any one time has been thirty-five. The patients are coming and going constantly, and the days are full of work. During the last month more children have been treated than at any time previous. The cool, clean place appeals to them, and they are never ready to leave our comfortable hospital. A good deal of Christian work is done among the in-patients, and patients that stay a week will get a good deal of religious instruction and will commit many Bible verses to memory. Eight patients have unbound their feet this year.

The six graduates of the Training-school are strong, consecrated Christian women. One has gone as a teacher, and five as Bible-women on the district. The woman's station class is having a better grade of women coming for instruction than in any previous year. At the last quarterly meeting five of these women were admitted into the Church, and three were baptized. Only one in the school is outside the fold of Christ. The plague has greatly interfered with village work. Added to her regular work Miss Bartlett has had charge of the boarding-school since Miss Trimble has been in America. Four girls have graduated, but are to remain as teachers. Here we have the hope of China; consecrated Christian girls, giving their lives for their own people. A kindergarten department has been added, with an enrollment of twenty. Eighteen Bible-women have been going in and out the homes of Hok-Chiang. Most encouraging reports come of their work. Twice the number could be used if it were possible to supply the demand. There are so many needy places. A new kitchen and bathroom, costing $500, is greatly needed at this place. For sanitary reasons this request should be granted. Early in the year Miss Bartlett had smallpox, and has not quite recovered her usual strength. Her summer vacation has greatly helped her. We pray that this consecrated worker may be spared for many years to work in this field.

KUCHENG.—The work here has been carried on by Miss Lorenze and Miss Peters, two missionaries doing the work where there should be four. Miss Lorenze writes: "The people are hungry for the truth, and would accept Christ if they knew Him. We have had a good year, and much encouragement. After the close of school a missionaries' institute was held for a month. This added materially to the work of the missionaries, but they felt that it was necessary for the best development of the Bible-women and teachers. The general health of the girls in the boarding-school has been good. Smallpox has been on every side, but the girls have thus far escaped. We have one hundred pupils enrolled. The industrial work started by Miss Rouse is still a factor in the developing of the Christian lives of the poor and helpless. Our missionaries and native workers visit them in their homes and teach and train them. Only those who are unable to do other work are given the chance to earn a living by the drawn-work. Self-support is slowly coming to the Kucheng District. One feature in the training-school is hailed with delight. A former student is now doing some teaching, and serving as matron. The standard is higher than ever before. Some new features have been inaugurated. In the final examination a number of the women received ninety-eight and ninety-nine per cent. During the year they have committed to memory Psalms ninety-first and thirty-first; Matthew, seventh chapter, and Revelations, seventh, twenty-first, and twenty-second chapters. Added to this, fifty hymns have been committed to memory, but best of all they are growing spiritual. One hundred dollars in fees has been received this year, which has been expended for school expenses. Speed the day when all expenses except the support of the missionary shall be given, and self-support is an actuality. Of the eighteen day schools, some are worthy of especial recognition, particularly one where the native teacher prepared the recitations and songs, not from books and papers, but from the Bible and her own fertile brain. Men listened and believed the gospel after hearing the children's Christmas entertainment. The Bible-women have greatly advanced the work the past year. Sacrifices have been made by these faithful women, giving out of their poverty $31 for district work in addition to their regular Church subscriptions.'

Foochow District—*Woman's Training and Romanized School.*— These two schools are under the care of Miss Jewell. Four women have graduated, and have gone out full-fledged Bible-women, and have received their diplomas. One is working at the Leper Chapel; two have gone into district work, and one will remain and teach in the Romanized School. Twenty-five dollars and fifty cents has been received for board, and $4 for rent for two little rooms, making a total of $29.50. The school has been taxed to its utmost capacity. In the Romanized School four have finished their course and are now enrolled in the training-school. The work of some of the women is exceptionally good. Miss Jewell says: "I was tempted to mark some of them 100 in everything, so nearly perfect were they." One hundred and seven dollars was received from these women during the year, a step toward self-support. They need a new building for this work, and double the number of women could be cared for in both the Training and Romanized School.

Report from Dr. Lyon for the year 1908 covers only six months. After her return from America she found many things needed. The hospital required repairing and much preparatory work done before it was possible to admit patients. Fortunately things moved slowly; had they not, her strength would not have been equal to the task, but now the hospital is full. During the past year there has been very little plague, but many cases of smallpox. Thousands of children have died. She says: "In our one little contagion ward many are being vaccinated. Never before have smallpox cases been brought to us. They have been cared for at home. Every private room is full—more are needed—which shows that the better class are being reached. Over 650 in-patients since November. One family rented a small ward. They brought in a baby six months old with bronchial pneumonia. They had tried the Chinese physician. The child had been pricked with needles, the idol had been besought, but to no avail. A few days after they came they asked for prayers for the child. Soon they saw an improvement. Both grandparents, mother, and wet nurse were here; the father came often. At first all faces were anxious; later all beamed and all gave the Lord praise and glory. Since the grandparents have gone, different members of the family have come and remained in the ward for treatment. No private room would hold them, and they pay the rent for the whole ward. Services are held daily in the hospital, and patients are taught to read and are personally taught by the Bible-reader, whose work it is to impart the gospel to the waiting ones. The time has come when some action must be taken regarding the rebuilding of the hospital. The demand for better quarters and the imperative need of stronger walls, safer floors, and tight roofs have brought the question somewhat in this shape, "Shall we rebuild the hospital, or build a new one?" Listen to a few statements from Dr. Lyon. She says: "Well I have put this in the Lord's hands; He knows the needs; He knows how it has been impossible to perform some operations because we have not had a fit place in which to perform them. He knows how the work is opening up, and how beds are on verandas, in rooms, and in every available place in the halls. He knows that although our work has increased five times, yet we receive no more from home than in 1890. He knows that our consulting and dressing room are one, and how it tries our nerves to go on prescribing while a youngster is screaming over a dose of castor oil, or the dressing of a sore head. He knows that our only surgical ward is 18 x 16 feet, cut off of the end of a veranda. He knows that I have tried to put the work on a self-supporting basis. He knows that the old instruments wore out and that I have saved and gotten new out of our receipts. I said to Him while in America, 'If Thou wantest me to have help send the helpers to me.' He sent them, and now I say if it is Thy will that the old hospital, with its rotten floors and beams, be removed, send money to rebuild it. Let not the plan be mine, nor let it be of selfish ambition, but let what is best for the work come to me. I confess it harder than ever to work, because I am so handicapped, but I realize that you ladies are overburdened and that the fields are ripe, but the laborers are few." Dr. Lyon's proposition is that the old building shall be torn down and the material sold and a new building put up. Ten thousand dollars is asked for this hospital. It should be granted. This hospital was the first one supported by the women of our Society in all China, and has done fine work with very little outlay.

HING HUA CONFERENCE.

Hing Hua Mission Conference was organized in 1896.
Official Correspondent, Mrs. A. N. Fisher.

The Hing Hua Mission includes the Hing Hua prefecture and adjoining territory, where the Hing Hua dialect is spoken, and the Ing-Chung prefecture and adjoining territory where the Amoy dialect is spoken.

MISSIONARIES AND THEIR STATIONS.

HING HUA.—Minnie E. Wilson, Lizzie W. Varney, *Pauline E. Westcott, †Mary M. Thomas, Lulu C. Baker, Edith L. Fonda.
SIENG-IU.—Martha Lebeus, Martha Nicholaisen, Emma J. Betow, M. D., Frances L. Draper, M. D., Paula Seidlmann.
TEK-HOE.—Althea M. Todd, Jessie A. Marriott, Gertrude Strawick.
WIVES OF MISSIONARIES IN CHARGE OF WORK.—Mrs. E. F. Brewster, Mrs. H. G. Dildine, Mrs. F. S. Carson.

During the session of the Hing Hua Conference one year ago, two of the native preachers were commissioned to bear greetings to the Woman's Conference held at the same time. One of these likened the situation in

* Home on leave. † Working in Japan.

his district to that of a person having but one arm. "We have," said he, "thirteen Hing Hua men as preachers; we wish you would send us thirteen Bible-women also, then we would be like having two arms, and the work would prosper."

HING HUA AND ANTAU DISTRICTS—HING HUA.—*Hamilton Girls' Boarding-school.*—The present enrollment is 110. In her circular letter to patrons Miss Varney outlines their plan as follows: "Beginning with the primary or day schools we have a course of study that requires fourteen years of work, and covers subjects corresponding, as nearly as we can adjust Chinese studies, to the work in our public schools, and in addition to secular studies Bible and religious books are in the course. The first two years' work is done in the day schools. A few years ago we had but seven grades. This signifies a wonderful change in the sentiments of Christians. They used to take the girls out to marry after five or six years. Next term I plan to have the more advanced girls begin work as pupil teachers, so that when they leave here they will have had some experience in school work. There are many country places asking for day schools. One feels in this land of unlimited demands for earnest, careful work, that life is not long enough nor strength great enough to half cover the things we long to do. I am glad my lot has been cast here, and rejoice to see the growth and development of the Master's kingdom." Miss Baker will assist in this work.

A class of five was graduated from the Bible training-school early in the year. The mid-summer normal school for Bible-women was attended by thirty and was a season of great profit. Some of the preachers in the city gave valuable instruction along certain lines, such as how to meet the questions and superstitions of those out of Christ, as well as how to influence those already Christians to give up harmful customs. The women themselves prepared talks for heathen or Christian audiences and received criticism or suggestion as needed.

The continued absence from the mission of Miss Thomas, for health reasons, is greatly regretted. Miss Westcott is on furlough, and Miss Fonda goes this fall as a new recruit.

SIENG-IU DISTRICT, SIENG-IU.—*Isabel Hart Girls' School.*—Miss Nicolaisen finds reason for rejoicing in the improvement noted in her girls, and especially in the spiritual atmosphere of the school and in the tokens of self-denial for the sake of Christ and His Church.

Miss Lebeus continues "in labors abundant," visiting every Circuit in the large District, superintending the woman's Bible training-school and holding a normal school with her workers. The last mentioned she considers the most profitable gathering of the sort she has held She chose the Epistle of James as a study for the daily morning devotions, and the practical lessons were of inestimable value to the women, who seemed so ready to recognize their own faults and to seek Divine aid to overcome them.

The year has been a very busy one in the Margaret Nast Hospital, under the care of Drs. Betow and Draper. The in-patients have increased from 294 of the preceding year, to 511. Many have been chronic cases, which afforded greater opportunity for teaching them the way of Truth. The majority come from heathen homes and would never have been reached without the hospital. There are many most interesting cases of persons who have given up their idols and become Christians.

Ing Chung and Dua Cheng Districts—Tek-hoe.—The girls' and the woman's schools are still carried on in the building erected for the training-school some years ago. It was hoped long since to have the new building for the girls' school, but the numerous difficulties which have arisen in securing land have delayed operations, and the end is not yet. Three girls—the first graduates—were sent forth in June. One will study medicine in Foochow; one will be married soon, and the third will teach until the young man she is to marry shall have finished his school work. The kindergarten under Miss Marriott and the children's church continue to flourish. Teachers are greatly needed for the day schools.

Miss Strawick will soon be ready for evangelistic work.

In writing of the obstacles they are encountering, Miss Todd says: "Things do not look very bright just now, but we know that God is planning for us and what He does is best. We are not discouraged, but getting a better idea of what faith means."

SUMMARY OF WORK IN THE HING HUA CONFERENCE.

NAMES OF STATIONS OR DISTRICTS.	Sieng Iu	Hing Hua	An-tau	Ing-cheong	Deh-hua	Dua-cheng	Totals
W. F. M. S. Missionaries	4	4			3		11
WOMEN IN THE CHURCH—							
Full Members	416	782	239				1,437
Probationers	183	230	98				511
Adherents	320	530	221				1,071
Women and Girls B'zed during Year	53	140	50				243
No. Bible-women Employed	22	26			7		55
SCHOOLS FOR TRAINING BIBLE-							
WOMEN—No. Schools	1	1			1		3
No. Missionaries	1	1			1		3
No. Native Teachers	4	4			2		10
Enrollment	40	37			10		87
VERNACULAR AND ANGLO-VERNAC-							
ULAR BOARDING SCHOOLS—							
No. Schools	1	1			1		3
No. Foreign Missionaries	1	1			1		3
No. Native Teachers	6	6			4		16
No. Day Students	10						10
Total Enrollment	80	62			30		172
DAY SCHOOLS—							
No. Schools	7	13					20
No. Teachers	7	13					20
Total Enrollment	112	193					305
KINDERGARTENS—							
No. Kindergartens					1		1
No. Foreign Kindergartners					1		1
Total Enrollment					30		30
MEDICAL WORK—							
No. Hospitals	1						1
No. Foreign Physicians	2						2
Eurasian or Native Nurses	6						6
No. Hospital Beds	70						70
No. Hospital Patients	511						511
No. Out-Patients	1,004						1,004
No. Dispensary Patients	5,372						5,372
Dispensary Receipts	*$198 14						*$198 14
Hospital Receipts	*$641 86						*$641 86

* Mexican.

KOREA.

Women's Work commenced in 1885. Organized as a Conference in 1904.

Official Correspondent, Louisa C. Rothweiler.

MISSIONARIES AND THEIR STATIONS.

CHEMULPO.—Josephine O. Paine, Gertrude E. Snavely, Mary R. Hillman, Lula A. Miller.

KONG JU.—Mrs. Alice H. Sharp, Miss Ora M. Tuttle.

PYENG YANG.—Mrs. Rosetta S. Hall, M. D., Mrs. Esther Kim Pak, *Miss Henrietta P. Robbins, Miss Emily I. Haynes, Miss Sarah B. Hallman.

SEOUL.—Mrs. M. F. Scranton, Lulu E. Frey, Mary M. Cutler, M. D., Emma Ernsberger, M. D., Jessie Marker, Millie M. Albertsen, Alta I. Morrison.

YENG BYEN.—Ethel M. Estey.

WIVES OF MISSIONARIES IN CHARGE OF WORK.—Mrs. G. H. Jones, Mrs. W. N. Noble, Mrs. D. A. Bunker, Mrs. F. E. C. Williams, Mrs. Corwin Taylor, Mrs. W. C. Rufus, Mrs. E. D. Follwell, Mrs. E. M. Cable, Mrs. J. Z. Moore, Mrs. C. Critchett, Mrs. A. L. Becker.

The Korea of to-day, the mental and spiritual attitude of its people, differs from the Korea of twenty-four years ago, when the first missionaries were appointed to go there, as the day differs from the night, as noonday brightness differs from midnight gloom.

Not only have 150,000 or more identified themselves with the different Protestant Churches, but many of these are Christians of the highest type, not Christian in outward form only, but men and women of deep spirituality.

A continual revival has been going on for the last two years. Christianity has so permeated the mass of the people that they have come to a wonderful realization of their needs, of the inefficiency of the old methods of education. Not only in regard to men and boys is this true, but all the old prejudice against education for girls and women seems to have vanished and in its place has come an earnest demand for educational privileges for their daughters, sisters, and wives. In order to receive these, fathers, husbands, and brothers are ready even to make personal sacrifice. Miss Frey writes, "I never dreamed that I would see the enthusiasm over education that now exists." We have over thirty day schools, in all of which more or less is being done toward self-support, besides a number which are entirely supported by the people. In Pyeng Yang tuition is now being charged all but those who are in their first year—for the mixed grades, 10 sen, and for the higher grade, 15 sen a month. In Chemulpo the native Church agreed to pay for one of the best teachers. In Ewa Haktang, our boarding-school, ten pupils were entirely self-supporting, seventy partly so, and only seventeen were entirely supported. During the last year no girl was admitted who could not at least read the native character. The grade of the school has been raised; a lower, a middle, and a higher course has been provided for. Five girls were graduated from the middle course last June. Of these, one goes out to teach, the others hope to complete the higher course. Calisthenics, formerly looked upon as entirely unbecoming for Korean girls,

*Home on leave.

are looked upon with favor—are even demanded. Photographs showing the entire school taking part in a May day festival, crowning their beloved Mrs. Scranton as May Queen, and going through various drills, look like dream pictures to one who saw and knew Korea many years ago.

Mrs. N. K. Ha, a former pupil, later a graduate of the Ohio Wesleyan University, has been a most efficient helper and teacher during the past year. Additional foreign help has become a necessity. Mrs. Hugh Miller, Mrs. Jones, Mrs. Bunker, and others have given regular instruction in music and calisthenics. In the north the problem of education for girls, beyond what can be obtained in the day schools, is to be solved by a girls' higher school, carried on by the Presbyterian and our own mission. Forty Methodist girls were in attendance during the past year. The number of boarders was small as there was no dormitory or other place which would serve the purpose. If only some kind friend could be found who would furnish $10,000 to put up a building to accommodate one hundred girls, this school, which for running expenses would be almost self-supporting, would be put on a firm basis. We are very grateful to Mr. Collins, who has promised the funds for several day school buildings.

If Pyeng Yang and Seoul could each be furnished with a missionary of experience as a teacher, a good musician—one who could devote herself to the supervision of day schools—it would be a boon to our work there. In Seoul especially she would not be restricted to our own day schools, but could easily gain access to Government and private schools for teaching the gospel, an opportunity which Japan never gave to missionaries. The crying need of the country is for teachers, and our mission schools should supply them.

The medical work has, of necessity, been greatly hampered. In Pyeng Yang, Dr. Hall and Miss Hallmann have worked in cramped rented quarters. But the hospital and dispensary will soon be completed so far as the money available will permit. Two thousand six hundred dollars will be required to finish and equip the building. In the meantime work is being carried on as well as can be done.

In Seoul, Dr. Cutler has been working at the old place near the boarding-school, and Dr. Ernsberger at the East Gate, both doing heroic work under the difficulties which lack of room and conveniences cause. The hope of soon having something better is being made daily more certain, as work is going on on the Lillian Harris Memorial Hospital. Less than one-half of the needed funds are in hand, but the other half must be furnished soon or work will have to stop. Another physician for our work in Korea must be sent soon or some work must be closed when one or other of the present force needs to come home.

The nurse's training-school is very fortunate in having secured in Miss Morrison an able and efficient successor to Miss Edmunds. A splendid foundation has been laid and the first class of nurses graduated.

The evangelistic work has been just as encouraging as ever. While perhaps not quite such large numbers have been gathered in as last year, the need to instruct those who had come in was very great. Miss Paine writes of wonderful meetings with large crowds of interested listeners and very good visible results. The need is so great that she and other workers feel overwhelmed by their inability to meet the demand. The large District which Miss Paine and Miss Snavely worked last year has been divided, Miss Miller and Miss Hillman being appointed to one part and Miss Paine and Miss Snavely to the other, comprising the work on the islands and in Haiju. Miss Paine, who has 130 groups of Christians in her District, writes of five groups visited, four of which did not have a single woman attending the services because no woman had ever been there. She sent a Bible-woman there and very soon

SUMMARY OF WORK IN KOREA.

NAMES OF STATIONS OR DISTRICTS.	Seoul (formerly Seoul and Chemulpo District)	Pyeng Yang	Kong Ju	Yeng Byent	Totals
W. F. M. S. Missionaries	10	4		1	15
Wives of Missionaries in Active Work	2	4	1	1	8
WOMEN IN THE CHURCH—Full Members					¶2000
Probationers					¶9000
Adherents					¶8500
Women and Girls Baptized during Year ¶					¶700
No. Christian Women under Instruction	*	*	*	*	*
No. Bible-women Employed	21	5	2	3	31
BIBLE INSTITUTES OR TRAINING CLASSES—					
No. of Institutes	2	11	2	6	21
No. Missionaries Teaching		5	1	2	8
No. Native Teachers	§§	10	4	6	20
Enrollment	§§	600	110	152	**862
SCHOOLS FOR TRAINING BIBLE WOMEN—					
No. Schools	1				1
SEMINARIES—No. Schools	§§	1			1
No. Foreign Missionaries	§§	1			1
Foreign or Eurasian Teachers	§§	1			1
Total Enrollment	§§	150			150
Receipts for Board and Tuition	§§	$32 00			$32 00
VERNACULAR AND ANGLO-VERNACULAR					
BOARDING SCHOOLS—No. Schools	1	1			2
No. Foreign Missionaries	2	‡			2
Foreign or Eurasian Teachers		‡			
No. Native Teachers	5	1			6
Self-Supporting Students	10	1			11
Wholly-Supported Students	17				17
Partly-Supported Students	70	5			75
No. Day Students	15	2			17
Total Enrollment	115	8			123
Receipts for Board and Tuition	§§	$14 00			$14 00
Donations of Foreigners	§§	4 50			4 50
DAY SCHOOLS—No. Schools	10	18	2	3	33
No. Teachers	10	20	2	5	35
Total Enrollment	464	673	50	45	1232
Average Daily Attendance	343	416	35	40	834
Receipts for Tuition	†	†	†	†	†
INDUSTRIAL SCHOOLS—No. Schools	1		1	1	3
No. Industrial Depts. in other Schools	§§	1	1	1	3
No. Foreign Missionaries	§§			1	1
Foreign or Eurasian Teachers	§§				
No. Native Teachers	§§		1	1	2
No. Pupils	§§		8	15	23
Receipts for Tuition and Board	§§		$14 00		$14 00
From Sale of Products	§§		18 35	$20 00	38 35
Donations from Foreigners	§§		4 50		4 50
MEDICAL WORK—No. Hospitals	(1) 1	(2)	(3)		1
No. Foreign Physicians	1	1	1		3
Eurasian or Native Physicians			1		1
No. Medical Students	2		1		3
No. Foreign Nurses	1		1		2
No. Nurse Students	5				5
No. Hospital Beds	16	8			24
No. Hospital Patients	61	158			219
No. Out-Patients	161		‖269		430
No. Dispensary Patients	1048	6752	¶¶810		8610
Dispensary Receipts	$45 50	$230 00	$39 26		$314 76
Hospital Receipts	66 60	187 75			254 35
Fees and Donations from Foreigners	38 00	39 50	$14 55		92 05
Government Grants		§	§		

* All members probationers and adherents.
† In almost all the schools the children pay for fuel, which is very expen-

the report came that forty-five women were now Christians. One old lady accompanied Miss Paine from place to place, walking over two hundred miles. When asked whether she was not very tired, she said, "O· no; it is like seeing Jesus to attend these meetings and having my soul fed."

The crying need of Kong Ju District has been met by the return of Mrs. Sharp and the appointment there of Miss Tuttle. These with Mrs. Cable will look after the work there, but a home for our workers is very much needed. In the far north Miss Estey is alone on a very large District. She should have an associate, but because there is no home there she has not asked for one. We rejoice in the hope that the home will be provided for during the coming year. In Pyeng Yang also another worker is very much needed for evangelistic work, since the growing school work should necessarily take the greater part of the time of Misses Robbins and Haynes.

Now is the day of opportunity in Korea; if not improved now it may be taken from us. Korea is not only willing to receive the gospel—it is hungering for it.   Respectfully submitted,

LOUISA C. ROTHWEILER.

JAPAN.

JAPAN CONFERENCE.

Woman's Work commenced in 1874.
Organized as a Conference in 1884.
Official Correspondent, Carrie J. Carnahan.

The Japan Conference includes the northern part of the Empire of Japan.

MISSIONARIES AND THEIR STATIONS.

HAKODATE.—*M. S. Hampton, Augusta Dickerson, *F. E. Singer, A. B. Sprowles.
HIROSAKI.—Mary B. Griffiiths, B. Alexander.
NAGOYA.—*R. J. Watson, *E. M. Soper, M. Lee.
SAPPORA.—L. Imhof, *A. V. Bing.
SENDAI.—E. J. Hewett, C. A. Heaton, Frances K. Phelps, *Georgiana Weaver.

* Home on leave.

sive; also pay the salary of a man who teaches Chinese; also, in Pyeng Yang District, the people have built new school houses costing more than $150.
† Schools for blind girls.
§ Extension of Lillian Harris Memorial Hospital site by a thirty-year lease.
‖ In nine months.
¶ Approximately. Because of Conference being held three months earlier than usual, the numbers in the church, especially the baptisms, are incomplete.
** Many women studied in the classes held by the men.
§§ No report.   ¶¶ In four months.
(1) Po Ku Nyo Koan, Seoul, report for six months: Received special gifts of $250 from Japanese Prince. Received special gift of $100 from Severance Hospital for Training School.
(2) Baldwin Dispensary, Seoul, report for twelve months. Received special gift of $250 from Japanese Prince; 10,000 women taught in Dispensary waiting room; three untrained helpers.
(3) Dispensary at Pyeng Yang, one untrained helper.

Tokyo.—M. A. Spencer, Amy Lewis, H. S. Alling, Ella Blackstock, E. Bullis, Miss Russell.

Yokohama.—Mrs. C. W. Van Petten, M. N. Daniel, *A. B. Slate, G. Baucus, E. Dickinson, Leonora Seeds.

Hakodate.—After all that our work in Hakodate has passed through, it is a great joy to us to know that on July 29th our new school buildings were dedicated under very delightful circumstances. Miss Sprowles, writing of the occasion, says, that the buildings have been completed sufficiently to dedicate them to the Master's use, is a cause of deep gratitude and thanksgiving. "Early on the morning of dedication day the guests began to arrive. Who were they? The girls who had received their education and had their Christian characters molded in the dear Iai Jo Gakko, some of them not alone, but bringing their babies. Who can tell how far and wide the influence of the school may reach—already to a second generation? Then the Mayor of Hakodate, the Vice-mayor, the Secretary of Education at Sapporo, lawyers, judges, school principals, and teachers—and so the chapel was full. We were disappointed not to have it permanently furnished, but the chairs from the classrooms had been transferred temporarily to the chapel, so we saw it for the first time with any furniture."

The exercises were most interesting. The oration was delivered by Bishop Honda, of the New Japan Methodist Church, the first Japanese to be elected by any denomination to the episcopal office, and a man who commands the respect of every one. He urged the necessity for the higher education of girls, insisting that they were of more value as teachers in the schools than men. "Educate our girls," he urged, "to serve their country by giving part of their lives to teaching, and also educate them so that they may become worthy mothers."

Mr. Yamaka, a former pastor of our Church in Hakodate, spoke of the value of educational work of the Woman's Foreign Missionary Society, and of what a great service our school and those of other mission boards had rendered to the nation.

The dedication service was conducted by the present pastor of Hakodate, who followed the form used by our Church for the dedication of Church edifices, making the necessary changes for the dedication of the school.

A set of photographs have been received, showing the buildings to be solid and substantial and at the same time attractive in appearance. They consist of a recitation hall, a dormitory, and a comfortable home for our missionaries. The latter was the gift of personal friends of Miss Dickerson, to whom our Society is most grateful, for it has required great economy and most careful planning to make the appropriation (made before the Russo-Japanese War and somewhat increased since the great fire which almost destroyed Hakodate) meet the cost of completion of the school buildings, because of the great increase in the price of labor and materials since the war. The great need now is for proper furnishing and equipment for these excellent buildings, so that the school may be an even greater power than it has been in the past.

Of the evangelistic work Miss Hampton writes: "The fire has made such a complete change in all our work and workers that it will take a few years to recover and know what we can do. There have been many compensations, however, for all our losses and we look forward to a future better than the past."

---

*Home on leave.

SAPPORO.—Miss Bing reports an interesting and growing evangelistic work. (The number of baptisms in the District is more than double that reported last year, and others are under instruction in all the Churches.)

Miss Imhof has had a Bible class among the nurses in the Red Cross Home and an interesting work among the girls in the linen factory, besides carrying on other kinds of city evangelistic work.

HIROSAKI.—Miss Alexander, in charge of our school, writes: "A complete change of the regular teachers in our higher department made the opening of the school seem a rather formidable affair. Among our new teachers this last year we were glad to have one of our own girls—Kudo O Tsune San—who, after six years' study at Aoyama, came back to us in the capacity of English teacher. She has done good work in her classes and taken an active interest in the religious life of the school.

"There are nine graduates for the past school year, four from the regular school department and five from the sewing department. Of the four, one goes to the Bible training-school at Yokohama, one into our kindergarten work, one to study in Tokyo, and one to be married soon.

"The interest taken in Bible study is encouraging and a cause for thankfulness. Among our Christian girls there is an earnest desire for growth in the spiritual life."

Of the kindergarten Miss Alexander writes: "The foundation of the new kindergarten was being laid when we started to Conference early in May last year, and we hoped the building might be ready for the opening of the fall term in September. The unexpected happened, though, and we actually moved into our new quarters the last day of June, had Sunday-school there on July 1st, and regular kindergarten work the next day. The building is on a corner lot and is set back from the street, with a playground in front. The outside presents a very neat appearance. In the building we have a large playroom thirty feet square, two classrooms, a small guest room or office, and a waiting room for the nurse girls, as well as servants' quarters. So we are very proud of our new and comfortable kindergarten home, and very grateful to the unknown friend of New England Branch whose kind gift made all this possible, and wish she could come some time and see the children as they play."

SENDAI.—A recent letter from Miss Hewett says: "A change in the Government schools has affected all our mission schools. Until recently only four years were required to complete the primary grades in the Government schools, but now it requires six years, and no pupils are allowed to leave the Government schools before finishing the primary grades. In Sendai we made a change in our course of study to adjust ourselves to the new regulation. We are sending four of our brightest girls to Hakodate to enter there in September. We sent one in April, and one sent two years ago has not yet graduated, so there will be six of our Sendai girls there. Another girl, who came two years ago, went this spring to the Yokohama school to prepare for Bible-women's work. One of our girls who graduated this spring is now in Miss Blackstock's industrial school. Two others are in St. Luke's Hospital learning to be nurses."

Of the city evangelistic work Miss Hewett writes: "The work in the various Sunday-schools and children's meetings has been continued in close connection with the school. The King's Daughters Circle conducts two Sunday-schools." Such work gives the older pupils in our school excellent practice and experience, and enables them to be little, efficient Christian workers when they go to their own home towns.

The orphanage under the care of Miss Phelps has had its times of difficulties and dangers, but also of victories and blessings. There are about 225 children in the institution.

"Our school has advanced very much, the work being directed by one of the normal school teachers. They have made this one of their practice schools and the result is that we have systematic teaching of the best, under the admirable school system of Japan, which is not so different from our own.

"Industrial work has been taught in gardening, pasting, basket making, and sewing, with a little knitting.

"The year has seen the erection of ten new cottages and a storehouse. The cottages were occupied just before Christmas, and now we do not need to spread bedding for fifty in one big room which must be used during the day for school and play. Each child has his own home, the girls on one side of the Compound and the boys on the other. These, with the little folks' home and the sick children's home, make twelve separate houses, with an average of about twenty in each.

"We will soon have a large class of young men and women, and we trust that they will go out into the world pure in heart and strong in spirit—God's own children—and His messengers of the true light which Christ brought to the earth."

TOKYO.—Last year we reported the need and the reason for obtaining land for our Aoyama Girls' School. During the latter part of the present year the committee having such purchases in charge on the field, and a special committee appointed by the Reference Committee in May, have been making earnest efforts to secure a suitable site. For a time the former committee had trouble to secure a satisfactory location, but seem now to have succeeded. The present pressing need is for money with which to make the required cash payment for the same. That we must soon have more room for the school is clearly shown in a very recent letter from Miss Lewis, the President, who writes: "Our school is growing constantly. Classrooms and dormitory are crowded, and with the recently received Government recognition, which gives our school a position held by no other mission school, we shall doubtless have a still larger number of applicants next year. We long to take in all who come and so bring them under Christian influence and instruction."

Last year the Educational Department in Japan made a new regulation, practically excluding from their special schools and from the examination for license to teach in their girls' high schools, graduates of schools not recognized by the department. Realizing that this exclusion would greatly affect the popularity of our school, a written statement, giving a history of the school, its rules, full information in regard to teachers, students, graduates, ground and buildings, finances, text-books, apparatus, etc., was carefully prepared, and our request for privileges similar to those held by graduates of Government high schools, was finally granted by the Educational Department. As Miss Lewis has said, ours is the only mission girls' school holding this privilege as yet.

It is most desirable that with the great opportunities before it in these days in Japan, and the popular position it now holds, that this school should be raised to full college grade; but to do this it will be necessary that we have a different location with suitable buildings and proper equipment. Our hearts echo the words of Miss Lewis when she says, "We are praying that some one to whom much has been given may see this opportunity of doing a great work." (By contributing generously for the purchase of land and erection of suitable buildings, etc.)

The Harrison Memorial Industrial School has an enrollment of 125, with an average attendance so great as to fill every available spot in dormitory and classrooms and create a constant cry for enlargement. Miss Blackstock writes: "We have thirteen graduates this year, and the way opens for them to fill honorable places in home life, in teaching, or in taking a higher course of study. Very little change has been made in industries taught and their related studies. The sewing department has been somewhat improved. We have a teacher of Japanese cooking, also one of foreign cooking, and the new kitchen adds to the efficiency of this department. Our experienced teacher of domestic economy is popular. The girls get enough mathematics to keep household accounts, and enough Japanese to enable them to read woman's magazines and easy books and, best of all, a half hour every morning for Bible study."

The day schools are under Mrs. Bishop's faithful superintendency, as also the work of the Tokyo-Shinano District.

The total enrollment of the Asakusa Day School is two hundred and fifty-five. The school is gaining continually in strength and usefulness, and as a means for spreading the knowledge of the gospel and teaching its principles; especially among the poor, we feel that its value can not be estimated.

The Sunday-school, which is carried on in connection with the day school and is an outgrowth of it, has an enrollment of two hundred and fifty-seven, though forty of these are from outside the regular attendance of the school. Through the gift of a kind friend in New England Branch, the new building for which teachers and friends of this school have long been praying, can now be built.

YOKOHAMA.—Mrs. Van Petten, while on her furlough, was greatly missed from the Higgins Memorial Home and Training-school, as also from many departments of Christian benevolence in Yokohama, with which for years she has been so closely identified. In her absence Miss Atkinson filled the place of principal of the school successfully, and the earnest, faithful work has gone on through the year.

"The present conditions and demands along educational lines in Japan are such, that it was deemed wise to raise the standard of requirements in this school and admit only high-school graduates, or girls who can pass examinations in that grade, into the regular course. We believe that the time has come in Japan when only the best material can be utilized in the training of Bible-women. There is, however, a special course provided for any Christian women who are too old or not well enough educated to take the regular course, but who desire Bible study as preparation for Sunday-school or home work; but such will not receive diplomas or be employed as Bible-women.

Miss Atkinson has been looking after the day schools during the absence of Miss Slate, and paying occasional visits to Nagoya, where Miss Lee is alone, while the Misses Watson and Soper are on needed furloughs.

So great is the need for more workers in Japan that the small force who are holding the fort, while some of their number are taking necessary furloughs, are in danger of breaking under the strain. Our work has not been so short-handed in this country in years.

While Methodist union in Japan does not affect the work of the Woman's Foreign Missionary Society, we should be ready to co-operate with the new Church in every practical way, and, as one missionary expresses it, we must send more missionaries to Japan soon, and continue to send them for another generation.

NAMES OF STATIONS OR DISTRICTS.	Hokkaido District	Sapporo City	Hakodate City	Aomori District	Hirosaki City	Sendai District	Sendai City	Tokyo-Shinano Dist.	Tokyo City	Tokyo-Yokohama Dist.	Yokohama City	Nagoya District	Nagoya City
W. F. M. S. Missionaries		2	3		2		3		4		4		3
Wives of Missionaries in Active Work		1					1		2		1		1
WOMEN IN THE CHURCH—													
Full Members	120	60	85	141	74	176	82	126	357	126	292	50	72
Probationers	36	10	7	52	19	59	37		26	46	92	11	10
Adherents			20	54	41	54	20			68		14	29
Women and Girls Baptized during Year	17	9	10	17	8		9	33	57	6		3	15
No. Christian Women under Instruction	111		5					95	264				1
Non-Christian Women under Instruction	57	96	12						210				6
No. Bible-women Employed	4		1	4	2	5	2	4	4	5	1	2	3
SCHOOLS FOR TRAINING BIBLE-WOMEN—													
No. Schools											1		
No. Missionaries											1		
No. Native Teachers											5		
Enrollment											24		
Receipts for B'rd and Tuit'n											$236 10		
VERNACULAR AND ANGLO-VERNACULAR B'RDING SCHOOLS—													
No. Schools			1				1		1				1
No. Foreign Missionaries			3				1		3				2
No. Native Teachers			16				7		32				14
Self-Supporting Students			14				1		62				26
Wholly-Supported Students							21		40				2
Partly-Supported Students			60				5		30				
No. Day Students			79				37		132				71
Total Enrollment			153				64		270				99
Receipts for B'd and Tuition			$600				$259 33		$3968 80				$869 63
Gov. Grants and Donations			D$100						D$80 80				D$151 54
ORPHANAGES—													
No. Orphanages							1						
No. Foreign Missionaries							1						
No. Native Teachers							6						
Total No. Orphans							180						
DAY SCHOOLS—													
No. Schools			1		1				2		4		
No. Teachers			1		11				9		16		
Total Enrollment			12		102				458		513		
Average Daily Attendance			9		79				427		411		
Receipts for Tuition					$201 38				$376 60		$605 71		
Gov. Grants and Donations											D$6 00		
KINDERGARTENS—													
No. Kindergartens			1		1						2		
No. Native Kindergartners			1		1						1		
Nat. Kindergartners in T'ing			2		5						3		
Total Enrollment			140		91						93		
Average Attendance			110		51						53		
Receipts for Tuition			$120		$148 42						$229 94		
Gov. Grants and Donations			D$40								D$218		
INDUSTRIAL SCHOOLS—													
No. Schools									1				
No. Ind. Depts in other Sch'ls									12				
No. Foreign Missionaries									1				
No. Native Teachers									19				
No. Pupils									125				
Receipts for Tuit'n and B'rd									$821 00				
From Sale of Products									$136 10				
Gov. Grants and Donations									D$50 00				

SOUTH JAPAN CONFERENCE.

Organized as a Mission Conference in 1899.
Organized as a Conference in 1905.
Woman's Work commenced in 1879.
Official Correspondent, Mrs. R. L. Thomas.

The South Japan Mission includes the Island of Kiushiu and the other islands south and east of the mainland, including Formosa and the Loochoo group.

MISSIONARIES AND THEIR STATIONS.

FUKUOKA.—Mabel K. Seeds, L. Alice Finlay.
KAGOSHIMA.—*Jean M. Gheer, Lida B. Smith, Hortense Long.
NAGASAKI.—Elizabeth Russell, Marianna Young, *Mary E. Melton, *Lola M. Kidwell, Hettie A. Thomas, Mary A. Cody, Daisy Byron Sutton, Adella M. Ashbaugh.
WIVES OF MISSIONARIES IN CHARGE OF WORK.—Mrs. J. C. Davison, Mrs. F. N. Scott.

NORTH KIUSHIU DISTRICT: *Evangelistic Work.*—Miss Alice Finlay writes that her ten Bible-women have been greatly blessed in two meetings, one held in the autumn, and the other in March. Before the meeting ended all the Bible-women testified to having received the blessing of the Holy Spirit. They are welcomed everywhere and have carried the gospel to hundreds of women. The city Sunday-schools are another power for good, and the next generation will be more easily brought to Him because of these schools.

Ei-Wa Jo Gakko.—The girls' boarding-school in Fukuoka being without a principal, Miss Kidwell was sent from Nagasaki to take charge. She reports a decrease in the enrollment, due to the new schools opened by the Government. The health of the girls has been good; they are fond of athletic sports. They were greatly blessed spiritually in special meetings held in November.

SOUTH KIUSHIU DISTRICT.—There are fifteen Bible-women in this District, under the supervision of Misses Smith and Long and Mrs. Davison. There has been advance along all lines. Throughout South Kiushiu the people are in a receptive mood, and gladly listen. The Sunday-schools are large and interesting. Miss Smith and Miss Long were asked to teach Christianity to a class of nurses at the Government Hospital. "Dr. Tanaka is not a Christian, but he thinks that Christianity would do the nurses good, would make them kinder to their patients, and more honest in their work. He said that he knew of nothing that had such a softening, refining, humanizing effect on character as Christianity. Already two of the women have said they want to become Christians." The doctrine has not lost the power that it had in the days of the apostles.

NAGASAKI: *Kwassui Jo Gakko.*—Great perplexity as to the work of the year was felt when college opened with three missionaries in place of seven. Miss Cody had the kindergarten so well mapped out that her faithful assistant, Miss Takamori, carried the work until Miss Cody's return, in November. Miss Russell, already heavily laden with duties, took charge of the Biblical department and city Sunday-school work. Miss Evington, daughter of the English Bishop, taught the most advanced pupils in music. Miss Mary Thomas, on health leave in Japan, has been doing

*Home on leave.

almost the work of a well woman while gaining strength to return to China. Mrs. Heicher, of the General Society, cheerfully supplied in some of the work which Miss Kidwell carried, and thus the Lord provided for their extremity. In January Miss Daisy Sutton was sent to their relief, and in October Miss Ashbaugh went out to take charge of the musical department. The enrollment for the Conference year was 432, 145 of whom were boarders. This includes forty-four pupils of the kindergarten at the Y. M. C, A. Last year two excellent girls graduated from the college course, both of whom are teaching in the school. This continues to be a cosmopolitan school. Chinese, Korean, Russian, English, German, Eurasian, Japanese, and American girls are found in the school. Ei-Wa Jo Gakko has sent us some excellent girls since the affiliation of the two schools. There have been *nine* girls in the kindergarten normal course. These girls have done splendidly, and the kindergarten work is a great success. There have been sixty in the Industrial department, sixty-five in the Musical department, and fourteen in the Biblical department. The spiritual life of the school has been excellent.

Four series of meetings have been held, and many girls received a great blessing. One day at chapel services almost the whole middle section moved forward, led by classmates and friends, to the altar for prayer. These were largely non-Christian day pupils. All the boarders are Christians. "This is a many-sided work, our girls are tremendously busy, but no part received more attention than the spiritual. Weekly class-meetings, semi-weekly prayer-services, the daily Bible study, the Sunday-school work, are instructive and practical. God has been with us in a wonderful way. He has taken the burdens too heavy for us to bear, has answered our prayers for health and strength and help, for this work is not ours, but the Lord's. For many years this school has stood a lighthouse upon a hill. Its beams have shone out into the heathen darkness far and wide and lit up hundreds of dark homes and hearts. The storms have beat about it, but the structure will stand, for God is our foundation. What the future will be none but God knows, but it is His cause, and we are glad to be co-workers with Him as long as He pleases to use us. We are not supplied with all that we need, but we go forward, trusting that He is able to carry us through. Blessed hope, precious faith, and trust in Him who is abundantly able to give the *all* things to those who will receive them."

Kwassui Jo En.—For the orphanage Miss Russell reports: "The Home is like all healthy homes, progressing quietly and steadily. The children are happy and well. A graduate of Kwassui Industrial Department teaches drawn work and embroidery. Another Kwassui girl has charge of the school. Twenty-five of the girls are Christians; the others are Christians as far as they know. God has raised up friends for the institution, and aid has come that we had not looked for, and from sources unexpected." She needs six more scholarships. Who will help?

Loo Choo Islands.—Miss Smith says: "The Loo Choo Islands form a most satisfactory mission field. The women are sensible, reliable, active, and intelligent. There are a quarter of a million of these noble creatures, who have never heard about Jesus. What are we going to do about it? We have only two Bible-women. There is a wonderful opportunity of preaching the gospel in the ancient capital. A number of the nobility have become interested. Baroness Io, a granddaughter of the former king, has received baptism."

We must have a missionary for these islands. We need two to live in the islands. The Loo Choo has passed out of the experimental stage. There is no doubt of its success. There is no doubt that the splendid women of Loo Choo can be reached with the gospel. The time is ripe for a persistent, systematic movement in their behalf.

MEXICO.

Woman's Work commenced in 1874.
Organized as a Conference in 1885.
Official Correspondent, Carrie J. Carnahan.

The Mexico Mission includes the Republic of Mexico, except the States of Chihuahua and Sonora, and the territory of Lower California.

MISSIONARIES AND THEIR STATIONS.

GUANAJUATO.—Effa M. Dunmore.
MEXICO CITY.—Harriet L. Ayres, Laura Temple, Grace A. Hollister.
PACHUCA.—Helen Hewitt, Blanche Betz.
PUEBLA.—Anna R. Limberger, Caroline M. Purdy, Ella E. Payne.

The general progress and real advancement which the Republic of Mexico is making in these days is shown not only in the strides the nation is taking in industry, commerce, and education, but even more in the growing spirit of religious toleration noticeable throughout the country, making it possible for Protestant missionary work to develop without any serious outward opposition.

One manifestation of this toleration is seen in the increased enrollment and self-support of all our mission schools, and in the fact that at the Commencement exercises of some of these institutions, government officials or their representatives were present and presided or distributed the diplomas. Another manifestation is that some of the graduates of our schools are finding it possible to obtain good positions as teachers in Government schools. During this past year four of the graduates of our Puebla Normal Institute applied for and succeeded in getting good positions in the Government schools of Mexico City. Already the number of our graduates is larger than the demand for teachers in our day schools (unless, as we are being urged to do, we increase our appropriations for such day schools), and as the number of graduates increases yearly it would seem that in Mexico, even as in Japan and elsewhere, it is a good thing for our Christian girls, whom we can not supply with work, to find service in other schools than our own, thus enabling them to spread Christian influences even where the laws may prevent direct Christian instruction. It behooves us to see to it, however, that the pupils in our schools are given not only the best intellectual training, but a well-grounded Christian foundation, if our graduates are to be able to meet and overcome the temptations and difficulties found in the environments outside our Protestant mission circles, where infidelity and lack of high moral ideals prevail. It is a sad fact that in our higher-grade schools, our force of missionaries is so small, that it is difficult for them to hold the schools up to the high standards necessary for them to compete with Government schools, and have sufficient time and strength left for systematic Bible instruction, and for the thorough cultivation of the spiritual life of the students.

MEXICO CITY.—The Sarah L. Keen College has had a quiet year, conducive to internal development. Two hundred and twenty-five pupils were enrolled, of whom seventy have been in the boarding department. There were twenty young women in the commercial school, which is a new department of the college. Eleven completed the grammar course, and two graduated from the normal department. The work done in the classroom during the past year by the Mexican teachers has been of high grade. Miss Temple writes: "It is gratifying to see the willingness with which the graduates of our normal schools remain in the mission schools for much lower salaries, than they could command in the Government schools."

"The self-support of the school has increased, the amount received the past year being over $10,000 silver. As a result of the efforts on the part of Miss Hollister to develop the various departments of the Epworth League, of which she is President, the spiritual life of the college was greatly quickened, and girls before indifferent became active in Christian service."

Miss Temple continues to plead for the industrial school, the obvious need for which grows from year to year.

PACHUCA.—The growth in our girls' school here has been remarkable. The matriculation during the year reached 530, and but for the often repeated "no room," it might have been much more, since from early in the year only the most promising pupils were received.

Some of the greatly needed new rooms have been added to the school during the year by the generous gift of a friend in the New England Branch, and sanitary conditions have been greatly improved. This school is the largest one our Society has in Mexico, and there is great need for an increased appropriation, in order that the force of teachers may be enlarged. Especially should they have additional well-trained help for the kindergarten, which numbers over two hundred.

"We are beginning this year to reap some of the benefits of our work," writes Miss Hewitt. "One of our own girls has returned to us as a teacher, after completing her normal course at Puebla, and is doing work such as only a thorough training could enable her to do."

Miss Betz's first year of work in Puebla has been very successful and beneficial to the school.

GUANAJUATO.—The building in which this school is located has been completed within the year, New England Branch having given the money for this purpose. A revival in the school, which continues to this writing, has brought rich blessings to many of the girls. "Their pleadings with God for pardon of sins, and their clear, ringing testimonies of victory make our hearts rejoice," writes Miss Dunmore.

The first graduate of the Bible-training department finished her course in April. She will go to help Miss Payne in her evangelistic work in Puebla.

The school has had its share of sickness during the year, but through it all strength has been given to Miss Dunmore, who, with a good corps of Mexican teachers, is caring for both the school and the Bible workers' training department. One of our most pressing needs in Mexico is an especially well qualified teacher-missionary to take charge of the boarding-school. It is not right that Miss Dunmore should be there alone, with the care of both schools devolving upon her.

PUEBLA.—The Puebla Normal Institute has had a busy year in its present crowded quarters, but teachers and pupils are looking forward with relief to obtaining possession on October 31st of the new property which we are purchasing immediately adjoining the school, and we hope the opening of the new term will find the Institute in its new quarters, with a chance to expand and develop.

During the year the school has opened two new departments—a commercial course and a four-year literary and scientific course—for students who do not care to take the normal course. These departments meet a long-felt need. The English department of the school has developed into a fully graded primary and grammar school, and it is from this department chiefly that the remarkable self-support of the Institute comes. This past year the income from self-support has amounted to over $19,000 silver.

A course of systematic Bible study, covering the years of the school course from the primary to the normal, was organized this year, and good effects were seen during the recent revival in the rapidity with which the girls could turn to desired references or quote texts appropriate to their experiences.

These special revival meetings, conducted for the school, were greatly blessed by the presence and power of the Holy Spirit. Evidences of genuine contrition for sin were manifested, and some of the most influential students in the school took the deciding step, consecrating themselves to Christ. Many of those who were already professing Christians were

SUMMARY OF WORK IN MEXICO.

NAMES OF STATIONS.	Guanajuato	Mexico City	Miraflores	Apizaro	Orizoba	Pachuca	Puebla	San Vicente	Tezontepec	Tlaxcala	Ayapango	Totals
?. M. S. Missionaries	1	3				2	3					9
lve Workers	4				2							6
MEN IN THE CHURCH—												
Full Members	82	140	48	14	34	65	85	5		4		477
Probationers	41	125	68	6	12	36	15	3		1		307
Adherents	160	200	100	12	157	400	16	3		15		963
men and Girls B'zed during y'r.	5	12			1	7	16					41
Chris'n Women under Instr'n,	44	50										94
-Chris'n Women under Inst'n,	20											20
Bible-women Employed	2	3					1					6
OOLS FOR TRAINING BIBLE-												
)MEN—No. Schools	1											1
No. Missionaries	1											1
No. Native Teachers	1											1
Enrollment	4											4
:NACULAR AND ANGLO-VER-ACULAR BOARDING SCHOOLS—												
No. Schools	1	1				1	1					4
No. Foreign Missionaries	1	3				2	3					9
Foreign or Eurasian Teachers		2					4					6
No. Native Teachers	4	14				11	11					40
Self-Supporting Students	5	150				14	169					338
Wholly-Supported Students	5	3				10	27					45
Partly-Supported Students	14	88				10	167					229
No. Day Students	139	110				515	254					1018
Total Enrollment	163	190				549	363					1265
Receipts for Board and Tuition,	$1,353.	$5,010.				$650.	$9,668.64					$16,681.64
' SCHOOLS—												
No. Schools			1	1				1		1	1	4
No. Teachers			3	1				1		1	2	8
Total Enrollment			162	24				23		64	28	301
Average Daily Attendance				13				20			21	54
Receipts for Tuition			$220.	$36.37						$31.		$287.37
'DERGARTENS—												
No. Kindergartens	1	1	1			1	1					5
No. Native Kindergartners	1	1				1	1					4
Nat. Kinder'ners in Training	1						1					2
Total Enrollment	55	17	42			287	45					446
Average Attendance	25	10				150	35					225
Receipts for Tuition	$14.81	$162.	$100.			100	$264.10					$640 91

greatly strengthened and refreshed. Some students belonging to Catholic families, and who had never before been under Protestant influence, went to the altar and gave their hearts to God.

The Epworth Leagues, both English and Spanish, under the efficient care of Miss Ella Payne, have been a real source of spiritual power.

The Auxiliary of the Woman's Foreign Missionary Society connected with the Institute has done nobly during the year, having increased their membership and having raised a thank-offering of $100 silver, besides sending more than $60 gold to the New England Branch treasury for work in the Orient.

Day Schools.—The appointment of a committee to have regular supervision of our day schools in small cities and villages has proven very beneficial. We are better informed as to the character of the teachers. and the conditions under which they are working. We hope the way is being paved for bringing to pass, as far as possible, a uniform curriculum in our schools of various grades. We have these day schools in San Vicenti, Apizaco, Tlaxcala, and Tezoutepec, and pastors are asking eagerly for them in some other places.

Our missionaries tell us the door of opportunity in Mexico is more widely open than ever before. The work of our Church has been unusually successful during the past two years. Surely we should follow up this success with workers and larger appropriations, that our opportunity as Christ's followers to win Mexico for Him may not be lost.

SOUTH AMERICA.

Woman's Work organized in 1874. Conference organized in 1893.
Official Correspondent, Mary E. Holt.

MISSIONARIES AND THEIR STATIONS.

BUENOS AYRES.—Eleanor LeHuray.
ROSARIO.—*Mary F. Swaney, Bertha E. Kneeland, Susie A. Walker.
MONTEVIDEO.—Lizzie Hewett, Jessie L. Marsh.
LIMA.—Elsie Wood.
CALLAO.—Alice McKinney.

BUENOS AYRES.—Miss LeHuray reports as follows: "As the time comes again for the forwarding of the estimates and the annual report, I have been thinking what I could write to bring clearly before you how the woman's work in this city is situated. We have been here so many years—twenty for which I am responsible, and other years under my predecessor—yet we have, apparently, nothing to show for our labor; no home, nothing that we can call our own, unless it be this rented property, on which we have a lease for one more year. Although this is only our second year in this neighborhood, we have clearly taken root and are beginning to be favorably known. We have a few more children than last year—between forty and fifty—and a few more friends among the parents of the children. Our Church services are more largely attended, the Sunday-school as well, and as for boarding pupils and self-support, this has been the best year of the twenty. The heavy rent of $250 gold per month we have been able to meet, as well as other expenses, not so much from help we receive from home as from the proceeds of

*Home on leave.

self-support. The twelve scholarships are filled and we have a number of paying boarders, some of native, others of Dutch, English, and German descent. Our Home is comfortably furnished. We have five reliable teachers and servants, who have been with us many years.

The constant moving from place to place is the cause of a lack of day pupils, whose tuition would help largely in defraying the expenses of the school. A permanent location, with property of our own, would obviate these difficulties, as the school would become more widely known to the people. The boarding pupils are mostly girls from the country, where there are but few school advantages, hence come with a very elementary knowledge and often most striking ignorance of everything they ought to know. A teacher is much needed for the English department which should be inaugurated."

Miss LeHuray completes next year twenty-five years of missionary service and naturally is anxious to see this school established on a firm basis in a suitable building of our own ere she takes a much-needed rest. The Bible-woman continues her work from house to house, bringing her report each quarter to Miss LeHuray.

ROSARIO.—In January Miss Kneeland sailed for South America to resume work in this city, her former field of labor. In May, Miss Swaney, after her long term of service, returned to the home land for her much-needed furlough, her sister, Miss Carrie, accompanying her.

The long-prayed-for school building is at last being erected, and at last accounts was progressing favorably. The contract stipulates that the building shall be completed in March, 1909. The corner-stone was.laid March 25th with appropriate ceremonies. Dr. Tallon, District Superintendent, conducted the exercises. Señor Miranda, an inspector representing the school authorities of the province, made an address. In addition to the members of the Methodist congregation there were present other friends of the school, including some old pupils. The plans are reduced to what is indispensable for the work. The sale of the old property helps materially on the expense, also the amount contributed during the year by the Branches; but there is still a large balance to be raised in order to complete the building without debt.

It has been arranged that the Children's Thank-offering for the coming year shall be devoted to this school, and the primary room is to be named for the. King's Heralds.

Both the boarding and charity schools opened favorably in March, the rooms being filled to overflowing and some being refused admission. One of the teachers in the charity school left, and her place is filled by a teacher from the boarding-school. A young lady who received her education in the Rosario and Buenos Ayres schools and is a recent graduate from the normal school in the latter city, has been secured for the vacancy in the boarding-school. She is a Christian and is taking up the work with enthusiasm.

Miss Walker was transferred from Buenos Ayres, to be with Miss Kneeland during the absence of Miss Swaney. Although suffering from ill-health, she is an interested and enthusiastic worker.

In a recent letter Miss Kneeland writes: "The girls keep coming into the school, even though the year is nearly half gone. I believe we have several more than last year. Just two days ago we had to refuse again to take girls into the home, but we always tell them we shall have room next year. It is a long time to wait. It is a delight to see the way the little children in the first and second grades enjoy the Bible lessons. We try to make them very practical. Our new scholarship girls are now getting on finely. It has taken much time and prayer to get them to the point where they are, but we feel that the foundation is now quite well placed." Miss Kneeland is seeing busy days, having on her hands teaching, the care of the two schools, oversight of the home, work of the treasurer, Sunday-schools, new building, etc.

She pays an appreciative tribute to the admirable leadership and efficiency of Miss Swaney and her sister, both of whom she greatly misses. The former helped her over many difficulties in the building matters, and the latter arranged the details of the housekeeping department in such a way as to give her the least possible anxiety.

MONTEVIDEO.—In 1907 six girls graduated from the school—four from the Spanish department and two from the English. The Commencement exercises were presided over by Dr. Cuhilo, a distinguished lawyer of the city and a loyal Methodist. The address was delivered by Dr. De Salterain, an eminent physician of the city and a senator in Congress. He has three daughters as students in the school. The program for the week consisted as usual of the literary and musical entertainment given by the pupils, Class Day, Commencement Day, and Alumni banquet.

The monthly temperance meetings have been held in the school as formerly, both those of the Woman's Christian Temperance Union and the Loyal Temperance Legions of both Spanish and English departments. Miss Hewett has given temperance lessons in the different Sunday-schools.

A special cause for gratitude has been the marked interest manifested by the pupils in the religious meetings of the school. The girls of the King's Daughters Band, under the care of Miss Marsh, have kept up their weekly devotional meetings and have also ministered to the sick and the poor. Miss Hewett's probationers' class of Spanish girls has met regularly, and the meetings have been occasions of spiritual uplifting. Miss Hewett mentions great satisfaction in watching the spiritual development of these girls, who have all their lives been under the cloud of superstition and error of the Romish Church. Nine of the girls have professed a change of heart and have united with the Spanish Methodist Church in full connection. They wished to do some work for the Lord, and, following Miss Hewett's suggestion, they went into the streets and gathered together children for a Sunday-school which was held every Sunday morning in the school. These girls gave the children a treat at Christmas time and still continue their interest in the work.

There are two Bible-readers in the city who are doing faithful work going from house to house distributing tracts, portions of Scripture, and winning many souls for Christ. One of these women was one of the first graduates from the school. A Spanish Ladies' Aid, named for Mrs. McCabe, still continues its work among the women of the Church. Since its organization, in 1903, this society has raised $2,534.18 gold, which has been passed over to the treasurer of the Spanish Church. Mrs. Hewett is now the President.

As a result of a visit from Miss Jessie Ackerman, who interested all in accounts of her travels and of her work in the slums of London, a Girls' Guild was organized in the school with some eighty members, who are being trained in Christian work.

There are nine Spanish Methodist Sunday-schools in Montevideo, in all of which there are good opportunities for work. In the school are thirteen teachers and 206 pupils, including boarders.

LIMA.—Miss Wood reports: "We have forty-four pupils registered in the regular classes, ranging in age from five to seventeen years, against twenty a year ago. Fourteen of these are in the new branch school, where I have one of our former pupils in Callao in charge. The money sent to

Lima pays the school rent. The income has just paid for the furniture, care, and assistants. The Sunday-school in two months increased from an attendance of eleven to twenty-seven on a recent Sunday. Most of the people have never attended such meetings before."

CALLAO.—At the last Conference Miss McKinney was again appointed director of the girls' department of the high school. The school year opened March 9th, after a vacation of two months during the warm period of the year. The present enrollment is twenty-six, of whom seven come from the lower grades and three from a private school. The improvement in the girls is noticeable and they really seem to enjoy order and quiet. There are nine English-speaking girls and the rest are Peruvians. Almost all are from Roman Catholic families and many of them are unwilling to attend our Church. About one-half attend some of the Church services, and the larger part go to the English Sunday-school, although they still claim to be Catholics. One of the teachers could not return, and her place is filled by Miss Ramsey, an English girl of Peruvian birth, who speaks Spanish fluently. Because of lack of room there is some confusion in changing classes, great vigilance being required to keep perfect order. There should be a separate entrance for the girls, but the necessary funds are not at hand.

Miss Wood comes each day to teach singing and calisthenics.

Miss McKinney longs to make an impression upon these girls spiritually, and during the vacation she visited the homes of many of the

SUMMARY OF WORK IN SOUTH AMERICA.

NAMES OF STATIONS OR DISTRICTS.	Buenos Ayres	Rosario	Montevideo	Total
W. F. M. S. Missionaries	1	1	2	4
Native Workers	4			4
No. Bible-women Employed	1		2	3
VERNACULAR AND ANGLO-VERNACULAR BOARDING SCHOOLS—				
No. Schools	1		†1	2
No. Foreign Missionaries	1		2	3
No. Native Teachers	4		13	17
Self-Supporting Students	10		†6	16
Wholly-Supported Students	12		†2	14
Partly-Supported Students			†1	1
No. Day Students	22		169	191
Total Enrollment	44		178	222
Receipts for Board and Tuition	*	*	*	*
DAY SCHOOLS—				
No. Schools		2	1	3
No. Teachers		8	13	21
Total Enrollment		185	§178	363
Average Daily Attendance		156	150	306
Receipts for Tuition		$250 00	§$1400 00	$1,650 00
KINDERGARTENS—				
No. Native Kindergartners			1	1
Total Enrollment			27	27
Average Attendance			20	20

*Incomplete.
† In Montevideo there is a day school with a boarding department.
‡ Boarding pupils.
§ Number and amount to date.

girls, asking their mothers to allow them to attend the English Sunday-school. Too often this invitation is met with the reply that their children are simply in the school to be educated, implying that conversion to Protestantism is not desired. However, it is cause for thankfulness that, in this country, where religious freedom is not allowed, some girls attend the Protestant school and Church services.

In addition to the teaching in the high school, Miss McKinney has a class in the Spanish Sunday-school and assists in the Junior League work.

That the gospel is finding an entrance into the hearts of the people is shown from the fact that the mother of two boys in the high school, who is not able to attend Church, gives a certain sum of money each month to the pastor to have him come to her home weekly for a service. Our prayers should be often ascending to God that religious freedom may be speedily granted throughout South America.

BULGARIA.

Woman's Work commenced in 1884.
Constituted a Mission Conference in 1892.
Official Correspondent, Mrs. F. P. Crandon.

MISSIONARIES AND THEIR STATIONS.

LOVETCH.—Miss Kate Blackburn, Miss Dora Davis.

In that which tells on the most vital interests of the cause, we feel there has been real advance in this year's work. The announcement that the course of study in our Lovetch Girls' School had been made equal to that of the Government gymnasia, seemed to be the signal for the clergy and other fanatical opposers to do all in their power to detract from our attendance. However, all their efforts God overruled for our profit. Though they succeeded in getting the city school for girls raised one grade higher, and thus reduced the number of our day pupils, yet this only made place for an increased number of boarding pupils, and *we still had as large an enrollment as the preceding year.* This, too, with a class of girls among whom we could do our best work. The local income exceeded that of the preceding year by 1,500 francs, or $300. The music pupils brought in a good proportion of this sum. This department is steadily developing under the wise and judicious care of Miss Davis, and our patronage is constantly widening.

The health of the school could scarcely have been better, and in this we recognize special reason for gratitude when we remember that last year many schools in Bulgaria were closed for months because of serious epidemics.

Deportment and scholarship were gratifying. Above all are we thankful for the abundant evidences of quickened spiritual life among the teachers and pupils. Two of our girls were received as probationers in the Church, two others taken into full membership, and seven became members of the Epworth League. The full attendance at class meetings and the earnest prayers and testimonies often warmed our hearts. But after all it is in the every-day and Christian life and deportment that we must look for the real development of character and Christian life, and judging by this standard, there is much to encourage. This is abundantly attested in the lives of girls who have left school and are witnesses for Christ amid non-Protestant surroundings.

We had no graduating class this last June, owing to the raising of the grade of the school. The class which would naturally have graduated then, proposes to return and complete the full seven years' course of study next year.

The Government school inspector visited us twice during the year, and the official inspector of school sanitation once. Both expressed hearty approval of what they saw. The inspector of school sanitation was accompanied by the city mayor. As they left the premises he remarked to the mayor: *"Our people can profit immensely and get great good out of schools like this."* United States Ambassador Hon. Horace G. Knowles, with his wife, favored us by a brief visit in June, bringing with them Baroness Rengers, wife of the Dutch Minister in Bucharest, Roumania.

Another welcome visitor during the year was Rev. Julian S. Wadsworth, of Brockton, Mass. (formerly of Jacksonville, Ill.), who on a flying visit through the Balkan Peninsula gave us two days of his valuable

SUMMARY OF WORK IN THE BULGARIAN CONFERENCE.

NAMES OF STATIONS.	Lovetch	Hotiantsa	Gabrovo	Rustchuk	Varna	Tirnovo	Sistov	Voyvodovo	Hibiee	Orchanta	Sevlievo	Vratza	Lom	Pleven	Shumen	Viddin	Total
				OTHER CHARGES REPORTING TO BULGARIA MISSION CONFERENCE.													
W. F. M. S. Missionaries	2																2
Wives of Missionaries in Active Work																	
Foreign or Eurasian Assistants																	
Native Workers	7	1	1														9
WOMEN IN THE CHURCH—																	
Full Members	20	12	2	14	8	8	7	45	11	3	5	1	6	15	7	2	166
Probationers	6		2		1			3	1	1	2	1	2	14	3		36
Adherents	60		1	2	25	15	1		4	1	12	10	3		20	5	159
Women and Girls Baptized during Year						2		7	1				2	3			15
No. Christian Women under Instruc'n	30	14	4	30	15	10	7	75	7	25	7	2	5	29	22		282
Non-Christian Women under Instru'n	30	7	6	5	8	3			1		10	3	4	45	20	1	143
No. Bible-women Employed		1	1	*1										*1			4
SCHOOLS OF COLLEGE GRADE—																	
No. Schools	1																1
No. Foreign Missionaries	2																2
Foreign or Eurasian Teachers																	
No. Native Teachers	6																6
Self-Supporting Students	12																12
Wholly-Supported Students	4																4
Partly-Supported Students	10																10
Total Enrollment	†36																36
Receipts for Board and Tuition	$1215 00																$1215 00
Govern't Grants and Donations																	
DAY SCHOOLS—																	
No. Schools		1															1
No. Teachers		1															1
Total Enrollment		20															20
Average Daily Attendance		18															18
Receipts for Tuition																	
Govern't Grants and Donations																	

* Employee of Bulgaria Mission Conference W. F. M. S.
† Day pupils, 10.

12

time. His presence and the intense interest manifested in our work proved a real inspiration.

The prospect for the next school year is unusually propitious. Already as many have been accepted as we had last year, and others are applying. If we take more we hardly know where to stow them.

The local School Board in Hotántsa has asked for the return of Miss Marika Ticheva as teacher of their primary school for next year. This speaks well for her services. Twenty pupils were enrolled the past year. In April Miss Davis and I visited Gabrovo, where Evanka Duinska has been so faithfully working as Bible-woman for some time past. It was truly gratifying to see her work and with her visit numerous homes. More than one hundred homes are now open to her visits. Of Evanka it may be truly said, "To know her is to love her." In the homes of the poor, by the bedside of the sick and dying, wherever her service is needed for body or soul, there she is ready to go. The Conference Woman's Society has also supported a Bible-woman, Miss Todorka Gancheva, for the greater part of the year. She has worked in Lom, and for six months the same Society employed a second Bible-woman. In Lovetch the work among the women has been growing. Three married women have recently united with the Church. Our local Woman's Foreign Missionary Society Auxiliary has increased its contribution this year. The weekly cottage meetings held for the women have been well attended, and new homes are opening to them. Here, as elsewhere, it is true that "all that will live godly in Christ Jesus shall suffer persecution." Young and old of both sexes have their peculiar trials and temptations. Just now one of our Lovetch families is under the fire of persecution. We earnestly pray that they may come off victorious.

Each year brings trials and compensations, and it is true beyond a question that each year binds our hearts closer to the work in this land.

We read with joy and eagerness the glowing accounts of success in other and more popular fields, and then we resolutely and hopefully set about our own God-given tasks, thankful that it is our privilege to labor in this "little corner," where there is so much need and so little glamor.

ITALY.

Organized as a Conference in 1881.
Woman's Work commenced in 1886.
Official Correspondent, Mrs. F. P. Crandon.

MISSIONARIES AND THEIR STATION.

ROME.—*Edith M. Swift, Edith Burt, Italia Garibaldi.

ROME: *Crandon Hall.*—No better report can be made of the work of Crandon Hall than that rendered by Misses Swift and Burt to the Annual Conference of Italy. From this we quote:

"Walking in the strength of God's promises, we have come to the close of another school year. Though we have not fully reached the goal upon which our hopes were set, yet, as we look back upon the way and note the many obstacles overcome, we can humbly thank God that the year has been one of real progress. The attendance on the opening day was larger than ever before, one hundred and seventy-five pupils being en-

*Home on leave.

rolled in the regular courses, and nearly one hundred more in the music school and language classes.

"The teachers have shown their usual zeal and faithfulness, and in addition to their regular class work have given their pupils many special talks on art and history in the various museums and galleries of Rome.

"The universal interest in all that pertains to the mission of woman, in the family and in society, is stirring the minds of our Italian young women, so that the course of Domestic Economy, inaugurated this year, was taken by numerous enthusiastic students.

"Crandon Hall has taken the initiative in this, as it is the first girls' school in Italy to introduce this useful branch of study.

"Many of our teachers and older pupils attended the meetings of the National Congress of Italian Women, held in Rome this spring. One of the chief topics of discussion was the attitude of the liberal-minded Italian women toward the Catholic religion.

"The manifest hostility of Italy's leading educators towards the Church that opposes Italian patriotism, could not but stimulate a desire on the part of many of our Catholic pupils to study more closely the principles of their own and the Protestant religion.

"Thus the congress opened the way for many talks upon spiritual subjects, and led to the formation of elective courses on comparative religion in the English, French, and Italian languages.

"This deeper interest in spiritual subjects was also revealed in the greater attention of the girls to the sermons of our Italian minister. This we are very grateful for.

"The kindergarten was well attended and, as usual, the children's songs and recitations called forth the admiration of our many visitors from the homeland.

"The music school has kept up its high standard, the frequent recitals before large Roman audiences being one way of showing the Italian people what Methodism is doing for Italy.

"Through the efforts of Miss Hill our library has been greatly enriched by many helpful books, the gifts of American friends.

"Unfortunately the building does not expand with the growing needs of the school, so that all branches of the work must suffer from the overcrowding. Our faith has been in the Lord. He has brought it to pass, the year marks another step toward the ideal set before us, and we know that our efforts, with His blessing, must bear fruits for His kingdom."

The Inspection Committee of the Italian Conference also add their testimony to the excellence of the school: "The Crandon Institute in Rome continues to fulfill its blessed mission with growing success. Miss Burt and Miss Swift have not only held the Institute up to that high standard it had attained in former years, but have given it even greater development and solidity. The one great need, however, becomes each year more imperative—more room. The school could easily fill a building four times the size of Crandon Hall. Crandon Institute is known not only in Rome, but in all Italy, as the best non-clerical school. Many people have spoken to us of its splendid organization, its order, the neatness of its pupils, its fine moral and spiritual influence upon the character of its pupils."

Countess Franchetti, speaking of Crandon Hall, said: "O, that is an ideal school for loyal Italians. The girls are taught to love God and also to love their country, and these two noble passions are not kept in constant war with each other as in the nuns' schools."

The pupils of Crandon Institute have regularly attended the Church services during the year, and have given very material aid to the pastor by visiting and raising money for the sick and poor.

The public recitals and musicales have been a means of drawing the attention of· many to Methodist institutions and the Methodist religion who otherwise would not know of our existence in Rome.

The attendance of about three hundred is in itself the best proof of the importance of the Institute.

We record with great regret the illness of Miss Swift and her enforced return to this country; but we most earnestly pray the Father that His healing hand may be laid upon her and that she may soon return to the work which she has so faithfully done and which so greatly needs her.

VIA GARIBALDI.—Miss Odgers, who for eight years has been connected with the Home School at Via Garibaldi, returned to this country in April, and Miss Italia Garibaldi was chosen to succeed her. She comes to us with many testimonials of her ability, and we confidently expect that her administration will be a success. Miss Garibaldi was sent to London to represent the Italian Sunday-schools at the great convention held last May. Truly a gratification to those who have watched her progress as a student.

The school has sixty girls in attendance. They come from all parts of Italy. Domestic instruction, as well as normal preparatory work, is given, and some are expecting to teach in Government schools, some in our Christian institutions. Thus little by little is the dawn brightening in the Papal land.

SUMMARY OF WORK IN THE ITALIAN CONFERENCE.

NAMES OF STATIONS OR DISTRICTS.	Rome, Italy	Montaldo, Italy	Milan, Italy	Totals
W. F. M. S. Missionaries	3			3
Wives of Missionaries in Active Work	3			3
No. Bible-women Employed		1	1	2
BIBLE INSTITUTES OR TRAINING CLASSES—				
No. Institutes	2			2
SCHOOLS OF COLLEGE GRADE—				
No. Schools	1			1
No. Foreign Missionaries	2			2
Foreign or Eurasian Teachers	5			5
No. Native Teachers	30			30
Self-Supporting Students	274			274
Wholly-Supported Students	3			3
Partly-Supported Students	3			3
Total Enrollment	280			280
Receipts for Board and Tuition	$11518 00			$11518 00
KINDERGARTENS—				
No. Kindergartens	1			1
No. Native Kindergartners	1			1
Total Enrollment	150			150
Average Attendance	80			80
Receipts for Tuition	$150 00			$150 00
INDUSTRIAL SCHOOLS—				
No. Schools	1			1
No. Foreign Missionaries	1			1
No. Native Teachers	2			2
No. Pupils	47			47
Receipts for Tuition	$340 00			$340 00
From Sale of Products	60 00			60 00

GERMANY AND SWITZERLAND.

Official Correspondent, Louisa C. Rothweiler.

As in former years, so again this year, five visiting deaconesses have been partially supported in as many different localities by the appropriation of $375 made by the Northwestern Branch.

An aggregate of 2,154 visits made to the homes; of 2,538 hours 32 nights and 36 days of nursing the sick; of 155 meetings held, and of 3,690 pieces of Christian literature distributed is reported. The real results of this work can not be given in figures—the future must show the fruitage—but to bring encouragement to the hearts of the workers, the Master allows them to see some of the results now. One sister tells of coming to a house in which she found the husband dying of consumption. The days of health had been spent by his wife and himself in dissipation. Now that the days of trial had come, instead of being drawn closer together, their hearts were filled with bitterness toward one another and they were becoming more and more estranged. The sister repeated her visits and finally love gained the victory; both turned to God; the husband's last days were spent in peace with his wife and his God.

Another sister tells of young girls kept from entering a life of sin and of others rescued from such a life. She tells of one who, having been betrayed, determined to end her misery by jumping into a lake. In some marvelous manner she was rescued and brought to the Home for girls, which one of our sisters supervises. She was persuaded to change her determination, and at last reports had returned to her home determined to lead a better life.

That these sisters are often called to work which calls for a great amount of self-denial we can easily understand. One tells of having spent three weeks in a home, the mother of which was in the hospital. Besides caring for the daily wants of the father and eight children, she instituted a complete cleansing of the bedding, clothing, and rooms. It took the entire time to accomplish this, but when the mother after her return noted the change, the object lesson had the desired effect and she is trying to make the home what it should be for husband and children.

The sister at Chemnitz, North Germany, was a faithful worker, but impaired health and other circumstances made it necessary for her to give up the work. Instead of employing another in this same place, it has been decided to ask permission to use the money in supporting a worker in Berlin. In this large city there is so much to be done, so many opportunities for work among girls who come to the city to work, as well as in the homes of the poor and the Christless, that it seemed wise to make this change.

While this work in Europe may not appeal to our people as much as work in heathen lands, it is certainly as necessary and as worthy of support as that is.

The contributions to our treasury are not quite so large as last year, not because our sisters have lost interest, but because they have found it imperatively necessary to raise funds to help some young women in their preparation for work in the foreign field to which they feel called. For this reason they were not able to do as much in the past year as they have done formerly and as they hope to do again in the future. May not the Lord be leading the Church to see that He has chosen workers in other lands as well as in America whom He wishes to have used in the foreign field? Who are we, to say that this may not be?

AFRICA.

Woman's work opened in 1890.
Official Correspondent, Mrs. S. F. Johnson.

MISSIONARIES AND THEIR STATIONS.

OLD UMTALI.—Sophia Jordan Coffin.
QUESSUA.—Susan Collins and Martha A. Drummer.

Africa is calling to us to-day in tones strong and emphatic. Shall we not respond with workers and money to carry to her people the gospel of Jesus Christ with all that that means in civilization, education and spiritual training?

So far we are doing comparatively little for these sisters of ours and their children. Just one missionary of our Society in all of East Africa and two in West Africa.

However, there are encouraging indications that new work will soon be begun. One apostle of generosity in the New England Branch has promised us $5,000 for the erection of a school in St. Paul de Loando, where we promised long ago to start our work for women and girls as soon as a missionary and building were supplied. We have plenty of land, well located, and now all we lack is a missionary and money to support the work which is so much needed among the thirty thousand people of that city, a large proportion of whom are part native, part Portuguese. Who will go and who will send?

Three hundred miles east and south of this coast town of Loanda we have a well-established work at Quessua, six miles from Melange. Our Church is undertaking to evangelize the whole district of Loanda; and Quessua, though so far away, is still within the bounds of this district, which is in the province of Angola.

Here our two missionaries, Miss Susan Collins and Miss Martha Drummer, are earnestly and lovingly working to win from darkness to light these people of their own race. They are using the new and nearly completed building, where they are so happy to have their thirty-two girls comfortably cared for, instead of being in the three-room house where they have had to be so long. This new building is a well-arranged adobe structure, with six rooms on the ground floor and three in the second story. Thus is provided a home for the missionaries and a dormitory for the girls.

Miss Collins is our faithful treasurer and mother to the girls, while Miss Drummer, besides teaching the school, frequently takes some of the larger girls with her to sing the gospel in the surrounding towns where sacred song has never been heard. In this way she wins the hearts of many people who listen gladly while she reads and explains the Bible to them. She writes: "The school is constant and the children are doing nicely with their studies. These outside trips are made on Saturdays and occasional afternoons during the dry season. Our native Christians have turned away from the witch-doctors and come to me so often for some simple remedies which I do not have and can not afford to purchase."

She, and Miss Collins, and the district superintendent plead with us for a hundred dollars to buy a "ricksha," which is a one-wheeled, purely African conveyance, and would be a wonderful help in their work and a real economy as well, for many of their necessities have to be carried long distances on the backs of the native men or in hammocks. Medicines and a conveyance are therefore the main needs now at this station.

Near the east coast of this great continent, in the Province of Rhodesia, we have a well-established school at Old Umtali. Here were fifty girls a few months ago being educated and trained in Christian character and only one missionary to carry the burdens incident to so large a work. The numbers were encouraging, but it was found as the weeks went by that it was impossible to properly care for so many without assistance, and it was finally decided to send twelve of the girls back to their homes until we can send another missionary to help Miss Coffin, who is surely doing the best she can under the circumstances.

Not only a new worker is needed, but more money to carry on the work. The new dormitory just completed needs furniture, and more scholarships are needed.

We are much indebted to Dr. Samuel Gurney, who has given the girls all medical attendance necessary without cost to us.

That in two years and a half this school has increased from ten to fifty is. a cause for great gratitude. Many more have sought admission, but have had to be refused.

Miss Coffin writes of her delight in receiving a Government grant of $150 this year. This was quite opportune, as the melio crop failed this years and melies are a staple article of food in that region.

A siege of chicken-pox and an occasional wedding add much to the labors of Miss Coffin. She asks for a typewriter and pleads most earnestly for a sewing machine; but the greatest of all her needs is a sister worker to share her burdens and responsibilities in this rapidly developing work.

Five young women graduates of last year have become the wives of pastor-teachers and are earnestly doing the work of Bible-women. One writes as follows: "I repented and was converted in the church at Old Umtali in August, 1906. God saved me and I am very glad He has helped me these two years to do His work. We were married last December. Then we came to Gondanzara's in the Makoni District. When we came here some women they were afraid to me, so I told them, 'Brethern, be not afraid of me, for I am your friend. I bring the message. from God to you, friends.' Now my work is to teach in school and help my husband in Sunday-school. Every Friday I spend much time in school to teach our girls to sew their clothes. Some of them now know how to sew their clothes even as I do. Some of them learn to wash and iron their clothes. Some of them learn to do cooking in our kitchen. I will try always to do best I can to help and to help them to do better things that Christians do in their life. Let us Christians remember to pray for this Africa and for our Bishops, because many, many people here they need the gospel. I hope they all have it soon."

In this Africa's Jubilee year may many of us turn our thought, our prayers, and our gifts to her needy children.

SUMMARY OF WORK IN AFRICA.

NAMES OF STATIONS OR DISTRICTS.	EAST AFRICA.		West Africa	Total
	Old Umtali	Umtaso Circuit Mission.		
W. F. M. S. Missionaries	1		2	3
Wives of Missionaries in Active Work		1		1
Native Workers		6		6
WOMEN IN THE CHURCH—				
Full Members	1	4		5
Probationers	†24	‡2		26
Adherents	†25			25
Women and Girls Baptized during Year			7	7
No. Christian Women under Instruction	8	2		10
Non-Christian Women under Instruction	4			4
No. Bible-women Employed		6		6
SCHOOLS FOR TRAINING BIBLE-WOMEN—				
No. Schools	1	1		2
No. Missionaries	1	§		1
Enrollment	1	2		3
VERNACULAR AND ANGLO-VERNACULAR BOARDING SCHOOLS—				
No. Schools	1	1		2
No. Foreign Missionaries	1	§		1
No. Native Teachers	5			5
Wholly-Supported Students	34			34
Partly-Supported Students	10			10
No. Day Students	11			11
Total Enrollment	55	6		61
Receipts for Board and Tuition	$620 00			$620 00
Government Grants and Donations	$154 88			$154 88
DAY SCHOOLS—				
No. Schools		1		1
No. Teachers		1		1
*Total Enrollment		15		15
Average Daily Attendance		13		13
ORPHANAGES—				
No. Orphanages			1	1
No. Foreign Missionaries			2	2
Total No. Orphans			23	23
MEDICAL WORK—				
No. Foreign Nurses	1			1

* Women in kraals won't enroll, hence no record yet.
† Girls.
‡ Women.
§ Wife of a Missionary,

EXPLANATORY NOTES TO TABLE ON FOLLOWING PAGES.

INDIA—a. .Gracey Home, Sitapur.
  b. Whitney Home, Nadiad.
  c. Budaon.
  d. Bhot, Dispensary.´
  e. Pakur.
  f. Rangoon.
  h. Bangalore.
  l. Delia Fuller Memorial.
  m. Vikarabad.
  n. Repairs in N. W. India.
  o. Repairs in South India.
  p. Property in Bengal.
  s. Raipur.
  t. Pithoragarh.

  u. Gonda.
  v. Brindaban.
  w. Kolar.
  x. Lee Memorial Hospital.

CHINA—g. Sieng Iu.
  r. Land and Repairs in West China.

JAPAN—j. Repairs in North Japan.
  k. Sappora.

KOREA—q. Yeng Byen.

SUMMARY OF DISBURSEMENTS FOR 1907–1908.

STATIONS.	New England	New York	Philadelphia	Baltimore	Cincinnati	Northwestern	Des Moines	Minneapolis	Topeka	Pacific	Columbia River
INDIA—											
For General Work	$17,501 92	$31,522 70	$17,653 05	$7,929 60	$25,878 35	$49,141 00	$19,072 96	$5,808 68	$19,987 93	$12,283 00	$7,509 00
Dwarahat Home	52 00		x 100 00	32 00	104 00	h 1,000 00	n 50 00		h 8,000 00	c 700 00	b 2,000 00
Shahjahanpur Roof	42 00	280 00		24 00	214 00		57 00		85 00	79 00	24 00
Baroda Hospital	800 00	2,500 00		s 1,808 00	m 50 00		m 5,000 00		i 500 00	d 400 00	
Godhra School Building	2,000 00	f 120 00	t 400 00		t 50 00		200 00		e 450 00	e 200 00	
Poona				110 00	u 57 00		765 00		495 00	f 3,000 00	
Bareilly Orphanage		125 00			w 3,000 00	1,000 00	o 25 00		10 00		12 00
Bareilly Hospital		100 00		10 00	75 00		p 700 00				
Bombay Day School	1,000 00	a 2,881 96			v 254 00						
Calcutta Girl's High School		750 00	300 00		575 00	1,350 00			248 00	500 00	
Total for India	$21,395 92	$38,229 66	$18,453 05	$8,605 60	$30,257 06	$52,491 00	$36,466 38	$5,808 68	$24,716 93	$16,817 00	$9,545 00
MALAYSIA—											
For General Work	$2,085 00	$975 00	$810 00	$810 00	$2,123 35	$3,270 00		$7,009 68	$645 00	$35 00	$854 00
Kuala Lumpur School	3,000 00						$30 00				
Penang					35 00	100 00					6 00
Total for Malaysia	$5,085 00	$975 00	$810 00		$2,158 35	$3,370 00	$30 00	$7,009 68	$645 00	$35 00	$860 00
PHILIPPINES		$100 00	$1,090 00	$100 00	$940 00	$2,455 00	$875 00	$9,762 00	$1,432 00	$2,744 00	$705 00
CHINA—											
For General Work	$10,760 10	$16,234 71	$6,078 83	$4,776 00	$11,847 30	$34,429 11	$11,810 56	$5,745 15	$5,559 00	$4,480 00	$1,750 00
Tai an Fu School Building	4,000 00									g 25 00	
Wuhu Day School	800 00			300 00	240 00	300 00	2,010 00	2,000 00			
Pekin		229 85				1,700 00	q 1,000 00				
Kiu Kiang		1,904 19			138 00						
Foochow										500 00	
Hing Hua							72 00				
Iong Bing Training School		450 00	1,000 00				r 400 00				
Nanchang		72 00			725 89						
Hai Tang				1,000 00	1,055 00					500 00	
do											
Total for China	$15,560 10	$18,890 75	$7,078 83	$5,076 00	$13,506 19	$36,429 11	$18,157 31	$7,745 15	$5,559 00	$5,505 00	$1,750 00

186

SUMMARY OF DISBURSEMENTS FOR 1907-1908—Continued.

KOREA—											
General Work	$1,480 00	$8,339 00	$2,618 50	$1,245 00	$7,279 25	$1,575 00	......	$173 00	$160 00	$550 00	$75 00
Pyeng Yang School	3,000 00	75 00			589 00						
Pyeng Hospital Building			3,000 00	400 00	150 00						
Chemulpo Building			1,000 00		200 00						
Kong Ju											
Total for Korea	$4,480 00	$8,414 00	$6,618 50	$1,645 00	$8,218 25	$1,575 00		$173 00	$160 00	$550 00	$75 00
JAPAN—											
General Work	$3,352 00	$10,850 00	$10,380 55	$2,505 00	$14,827 90	$12,881 03	$4,517 50	$2,177 00	$3,092 00	$1,931 00	$435 00
Asakusa School Building	3,000 00				k 50 00	k 50 00	j 25 00				
Hakodate School		1,000 00	3,500 00		500 00	4,350 00		36 00	55 00		$50 00
Nagasaki Debt			90 00			85 00	85 00				
Omura Orphanage					1,500 00	240 00	k 25 00		2,500 00		100 00
Nagoya											
Total for Japan	$6,352 00	$11,860 00	$18,970 55	$2,505 00	$16,877 90	$17,421 00	$4,627 50	$2,213 00	$5,647 00	$1,931 00	$585 00
MEXICO—											
General Work	$1,922 25	$3,850 00	$6,175 00	$125 00	$4,495 00	$7,459 00	$1,533 00	$30 00	$40 00		
Mexico Land	500 00	685 00									
Pachuca Room Sch'l Bldg.	1,000 00		160 00		100 00		100 00				
Industrial School, Mexico						2,650 00					
Puebla School		1,150 00	5,800 00								
Total for Mexico	$3,422 25	$5,685 00	$12,125 00	$125 00	$4,595 00	$10,109 00	$1,633 00	$30 00	$40 00		
SOUTH AMERICA—											
General Work	$2,806 45	$4,675 00	$973 00	$36 00	$75 00	$6,178 00	$100 00	$301 00	$3,097 00	$1,426 00	
Rosario School Building	350 00	375 00	500 00			2,697 00	262 00		39 00		
Montevideo School		414 00									
Total for South America	$3,156 45	$5,464 00	$1,473 00	$36 00	$75 00	$8,875 00	$362 00	$301 00	$3,136 00	$1,426 00	
AFRICA—											
West Central	$40 00	$743 00	$33 00	$25 00	$490 00	$505 00	$60 00		$60 00	$1,382 00	$20 00
East Central, Gen. Work						950 00					
Old Umtali School Build'g	1,000 00										
Total for Africa	$1,040 00	$748 00	$33 00	$25 00	$490 00	$1,455 00	$60 00		$50 00	$1,382 00	$20 00
ITALY—General Work	$250 00	$950 00	$328 00	$130 00	$265 00	$5,267 00	$200 00		$50 00	$1,382 00	$20 00
Rome						2,500 00					
Total for Italy	$250 00	$950 00	$328 00	$130 00	$265 00	$7,767 00	$200 00		$50 00	$1,382 00	$20 00

STATIONS.	New England	New York	Philadelphia	Baltimore	Cincinnati	Northwestern	Des Moines	Minneapolis	Topeka	Pacific	Columbia River
BULGARIA	$436 00	$560 00	$240 00			$2,875 00		$48 00			
SWITZERLAND						$150 00					
NORTH GERMANY						$125 00					
NORWAY										$50 00	
MISCELLANEOUS—											
Folts Mission Institute	$85 00	$1,586 35	$250 00	$3,506 00	$57 50		$47 50	$20 00	$30 00	$20 00	$10 00
Contingent Funds	3,144 20	4,279 56	2,092 48	5 10	20,597 91		783 80	2,225 71		1,478 00	195 20
Interest on Annuities, etc.	489 00	677 50	1,566 13	1,657 00	44 40		401 50			160 00	6 00
Knickerbocker Emergency Loans		194 56									
General Tr ney											75 00
Total for Miscellaneous	$3,668 20	$6,627 97	$3,908 61	$5,168 10	$20,699 81		$1,232 80	$2,245 71	$30 00	$1,058 00	$286 20
Total	$64,845 92	$98,489 88	$66,228 54	$28,415 70	$98,032 56	$145,097 14	$63,543 99	$35,345 54	$41,425 93	$32,198 00	$13,886 20
Grand Total											$682,504 90

Appropriations for 1908-1909.

NEW ENGLAND BRANCH.

NORTH INDIA.

Naini Tal, Schools, conveyance, and teachers	$110
Dwarahat, First assistant	280
Three scholarships	60
Pithoragarh, Miss McMullen	300
Conveyance	60
Two scholarships	40
Bhot, Bible-women	24
Medicines	33
Itinerating	34
Moving	17
Expenses to Conference	33
Bareilly, Twenty scholarships	300
Hospital roof	105
Shahjahanpur, Four scholarships	60
Moradabad, Miss C. M. Organ	600
First assistant	300
Fifty scholarships	750
Two Agra medical scholarships	80
Twelve city schools	168
Inspectress	60
Conveyance	80
Bible-women	200
Rent	120
Furniture	100
District work	1,160
Mrs. Core's itinerating	33
Bijnour, Second assistant	200
Twelve scholarships	180
City workers	160
Conveyance	66
Circuit Bible-women and teachers	84
District work	800
Lucknow, Miss Ada Mudge	600
Two memorial scholarships	80
Three high school scholarships	120
Lois S. Parker Memorial	910
Budaon, Miss E. M. Ruddick	600
Hardoi, Assistant	300
Two scholarships	30
Home	140
Total	$9,377

NORTHWEST INDIA.

Phalera, Two scholarships	$30
Cawnpore, First assistant	240
Ten scholarships	150
Two one-half scholarships	80
Meerut, First assistant	275
Muttra, First assistant	240
Conveyance	40
Thirteen scholarships	195
Allahabad, Miss B. F. Crowell	600
Total	$1,850

SOUTH INDIA.

Hyderabad, City schools	$275
Miss M. Elias	260
Conveyance	25
Four scholarships	80
Madras, Miss D'Jordan	300
Miss Young	300
Conveyance	80
Ten scholarships	200
Meenambal	100
Total	$1,620

CENTRAL PROVINCES.

Basin, Assistant	$240
Bible-women	275
Fifty scholarships	840
Rent	200
Raipur, Miss E. L. Harvey	600
Conveyance	60
Debt on furniture	17
Total	$2,232

BOMBAY.

Telegaon, Three scholarships	$60
Baroda, Dr. B. J. Allen	600
Conveyance	150
Drugs	200
Compounder	100
	200
Total	$1,310

BENGAL.

Calcutta, High school (property) conditional	$370
Darjeeling, Miss E. L. Knowles	300
Pakur, Building	300
Total	$970

BURMA.

Rangoon, Sewerage connections	$56
Total	$56

MALAYSIA.

Malacca, One scholarship	$25
Singapore, Seven scholarships	175
Miss Meyer	250
Rent, Teluk Ayer	216
Conveyance	125
Teacher	100
Miss E. A. Hemingway	600
Kuala Lumpur, Two scholarships	50

Conference transit 40
Contingencies 120
Support of conveyance....... 100
Penang, First teacher.......... 200
Sanitarium repairs 10

Total $2,011

PHILIPPINES.

Manila, Land $115

Total $115

NORTH CHINA.

Peking, Miss E. G. Young...... $650
Miss G. Gilman 650
Tartar city school.......... 60
Hospital current expenses.... 400
Medical student 50
Thirty scholarships 900
Ch'ang-Li, Miss E. E. Glover... 650
Miss C. P. Dyer............. 650
Furniture 50
Day schools 100
Training-school 300
Hospital current expenses.... 275
Nineteen scholarships 570
Mrs. Ts'ao 40
T'ai An fu, Dr. E. G. Terry.... 650
Conference reports 25

Total $6,020

CENTRAL CHINA.

Nanking, Seven scholarships.... $210
Day school 50
Kiu Kiang, Building debt...... 70

Total $330

WEST CHINA.

Chung King, Bible-woman...... $40
Chentu, Miss C. J. Collier...... 650
Miss M. A. Simester 650
Ten scholarships 250
Itinerating 70

Total $1,660

FOOCHOW.

Foochow, Twelve scholarships... $240
One orphan 30
Ku Cheng, Ten scholarships.... 150
Bible-women 50
Day school 30
Repairs 25
Iu Ka, Miss M. C. Hartford.... 600
Five scholarships 100
Hai Tang, Ten scholarships.... 200
Three day schools.......... 90
Bible-women 50
Conference reports 10

Total $1,575

HING HUA.

Deh hua, Miss A. M. Todd...... $600
Miss J. A. Marriott 600
Bible-women 75
Messenger 25
Expenses 10

Total $1,310

KOREA.

Seoul, House steward $50
West Gate day school....... 25
Repairs Scranton Home...... 25
Itinerating 25
Twelve scholarships 420
Sang Dang, Gateman, Mrs. Scran-
ton 50
Keesu, Mrs. Scranton........ 50
Chemulpo, Miss J. O. Paine.... 700
Itinerating 200

Total $1,545

NORTH JAPAN.

Hakodate, Teacher of literature. $270
Teacher first and second grades 115
Seven scholarships 280
Hirosaki, Teacher third and
fourth grades 100
Assistant 60
Bible-woman 90

Total $915

CENTRAL JAPAN.

Tokyo, Aoyama, Science teacher. $235
Eight scholarships 320
Two industrial scholarships... 80
Land 381
Yokohama, Preparatory teacher. 75
Ground rent 50
Insurance and taxes........ 150
Fuel and lights 75
Mrs. Inagaki 90
Seven scholarships.......... 280
Yamabukicho day school...... 650
Blind school 25
Literary work 40
Nagoya, Translation teacher.... 150
Sewing teacher 200
Matron 100

Total $2,901

SOUTH JAPAN.

Nagasaki, Seven scholarships.... $280
Conference reports 10

Total $290

MEXICO.

Mexico City, Three scholarships. $150
Bible-woman 50
School supplies 100
Land 98
Miraflores, A. S. Ortiz........ 240
J. Ramirez.............. 240
Pachuca, Miss Orozco........ 275
Miss A. Martinez........... 200
Water tax and repairs....... 80
One scholarship 50
Puebla, Miss J. Palacios 500
Three scholarships 150

Total $2,133

SOUTH AMERICA.

Buenos Ayres, Rent.......... $200
Assistant teacher 200
One scholarship 80

Rosario, Miss B. E. Kneeland... 750
  Assistant 400
  Taxes 200
  School supplies 30
  Fuel and lights 50
  Furniture 50
  Two scholarships 200
  Children's thank-offering ... 105
Montevideo, Taxes 100
  Insurance 40
  School supplies 100

        Total $2,505

ITALY.

Rome, via Garibaldi, Five scholarships $250

        Total $250

BULGARIA.

Lovetch, Matron and other
  service $240
  Two scholarships 90
  Taxes 35

        Total $365

AFRICA.

Old Umtali, Two scholarships... $40

        Total $40

SUMMARY.

North India $9,377
Northwest India 1,850
South India 1,620
Central Provinces 2,232
Bombay 1,310
Bengal 970
Burma 56
Malaysia 2,011
Philippines 115
North China 6,020
Central China 330
West China 1,660
Foochow 1,575
Hing Hua 1,310
Korea 1,545
North Japan 915
Central Japan 2,901
South Japan 290
Mexico 2,133
South America 2,505
Italy 250
Bulgaria 365
Africa 40
Contingencies 620

                            $42,000
Contingent Fund 2,000

        Total $44,000

NEW YORK BRANCH.

NORTH INDIA.

Kumaon, Naini Tal, Bible-woman $64
  Mrs. Newman's Bible-woman. 50
  Rent for Bible'woman's
    Homes 33

Dwarahat, Four scholarships, at
  $20 80
  Medical scholarship 40
Pithoragarh, Eight scholarships,
  at $20 160
  Support of women 100
  Industrial work ....: 320
  Miss Annie Budden, salary
    (cond.) 600
  Assistant, Miss Ellen Hayes
    (cond.) 300
  Two village schools........ 40
  Training class 64
  Rent for Miss Budden (cond.) 120
  Six Bible-women 125
  Conveyances 80
  Itinerating 125
  Mrs. Newman's Bible-woman.. 100
  Repairs 20
Bareilly District, Bareilly Orphan-
  age and first assistant..... 300
  Bareilly Orphanage and second
    assistant 240
  Bareilly Orphanage and third
    assistant ....: 220
  110 scholarships 1,650
  City schools, 5, at $20..... 100
  Mohulla and village Bible-
    woman 165
  Four city Bible-women...... 160
  Conveyances 160
  Special Bible-woman........ 25
  Itinerating (Sadar Bazaar).. 40
  Woman's School and teachers. 120
  Books and incidentals 12
  Scholarships, students' wives,
    at $12 50
  Two hospital beds.......... 40
Shahjahanpur, Boarding school,
  six scholarships 90
  Miss Fannie M. English...... 600
Shahjahanpur West, Bible-woman 72
  Mrs. West's itinerating and
    medicine 50
  City work, four Bible-women. 140
  Conveyances 60
  Widows 64
  Repairs 20
  City schools 40
  Katra Circuit 48
  Khera Bajhera Circuit....... 62
  Faridpur Circuit 67
Garhwal Pauri, Six scholarships. 120
  Mrs. Newman's two Bible-wo-
    men 100
Moradabad, Five scholarships... 75
  Evangelistic work, convey-
    ances 75
  Five Bible-women 140
  Medicines 25
Budaon, Kakrala Circuit 120
  Ujhaini Circuit 120
  Dataganj Circuit 100
  Bhamora Circuit 112
  Aonla Circuit 155
  Bilsi Circuit 156
  Bisauli Circuit 132
  Summer school 25
Bijnour, Assistant 120
  Itinerating 50
  Two scholarships 30
Pilibhit, Pilibhit Circuit........ 180
  Fatehganj Circuit 144
  Mirganj Circuit 88
  Shahi Circuit 88
  Bisalpur Circuit 72

Nawabganj Circuit	68
Puranput Circuit	60
Rampur Circuit	76
Sirauli Circuit	96
Baheri Circuit	128
Itinerating	32
Summer school	25
Mrs. Wilson's itinerating....	13
Hardoi, Twenty scholarships....	300
Fifteen Bible-women	200
Tax on land for Home......	10
Sandila Circuit	68
Safipur Circuit	60
Sandi Circuit	52
Mallawan Circuit	68
Bilgram Circuit	80
Unao Circuit	80
Pahani Circuit	68
Shahabad Circuit	124
Summer school	25
Oudh, Lucknow College repairs..	100
Conveyances	100
Bible-woman, Caroline Rich-ards	40
Zenana and village, three Bible-women, and rent..........	144
Conveyances	80
Circuit Bible-woman	60
Sitapur, Miss Ida G. Loper.....	600
Ten scholarships, at $15.....	150
Bible-woman, Georgia Dempster	40
Gonda, Ellenpur and Mankipur Bible women	100
Bahraich (Nanpara) schools..	80
Conveyances	93
Rent	40
Bible-women	155
Kaisarganj Circuit Bible-woman	68
Bhinga Circuit Bible-woman..	84

Total for North India..$12,810

NORTHWEST INDIA.

Ajmer-Phalera, One scholarship..	$15
Allahabad, Twelve scholarships, at $15	180
Assistant	220
Tilonia, Sanitarium, Medical Assistant	180
Cawnpore, Thirty-five scholarships, at $15..........	525
High school, two scholarships.	160
High school repairs..........	50
Five Cawnpore city Bible-women and conveyances.	125
District Bible-woman and itinerating	350
Meerut, Eight Bible-women and itinerating	200
Muttra-Agra, Assistant	240
Four Bible-women and conveyance	200
Day school	25
Jinrickshaw	40
Brindaban, Two Bible-women...	95
Bengali evangelist (half)....	120
Muttra, Miss Agnes Saxe.......	600
Training-school, five native scholars	100
Boarding-school, five scholarships	75
Two District Bible-women....	50

Total for Northwest India. $3,550

SOUTH INDIA.

Bangalore, Kolar, Eighteen scholarships, at $20.......	$360
Assistant, Miss Gladys Curties	260
Conveyance	100
Two Bible-women	50
Hyderabad, Assistant, Miss Mary Smith	260
Conveyance (partial)	50
Village school	40
Industrial work	25
Secunderabad, Bible-woman	40
Bowenpalli School..........	80
Madras, Taxes (half)	65
Seventy scholarships, at $20.	1,400
Matron	200
Three city and nine village schools	468
Miss Lydia Lewis..........	240
Miss Clara Betreen.........	220
Munshi	20
Four Bible-women...........	160
Conveyances	160
Raichur District work, Mrs. Beal Bible-woman	$25
City, Mrs. Scharer, conveyance	15
City Marathi Girls' School...	125
Belgaum, School assistant......	250
Munshi	25
Matron (in part)..........	80
Fifteen scholarships, at $20..	300
Gulbarga, B. W. Martha......	50
Bible-woman	25
Raichur, Mrs. Cook, three Bible-women: Louisamma, Nágami, Grace Pillai	75
Five scholarships, at $20....	100

Total for South India.... $5,268

CENTRAL PROVINCES.

Jabalpur, One scholarship......	$20
Narsinghpur, Six Bible-women..	250
Nagpur-Basim, Two scholarships..	30
Raipur, Two scholarships......	40
School furniture	36

Total for Central Provinces $376

BOMBAY.

Bombay, Miss Elizabeth Nicholls	$650
Mrs. Sakerbai Sorabje.......	280
Mrs. Bhimjibhoy	160
Agnesbai Silas	80
Mrs. Nathan	95
Bible-woman and conveyances.	230
City schools, Miss Robinson..	650
Teachers, Colaba School.....	280
Itinerating	25
Taxes and insurance.......	160
Poona, Mrs D. F. Fox for 1908.	100
Mrs. D. F. Fox for 1909......	100
Miss Files' Home salary.....	300
Twelve scholarships, at $20..	240
Interest on school debt......	150
Telegaon-Dabhada, Miss C. H. Lawson	600
Assistant matron	56
Nurse	60
Thirty scholarships, at $20...	720
Taxes, insurance, and upkeep	50

Keep for conveyance........	140
Miss Durant	340
Two Bible-women	100
Drugs	50
Gujarat, Ahmedabad, Three Bible-women	90
Baroda, Twenty-four scholarships, at $20.............	480
Industrial work	50
Godhra, Thirty-seven scholarships, at $20.............	740
Industrial work	100
Engine for well........\....	100

Total for Bombay...... $7,176

BENGAL.

Asanol, Six scholarships, at $20.	$120
Balpur, Three Bible-women.....	120
Three teachers	80
Two Jhees	12
Village schools	20
Repairs	20
Drivers and bullocks........	48
Pakur, Ten scholarships.......	200
Assistant	30
Bible-woman Rebecca	40
Bullock cart	20
Calcutta, Five orphans, at $40..	200
Miss Elizabeth Maxey........	400
Deaconess Home, interest on debt	400
Hindustani work, One Bible-woman	40
Two teachers	64
One teacher	40
Rent for schools	60
Kidderpur, One Bible-woman...	40
Bengali Work, Four Bible-women	180
Seven scholarships	175
Nogendro and Shoju..........	50
Horse and garri keep........	150
Tamluk, Miss Moyer, Home salary	300
Three teachers and Jhce.....	140
District and Sunday-schools..	80
One Bible-woman and scholarship	55

Total for Bengal........ $3,084

BURMA.

Rangoon, Scholarship, Emma Kunzl	$80
Sewer connection	32

Total for Burma........ $112

MALAYSIA.

Kuala Lumpur, Matron........	$144
Six scholarships, at $25.....	150
Insurance	45
Penang, Repairs on C. S. Winchell Home..............	50
Teacher Tamil Girls' Orphanage	87
Malacca, Miss Jessie Brooks' salary	600

Total for Malaysia...... $1,076

PHILIPPINE ISLANDS.

Manila, Training-school repairs..	$25
Bible-woman	75
Lingayen, Two Bible-women....	150
Toward Conference Minutes..	5

Total for Philippines.... $255

NORTH CHINA.

Peking, Mrs. C. M. Jewell......	$650
Miss Alice Powell..........	650
Mary Porter Gamewell School, twenty-two scholarships, at $30	660
Rondout Day School........	50
Bible-woman, Mrs. Phoebe Li.	40
Bible-woman, Mrs. Hsieh-Chao	40
Training-school, Mrs. Wang Wen Jung	40
Nurse	40
Tein-Tsin, Bible-woman, Mrs. Kuo Wei..................	40
Bible-woman, Mrs. Yang Hsu.	40
Chang-Li, Fourteen scholarships, at $30	420
Bible-woman, Mrs. Ch'in-Yang	40
Bible-woman, Mrs. Wang-Chou	40
Training-school teacher	40
Shan-Tung, Bible-woman, Old Lady Wang	40
Bible-woman, Clara Wang....	40
Bible-woman, Mrs. Liu Chi Hsien	40
Publishing Conference reports (partial)	25

Total for North China... $2,935

CENTRAL CHINA.

Chinkiang, Dr. Lucy H. Hoag...	$650
Drugs and supplies (partial).	100
Nurse	50
Fourteen scholarships, at $30.	420
Mrs. Longden's Bible-woman..	50
Hospital bed	40
Nankin, Four scholarships, at $30	120
One Bible-woman	50
Wuhu, Two Bible-women......	100
City evangelistic work and Itinerating	100
Two day schools............	100
Rent for day school building..	50
Insurance on Second Street Day School	15
Gateman	25
Kiu Kiang, Miss J. V. Hughes..	650
Twenty scholarships and orphans, at $30............	600
Knowles Training-school, one teacher	60
Ten scholarships, at $25.....	250
Three Bible-women, at $50...	150
Two day schools............	100
Itinerating	40
Danforth Hospital, five nurses	250
Four teachers	100
Medical students	70
Nanchang, Miss W. B. Honsinger	650
Seventeen scholarships	510
Medical assistant	70
Day school teacher	50

Miscellaneous, Miss Alethea W. Tracy, outfit, passage, and salary 1,000
Printing Conference Minutes.. 25

Total for Central China.. $6,445

FOOCHOW.

Foochow, Woman's Training-school, three scholarships, at $20 .... $60
Woman's station class, three, at $20...................... 60
Miss Phebe Wells' salary 600
Four Bible-women 100
Two day schools............ 60
Special for old Bible-women.. 12
Miss Florence Plumb, Home salary 350
Girls' School, seven scholarships 140
Nine orphans, at $30........ 270
Miss Elizabeth Strow........ 600
Repairs, Tai Maiu Home..... 50
Preparatory department, Miss Travis' salary 600
Miss Travis's passage out.... 300
Furniture 100
Ming-Chiang, Dr. Mary E. Carleton, Home salary.......... 350
Hospital beds.............. 300
Medical students 125
Medical assistant 75
Watchman 30
Repairs 50
Ku-Cheng, Messenger (in part).. 25
Woman's school (half), seven scholarships 150
Boarding-school, seven, at $20 140
Boarding-school repairs 50
Ku-De, Eight day schools..... 200
Eight Bible-women 200
Yeng Ping, Miss Linam........ 600
Messenger 50
Woman's Training-school, twelve scholarships, at $20. 240
Two Bible-women 50
Furniture for Training-school. 50
Repairs 50
Ngucheng, Dr. Li Bi Cu........ 300
Hospital expenses (in part).. 350
Hospital assistant 75
Hospital student and nurses.. 120
Hospital matron 25
Hospital Bible-women 25
Hospital watchman 25
Hospital gateman 25
Hospital repairs 50
Haitang, Scholarships, four, at $20 80
Furnishings 40
General Work, Insurance...... 100
Business agent's expenses.... 50

Total for Foochow...... $7,302

HING HUA.

Hing Hua, Leper work and day schools $50
Two Bible-women 60
Sieng Iu—Isabel Hart School—two scholarships 40

Total for Hing Hua...... $150

KOREA.

Seoul, Ewa Haktung, sixteen scholarships $560
Eunmun teacher 75
Industrial teacher 100
Chong Dong, Bible-woman, Theresa 50
Bible-woman, Delia 50
Hospital, Dr. Mary Cutler.... 700
Eight free beds, at $35...... 280
Repairs and incidentals...... 175
Drugs and instruments....... 300
Medical student assistant..... 35
Sang Dong, Mrs. M. F. Scranton 500
Bible-woman, Hannah Chung. 50
Bible-woman, Alice Barr..... 50
Bible-woman, Lucy Pak...... 50
Sang Dong Day School....... 50
School supplies and fuel...... 100
Chemulpo, Miss Miller, salary.. 700
Miss Miller, itinerating...... 200
Miss Miller, Bible-woman.... 50
Bible-woman, Hannah Yi.... 50
Bible-woman, Helena 50
Kang Wha Bible-woman Frances Mary 50
Bible-woman, Sarah Kim..... 50
Muchinai Day School........ 50
Kong Ju, Mrs. Sharp, salary... 700
Mrs. Sharp, itinerating...... 150
Day school 50
Pyeng Yang, Miss Robbins, salary 700
Miss Robbins, itinerating.... 125
Miss Robbins' Bible-woman.. 60
Ham Chong Day School and supplies 100
Pong Nong Dong Day School (Edward M. Blake) 75
Miss Irene Haynes' salary.... 700
Miss Haynes, itinerating..... 65
Miss Haynes' Bible-woman... 60
Chinnampo Day School and supplies 75
Woman's Hospital, R. S. Hall, M. D. 700
Drugs and instruments....... 300
Hospital and dispensary assistant 200
Hospital Bible-woman 60
Hospital matron, Susan Noe.. 60
Hospital repairs 50
Hospital fuel 150
Hospital in-patients 100
Hospital insurance 50
Blind class teacher.......... 40
Insurance on Home 75
Running expenses of Union Seminary 75
Yeng Byen, Miss Estey's salary. 700
Miss Estey's itinerating 250
Bible-woman 60
Day school 60
Two Bible-women 120
Gateman 50
Freight 50
General: Medical traveling.. 75
Printing annual report....... 15

Total for Korea.........$10,425

NORTH JAPAN.

Hakodate, Caroline Wright Memorial School, Miss M. S. Hampton, Home salary.... $350

Miss Hampton's passage home	300
School taxes	100
School insurance	300
Fifteen scholarships, at $40..	600
Teachers, Chinese—Mr. Uno..	350
Teachers, Music and English, Matsui Kiyo	145
Matron	115
Dickerson Memorial Kindergarten, second assistant.	100
Industrial and blind school teacher	60
Industrial and blind school rent	25
City work, Bible-woman, and teachers' rent	40
Bible-woman, salary, Teru Orikasa	90
Tracts and city work	25
Hirosaki, Girls' school, assistants, first and second grades	60
Teachers, eighth grade	365
Teachers, sewing	110
Teachers, first assistant	100
Teachers, second assistant	60
Teachers, drawing	60
Mary Alexander Memorial Kindergarten, head teacher	220
Bible-woman at Aomori, Ura Sakairi	90
Nurse Girls' School	75
Yoshida children's meetings	30
Monthly meetings (travel)	30
Total for North Japan	**$3,800**

CENTRAL JAPAN.

Sendai, Evangelist Georgiana Weaver, Home salary	$350
Return passage	300
Bible-woman, Sendai, Mrs. Hirabayshi	90
Repairs	50
Tokyo, Insurance	150
Four scholarships, at $40	160
Harrison Memorial Industrial School, two scholarships	80
Yokohama, Miss Anna P. Atkinson	700
Income tax	30
Higgins Memorial Training-school, two scholarships	80
Blind School	25
Bible-woman, Tokyo Central Church	90
Bible-woman at Mita, Mrs. Jaliyama	90
Bible-woman, Kamakura	90
Literary work, "Tokiwa"	150
Nagoya, Teachers, history and geography	300
Teachers, intermediate department	160
Teachers, second assistants	150
One scholarship	50
Bible-woman at Second Church	90
District travel (cond.)	70
Conference Minutes (partial)	10
Total for Central Japan	**$3,265**

SOUTH JAPAN.

Nagasaki, Kwassui Jo Gakko, teacher Japanese literature.	$250
Fifteen scholarships, at $40..	600
Treasurer's stationery, postage, etc.	15
Toward painting school	25
Fukuoko-Ei Wa Jo Gakko, Two scholarships	80
South Kiushu District, Miss Lida B. Smith	700
Miss Jennie M. Gheer	700
Miss Hortense Long	700
Bible-woman, Mrs. Oshima, Kumamoto	130
Miss Yamada or Miss Matsunobu, Yatsushiro	105
Mrs. Yamaki, Omura	115
Mrs. Tsuchihashi, Kagoshima.	115
Mrs. Kubo, Kagoshima	65
Mrs. Nakamura	55
Matsumoto, Kagoshima	95
Miss Hori, Shuri, Loo Choo..	115
Mrs. Yoneyama, Naha, Loochoo	95
Miss Ito at Loochoo	35
Tracts, literature, etc.	50
Sunday-school and supplies	50
District and city travel and work	300
Kagoshima, House rent, taxes, and repairs	315
Total for South Japan	**$4,710**

MEXICO.

Mexico City, Miss Temple	$750
Miss Dora Gladen	500
Srita Concepcion Perez (cond.)	500
Normal department, Prof. Cervantes Imaz	300
French, Prof. Madame Diffon.	200
Insurance	75
Seven scholarships, at $50	350
Mrs. Newman's Bible-woman..	50
Treasurer's expenses	50
Land for Industrial School	56
Pachuca, Elisa Salinas (high school)	275
Kindergarten assistants	300
Three scholarships, at $50	150
Mrs. Newman's Bible-woman..	50
Puebla, Miss M. Tovar, primary	160
Miss Manriquez, intermediate.	190
Matron	210
Four scholarships, at $50	200
Repairs	70
Guanajuato, Matron	100
Total for Mexico	**$4,536**

SOUTH AMERICA.

Buenos Aires, House rent	$750
Miss Eleanora Le Huray	750
Assistant teacher	400
Servants	275
Taxes and repairs	300
Physician	75
School supplies	200
Mrs. Newman's Bible-woman..	50
Eight scholarships, at $85	670
Matron's assistant	50
Montevideo, Mrs. Newman's Bible-woman	50
Total for South America.	**$3,570**

NORTH ANDES.

Lima, Peru, Miss Elsie Wood....	$750
Rent for Lima High School (partial)	50
Miss Alice McKinney (with Philadelphia' Branch)......	375
Total for North Andes...	**$1,175**

BULGARIA.

Lovetch, Teacher of mathematics	$240
Miss Leona Vasileva........	240
Scholarship	45
Taxes	35
Total for Bulgaria......	**$560**

ITALY.

Rome, Isabel Clark creche......	$150
Via Garibaldi, five scholarships	250
Via Garibaldi, matron (part)	200
Via Garibaldi, day teachers..	100
Via Garibaldi, repairs.......	100
Total for Italy..........	**$800**

EAST AFRICA.

Old Umtali, Miss Sophia J. Coffin	$500
Five scholarships, at $20....	100

WEST AFRICA

Quessua, One scholarship.......	20
Total for Africa........	**$620**

SUMMARY.

North India	$12,810
Northwest India	3,550
South India	5,268
Central Provinces	376
Bombay.	7,176
Bengal	3,084
Burma	112
Malaysia	1,076
Philippines	255
North China	2,935
Central China ....: ...	6,445
Foochow	7,302
Hing Hua	150
Korea	10,425
North Japan	3,800
Central Japan	3,265
South Japan	4,710
Mexico	4,536
South America, Buenos Aires...	3,520
Montevideo	50
Peru.......................	1,175
Bulgaria, Lovetch.............	560
Italy, Rome ....:.........	800
Africa	620
	$84,000

THANK-OFFERING.

North India, Bareilly Hospital repairs	$275
Hardoi Home	460
Lucknow High School.......	2,000

Bengal, Calcutta High School....	800
Pakur Orphanage	250
Philippines, Manila Hospital land	320
Central China, Wuhu Home....	1,000
Kiukiang, Knowles Training-school	1,650
Nanchang, furniture for Baldwin School	200
Korea, Yeng Byen Home.......	3,000
South America, Land for Buenos Aires School	2,000
Land for Tokyo College (Y. W. & S. B.)...............	820
Rosario School, King's Heralds' Room	225
	$13,000
Branch Contingent Fund......	3,000

Total appropriations New York Branch $100,000

PHILADELPHIA BRANCH.

NORTH INDIA.

Dwarahat, Scholarships	$60
Pithoragarh, Scholarships	100
Support of women	100
Bible-women	50
Bareilly, Scholarships	135
Assistants	104
Students' wives' scholarships.	120
Kindergarten	72
Pauri, Miss Kyle's salary......	600
Assistants	240
Water supply	75
Scholarships	300
Medical scholarships	40
Village schools	100
Moradabad, Salary, Miss Blackstock	600
Assistant	50
Scholarship	15
Bijnour, Scholarships	105
Hardoi, Scholarships..........	150
Rent	50
Lucknow, Miss Hill's salary....	600
Doctor and medicine........	125
Schools and conveyances.....	150
Gonda, Scholarships	150
First Assistant	240
Bible-women	175
Conveyance	80
Balrampur, Circuit work.......	130
Total	**$4,716**

NORTHWEST INDIA.

Phalera, Widows' support......	$45
Telonia, Six beds in consumptives hospital	120
Allahabad, Scholarships	90
Aassistants	160
Bible-women	250
Conveyance and Itinerating...	150
Cawnpore, Scholarships	225
Margaret Peale Scholarship..	80
Bible-women	100
Agra, Repairs	100
Brindaban, Bengali evangelists..	120
Muttra, Bible-women	350
Itinerating	70
Conveyance	85
Total	**$1,945**

SOUTH INDIA.

Kolar, Scholarships $80
  Partial support of Linda
    Lewis 60
  Two day schools 120
Bidar, Miss Fenderich's home
  salary 350
  Passage money, etc. 300
  Assistant 260
  Second assistant (partial).... 120
  Munshi 30
  Bible-women 180
  Conveyance 50
  Itinerating 50
  Scholarship 20
Hyderabad, Bible-women 230
  Conveyance 50
  Industrial work 25
  Scholarships 100
Vikarabad, Scholarship 20
Belgaum, Scholarships 60
Raichur, Scholarships 40
  Conveyance 50

    Total $2,195

CENTRAL PROVINCES.

Jabulpur, Bible-women $120
  Conveyance 40
  Tent 85
  Bible-woman and school...... 72
  Assistant 120
Raipur, Scholarship 15
  Debt 24

    Total $476

BOMBAY.

Gujarat District, Miss Williams'
  salary $600
Baroda, Miss Crouse's salary... 600
  First assistant 210
  Second assistant 190
  Matron 240
  Pundit 40
  Scholarships 2,300
  Rent. 120
  Taxes, insurance, and repairs. 250
  Industrial wo k 50
  Medicine ....r............ 50
  Medical assistant (conditional) 300
  Second medical assistant (con-
    ditional) 75
  District Training-school
    scholarships 600
  Head teacher 100
  Taxes and current expenses... 100
Bombay, Assistant 280
Godhra, Scholarships 200
Poona District, Bible-women.... 75
  Mrs. Stephens' itinerating.... 100

    Total $6,480

BENGAL.

Calcutta, Lee Memorial scholar-
  ships $75
Mazuffarpur, Scholarship 20
Tamluk, Bible-woman 25

    Total $120

BURMA.

Rangoon, Scholarship $20
Thandaung, Scholarships 120
  Miss Illingworth's salary.... 600
  Interest 50
  Printing Conference Minutes.. 15

    Total $805

MALAYSIA.

Singapore, Scholarships $200
  Miss Fox's salary 280
  Itinerating 30
  Bible-woman 80
  Contingencies 50
  Repairs, Deaconess Home.... 20
Malacca, Rent on Bible Training-
  school 180

    Total $840

PHILIPPINES.

Manila, Deaconess Home, light
  and fuel $25
Le Singayen, Purchase of property 500

    Total $525

NORTH CHINA.

Peking, Scholarships $120
  Bible-woman 36
Tientsin, Bible-woman 40
  Gateman 40
Chang-li, Scholarships 240
  Bible-woman 40
Tai-an-fu, Scholarships 240
  Hospital expenses 300
  Dr. Stryker's salary 650
  Dr. Stryker's outfit and pas-
    sage 450
  Dr. Koon's salary 650
  Repairs 100
  Bible-woman 40
  Dr. Benn, home salary...... 350

    Total $3,296

CENTRAL CHINA.

Nanking, Miss White's salary... $650
  Scholarships 120
Kiu Kiang, Scholarships 210
  Bible-women in training...... 50
Chin Kiang, Scholarships 180

    Total $1,210

FOOCHOW.

Foochow, Scholarships.......... $160
  Medical student 80
  Dr. Hu's salary 450
  Hospital expenses 500
  Assistant 50
  Instruments 50
  Medical student 40
  Matron 30
  Repairs 50
  Watchman 50
  Support of orphans.......... 150
Ku Cheng, Scholarships........ 180
  Scholarships in deaf and dumb
    school 50

Hai Tang, Scholarships 40
School furnishings 40
Printing Conference Minutes.. 10

Total $1,930

KOREA.

Seoul, Scholarships $280
Fuel 50
Bible-woman, Hannah 50
Bible-woman, Drusilla Yi 50
Bible-woman, Hester 50
Shares in Nurses' Training-
school 210
Insurance 20
Dispensary assistant 60
Head nurse 75
Shares in Evangelistic Train-
ing-school 60
Chemulpo, Miss Snavely's salary 700
Miss Snavely's itinerating.... 175
Miss Snavely's Bible-woman.. 50
Teacher in school 60
Gateman 50
Pyeng Yang, Bible-woman...... 60
Bible-woman's Institute...... 40
Dr. Pak's salary 240
Laura Arner's Day School.... 50
Supplies 25
Kang Syo, Day school and sup-
plies 75

Total $2,430

NORTH JAPAN.

Sappora, Bible-woman $90
Hakodate, Miss Dickerson's
salary 700
Miss Dickerson's income tax.. 30
Miss Sprowles' salary....... 700
Miss Sprowles' income tax... 30
Ladies' Home, ground tax.... 30
Ladies' Home, insurance..... 50
Ladies' Home, repairs...... 50
Fuel for school 150
Scholarships 360
Registration in Shadan...... 50
Blind school 150
Miss Singer's home salary.... 75
Miss Singer's passage and
salary 800
Hirosaki, Repairs 25
Teacher 65
Tracts and Gospels 30

Total $3,385

CENTRAL JAPAN.

Sendai, Miss Hewitt's salary... $700
Miss Hewitt's income tax.... 30
Repairs 50
City evangelistic work....... 30
Tracts and Sunday-schools.... 30
Aoyama, Teacher 250
Assistant 60
Scholarships 480
Asakusa Day School........ 400
Day school teacher.......... 90
Travel of teacher........... 10
Bible-woman 90
Mrs. Bishop's travel 100

Mrs. Bishop's assistant 30
Miss Spencer's home salary.. 90
Miss Spencer's passage and
salary 800
Yokohama, Miss Slate's home
salary 350
Miss Quantee's salary 585
Miss Quantee's income tax.... 30
Miss Quantee's passage 300
Bible Training School teacher 80
Evangelistic work and travel
(partial) 100
Assistant 30
Tokiwa and literature 100
Nagoya, Miss Soper's home
salary 350
Assistant 60
Bible-woman 90

Total $5,315

SOUTH JAPAN.

Nagasaki, Scholarships $200
Orphanage scholarships 40
Kiushu District, Bible-woman... 90
Sendai, Bible-woman 90

Total $420

MEXICO.

Mexico City, Teacher in S. L.
Keen College $250
Teachers of science and litera-
ture 360
Matron, Srita Ramerez 250
Scholarships 250
Pachuca, Scholarship 50
Puebla, Miss Limberger's salary. 750
Miss Purdy's salary........ 750
Miss Paynes' salary 750
Miss Duartes' salary 250
Bible-woman 105
Taxes 35
School supplies 80
Bookkeeper's salary 75
Scholarships 250
Guanajuato, Miss Dunmore's
salary 750
Water tax and repairs...... 100
Scholarships 200
School supplies 65
Two teachers 500
Light 50
Bible training scholarships.... 100
San Vincenti, Day school 200

Total $6,170

AFRICA.

Quessua, Scholarship.......... $20
Rickshak and school supplies. 100

Total $120

BULGARIA.

Hotantsa, Teacher $90
Bible work 140

Total $230

ITALY.

Rome, Via Garibaldi, scholarships	$200
The Creche	125
Total	**$325**

SOUTH AMERICA.

Buenos Aires, Scholarships	$80
Rent	200
Teacher	200
Lima, Peru, Rent	50
Miss McKinney's salary (half)	375
Total	**$905**

SUMMARY.

North India	$4,716
Northwest India	1,945
South India	2,195
Central Provinces	476
Bombay	6,480
Bengal	120
Burma	805
Malaysia	840
Philippines	525
North China	3,296
Central China	1,210
Foochow	1,930
Korea	2,430
North Japan	3,385
Central Japan	5,315
South Japan	420
Mexico	6,170
Africa	120
Bulgaria	230
Italy	325
South America	905
Total	**$43,838**
Conditional	1,090
	$44,928
Thank-offering	15,000
Grand total	**$59,928**

BALTIMORE BRANCH.

NORTH INDIA.

Dwarahat, Scholarships	$80
Bible-women	140
Itinerating	25
Pithoragarh, Bible-women	50
Bareilly, Scholarship	150
Moradabad, Scholarships	135
Lucknow, Miss Ruth E. Robinson's salary	600
Scholarship	26
Scholarship	30
Gonda, Scholarships	120
Total	**$1,356**

NORTHWEST INDIA.

Tilonia, Nurse	$40
Muttra, Bible-women	88
Conveyance	30
Total	**$158**

CENTRAL PROVINCES.

Sironcha, Scholarships	$80
Conveyance	30
Land tax	16
Raipur, Miss Manuel (school assistant)	260
Scholarships	500
Bible-women	100
Conveyance	60
Mrs. Gilder's itinerating	50
Furniture	109
Bible-women	160
Total	**$1,365**

SOUTH INDIA.

Kolar, Scholarships	$260
Keep of conveyance	25
Miss Linda Lewis's salary	65
Day schools	120
Bidar, Bible-woman	40
Hyderabad, Conveyance	25
City schools	80
Miss Murray (assistant)	260
Bible-women	80
Miss Elias (assistant, industrial work)	200
Matron	100
Scholarships	80
Assistant	80
Vikarabad, Bible-women	168
Belgaum, Bible-woman	25
Scholarships	100
Rent	300
Madras, Taxes	65
Scholarships	680
Elizabeth (evangelist)	56
Guilford Avenue School	40
Bible-woman	40
Miss Marston	220
Sooboonagam Ammal	124
Miss Grace Stephens' salary	600
Total	**$3,833**

BOMBAY.

Poona, Medical compounder and Bible-woman	$50
Scholarship	40
Drugs	100
Itinerating	25
Rents	60
Bible-woman	65
Keeper of cart, etc.	65
Gujarat, Bible-woman	24
Total	**$429**

BENGAL.

Calcutta	$412

NORTH CHINA.

Peking, Scholarships	$180

CENTRAL CHINA.

Chinkiang, Scholarships	$120
Beds	25
Drugs	100
Nurse	50
Hospital bed	40

Nanking, Scholarship	80
Kiukiang, Scholarships	150
Total	$515

FOOCHOW.

Foochow, Woman's Station Class	$40
Hospital Bible-woman	25
Leper work	50
Running expenses	25
Miss Wallace's salary	600
Girls' Boarding-school scholarships	240
Hospital students	80
City hospital expenses	100
City hospital student	40
City hospital Bible-woman	25
Mrs. Tippets' salary	300
Miss Edna Jones's salary	600
Orphans	360
Kindergarten	75
Ming Chiang, Training-school	200
Matron and Bible-woman	30
Ku-Cheng District, Day schools	200
Bible-women	50
Scholarship	20
Iu-Ka District, Women's Training Class	80
Yen Ping District, Bible-women	75
Bible-woman's Training-school	350
Haitang, Girls' Boarding-school	80
Furnishing, Girls' School	20
Treasurer's expenses	20
Publishing Conference Minutes	10
Insurance	65
Total	$3,760

HING HUA.

Hing Hua, Hamilton Boarding-school	$20
Juliet Turner Woman's School	300
Isabel Hart Girls' School	60
Total	$380

KOREA.

Seoul, Scholarships	$315
Matron	50
Aogi Day School	50
Two hospital beds	70
Room in hospital	100
Pyeng Yang, Chili San Li Day School	60
Miss Sarah B. Hallman's salary	700
Total	$1,345

JAPAN.

Hakodate, Scholarships	$160
Sewing teacher	60
Hirosaki, Bible-woman	90
Total	$310

CENTRAL JAPAN.

Tokyo, Amy G. Lewis's salary	$700
Aoyama	218
Income tax	30
Scholarships	240

Harrison Industrial School	40
Teacher of penmanship	65
Teacher of embroidery	75
Yokohama, Fuel and lights	50
Simon Memorial	300
Assistant's salary	200
Poor school	60
Day school visitor	80
Taxes	25
Literary work	25
Total	$2,108

SOUTH JAPAN.

Nagasaki, Kindergarten assistant	$135
Scholarships	120
Painting	25
Conference reports	10
Total	$290

ITALY.

Rome, Isabel Creche	$35
Bible-woman	90
Total	$125

AFRICA.

Missionary's salary	$25

MEXICO.

Scholarships	$100

SOUTH AMERICA.

Total	$204

PHILIPPINES.

Manila, Scholarships	$45
Bible-woman	60
Total	$105

SUMMARY.

India	$7,553
China	4,835
Korea	1,345
Japan	2,708
Italy	125
Mexico	100
Philippines	105
Africa	25
South America	204
Total	$17,000
Conditional	2,000
Total for Baltimore Branch	$19,000

CINCINNATI BRANCH.

NORTH INDIA.

New missionary, outfit and passage	$450
Naini Tal, Teacher and conveyance	110

Pithoragarh, Miss Lucy Sullivan's
salary .... | 600
First assistant .... | 240
Two special scholarships..... | 25
One scholarship .... | 20
Women's Home Bible-woman.. | 25
Medical - work, Miss Mary
Means' salary .... | 600
Village work, four village
schools .... | 80
Two Bible-women .... | 50
Bareilly, Orphanage, scholarships | 195
City and village work, Alice
Means' salary .... | 600
City schools .... | 83
Assistant, Mrs. Tucker...... | 300
Three special Bible-women.... | 75
Itinerating village work..... | 20
Horse for Miss Alice Means.. | 50
Bareilly Hospital (pro rata
appropriation) .... | 170
Two beds .... | 40
Shahjahanpur, First assistant.. | 240
Second assistant .... | 200
Sixty-four scholarships...... | 960
Three Bible-women (cond.)... | 75
Bareilly District Work, Tilhar
Circuit .... | 92
Jalahabad Circuit .... | 68
Powayan Circuit .... | 68
Panahpur Circuit .... | 52
Mohamdi Circuit .... | 44
Moradabad, Miss Waugh's salary | 600
Boarding school, twenty-six
scholarships .... | 890
Normal school, three scholar-
ships .... | 45
City and village work, rent
for Ladies' Home........ | 120
Three Bible-women .... | 75
Evangelistic work, assistant.. | 240
Itinerating .... | 100
Medicines .... | 25
Budaon, Boarding school, first
assistant .... | 260
Nine scholarships .... | 135
Bijnour, Boarding school, fifteen
scholarships .... | 225
District work, Bible-women
(conditional) .... | 125
Hardoi, W. F. M. S. (pro rata
(appropriation) .... | 250
Lucknow, College, Persian
teacher .... | 100
College scholarship .... | 60
High School, first assistant.. | 300
High School, second assistant. | 300
High School, scholarships.... | 400
High School, secretary's salary | 200
Repairs .... | 100
Home for Homeless Women,
Miss Hardie's home salary. | 300
Assistant .... | 240
Repairs .... | 40
Conveyance .... | 50
Matron and teachers....... | 225
Sitapur, Boarding School, first
assistant .... | 220
Second assistant .... | 180
Sixty-two scholarships ...... | 930
Zenana and circuit work, as-
sistant .... | 200
Conveyance .... | 120
Bible-women .... | 190
Oudh District, Bara Banki, Ten
Bible-women .... | 250

Lakhunpur, Nine Bible-women. | 225
Sedhauli, Bible-women ...... | 175
Gonda, Boarding School, Miss
Hoge's salary .... | 600
Thirty-one scholarships ...... | 465
Circuit work, Bible-women
(conditional) .... | 75
Repairs and medicines ...... | 16
Marietta Bible-woman....... | 25
Village conveyance .... | 53
Day school .... | 20
District work, Colonelganj,
Bible-women .... | 40
Frances Scott, salary and
travel .... | 900

Total for North India....$15,071

NORTHWEST INDIA.

Phalera, Circuit Bible-woman... | $20
Brindiban, Medical work, Dr.
Emma Scott .... | 600
Miss Linnie Terrell's salary.. | 500
Traveling .... | 300
Medicines .... | 350
Assistant .... | 200
Compounder .... | 50
Nurse .... | 60
Servants .... | 40
Beds, ten .... | 200
Conveyance .... | 100
Itinerating .... | 34
Hospital furniture .... | 215
City work, Zenana assistant... | 220
Rescue work .... | 90
Muttra, Training-school, four
scholarships .... | 80
Boarding School, twenty
scholarships .... | 400
Evangelistic teachers and
Summer School .... | 1,330
Contingent fund .... | 35

Total for Northwest India $4,824

SOUTH INDIA.

Bangalore, Baldwin High School,
two scholarships .... | $80
City and village work, Miss R.
Davids, assistant Canarese. | 200
Mrs. P. Davids, Tamil assist-
ant .... | 200
Conveyance .... | 100
Kolar, Boarding School, twenty-
four scholarships .... | 480
Zenana and village work, Miss
B. Smith .... | 260
Day School .... | 50
Bidar, Two day schools........ | 50
Boarding School scholarships.. | 80
Hyderabad, Ten scholarships.... | 200
Vikerabad, Girls' School, fourteen
scholarships .... | 280
Land tax .... | 60
Evangelistic work, Bible-wo-
men .... | 236
Day School .... | 24
Conveyance .... | 60
Secunderabad, Bible-woman .... | 24
Belgaum, Boarding School, seven
scholarships .... | 140
Raichur, District work, Mrs.
Ernsberger, itinerating .... | 50

City work, three Bible-women under Mrs. Cook 75
Primary Boarding School, one scholarship 20

Total for South India.... $2,669

CENTRAL PROVINCES.

Nagpur, Bible-woman $25
Sironcha, Eight scholarships... 160
Three widows 45
Six Bible-women 150
One new tonga and two pair oxen 200
Raipur, Mrs. Williams, matron.. 240
Scholarships 120
Miss Thomas, assistant...... 260
Pundit 40

Total for Central Provinces $1,240

BOMBAY.

Taylor High School, Mrs. Eddy, home salary....... $350
Mrs. Fox's salary 250
Three scholarships 60
Gujarat, Five Bible-women (one conditional) 125
Godhra, Four scholarships ... 80
Baroda, Seventeen scholarships.. 340
Poona, Marathi evangelistic work 300

Total for Bombay....... $1,505

BENGAL.

Asansol, One scholarship...... $20
Darjeeling, Miss Wisner, home salary 350
Calcutta, Bengali work, teachers 120
Bible-women 150
Ten scholarships 250
School 50
Medicines 20
Pakur, Seventeen scholarships.. 340
Matron 25
Two Bible-women and conveyance 160
One Bible-woman (Rampore Hat) 40
Dispensary and servants..... 150
Four village schools........ 110
Tamluk, Miss Kate Blair, home salary 350
Land rent and taxes........ 25
Two scholarships 40
Bible-women 120
Conveyance 60

Total for Bengal $2,380

BURMA.

Rangoon, Two scholarships..... $40
Sewerage connection (pro rata) 92

Total for Burma........ $132

MALAYSIA.

Malacca, Two Training-school scholarship $70

Singapore, Taxes and insurance. 86
Deaconess Home, twelve scholarships 300
Evangelistic, Miss Norris.... 180
Traveling and incidentals 30
Methodist Girls' school repairs 10
Telok Ayer, General work...... 200
Kuala Lumpur, Three scholarships 75
Penang, Contingencies 100
Boarding School teacher...... 200
Tamil Girls' Orphanage...... 250
Matron 72
Taiping, Miss Anderson's salary 600
Two scholarships 60
Sanitarium repairs 15

Total for Malaysia...... $2,198

PHILIPPINES.

Manila, Miss Crabtree's salary.. $750
Matron 30
Water 75
Incidentals and repairs...... 15
Scholarships 90
Conference Minutes 10
Hospital land in Manila (pro rata) 188

Total for Philippines.... $1,158

NORTH CHINA.

Peking, Mary Porter Gamewell High School, twenty-seven scholarships $810
Bible-woman, Tien Su E..... 40
Tientsin, Ting Chuang Day School 40
Bible-woman, Chao Wang.... 40
Watchman 40
Ch'ang-li, Five scholarships..... 150
Tsun Hua District Day School. 50

Total for North China... $1,170

WEST CHINA.

Chung King, Dr. Mary Ketring, salary $650
Furniture and repairs........ 50
Bedding and gowns 50
Nurses and helpers 90
Two beds 40
Evangelistic work, Bible-woman 40
Itinerating 50
Insurance 25
Chentu, Boarding School, four scholarships 100
Tsicheo, Bible-woman, Mrs. —— 40
Itinerating work 50
DeWitt Training-school, two scholarships 50
Insurance 50
Suiling, Evangelistic work, Bible-woman 40

Total for West China.... $1,325

FOOCHOW.

Foochow, Woman's Training-School, Miss Jewell's salary $600
Sixteen scholarships 320

Woman's Station Class, five scholarships 100
Repairs 60
Nine Bible-women 225
Boarding School, Miss Bonafield, salary 600
Thirty-five scholarships 700
Repairs 50
Liang-au Hospital, medical students 80
Hai Tang, Two scholarships.... 40
Insurance 25

Total for Foochow....... $2,800

HING HUA.

Hing Hua, Hamilton Girls' School, eight scholarships.. $160
Training-schools, twelve scholarships 300
Leper day schools.......... 200
Day School and traveling.... 550
Fourteen Bible-women and itinerating 420
Miss Lulu C. Baker, salary... 600
Miss Mary Thomas, salary.... 600
Sieng Iu, Training-school:..... 550
Day Schools and travel...... 300
Eighteen Bible-women 540
Itinerating 100
Miss Lebeus 600
Dr. Emma Betow 600
Miss Seidlmann 500
Isabel Hart Girls' School, fourteen scholarships 280
Hospital beds and nurse...... 65
Messenger and freight....... 15

Total for Hing Hua..... $6,380

KOREA.

Seoul, Ewa Haktang, Miss Frey, salary $700
Miss Marker, salary......... 700
Second Chinese teacher...... 75
Thirteen scholarships........ 455
Gateman 50
Books and stationery........ 50
Chong Dong, Bible-woman, Susanna 50
Bible-woman, Amanda....... 50
Training-school, Miss Morrison 200
Two scholarships 120
Baldwin Dispensary, Dr. Ernsberger, salary 700
Doctor's Bible-women 100
Dispensary 100
Dispensary fuel 100
Dispensary gateman 50
Dispensary repairs 75
Drugs and instruments 225
Insurance 50
Day School 50
Bible-woman's Training-school, Miss Albertson's salary.... 700
Two shares in Training-school. 60
Chemulpo, Miss Hillman, salary. 700
Miss Hillman's itinerating... 200
Miss Hillman's Bible-woman.. 50
Bible-woman, Frances Mary.. 50
Bible-woman, Mary Cho..... 50
Bible-woman, Elizabeth...... 50
Day School 60
Day School supplies......... 25

Insurance and taxes......... 60
Poo Pyeng Bible-woman...... 30
Kong Ju, Miss Ora May Tuttle, salary 700
Miss Tuttle's itinerating..... 150
Two Bible-women 100
Pyeng Yang, Mrs. Moore's Bible-woman 60
Yeng Byen District, Mrs. Morris' Bible-woman 60

Total for Korea........ $7,005

JAPAN.

Sappora, City evangelistic work, taxes, and insurance....... $35
District evangelistic work, Anna Bing, home salary.... 350
Bible-woman's salary, Sappora District 90
Hakodate, Caroline Wright's Memorial School, five scholarships 200
Hirosaki, Miss Bessie Alexander, home salary 350
Tokyo, Aoyama Jo Gakuin, eight scholarships 320
Teacher, sewing and etiquette. 130
Teacher, drawing 60
Matron 75
Sunday-schools 30
Harrison Memorial Industrial School, teacher sewing...... 80
District evangelistic work, three Bible-women in Shinano 270
Travel 25
Bible-woman, Lida.......... 40
Mrs. Alexander, Mothers' Meeting 20
Yokohama, Miss Leonora Seeds, salary and travel.......... 800
Higgins Memorial Training-school, two scholarships.... 80
Blind School 25
Nagoya, Teaching, drawing, and penmanship 125
Bible-woman, Gifu 90

Total for Japan........ $3,195

SOUTH JAPAN.

Nagasaki, Kwassui Jo Gakko, Miss Russell, travel and home salary $650
Miss Young 700
Miss Thomas 700
Miss Cody 700
Miss Sutton 680
Miss Ashbaugh 350
Penmanship and art......... 250
Science teacher 400
Industrial Japanese sewing... 100
Industrial drawn work and embroidery 100
Translation 100
Chinese literature 100
Principal's secretary 120
Scholarships, twenty-three ... 920
Ground rent 150
Insurance 200
Water rent 50
Dispensary 100
Repairs 300

Kindergarten supplies	50
Conference reports ...:......	10
Painting	200
Fukuoka, Ei Wa Jo Gakko, teachers' salaries	800
Six scholarships ....!...	240
Insurance ....!...	120
Evangelistic work, North Kiusiu District, Miss Finlay, salary	700
Bible-woman, Miss Sada Tagagi	87
Bible-woman, Mrs. Kato....	122
Bible-woman, Mrs. Saruta....	122
Bible-woman in Kureme......	120
Bible-woman, North District, Miss Aihara	77
Miss Finlay's assistant......	50
City Sunday-schools	50
District travel	100
Tracts and Bible...........	30
Omura, Kwassui Jo En, twenty-four scholarships	480
Teacher	60
Matron	40
Evangelistic work, South Kiusiu, Bible-woman, Mrs. Walenak	105
Bible-woman, Mrs. Tokunami.	105
Bible-woman, Miss Nebara....	60

Total for South Japan...$10,400

MEXICO.

Mexico City, Sarah L. Keen College, Miss Hollister, salary.	$750
Miss Pilar Aragon..........	210
Miss Velasco	210
Porter	210
Sewing teacher	90
Street, water, and property taxes	200
Cook	90
Five scholarships	250
Debt on land (pro rata)......	161
Evangelistic work, Harriet Ayres	750
Bible-woman, Concha	50
Bible-woman	150
Pachuca, One scholarship......	50
Puebla, Miss Palacios..........	500
Music teacher	120
Porter	140
Taxes	240
School supplies	100
Orizaba, Miss Refugio Hernandez	210
School supplies	60
Porter	60
Guanajuato, Bible-woman	50

Total for Mexico........ $4,651

ITALY.

Rome, Isabel Creche, Day Nursery	$90
Via Garibaldi, three scholarships	150
Evangelistic work, Bible-woman, in part.............	35

Total for Italy........ $275

AFRICA.

Old Umtali, Scholarships......	$460
Man service on the farm....	60
Bible-women	125

Total for Africa........ $645

Total appropriations $69,023

Pro rata appropriations:	
South America, Montevedio (not paid last year)......	$1,000
All pledged:	
Special appropriations, Kong Ju Home	1,000
Special appropriations, Gonda Home	1,000
Lucknow High School......	2,500
New work	1,000

$6,500
$69,023

Total appropriations $75,523

NORTHWESTERN BRANCH.

NORTH INDIA.

Naini Tal, Mrs. Worthington....	$400
Rent	100
Dwarahat, Second assistant....	240
Bible-women	100
Scholarships	280
Medicines	50
Pithoragarh, Second assistant...	200
Scholarships	380
Day schools	40
Bible-women	100
Medicines	20
Repairs	100
Bareilly, Doctor Gimson	600
Medical assistant	400
Medical work and repairs....	600
Beds in hospital............	240
Trained nurses	160
Hospital scholarships	100
Hospital Bible-women	75
Conveyance	80
Hospital roof	385
Bareilly Home, final payment.	1,200
Orphanage	450
Pauri, Second assistant........	220
Scholarships	340
Medical scholarships	80
Miss Wilson	600
Bible-women	60
District Bible work..........	500
Moradabad, Second assistant....	240
Scholarships	345
Normal School scholarship....	30
Training class	120
Circuit and village work and conveyance	280
District work	420
Budaon, Miss Wright..........	600
Second assistant	200
Scholarships	300
School and Zenana work.....	120
Bible-women and village work	280
Itinerating and conveyance...	200
Incidentals	25
Building	5,000

Bijnour, First assistant........	240
Scholarships	255
District work and conveyance.	200
Kiratpur Circuit Bible-women	80
Gonda, Zenana assistant........	220
Scholarship	20
Hardoi, Mrs. Parker's Home..	670
Lucknow, Miss Northrup (one-half year)	300
Traveling expenses	300
Miss Singh's home salary....	300
Normal School assistant......	400
Third assistant	300
Winslow scholarships	75
Farwell scholarship	50
Support of blind women.....	75

Total $19,745

NORTHWEST INDIA.

Phalera, Miss Hoffman	$600
Miss Forsyth	600
Assistant	200
Scholarships	100
Tilonia, Matron at Sanitarium...	200
Medicines	80
Allahabad, Scholarships	345
Cawnpore, Miss Greene........	600
Miss Logeman	600
English scholarships	160
Native girl scholarships......	540
Day School	40
Bible-women and itinerating..	175
Support of work	125
Meerut, Scholarship	20
Bible-women, itinerating, and conveyance	500
Aligarh, Miss Kipp............	600
Assistant	240
Scholarships	3,000
Mrs. Matthews	400
Assistant	240
Second assistant	200
Industrial work	1,400
Repairs	100
New dormitory	1,000
Muttra, English scholarships....	160
Boarding School scholarships..	345
Munshi	60
Evangelistic band	50
Second assistant	220
Zenana assistant	240
Bible-women	75
Rent, repairs, and incidentals.	120

Total $13,335

SOUTH INDIA.

Bangalore, Miss Benthein......	$600
Miss Toll	600
Kolar, Miss Peters............	260
Miss Anderson	240
Miss Mann	200
Mrs. Hall	200
Munshi	20
Scholarships	1,000
Bible-woman	50
Brahmin Day School........	120
Kindergarten	20
Miss Holland	600
Miss Fisher (one-half year)..	300
Miss Fisher's traveling expenses	300

Miss Fisher's home salary (one half year)	150
Doctor	600
Traveling expenses	300
Raichur, Scholarships	80
Belgaum, Miss Wood's home salary	250
Traveling expenses	300
Bible-woman	75
Day School assistants.......	180
Canarese Girls' School.......	75
Conveyance	100
Girls' School, Shaupur.......	25
Kindergarten	25
Matron	100
Madras, Miss Doyle	300
Pupil assistants	300
Conveyances	100
Scholarships	400
Munshis	40
Bible-women	200
Cingamah at Nicodemus Home.	40

Total $8,145

CENTRAL PROVINCES.

Raipur, Scholarship	$20
Furniture	55

Total $75

BOMBAY.

Poona, Mrs. Fox..............	$200
Mrs. Grove	300
Head mistress	350
Scholarships	80
Taxes	115
Building debt	2,000
Interest	150
Medical scholarships	50
Scholarship in Mrs. Hutching's School	50
Godhra, First assistant........	220
Second assistant	200
Matron	260
Pundit	40
Scholarships	1,420
Incidentals	360
Bombay, Miss Abbott..........	600
Assistants	160
Bible-women and itinerating..	150
Conveyance	190
Taxes and insurance........	165
Telagaon, Assistant High School teachers	360
Scholarships	800
Incidentals	75

Total $8,355

BENGAL.

Asansol, Miss Hoskings........	$200
Girls' School, Miss Verneaux.	160
Scholarships	1,200
Rent and repairs	100
Buildings	1,000
Evangelistic work, Miss Norberg	600
Bible-women	165
Conveyances	200
Zenana and Miss De Ilone....	200
Day School Bible-woman.....	50
Widows' Home, Miss Moore..	180

Mrs. Mondle, matron........	80
Widows	25
Pakur, Miss Swan (partial)....	200
Scholarships	280
Bible-woman	80
Santali, Bible-woman	40
Widows	60
Darjeeling, Miss Creek........	600
Calcutta, Miss Bennett.........	500
Traveling expenses	300
Scholarships	360
Deaconess Home	400
Miss Johnson's Bible-women.	100
Assistant to Mrs. Lee........	230
Mazefferpur, Miss Peters.......	600
Miss Voight	500
Traveling expenses	300
Furniture	100
Scholarships	900
Repairs, taxes, and land rent.	165
Matron	200
Assistant	240
Bible-women	200
Day schools	180
Medical work	450
Conveyances	175
Total $11,320	

BURMA.

Rangoon, Miss Stahl, home salary	$350
Traveling expenses	300
Sewers	215
Total	$865

MALAYSIA.

Singapore, Bible-woman	$80
Contingencies	50
Deaconess Home repairs......	100
Matron	125
Scholarships	175
Girls' School, Miss Bunce....	500
Furniture	100
Repairs	50
Taipeng, Miss Jackson, home salary	350
Traveling expenses	300
Miss Craven (partial).......	200
Scholarships	300
Bible-woman	75
Expenses to Conference......	80
Assistant's salary	270
Conveyance	100
Miscellaneous, Sanitarium......	80
Publishing Minutes	25
Total	$2,910

PHILIPPINES.

Manila, Scholarships	$90
Bible-woman	75
Hospital, Dr. Parish	750
Hospital supplies	1,000
Conveyance	245
Incidentals	200
Land	440
Native deaconess	60
Lingayen, Bible-woman.......	75
Total	$2,935

CHINA.

North China, Dr. Gloss........	$650
Dr. Manderson	650
Miss Wheeler	650
Scholarships	450
Lettie Mason Quine Day School	60
Medical students	50
Nurses	80
Tientsin, Dr. Martin	650
Mrs. Knox	650
Bible-woman	40
Medical work	200
Chang Li, Scholarships	40
Country evangelistic work....	100
Tai Au, E. E. Martin, home salary	300
Scholarships	1,200
Country schools	100
Lettie Mason Quine Day School	25
Bible-woman, Mrs. Liu.......	40
Training-school	75
Expenses to Conference......	50
Miscellaneous, Miss Jaquet	550
Traveling expenses and furniture	400
Total	$7,010

CENTRAL CHINA.

Chinkiang, Miss Crook........	$650
New missionary............	550
Traveling expenses and furniture	400
Scholarships	300
Bible-woman, hospital.......	50
Iron beds	100
Nanking, Miss Shaw..........	650
Traveling expenses	300
Miss Alice Peters	650
Miss Sarah Peters, home salary	300
Miss Peters, home salary.....	300
Scholarships	900
Bible-Woman's School	350
Kindergarten supplies	50
Bible-women	200
Day schools	100
Kiu Kiang, Miss Merrill.......	650
Miss Smith	650
Scholarships	600
Training-school scholarships..	200
Bible-woman	50
Lettie Mason Quine Day School	50
Esther Clark Day School......	50
Elizabeth Skelton Danforth Hospital and drugs........	600
Nurses and free beds	200
Kindergarten supplies	50
Purchase of land...........	270
Wuhu, Miss Crane...........	650
Traveling expenses	300
Nan Chang, Miss Howe, half year	375
Miss Howe, home salary.....	175
Dr. Kahn's home salary......	350
Medical assistant	70
Day-school teacher	50
Hospital	3,000
Total $14,190	

WEST CHINA.

Chun King, Medicines and instruments	$350
Supplies	50
Furniture and repairs	100
Charity beds	60
Bible-woman	40
Insurance	40
Chentu, Miss Stout	650
Miss Jones, traveling expenses	350
Miss Jones, home salary	350
Scholarships	500
Chentu Day School	75
Gien Dsei Day School	75
Bible-women	80
Insurance	60
Hospital beds	80
Tschieo, Bible-women	80
Bible-women in training	150
Day schools (district)	100
Itinerating	100
Incidentals	25
Suiling, Bible-women	40
Rogers Day School	75
Incidentals	10
Day school	400
Total	$3,840

FOOCHOW.

Foochow, Dr. Lyon	$600
Dr. Manderson	600
Miss Simpson	600
Hospital evangelistic work	50
Preparatory scholarships	50
Scholarships in boarding-school	200
Day schools and traveling	420
Lettie Mason Quine Day School	30
Liang Au Hospital expenses	980
Hospital repairs	150
Orphans	330
Ming Chiang, Miss Longstreet	600
Miss Longstreet, home passage	300
Training-class	200
Bible-women	325
Repairs	100
Boarding-school	240
Day schools and traveling	240
Watchman and messenger	75
Ku Cheng, Miss Peters	600
Woman's training-class	300
Girls' boarding-school	300
Messenger	25
Yen Ping, Woman's training-school scholarships	120
District day schools and traveling	180
Bible-women	175
Boarding-school	400
South Yen Ping, Day schools and traveling	180
Ngu Cheng, Woman's Station class	100
Day schools and traveling	30
Boarding-school	40
Hospital	200
Haitang Boarding-school	40
Miscellaneous, printing	25
Insurance	85
Total	$8,890

HING HUA.

Hing Hua, Hamilton Girls' Boarding-school	$200
Juliet Turner Woman's School	100
Bible women and traveling	300
Miss Wilson	600
Miss Westcott's home salary	200
Miss Westcott's traveling expenses	300
Miss Fonda	500
Traveling expenses and furniture	400
Messenger and freight	50
Sieng Iu, Scholarships	100
Dr. Draper	600
Country medical work	275
Ing Chung, Boarding and training-school	500
Districts, Day schools and evangelistic	150
Bible-women	200
Miss Strawick	600
Messenger and freight	25
Total	$5,100

JAPAN.

Hakodate, Scholarships	$240
Teacher, mathematics	320
Teacher, history	145
Teacher, sewing, etiquette, and cooking	180
Hirosaki, Insurance and taxes	50
Kindergarten assistant	125
Sendai, Scholarships	25
Miss Heaton	700
Traveling expenses	300
Bible-woman, Sendai District	60
District work	100
Tokyo, Miss Bullis	700
Income taxes	30
Scholarships	640
Teacher, Chinese	270
Teacher, literature	100
Teacher, translation	200
Teacher, English	200
Teacher, primary	115
Teacher, assistant	60
Teacher, normal	200
Payment on land	1,350
Industrial scholarship	40
Miss Alling	700
Income tax	30
Traveling expenses	300
Incidentals	200
Fukagawa, Day school	400
Yokohama, Mrs. Van Petten	700
Income tax	30
Books, tracts, and travel	90
Fuel, light, and repairs	250
Scholarships	280
Teacher, theology	330
Teacher, music	80
Teacher, sewing and etiquette	90
Aizawa and Ranagawa, Day school	400
Rent and taxes	130
Day school visitor and travel	160
Mothers' meetings	20
Nagoya, Insurance and supplies	200
Teacher, mathematics and science	250

Teacher, literature and composition 200
Teacher, music 180
Bible-woman, First Church... 90
Bible-woman, Toyohashi...... 90
City work 40
New building 750
Miscellaneous, literature work.. 100

Total $12,240

SOUTH JAPAN.

Nagasaki, Miss Melton........
Teacher mathematics $350
Biblical assistant 100
Primary teacher 65
Scholarships 240
City work 150
Kindergarten rent and supplies 150
Stationery and postage...... 15
Omura, Scholarships 20
Fukuoka, Miss Seeds 700
Traveling expenses 275
Teachers 125
Scholarships 280
Incidentals 270
Mrs. Sakomato............. 85
Mrs. Saruta................ 80

Total $2,905

KOREA.

Seoul District, Scholarships.... $420
Teacher 75
Repairs, insurance, and fuel.. 675
Hospital children's thank-offering 275
Hospital bed 35
Visiting nurse 50
Teacher 240
Pyeng Yang, Teachers........ 115
Bible-woman 60
Itinerating 50

Total $1,995

MEXICO.

Mexico City, Kindergarten teacher $250
Primary teacher 200
Scholarships 300
Pachuca, Miss Hewitt 750
Miss Betz 750
Miss Lopez 210
Miss Ester Garcia........... 210
Miss Chagoyan 250
Miss Martiarena 275
Miss Jimenez 175
School and dormitory supplies 250
Porter and repairs.......... 280
High school assistant........ 200
Scholarship 150
To complete building 500
Puebla, Normal teacher....... 280
Kindergarten teacher 250
Taxes and dormitory supplies 100
Scholarships 250
Guanajuato, Teachers 450
School supplies 120
Porter 120
Bible-woman 50
Miraflores, Miss Valverde...... 210
Rent and school supplies.... 70

Apizaco, Miss Castaldi........ 210
Support of school 220
Flaxcala, Teacher and support of school 270
Leon, Bible-woman 60

Total $7,510

SOUTH AMERICA.

Montevideo, Miss Hewitt...... $750
Miss Marsh 750
Teachers 1,000
Scholarships 200
Porter 100
Taxes 250
Repairs 150
Bible-woman 50
Buenos Ayres, House rent..... 400
Scholarships 170
Rosario, Scholarships 500
Assistants 900
Miss Walker 750
Traveling expenses 300
To complete building........ 400
Lima, Rent 150

Total $6,280

BULGARIA.

Lovetch, Miss Davis........... $600
Miss Blackburn 600
Miss Ralcheva 295
Miss Gouloumanova 280
French teacher 280
New teacher 240
Russian and sewing teacher.. 125
Incidentals and repairs...... 200
Books and apparatus........ 50
Traveling expenses 50
Scholarships 270

Total $2,990

ITALY.

Rome, Miss Swift, home salary.. $350
Crandon Hall, Miss Burt....... 700
Mlle. DeLord 500
Scholarships 300
Repairs 500
Home School, Miss Garibaldi ... 700
Matron 100
Scholarships 300
Teachers 500
Taxes and insurance 500
Repairs 300
Deaconess work 600

Total $5,650

AFRICA.

Quessua, Scholarships $180
Umtali Ct., Bible-woman 25

Total $205

NORTH GERMANY.

Bible women and work...... $150

SWITZERLAND.

Bible women and work...... $150

For emergencies............ $3,435

SUMMARY.

North India	$19,745
Northwest India	13,335
South India	8,145
Central Provinces	75
Bombay	8,355
Bengal	11,320
Burma	865
Malaysia	2,910
Philippines	2,935
North China	7,010
Central China	14,190
West China	3,840
Foochow	8,890
Hing Hua	5,100
Korea	1,995
Japan,	12,240
South Japan	2,905
Mexico	7,510
South America	6,820
Bulgaria	2,990
Italy	5,650
Africa	205
North Germany	150
Switzerland	150
Contingencies	3,435

Total $150,000

DES MOINES BRANCH.

NORTH INDIA.

Pithoragarh, Scholarships	$320
Bareilly, Scholarships	135
Hospital roof	145
Shahjahanpur, Scholarships	300
Pauri, Scholarships	200
Moradabad, Third assistant	200
Scholarships	60
Budaon, Scholarships	285
Lucknow, Miss Sircar	360

Total $2,005

NORTHWEST INDIA.

Cawnpore, Miss Pool	$600
Assistant mathematics	100
Scholarships, girls' high school	560
Repairs	50
Kasganj District	700
Meerut, Second assistant	240
Scholarships	15
Bible-woman and conveyance	90
Aligarh, Bible-women	88
Conveyance	100
Muttra, Miss Gregg	400
Assistant	300
Scholarships, woman's training-school	120
Boarding-school	90
Miss McLeary	240
District Bible-women	400
Miss Bobenhouse	900
Miss Lawson	800

Total $5,853

SOUTH INDIA.

Kolar, Miss Maskell	$600
Bible-women	144
Conveyances	100

14

Miss Linda Lewis, in part	75
Day school	75
Scholarships, boarding-school	320
Hyderabad, Miss Wood	600
Miss C. Smith	260
Conveyances	75
Bible-women	80
Village school	40
Industrial work	25
Repairs, Zenana Home	25
Miss Evans	600
First Assistant	260
Pupil assistants	260
Miss Ottley	260
Matron	100
Conveyance	50
Scholarships	1,000
Vikarabad, Miss Simons	600
Assistant	160
Scholarships	620
Evangelist assistant	260
Bible-woman	120
Day school	24
Conveyances	75
Miss Wells	850
Property	2,000

Total $9,658

CENTRAL PROVINCES.

Sironcha, Miss Lauck	$600
Assistant, Miss Daniel	200
Village school	100
Conveyance	45
Jabalpur, Mrs. Holland	600
Miss Reynolds	600
Scholarships	3,400
High school	125
Insurance	60
Training-school assistant	200
Bible-women	40
Evangelistic work, Bible-women	200
Conveyances	40
Khandwa, Miss Lossing	600
Miss Liers	600
First Assistant	200
Second assistant (conditional)	160
Scholarships	1,200
Miss Elieker	600
Assistant	100
Itinerating	30
Bible-women	180
Training-class	50
Burhanpur, Bible-women	100
Marsinghpur, Bible-women	100
Gadarwara, Bible-women	120
Raipur, Teacher	24
Bible-women	20
Debt on furniture	23

Total $10,317

BOMBAY.

Bombay, Miss Davis, home salary	$300
City schools	80
Goodhra, Scholarships	200
Poona, Interest	60

Total $640

BENGAL.

Calcutta, Miss Henkle.........	$600
Miss Aaronson	300
Property	475
Pakur, Scholarships	260
Assistant	25
Asansol, Scholarships..........	100
Bible-woman, Retu	16
Bible-woman, Kemti	16
Total	$1,792

BURMA.

Rangoon, Miss Robinson.......	$600
Miss Rigby	600
Miss Stockwell	600
Lease	100
Scholarships	140
Sewerage connections	76
Itinerating	100
Interest on loan	25
Sunday-schools	35
Village schools	25
Bible-woman	80
Thandaung, Miss Perkins.......	600
Scholarships	280
Conference Minutes	15
The Hagerty Home.........	5,000
Total	$8,276

PHILIPPINE ISLANDS.

Miss Crawford	$750
Training-school	90
Property	156
Total	$996

NORTH CHINA.

Peking, Miss Boddy...........	$650
Scholarships	360
Tientsin, Miss Wilson.......	650
Training-school	150
Country work	140
Chang Li, Scholarships	210
Bible-woman	40
Tai Au Fu....................	60
Total	$2,260

CENTRAL CHINA.

Wuhu, Miss Ogborn...........	$650
Itinerating	100
Kiu Kiang, Scholarships.......	360
Land	95
Dr. Stone	450
Nurses	100
Drugs	50
Free Beds	125
Bible-woman	50
Medical student, assistant.....	70
Nan Chang, Scholarships.......	660
Bible-women	100
Conference Minutes.........	25
Total	$2,835

WEST CHINA.

Chung King, Miss Galloway, passage and home salary.....	$725
Miss Wells	650

Dr. Edmunds	900
Medicines and instruments...	200
Beds	80
Bedding	10
Nurses and helpers.........	70
Day schools for women......	50
Day schools for girls........	75
Itinerating	50
Insurance	25
Chentu, Scholarships	300
Tsi Cheo, Miss Manning........	650
Scholarships, woman's school.	100
Itinerating	50
Medicines	25
Repairs and incidentals......	30
Freight	15
Salary, furniture, and passage, Miss Golisch	1,000
Total	$5,005

FOOCHOW.

Foochow, Miss Trimble	$600
College, Preparatory.........	40
Furniture	150
Miss Hu	300
Scholarships	400
Orphans	60
Ngu Cheng, Miss Allen	600
Miss Ankeny, passage, salary and furniture	900
Woman's school	400
Bible-women	375
Day schools, travel..........	420
Boarding-school	900
Medical student in Canton....	50
Repairs	50
Messenger	50
Hai Lang, Miss Glassburner.....	600
Miss Bartlett, passage and home salary	700
Boarding-school	40
Woman's station class	120
Bible-women	175
Day schools and travel......	330
Messenger	50
Conference Minutes	20
Insurance	50
Boat expenses	50
Total	$7,430

HING HUA.

Sieng Iu, Scholarships........	$180
Hospital	20
Total	$200

KOREA.

Translating and printing textbooks	$50
Miss Paine's Bible-women....	50
Hai Ju, Day school............	50
Mrs. Cable's itinerating......	50
Total	$200

NORTH JAPAN.

Hakodate, Scholarships	$120
Teacher, science............	215
Teacher, translation.........	145
Teacher, Japanese	145

Hirosaki, Miss Griffith's passage
and salary 925
Income tax 30
Repairs 25
Teachers, fifth and sixth grade 150
Teachers, seventh grade...... 360
Bible-woman, Kuroishi....... 90
Travel, district superintendent 75

Total $2,280

CENTRAL JAPAN.

Sendai, Scholarships $500
Teachers and supplies....... 275
Interest and taxes.......... 80
Insurance 40
Miss Phelps 700
Income tax 30
Yamagata, Bible-woman........ 90
Tokyo, Scholarships 280
Teacher, mathematics 235
District travel 25
Yokohama, Bible-women 65
Nagoya, Miss Daniel........... 700
Income tax 30
Property 300

Total $3,350

MEXICO.

Scholarships $200
Light 180
Industrial property 133
Puebla, Scholarships.......... 200
Guanajuato, Matron 100
Ayapanges, Teacher's supplies.. 375
Tezontepec, teacher's supplies.. 360
Orizaba, rent.............. 100

Total $1,648

SOUTH AMERICA.

Montevideo, property.......... $200
Lima, rent 100
Rosario 142

Total $442

AFRICA.

Quessua, Scholarship.......... $80

Total $80

ITALY.

Rome, via Garabaldi, Scholarships $200

Total $200

German thank-offering (cond.).. $300

Total $300

SUMMARY.

North India $2,005
Northwest India 5,853
South India 9,658
Central Provinces 10,317
Bombay 640

Bengal 1,792
Burma 8,276
Philippine Islands 996
North China 2,260
Central China 2,835
West China 5,005
Foochow 7,430
Hinghua 200
Korea 200
North Japan 2,280
Central Japan 3,350
Mexico 1,648
South America 442
Italy 200
Africa 80
German thank-offering (condi-
tional and unassigned)....... 300

Grand Total $65,767

MINNEAPOLIS BRANCH.

NORTH INDIA.

Pithoragarh, Ten scholarships... $200
Bareilly, Eight scholarships..... 120
Hospital roof 60
Pauri, Four scholarships....... 80
Budaon, Twelve scholarships... 180
Bijnour, Three scholarships..... 45
Hardoi, Home............. 90
Lucknow, Medicines.......... 25
Conveyance for English work. 150
Gonda, Nine scholarships...... 120

Total $1,070

NORTHWEST INDIA.

Ajmere, Repairs for roof....... $20
Twelve scholarships 180
Allahabad, Three scholarships... 45
Cawnpore, High school scholar-
ship 40
Muttra, Mrs. Ogilvie.......... 240
Five training-school scholar-
ships 100
Mussoorie, Two Bible-women,
itinerating, and conveyance. 68
Lahore, Thirteen Bible-women... 420
Roorkee, Seventeen Bible-women
and itinerating 316

Total $1,429

BOMBAY.

Bombay, City schools.......... $200
Poona, Two Bible women and
itinerating 175
Summer school 25
Telegaon, Four scholarships..... 80
Mrs. Crisp 280
Godhra, Two scholarships...... 40

Total $800

CENTRAL PROVINCES.

Jabalpur, Two scholarships..... $40
Patan Circuit, Four Bible-
women 100
Raipur, Furniture 9

Total $149

SOUTH INDIA.

Kolar, Five Scholarshipss......	$100
Two Bible-women	50
Madras, Two scholarships......	40
Total	$190

BENGAL.

Pakur, Salary for assistant	$40
Eleven scholarships	220
Eight widows	100
Matron's salary	120
Keep of conveyance	60
Day school	25
Stable	300
Debt	190
Total	$1,055

BURMA.

Rangoon, Miss Whittaker's salary	$600
Assistant	200
Three scholarships	60
Repairs on Burmese Girls' School	32
Thandaung, Scholarships.......	120
Total	$1,012

PHILIPPINES.

Manila, Matron...............	$37
Conveyance	175
Insurance	43
Repairs, incidentals	25
Scholarships	180
Bible-woman	75
Institutes	50
Miss Stixrud, salary in part..	750
Lingayen, Scholarships	100
Lights and fuel.............	50
Conference Minutes	10
Miss Erbst, salary half year (conditional)	325
Total	$1,820

MALAYSIA.

Malacca, Miss Pugh's salary...	$450
Conveyance	180
Contingencies	100
Girls' school expenses.......	200
Bible-women training teacher.	72
Bible-women school scholarships	35
Three girls' school scholarships	75
Singapore, Contingencies	100
Miss Blackmore's salary.....	600
Deaconess Home repairs......	100
Conveyance	144
Scholarships	300
Miss Olson's salary and transit	650
Teachers	648
Repairs	50
Penang, Transit to Conference..	60
Miss Martin's salary........	600
Insurance	54
Three Bible-women..........	225

Conveyance	180
Matron	144
Twenty-five scholarships	600
Teacher	144
Caretaker	72
Taipeng, Miss Sutton's salary..	600
Vernacular teacher	58
Contingencies	60
Second and third standard teachers	350
Conveyance	80
Insurance	45
Matron	85
Bible-woman	75
Kuala Lumpur, Miss Rank's salary	600
Total	$7,736

NORTH CHINA.

Peking, One scholarship, May Porter Gamewell School....	$30

WEST CHINA.

Chung King, Hospital work, bedding, and gowns..........	$40
Two nurses, or helpers.......	40
Three charity beds..........	60
Chentu, Four scholarships......	100
Tsi Cheo, Miss Brethorst's salary	650
One Bible-woman	40
One day school	75
One district school, "Frankie Grout"	50
Miss Brethorst's itinerating..	100
Total	$1,155

CENTRAL CHINA.

Chin Kiang, Four scholarships...	$120
Nanking, Miss Huelster's salary.	540
ary	540
Two scholarships	60
Kiukiang, Two Bible-women at $50	100
Six Bible-women scholarships.	150
One "Rulison Fish" scholarship	30
Nurse	50
Itinerating	60
One day school.............	50
Land	40
Nan Chang, Miss Tang's salary..	450
Total	$1,650

FOOCHOW.

Foochow, Woman's training-school, two scholarships...	$40
Girls' boarding-school, eight scholarships	160
One Bible-woman	25
Three medical students......	100
Kucheng, Miss Lorenz's salary..	600
Two Bible-women..........	50
Thirty-two boarding-school scholarships	640
Two deaf and dumb pupils...	50
Eight day schools...........	240
Repairs	50
Total	$1,955

HING HUA.

Sieng Iu, Miss Nicolaisen's salary	$600
Isabel Hart Girls' School, fourteen scholarships	280
Eighteen hospital beds	360
Hing Hua, Hamilton Girls' Boarding-school, eight scholarships	140
Messenger	10
Total	$1,390

JAPAN.

Hakodate, Three scholarships	$120
One pupil teacher	60
Tokyo, Miss Blackstock's salary	700
Miss Blackstock's government tax	80
Land	220
Harrison Memorial, ten scholarships	400
Nine teachers and matron	615
Insurance, repairs, and watchman	175
Publication Tokiwa, etc	25
Nagoya, Miss Lee's salary	700
Miss Lee's government tax	30
Total	$3,075

KOREA.

Seoul, Three scholarships	$105
Chinese teacher	75
Bible-woman, Mrs. Kim	50
Hospital	125
Peng Yang, Day school teacher, Helen	55
Total	$410

BULGARIA.

Bulgaria, One scholarship	$45

SOUTH AMERICA.

Buenos Ayres, One pupil teacher	$250
Rosario, Fuel and lights	25
Corridor	60
Total	$335

MEXICO.

Mexico, Debt	$56
Contingencies	$238
Grand total for Minneapolis Branch	$25,600

TOPEKA BRANCH.

NORTH INDIA.

Pithoragarh, Scholarships	$100
Bible-woman	25
Medicines	100
Hospital helpers	100
Conveyance	80
Moradabad, Teacher's salary	100
Scholarships	60
Shajahanpur, Scholarships	150
Pauri, Scholarships	400
Bible-women	50
Budaon, Scholarships	300
Lucknow, Bible-women	100
Lois Parker High School building	400
Sitapur, Miss Widney	600
Bible-women	50
Rae Bareli, Bible-women	242
Itanja, Bible-women	68
Bareilly, Hospital roof	90
Hardoi, Home	130
Outgoing, Miss Oldroyd	500
Total	$3,645

NORTHWEST INDIA.

Ajmer, Miss Lavinia Nelson	$600
Scholarships	870
Circuit Bible-women	96
Conveyance	100
Teacher	40
District Bible-women	400
Repairs on roof	50
Phalera, Scholarships	1,020
Repairs	40
Tilonia, Dispensary	60
Meerut, Miss Livermore	600
Miss Nelson	600
Scholarships	1,185
Bible-women	910
Bible-women, special, under Miss Livermore	50
Muttra, Miss McKnight	600
Scholars in training-school	225
Scholars in boarding-school	330
Punjab District, Bible-women	675
Evangelistic teachers	195
Out-going and salary of Miss Gabrielsen	900
Total	$9,546

SOUTH INDIA.

Bangalore, Rent	$600
Bible-women	275
Day school, Blackpully	125
Kolar, Scholarships	240
Assistant, Miss Lewis	60
Bible-women	30
Belgaum, Miss Ericson	600
Miss Montgomery, home salary	300
Bidar, Bible-women	180
Conveyance	40
Day schools	60
Assistant	60
Hyderabad, Scholarship	20
Raichur District, Bible-women	150
Godabe Circuit, Bible-women	50
Canarese, Girls' School	60
Gulbarja, Bible-women	100
Raichur City, Bible-women	25
Total	$2,975

CENTRAL PROVINCES.

Sironcha, Mrs. Turner, homecoming and salary	$600
Assistant	260
Scholarships	140
Conveyance	75

Pundit 40
Bible-women 185
Bassim, Scholarships.......... 200
Raipur, Scholarships.......... 120
Bible-women 60
Mrs. Gilder's itinerating..... 50
Bible-woman 20
Balaghat, Bible-women 80
Debt on Raipur furniture..... 14

Total $1,844

BOMBAY.

Nadiad, Miss Morgan.......... $600
Assistant 220
Pundit 40
Itinerating 150
Furniture for new building... 75
Taxes and insurance........ 65
Baroda, Scholarships 240
Mrs. Parker's assistant...... 60
Mrs. Parker's teacher....... 30
Godhra, Scholarships 920

Total $2,400

BENGAL.

Asansol, Scholarships $380
Nolina Sircar, Bible-woman..... 40
Pakur, Miss Swan............ 400
Assistant 20
Scholarships 120
Bible-women 40
Rampore, Hat Bible-women..... 40
Santali, Bible-women 80
Driver and bullocks......... 20
Beg Began Circuit........... 330
Calcutta, Girls' High School debt 300
Mrs. Bose 180
Kidderpur, Hindustani work.... 244
Bengali work under Mrs. Lee. 360
Scholarship, "Gungli"...... 15

Total $2,569

BURMA.

Rangoon, Miss James.......... $600
Land lease 100
Scholarships' 200
Sewer connection 45
Conveyance 25

Total $970

MALAYSIA.

Kuala Lumpur, Miss Holland... $600
Conference transit 25
Painting building 125
Contingencies 50
Assistant, salary 200
Teacher, special 100
Penang, Matron 180
Taxes 20
Insurance 20
Repairs on sanitarium....... 10
Malacca, Scholarships 75

Total $1,405

PHILIPPINES.

Manila, Training-school cook... $67
Furnishings 75
Scholarships 280
Bible-women 225
Hospital, Miss Dreisbach.... 750
Hospital expenses 125
Hospital site 100
Conference Minutes........ 10

Total $1,632

NORTH CHINA.

Tientsin, Dr. Stevenson........ $650
Medical work 200
Ch'an Li, Scholarships 180
Bible-women 40

Total $1,070

CENTRAL CHINA.

Nanking, Scholarships $60
Bible-women 150
Itinerating 60
Kiu Kiang, Scholarships....... 300
Chin Kiang, Scholarships...... 270
Debt on Kiu Kiang land..... 60

Total $900

WEST CHINA.

Chung King, Miss Borg........ $650

Total $650

FOOCHOW.

Foochow, Scholarships $120
Bible-women 50
Kucheng, Bible-women 200
Scholarships 400
Bible-woman 25
Yenping District, Bible-women.. 100
Kude District, Bible-woman.... 25
Iuka District, Bible-women.... 100
Outgoing and salary of Miss
Frazey 900

Total $1,920

HING HUA.

Sieng Iu, Scholarships $40
Hospital beds 200
Hing Hua, Scholarships........ 660
Miss Varney 600
Bible-women 120

Total $1,620

JAPAN.

Sappora, Miss Imhof.......... $700
Income tax 30
Assistant 90
City work 10
District Sunday-school 15
Otaru Bible-woman 90
Hakodati, Scholarships 240
Pupil assistants 120
Sunday-school 25

Tokyo, Purchase of land...... 327
  Scholarships 200
  Penmanship teacher 80
  Miss Stubiata 300
  Miss Gardner, outgoing and
    salary 900
Yokohama, Bible-women 80
Nagoya, Miss Watson, home
    salary 300
  Supplies 60
  Scholarships 40
  Building Nagoya Home...... 4,000

    Total $7,607

SOUTH AMERICA.

Rosario, Scholarships $400
  Assistants 240
  Matron 450
  Repairs and taxes.......... 200
  Interest 500
  Cook 180
  Furniture 100
  Supplies 50
  Home salary and return, Miss
    Mary I. Swaney 750
  Return, Miss Carrie Swaney.. 250
  Extra for Rosario building.. 90
Peru, Lima, rent.............. 100

    Total $3,310

KOREA.

Seoul, Scholarships $110
  Bible-women 50

    Total $160

MEXICO.

Mexico City, Scholarship...... $50
  Debt on land.............. 84

    Total $134

AFRICA.

Old Umtali, Scholarships...... $60

    Total $60

SUMMARY.

North India $3,645
Northwest India 9,546
South India 2,975
Bombay 2,400
Central Provinces 1,844
Bengal 2,569
Burma 970
Malaysia 1,405
Philippines 1,632
North China 1,070
Central China 900
Foochow 1,920
Hing Hua 1,620
West China 650
Korea 160
Japan 7,607
South America 3,310
Mexico 134
Africa 60

    Total $44,417
  Contingent 1,583

    Grand total $46,000

PACIFIC BRANCH.

NORTH INDIA.

Bhabar, Bible-women $100
  Day schools (two) 50
Dwarahat, Scholars........... 80
Pithoragarh, Scholars 200
  Bible-women 100
Bhot, Dispensary 100
Bareilly, Miss Easton's salary.. 600
  Scholars 225
  Repairs 50
  Hospital beds 40
  Hospital roof 60
Shahjahanpur, Scholars........ 120
Pauri, Scholars 160
Moradabad, Scholars 150
  Bible-women 75
Budaon, Scholars 180
  Property 700
Bijnour, Scholars............ 135
Hardoi, Home for Missionaries.. 550
  Mrs. Parker's itinerating.... 50
Lucknow, Inspectress 60
Sitapur, Scholars 150
Barabanki, Bible-women 75
Gonda, Assistant 220
  Scholars 200
  Lucknow High School building 2,000

    Total $6,430

NORTHWEST INDIA.

Ajmore, Scholars $930
  Roof 70
  First assistant 240
  Second assistant 220
  Water supply and taxes...... 40
  Bible-women and itinerating.. 215
Phalera, Medical assistant...... 100
  Medicines 75
  Medical itinerating 25
  Scholars 1,350
  Matron 200
  Repairs 40
  Widows 150
  Bible-women and itinerating.. 145
Tiloma, Sanitarium 45
Cawnpore, Scholars 495
  Bible-women and conveyance
    (city) 175
  Five Bible-women and itinerat-
    ing (district) 125
Meerut, Scholars 75
  Bible-women and conveyance.. 135
Agra, Miss Holman's salary.... 600
  Taxes 25
Aligarh, Scholars 60
Muttra, Training scholars...... 40
Lahore, Bible-woman 100
Roorkee, Bible-woman 200

    Total $5,875

SOUTH INDIA.

Kolar, Scholars $100
  Day School 50
  Conveyance 50
Hyderabad, Scholars 60
Vikarabad, Bible-women 50
Belgaum, Bible-women and con-
    veyance 75

Gokak, Bible-woman 25
Raichur, Bible-women (district). 125
Belgaum, School building...... 2,000
Madras, Scholars 140

Total $2,675

CENTRAL PROVINCES.

Sironcha, Assistant, Rhoda Burt. $200
Scholars 40
Balaghat, Bible-women 60
Kampti, Mrs. Butterfield's salary 260
Bible-women 150
Schools 190
Raipur, Bible-women 65
Furniture 10
Nagpur, Bible-women ...., 125
New Tonga 50
Day Schools 80

Total $1,230

BOMBAY.

Baroda, Scholars $100
Hospital building 500
Teachers in Woman's Theolog-
ical School 50
Godhra, Scholars 200
Outgoing expenses of new mis-
sionary 300

Total $1,150

BENGAL.

Asansol, Scholars $100
Widows 100
Pakur, Scholars 400
Building and repairs........ 80
Assistant 50
Widows 100
Matron 25
Santali Day School.......... 25
Calcutta, Bible-women under Mrs.
Lee 80
Scholarships under Mrs. Lee.. 75
Girls' High School building.. 200

Total $1,235

BURMA.

Rangoon, Burmese School...... $200
Land 150
Burmese School sewerage con-
nection 35
Thandaung, Scholar........... 80

Total $465

MALAYSIA.

Malacca, Bible-women in training $35
Singapore, School dormitories... 400

Total $435

PHILIPPINES.

Manila, Miss Decker's salary... $750
Bible-woman 75
Training scholars 135
Land lease (Training-school). 150

Repairs 25
Land for hospital 70
Dagupan, Miss Parkes' salary... 750
Miss Parkes' itinerating...... 100
Bible Institute 25
Medicines 25
Outgoing expenses of Miss Wil-
helmina Erbst 300
Publishing Conference Minutes 10

Total $2,415

NORTH CHINA.

Peking, Miss Baugh's salary.... $650
Miss Baugh's furniture...... 50
Scholars 60
Chang-li, Scholars 30

Total $790

CENTRAL CHINA.

Chinkiang, Dr. Taft's home salary
and return $600
Hospital nurse 50
Hospital bed 40
Medicines 100
Scholars 180
Kiukiang, Bible-women in train-
ing 100
Teachers in Training-school.. 80
Bible-women in Hospital..... 50
Land for Hospital 40
Scholars 120
Wuhu, Day School building..... 200
Nanchang, Hospital 1,000

Total $2,560

WEST CHINA.

Cheutu, Scholars $175
Woman's School 50
Tsi-cheo, Woman's scholarships 50
Day School building........ 500
Suiling, Bible-woman 40

Total $815

FOOCHOW.

Foochow, College building...... $5,000
Orphans 120
Mingchiang, Scholars 260
Kucheng, Scholars 20
Bible-women 50
Kude, Day Schools........... 120
Bible-women 175
In-ka, Bible-women 150
Yeng Ping, Bible-women 75
Furniture for Training-school. 50
Ngn-cheng, Scholars 100
Haitang, Scholars 80
Bible-women 100
Medical work 25

Total $6,325

HING HUA.

Hing Hua $120
Sieng-iu 200
Hospital beds 50

Total $370

KOREA.

Seoul, Miss Morrison's salary..	$200
Hospital building	115
Scholars	70
Fuel for school	50
Day School	50
Translating text-books for nurses	50
Kong Ju, Bible-women	100
Chemulpo, Bible-woman	50
Pyeng Yang, Scholar	20
Hospital building	1,000
Support of blind girls	60
Expenses of Seminary	50
Publishing annual reports....	15
Total	$1,830

NORTH JAPAN.

Hakodate, School insurance....	$50
Hirosaki, Sunday-schools	30
Total	$80

CENTRAL JAPAN.

Tokio, Miss Russell's salary....	$700
Miss Russell's income tax....	30
Land for school, Young Peoples' Thank-offering	220
Bible-woman	40
Scholar	40
Sendai, Mothers' meetings	20
Yokohama, Scholar	40
Nagoya, Bible-woman	90
Taxes	50
"Tokiwa" and other publications	25
Publishing reports	10
Total	$1,265

SOUTH JAPAN.

Nagasaki, Scholars	$80
Bible-woman	60
Painting College	50
Total	$190

MEXICO.

Pachuca, Scholars	$100
Mexico land for School	55
Total	$155

SOUTH AMERICA.

Montevideo, Scholar	$100
Rosario, Furniture	100
Fuel	50
Children's thank-offering	60
Buenos Aires, School building...	1,000
Total	$1,310

AFRICA.

Quessua, Miss Collins' salary...	$500
Miss Drummer's salary	500
Scholars	340
Medicines and supplies	10
Total	$1,350

NORWAY.

	$50
Contingencies	$1,000
Grand total	$40,000

COLUMBIA RIVER BRANCH.

NORTH INDIA.

Dwarahat, Scholarships	$40
Pithoragarh, Scholarships	80
Bible-women	80
Budaon, Scholarships	150
Bareilly, Scholarships	90
Hospital roof	30
Shajahanpur, Scholarships	120
Lucknow, Mrs. Ward	160
Gonda, Scholarships	120
Rae Bareli, Bible-woman	25
Hardoi, Lois Parker Home	30
Total	$925

NORTHWEST INDIA.

Meerut, Scholarships	$600
Muttra, Scholarships	90
Aligarh, Scholarships	180
Total	$870

SOUTH INDIA.

Vikarabad, Bible-woman	$25
Total	$25

CENTRAL PROVINCES.

Jagdalpur, Bible-women	$60
Sironcha, Scholarships	40
Widow	15
Jabalpur, Scholarships	120
Raipur, Scholarship	20
Furniture	5
Total	$260

BOMBAY.

Gujarat, Village work	$2,900
Miss Williams' assistant	240
Miss Holmes, home salary and passage	650
Nadiad, Taxes, insurance, and rent	130
Baroda, Scholarships	200
Godhra, Miss Austin	600
Scholarships	300
Telegaon, Scholarships	100
Teacher, Bhimabai	60
Total	$5,180

BENGAL.

Pakur, Scholarships	$40
Assistant	10
Total	$50

BURMA.

Rangoon, Sewerage connections..	$16
Total	$16

MALAYSIA.

Singapore, Scholarships	$100
Teacher, Miss Watts	86
Repairs, school and sanitarium	20
Malacca, Bible training scholarships	70
Penang, Miss Lilly, salary and transit	650
Scholarship	25
Total	$951

PHILIPPINES.

Manila, Hospital, Miss Dudley..	$750
Incidentals	50
Nurse in training	60
Land for hospital	35
Total	$895

CENTRAL CHINA.

Kiukiang, Hospital beds (cond.)	$75
Hospital, land	20
Nang Chang, Scholarships	60
Total	$155

WEST CHINA.

Tsicheo District, Day School....	$50
Total	$50

FOOCHOW.

Foochow, Scholarships	$40
College dept. scholarships....	80
Running expenses	25
Bible-woman	25
Bible training scholarships...	20
Day School	30
Miss Parkinson, home salary.	225
Laura Cranston Memorial....	2,000
Ming Chiang, Scholarships	200
Kucheng, Scholarships	100
Ngu Cheng, Bible-women	125
Medical and kindergarten students	250

Haitang, Scholarships	200
Station Class	80
Medical work	150
Total	$3,550

HING HUA.

Sieng Iu, Bible-women	$120
Scholarships	60
Hospital beds	40
Building (cond.)	10
Total	$230

KOREA.

Chemulpo, Nam Yang, Bible-woman	$50
Pyeng Yang, Bible-woman	50
Total	$100

NORTH JAPAN.

Hakodate, Scholarships	$80
Hirosaki, Prize scholarship	40
Kindergarten	60
Total	$180

CENTRAL JAPAN.

Tokyo, Aoyama land	$100
Industrial scholarship	120
Teacher, wood carving	40
Yokohama, Scholarships	80
Tokiwa	25
Total	$365

MEXICO.

Mexico City, Industrial School..	$28
Total	$28

SOUTH AMERICA.

Rosario (cond.)	$30
Total	$30

AFRICA.

Old Umtali, Scholarship	$20
Total	$20
Contingent	120
Total	$14,000

CONFERENCES.	NEW ENGLAND	NEW YORK	PHILADELPHIA	BALTIMORE	CINCINNATI	NORTH-WESTERN	DES MOINES	MINNEAPOLIS	TOPEKA	PACIFIC	COLUMBIA RIVER	TOTALS
INDIA: North India	$9,877	$15,545	$4,716	$1,856	$15,071	$19,745	$2,005	$1,070	$3,645	$6,430	$925	$79,885
Northwest India	1,960	3,550	1,945	168	4,824	13,385	5,853	1,429	9,546	5,875	870	49,285
South India	1,620	5,298	2,195	3,883	2,669	8,145	9,658	190	2,975	2,675	25	39,253
Bombay	1,810	7,176	6,480	429	1,505	8,355	640	800	2,400	1,150	5,180	35,425
Central Provinces	2,232	378	476	1,365	1,240	75	10,811	149	1,844	1,290	260	19,564
Bengal	970	4,134	120	120	2,380	11,320	1,792	1,055	2,569	1,285	50	26,083
Burma	56	112	805	412	182	805	8,270	1,012	970	466	16	12,709
Total	$17,415	$36,161	$16,737	$7,553	$27,821	$61,840	$38,541	$5,705	$23,949	$19,060	$7,326	$262,108
Malaysia	$2,011	$1,076	$840	$105	$2,198	$2,910		$7,736	$1,405	$435	$951	$19,502
Philippines	115	575	525		1,158	2,085	$996	1,820	1,682	2,415	895	13,171
CHINA: North China	$6,020	$2,995	$3,296	$180	$1,170	$7,010	$2,260	$80	$1,070	$790	$155	$24,761
Central China	330	9,295	1,210	515	1,825	14,190	2,835	1,650	900	2,500	50	33,640
West China	1,660					3,840	5,045	1,155	650	815		14,500
Foochow	1,575	7,302	1,980	3,760	2,810	8,800	7,430	1,955	1,920	6,320	3,550	47,437
Hing Hua	1,310	150	380	380	6,380	5,100	200	1,390	1,620	970	230	17,180
Total	$10,895	$19,682	$6,436	$4,835	$11,675	$39,080	$17,730	$6,180	$6,160	$10,800	$3,985	$137,468
Korea	$1,545	$13,425	$2,430	$1,345	$7,005	$1,995	$200	$410	$160	$1,880	$100	$30,445
JAPAN: Japan	$915			$310	$3,195	$12,240	$2,290	$3,075	$7,607	$80	$180	$26,427
North Japan	2,901	3,800	3,385							1,285	365	10,640
Central Japan		4,085	5,315	2,108	10,100		3,350					19,389
South Japan	290	4,710	420	290		2,905				190		19,205
Total	$4,106	$12,595	$9,120	$2,708	$13,595	$15,145	$5,630	$3,075	$7,607	$1,535	$545	$75,661
Mexico	$2,183	$4,596	$6,170	$100	$4,651	$7,510	$1,618	$58	$184	$155	$58	$27,151
South America	2,505	6,970	905	204	1,000	6,820	442	335	3,310	1,310		23,801
Bulgaria	885	560	230			2,990	200	45				4,190
Italy	250	800	325	125	275	5,650	80					7,625
Africa	40	620	120	25	645	205			60	1,350	20	3,165
Switzerland						150						150
North Germany						150						150
Norway										50		50
Contingent	2,620	8,000		2,000		2,670		288	1,583	1,000	120	13,231
Conditional			1,090									1,090
Thank Offering			15,000				300					15,300
Special Appropriations					5,500							5,500
Grand Total	$44,000	$100,000	$59,928	$19,000	$75,628	$150,000	$65,767	$25,600	$46,000	$40,000	$14,000	$689,818

REAL ESTATE

Belonging to The Woman's Foreign Missionary Society of the Methodist Episcopal Church.

NORTH INDIA.

Almorah, Epworth Sanitarium..	$4,000
Bareilly, Hospital	15,000
Bareilly Orphanage	11,000
Bhot, at Dharchula, Flora Deaconess' Home	1,900
Chandra, Deaconess' Home	1,100
Bijnour, Boarding School	3,000
Budaon, ...	5,650
Gonda, ...	2,500
Hardoi, Boarding Home	3,000
Lucknow, Isabella Thornburn College and High School...	53,334
Moradabad	9,500
Naini Tal, Boarding-school.....	30,000
Wellesley Hospital	1,000
Pauri, Boarding School and Orphanage	11,000
Pithoragarh, Boarding School and Woman's Home......	6,441
Shajahanpur, Bidwell Memorial School and Bungalow	7,000
Sitapur, Boarding School.......	8,801
Total :..............	**$174,226**

NORTHWEST INDIA.

Agra, Medical Home	$2,720
Ajmere, Boarding School and Marks Hall	13,335
Aligarh, Louisa Soule's Orphanage	12,528
Brindaban, Mabel Calder Home and Dispensary	4,600
Cawnpore, Hudson Hall and English School	23,300
Meerut, Howard Plested Memorial School	10,860
Muttra, Blackstone Institute...	16,800
Phalera, Orphanage and Industrial School	7,600
Total	**$91,743**

SOUTH INDIA.

Haiderabad, Stanley Home	$10,000
Zenana Home	6,000
Kolar, Wm. Gamble Deaconess Home.	5,000
Orphanage and Darby Hall..	5,000
Widows' Home	2,103
Madras, Harriet Bond Skidmore School, Baltimore Memorial Home and Northwestern Memorial Home	33,333

RAIPUR

Raipur, ...	500
Sironcha, Mary J. Clark Memorial	6,800
Vikarabad	1,000
Total	**$69,736**

BOMBAY.

Baroda, Orphanage	$22,000
Bombay, Boarding School and Home	25,000
Stevens Hall	16,666
Khandwa, ...	500
Jabalpur, Orphanage and Boarding School	12,000
Deaconess Home	5,000
Total	**$81,166**

BENGAL.

Asansol, Widows' Home	$1,500
Evangelistic Home	1,000
Darjeeling, Queen's Hill School (Crandon Hall, The Repose, Almira Hall and Pierce Building)	33,000
Muzaffurpur, Dispensary	3,516
Total	**$39,016**

BURMA.

Rangoon, High School.........	$40,000
Charlotte O'Neal Institute...	30,000
E. Rangoon, Burmese Girls' School	600
Pegu, Mission	150
Total	**$70,750**

MALAYSIA.

Kuala Lumpur, School	$15,000
Penang, ...	7,000
Singapore, Mary C. Nind Home.	25,000
Singapore School	7,500
Taiping, School	10,000
Total	**$64,500**

PHILIPPINES.

Manila, "Harris Memorial Deaconess Home"............	$14,000
Mary J. Johnston Memorial Hospital	13,575
Bungalow	1,000
Lingayen	3,000
Total	**$31,575**

NORTH · CHINA.

Peking, ...	$19,000
Tientsin, Isabel Fisher Hospital	19,000
Tsun Hua	8,000
	$46,000

CENTRAL CHINA.

Nan Chang, Baldwin Memorial..	$10,000
Dispensary and Home	8,000
Chin Kiang, Home, School, Hospital	13,916
Letitia Mason Quine Memorial	5,000
Dispensary at West Gate....	1,230
Kiu Kiang, Elizabeth S. Danforth .Hospital	7,850
The Home	3,500
Boarding School	2,500
Woman's Bible Training School	2,500
Kungling Day School.......	250
Rulison Fish Memorial School	8,000
Nan King, The Adeline Smith Home	5,500
High School	8,000
Amilla Lake School..........	1,638
Wuhu, Home	1,000
Total ....:	$78,884

WEST CHINA.

Chung King, Flora Blackstone Deaconess Home	$6,000
Holt Country Boarding School	1,100
Wm. A. Gamble Hospital....	6,700
Bungalow, Rest Cottage......	1,500
Chang Li Hospital	1,250
Total	$16,550

FOOCHOW.

Foochow, Boarding School and Residence	$14,000
Woman's School and Residence	4,500
Liang-au Hospital and Woolston Memorial Hospital and Residence	11,100
Mary E. Crook Memorial Orphanage	3,100
Hok Chiang, School..........	4,500
Ku Cheng, School.	3,950
Woman's Training-school.....	2,250
School compound	722
Total	$44,122

HING HUA.

Hing Hua, Juliet Turner Memorial School	$3,300
Hamilton Boarding-school....	8,500
Packard Home	5,500
Bible-women's School.......	1,500
Anton	513
Sieng Iu, Isabel Hart Memorial School	5,400
Margaret E. Nast Hospital...	10,000
German Memorial Home......	2,000
Tek-Hoe, Woman's School......	4,281
Total	$40,994

KOREA.

Seoul, Home and School....:..	$13,000
Dispensary	600
East Gate, Scranton Home...	2,000
East Gate Dispensary........	300
East Gate Baldwin Chapel...	250
Pyeng Yang, Home, Hospital, and Dispensary	1,500
Total	$17,650

NORTH JAPAN.

Hakodate, School and Home....	$13.500
Hirosaki, Home	1,000
Sappora	1,400
Total	$15,900

CENTRAL JAPAN.

Nagoya	$10,000
Sendai, Ladies' Home and Industrial School	7,495
Tokyo, Industrial School.......	3,000
Aoyama	20,000
Tsukiji	8,500
Asakusa Day School	500
Yokohama, Maud E. Simons Memorial.	4,000
Higgins Memorial Home and Training-school'	12,500
Yamabukicho School	1,200
Kanagawa, kindergarten	50
Don Tarbox School..........	200
Total	$67,445

SOUTH JAPAN.

Fukuoka	$15,000
Koga, Orphanage..............	5,000
Nagasaki, Home and School....	50,000
Total	$70,000

MEXICO

Guanajuato, School	$10,000
Mexico City, Orphanage........	50,000
Miraflores, School.............	1,000
Pachuca, School	20,000
Puebla, Normal Institute.......	25,000
Total	$106,000

SOUTH AMERICA.

Montevideo, School and Home...	$22,700
Rosario, Home	9,300
Total	$32,000

BULGARIA.

Lovetch, School and Home.....	$6,500

ITALY.

Rome, Crandon Hall...........	$75,000
Home	20 000
Total	$95 000

AFRICA.

Hartzell Villa ....'. $6,250

UNITED STATES,

Herkimer, N. Y., Folts Mission
    Institute $50,000
    Endowment 70,000
    Permanent fund ....·... 45,000

    Total $124,500

SUMMARY.

North India Conference.......'...$174,226
Northwest India 91,743
South India 69,736
Bombay 81,166
Bengal 39.016
Burma 70,750
Malaysia 64,500

North China .....!.......... 46,000
Central China 78,884
West China 16,550
Foochow 44,122
Hing Hua 40,994
Philippines 31,575
Korea 17,650
North Japan 15,900
Central Japan 67,445
South Japan 70,000
Mexico 106,000
South America 32,000
Bulgaria 6,500
Italy 95,000
Africa 6,250
United States 124,500

    Total $1,390,507

MRS. WM. B. DAVIS,
MRS. CYRUS D. FOSS,
Committee on Titles of Real Estate.

QUESTIONS FOR MISSIONARY APPLICANTS.

1. Full name.
2. Residence.
3. Place and date of birth.
4. Have you an experimental knowledge of salvation through the atonement of Jesus Christ our Lord? Answer this question somewhat in detail.
5. Are you a member of the Methodist Episcopal Church and a regular attendant upon its services, and are you fully in accord with its doctrines as set forth in Part 1, Division 1, of the Discipline?
6. Have you had special systematic study of the Scriptures?
7. Have you an earnest desire to win souls to Christ, and how has this desire been manifest in the past?
8. Do you trust that you are inwardly moved by the Holy Ghost to take upon you the work of a foreign missionary?
9. How long have you entertained this conviction?
10. Do you desire and intend to make this your life work, and are you willing to labor in any field?
11. To what extent are you acquainted with the work of the Woman's Foreign Missionary Society?
12. Have you any views which would prevent your cordial co-operation with the missionaries of the Methodist Episcopal Church?
13. Would you be willing to give up any personal habit which might grieve your fellow missionaries and lessen the influence of your example over the native Christians?
14. Are you a total abstainer from all forms of alcoholic beverages and from opium, cocaine, and other narcotics?
15. What is the condition of your health? (Answer question in Form II and procure testimony of a competent physician according to Form III.)
16. Outline the character and extent of your education. Name the institutions in which you were educated, the course or courses pursued, and date of graduation.
17: What languages other than English have you studied, and with what facility do you acquire them?
18. Have you a knowledge of music, vocal or instrumental?
19. Have you had business training, and in what line?
20. What positions have you held in business or professional life?
21. Executive ability. Provide testimonials relative to your success in teaching and in the management of financial matters.
22. Have you been married? If so, is your husband living?
23. Are you engaged to be married?
24. Are you liable for debt?
25. Is any one dependent upon you for support?
26. Gives names and addresses of at least ten persons, including pastors, instructors, and others who are able to give information relative to your Christian usefulness, your adaptability to people and circumstances, and your general fitness for the work.
27. A photograph should accompany your application.
28. Have you read the rules applying to missionaries, and do you promise to abide by them?

Signed...

Date...............................

DIRECTORY OF MISSIONARIES.

APPOINT-MENT.	MISSIONARY.	FOREIGN STATIONS.	BRANCH.	HOME ADDRESS.
1872	Hoag, Lucy, M. D.,	Chin Kiang, China,	New York,	Albion, Mich.
1872	*Howe, Gertrude,	Nan Chang, China,	Northwestern,	Lansing, Mich.
1878	Easton, S. A.,	Naini Tal, India .	Self-supporting,	Washington, D. C.
1878	*Spencer, Matilda A.,	Tokyo, Japan,	Philadelphia,	Germantown, Pa.
1878–90	*Swaney, Mary F.,	Mexico, Rosario, S. A.,		Manhattan, Kan.
1879	*Gheer, Jean M.,	Kagoshima, Japan,	New York,	Bellewood, Pa.
1879	Russell, Elizabeth,	Nagasaki, Japan,	Cincinnati,	Delaware, O.
1879	Budden, Annie,	Pithoragarh, India,	New York,	Almora, India.
1881	Hampton, Mary S.,	Hakodate, Japan,	New York,	Albion, Mich.
1881	*Knowles, Emma L.,	Darjeeling, India,	New England,	Tilton, N. H.
1881	Van Petten, Mrs. Caroline,	Yokohama, Japan,	Northwestern,	Neponset, Ill.
1882	Atkinson, Anna P.,	Peking, China,	New York,	Cazenovia, N. Y.
1884	Jewell, Mrs. Charlotte M.,	Nagoya, Japan,	New York,	Etna Mills, Cal.
1883	*Watson, Rebecca J.,	Shahjahanpur, India,	Topeka,	Lincoln, Neb.
1884	English, Fannie M.,	Raipur, India,	New York,	Seneca Falls, N. Y.
1884	Harvey, Emily L.,	Sendai, Japan,	New England,	St. Johnsbury, Vt.
1884	Hewett, Ella J.,	Foochow, China,	Philadelphia,	Gilead, Mich.
1884	Jewell, Carrie I.,	Buenos Ayres, S. A.,	Cincinnati,	Chicago, Ill.
1884	Le Huray, Eleanor,	Chandag Heights, India,	New York,	Summit, N. J.
1884	Reed, Mary,	Peking, China,	Cincinnati,	Becket.s, O.
1885	Gloss, Anna D., M. D.,	Pauri, India,	Northwestern,	Evanston, Ill.
1885	Kyle, Theresa J.,	Seoul, Korea,	Philadelphia,	Mount Pleasant, Pa.
1885	Scranton, Mrs. M. F.,	Kagoshima, Japan,	New York,	East Hartford, Conn.
1885	Smith, Lida B.,	Darjeeling, India,	New York,	Binghamton, N. Y.
1885	*Wisner, Julia E.,	Mexico City, Mexico,	Cincinnati,	Berea, O.
1886	Ayres, Harriett L.,	Montevideo, S. A.,	Cincinnati,	Hillsboro, O.
1886	Hewett, Lizzie,		Northwestern,	Gilead, Mich.

* Home on leave.

DIRECTORY OF MISSIONARIES.—Continued.

APPOINTMENT.	MISSIONARY.	FOREIGN STATIONS.	BRANCH.	HOME ADDRESS.
1886			DesMoines,	Ottumwa, Ia.
1887	*Bing,	Sappora,		Sydney,
1887	, Sophia,	Singapore, Sts. S.,		
1887	, Mary E., M. D.,	, China,		Dover, N. H.
1887	C.,	-ping,	New England,	
1887	w, Ella C.,		New England,	
1888	, Edna G., M. D.,	T'ai n Fu,	New England,	
1888-1907	J., M. D.,		New England,	
1888	, Kate A.,	Tamluk, India,		, O.
1888	, Augusta,			W. Va.
1888	Fa Estelle M.,			Pa.
1888				N. Y.
1888	, Sarah,	, China,	New	O.
1888	, Martha A., M. D.,	g, China,		Ill.
1888			Self-supporting,	Cal
1888		Pithoragarh,		O.
1889			Des	Ind.
1889		Sappora,		Neb.
1889	es E.,	Sendai,	Des	
1889	*Scott,			O.
1889	Sellers, le E.,	Ni Tal,	Self-supporting,	New ras, O.
1889	Trimt , Lydia A.,	Ngu-cheng,	Des	Ia.
1889	, O.	Ch	Des	
1889	, Georgiana,	, S. A.,	Self-supporting,	Corning, Ind.
1890				N. Y.
1890	, R., M. D.,	T'ai An Fu, Shantung, Ch.		R
1890	, , M. D.,	Pyeng ng,	New	N. Y.
1890	*Limberger, nna R.,	, Mexi ,		
1890	Lyon, Ella M., M. D.,	, China,		Alden,

15

DIRECTORY OF MISSIONARIES.—Continued.

APPOINT-MENT.	MISSIONARY.	FOREIGN STATIONS.	BRANCH.	HOME ADDRESS.
1890	Perkins, Fannie A.,	Thandaung, Burma,	Des Moines,	Mt. Ayr, Ia.
1890	Seeds, Leonora H.,	Yokohama, Japan,	Cincinnati,	Delaware, O.
1890	Stevenson, Ida M., M. D.,	Tientsin, China,	Topeka,	Monroe, Wis.
1891	Dunmore, Effie,	Guanajuato, Mexico,	Philadelphia,	Kreshoppen, Pa.
1891	Heafer, Louisa,	Jabalpur, India,	Philadelphia,	Philadelphia, Pa.
1891	Ogborn, Kate L.,	Wuhu, China,	Des Moines,	New Sharon, Ia.
1891	White, Laura M.,	Chin Kiang, China,	Philadelphia,	Philadelphia, Pa.
1892	Blackburn, Kate B.,	Lovetch, Bulgaria,	Northwestern,	Jacksonville, Ill.
1892	Cutler, Mary M., M. D.,	Seoul, Korea,	New York,	Grand Rapids, Mich.
1892	Glover, Ella E.,	Ch'ang, Li, China,	New England,	Boston, Mass.
1892	Hoge, Elizabeth,	Gonda, India,	Cincinnati,	Bellaire, O.
1892	*Lawson, Christine,	Telagaon, India,	New York,	Green Island, N. Y.
1892	Lauck, Ada J.,	Sironcha, India,	Des Moines,	Indianola, Ia.
1892	Paine, Josephine O.,	Chemulpo, Korea,	New England,	Roxbury, Mass.
1892	*Stahl, Josephine,	Rangoon, Burma,	Northwestern,	Diagonal, Ia.
1892	Stephens, Grace,	Madras, India,	Baltimore,	India.
1892	Wood, Catherine,	Hyderabad, India,	Des Moines,	Humeston, Ia.
1892	Young, Effie G.,	Peking, China,	New England,	Waltham, Mass.
1892	Frey, Lulu E.,	Seoul, Korea,	Cincinnati,	Bellefontaine, O.
1893	Heaton, Carrie A.,	Sendai, Japan,	Northwestern,	Seymour, Ind.
1893	*Singer, Florence E.,	Hakodate, Japan,	Philadelphia,	Philadelphia, Pa.
1893	Wilson, Minnie E.,	Hing Hua, China,	Northwestern,	Shelbyville, Ind.
1894	Allen, Mabel,	Ngu-cheng, China,	Des Moines,	Early, Ia.
1894	Alling, Harriet S.,	Aoyama, Japan,	Northwestern,	Chicago, Ill.
1894	Elicker, Anna R.,	Khandwa, Japan,	Des Moines,	Muscatine, Ia.
1894	Galloway, Helen R.,	Chung King, China,	Des Moines,	Mt. Ayr, Ia.
1894	Greene, Lily D.,	Cawnpore, India,	Northwestern,	Greencastle, Ind.
1894	Kidwell, Lola May,	Nagasaki, Japan,	Cincinnati,	National City, Cal.
1894	*Nichols, Florence L.,	Lucknow, India,	New England,	Lynn, Mass.
1894	Peters, Mary,	Kucheng, China,	Northwestern,	Princeville, Ill.

DIRECTORY OF MISSIONARIES.—Conti d.

APPOINT-MENT.	MISSIONARY.	FOREIGN STATIONS.	BRANCH.	HOME ADDRESS.
1894	▨n, ▨ry E.,	▨ri, India,	N ▨ern,	▨,
1895	Collier, C▨ra J.,	▨tu, ▨▨,	New 1 ▨d,	Chester, ▨.
1895	Evans, ▨e A.,	▨d, India,	Des ▨.	▨, Ia.
1895	* ▨de, Eva M.,	▨▨w, India,	1 ▨i	Nw ▨rk City.
1895	▨, King Eng, M. D.,	▨w, China,	▨a,	▨a.
1895	▨u, ▨de,	Yen-ping, China,	New ▨k,	Leesburg, Ind.
1895	Purdy, ▨e M.,	Puebla, Mo.,	Philadelphia,	Sunbury, ▨.
1895	▨ft, ▨e, M. ▨.,	▨n ▨, ▨ina,	Pacific,	▨s Angeles, ▨l.
1895	▨d, Althea M.,	▨ty, China,	New England,	Boston, ▨s.
1895	Wells, ▨▨be C.,	▨w, China,	New ▨k,	S. ▨s Falls, N. Y.
1895	▨ght, Laura S.,	1 ▨n, India,	Northwestern,	▨, Ind.
1896	Benthein, Elizabeth M.,	Bangalore, India,	▨rn,	▨k, Ill.
1896	* ▨r, ▨e F.,	▨g, ▨a,	N ▨rn,	Danville, Ill.
1896	▨n, ▨e,	▨r, India,	New England,	▨d, Vt
1896	* ▨n, Ida, M. D.,	Nanchung, ▨,	N ▨rn,	▨a.
1896	▨s, Mary,	Pithoragarh, India,	Cincinnati,	Akron, O.
1896	Merrill, Clara E.,	Kiu Kiang, China,	▨rn,	Flint, Mich.
1896	Nicholls, Eliz ▨h,	1 ▨ly, ▨ia,	New York,	New York City.
1896	Scott, ▨, M. D.,	Brindaban, ▨ia,	Cincinnati,	▨s, O.
1896	S▨, ▨ry, M. D.,	Kiu Kiang, ▨a,	Des ▨s,	Kiu ▨g, China.
1897	▨e, ▨a G.,	▨h, ▨d,	Des ▨s,	Cambria, Ia.
1897	▨l, N.,	▨o, ▨n,	Self-supporting,	Traer, Ia.
1897	▨an, ▨a E.,	▨a, ▨a,	Self-supporting,	
1897	▨s, ▨,	▨au,	▨ti;	Cincinnati, O.
1897	Lilly, ▨y B.,	▨g Iu, ▨a,	▨a River,	Menlo Park, Wash.
1897	▨e, ▨a A.,	▨g, ▨. ▨tlement,	Topeka,	Smith Center, Kans.
1897	Martin, Clara,	▨t, India,	Minneapolis,	Hamline, Minn.
1897	▨s, ▨de,	Penang, Sts. Settlement,	Cincinnati,	Akron, O.
1897	* ▨, ▨ry E.,	▨d, India,	▨	Jacksonville, Ill.
1897	▨, ▨a,	Nagasaki, Japan,	N ▨rn,	Marysville, O.
1898	Young, ▨y, ▨th A.,	Nagasaki, ▨n,	1 ▨i	
1898		Singapore, Mysia,	New England,	South Braintree, Mass.

DIRECTORY OF MISSIONARIES.—Continued.

APPOINT-MENT.	MISSIONARY.	FOREIGN STATIONS.	BRANCH.	HOME ADDRESS.
1898	Illingworth, Charlotte,	Thandaung, Burma,	Philadelphia,	Burma.
1898	Ingram, Helen,	Lucknow, India,	Self-supporting,	Brighton, Eng.
1898	Lewis, Amy G.,	Tokyo, Japan,	Baltimore,	Jamestown, N. Y.
1898	Longstreet, Isabella D.,	Ming Chiang, China,	Northwestern,	Bay City, Mich.
1898	Loper, Ida Grace,	Sitapur, India,	New York,	Marilla, N. Y.
1898	Varney, Elizabeth W.,	Hing Hua, China,	Topeka,	Pueblo, Col.
1898	Ernsberger, Emma, M. D.,	Seoul, Korea,	Cincinnati,	Rice, O.
1899	Gregg, Mary Eva,	Muttra, India,	Self-supporting,	Mt. Pleasant, Ia.
1899	Manning, Ella,	Chung King, China,	Des Moines,	Canada.
1899	Maskell, Florence W.,	Kolar, India,	Des Moines,	Madras, India.
1899	*Moyer, Jennie,	Tamluk, India,	New York,	Cortland, N. Y.
1899	Nicolaisen, Martha L.,	Sieng Iu, China,	Minneapolis,	Germany.
1899	*Parkinson, Phoebe A.,	Foochow, China,	Columbia River,	Spokane, Wash.
1899	Adams, Jeanette,	Foochow, China,	Self-supporting,	Pittsburg, Pa.
1900	Anderson, Luella R.,	Kuala Lumpur, Malaysia,	Cincinnati,	Ada, O.
1900	Davis, Dora,	Lovetch, Bulgaria,	Northwestern,	Kalamazoo, Mich.
1900	Estey, Ethel M.,	Pyeng Yang, Korea,	New York,	Waterville, N. B.
1900	Hillman, Mary R.,	Seoul, Korea,	Cincinnati,	Newark, O.
1900	Holman, Charlotte T.,	Agra, India,	Pacific,	Prince Edward Island.
1900	Kneeland, Bertha E.,	Rosario, S. A.,	New England,	Sprague's Mills, Me.
1900	*Martin, Elizabeth,	Peking, China,	Northwestern,	Otterbein, Ind.
1900	Martin, Emma E., M. D.,	Tientsin, China,	Northwestern,	Otterbein, O.
1900	*Rodgers, Eva,	Rome, Italy,	New England,	Chicago, Ill.
1900	Organ, Clara M.,	Moradabad, India,	New England,	Groveland, Mass.
1900	Pak, Esther K., M. D.,	Pyeng Yang, Korea,	Philadelphia, Pa.	Seoul, Korea.
1900	*Plumb, Florence J.,	Foochow, China,	New York,	Foochow, China.
1900	Rigby, Luella,	Rangoon, Burma,	Des Moines,	Mechanicsville, Ia.
1900	*Robinson, Ruth E.,	Lucknow, India,	Baltimore,	Calcutta, India.
1900	*Singh, Lilavati,	Lucknow, India,	Northwestern,	India.
1900	Williams, Mary E.,	Baroda, India,	Philadelphia,	Grove City, Pa.

DIRECTORY OF MISSIONARIES.—Continued.

APPOINT-MENT.	MISSIONARY.	FOREIGN STATIONS.	BRANCH.	HOME ADDRESS.
1901	Abbott, Anna Agnes,	Bombay, India,	Northwestern,	Chicago, Ill.
1901	Bennett, Fannie A.,	Calcutta, India,	Northwestern,	Bloomington, Ill.
1901	Collins, Susan,	Quessua, Africa,	Pacific,	Pasadena, Cal.
1901	*Edmonds, Agnes M., M. D.,	Chung King, China,	Des Moines,	Tina, Mo.
1901	*Foster, Carrie,	Rangoon, Burma,	Des Moines,	Omaha, Neb.
1901	Henkle, Nainette,	Calcutta, India,	Des Moines,	Des Moines, Ia.
1901	Lewis, Margaret D., M. D.,	Bareilly, India,	Northwestern,	Chicago, Ill.
1901	Limburger, Anna R.,	Puebla, Mexico,	Philadelphia,	Danville, Pa.
1901	Marriott, Jessie A.,	Tek Hoe City, China,	New England,	Osage City, Mo.
1901	McKnight, Isabel,	Muttra, India,	Topeka,	Gothenberg, Neb.
1901	Miller, Lula A.,	Chemulpo, Korea,	New York,	Little Falls, N. Y.
1901	Ruddick, Elizabeth May,	Budaon, India,	New England,	Eldorado, Kan.
1901	*Slate, Anna B,	Yokohama, Japan,	Philadelphia,	Williamsport, Pa.
1901	Stockwell, Grace,	Rangoon, India,	Des Moines,	Rowan, Iowa.
1901	*Tippet, Mrs. Susan,	Foochow, China,	Baltimore,	Glidden, Ia.
1901	*Wells, Elizabeth J.,	Vikarabad, India,	Des Moines,	Carlisle, Ark.
1901	*Winslow, Annie M.,	Meerut, India,	Topeka,	Morgan Park, Ill.
1901	*Woods, Grace M.,	Belgaum, India,	Northwestern,	Quincy, Ill.
1902	*Davis, Joanna,	Bombay, India,	Des Moines,	Fayette, Ia.
1902	*Eddy, Mrs. S. M.,	Poona, India,	Cincinnati,	Berea, O.
1902	*Jackson, C. Ethel,	Taipeng, Malaysia,	Northwestern,	Greencastle, Ind.
1902	*Montgomery, Urdell,	Bangalore, India,	Topeka,	Hastings, Neb.
1902	Robbins, Henrietta,	Pyeng Yang, Korea,	New York,	Northport, N. Y.
1902	Robinson, Helen,	Bombay, India,	New York,	India.
1902	Seeds, Mabel K.,	Fukuoka, Japan,	Northwestern,	Delaware, O.
1902	*Swift, Edith M.,	Rome, Italy,	Northwestern,	Newtonville, Mass.
1902	*Weaver, Georgiana,	Sendai, Japan,	New York,	Syracuse, N. Y.
1902	*Westcott, Pauline E.,	Hing Hua, China,	Northwestern,	Grand Rapids, Mich.
1903	*Alexander, Bessie,	Hirosaki, Japan,	Cincinnati,	Stanhope, P. E. I.
1903	Fenderich, Norma H.,	Bidar, India,	Philadelphia,	Atlegheny, Pa.

DIRECTORY OF MISSIONARIES.—Continued.

APPOINT-MENT.	MISSIONARY.	FOREIGN STATIONS.	BRANCH.	HOME ADDRESS.
1903	*Guthapfel, Minerva L.,	Seoul, Korea,	Philadelphia,	Philadelphia, Pa.
1903	Jones, Dorothy,	Chentu, China	Northwestern,	Joliet, Ill.
1903	Lee, Mabel,	Nagoya, Japan,	Minneapolis,	Grand Forks, N. D.
1903	Northrup, Alice M.,	Lucknow, India,	Northwestern,	Braceville, Ill.
1903	Olson, Mary E.,	Penang, Malaysia,	Minneapolis,	Afton, Minn.
1903	Parkes, Elizabeth,	Dagupan, Philippine Is.,	Pacific,	England.
1903	Peters, Jessie,	Muzafferpur, India,	Northwestern,	Chicago, Ill.
1903	Pool, Lydia S.,	Cawnpore, India,	Des Moines,	Mount Pleasant, Ia.
1903	*Soper, Ethel M ad,	Tokyo, Japan,	Philadelphia,	Japan.
1903	Temple, Laura,	Mexico City, Mexico,	New Y rk,	Hoboken, N. J.
1903	Thomas, Hettie A.,	Nagasaki, Japan,	Cincinnati,	Lancaster, O.
1903	*Travis, face B.,	Ku Cheng, China,	New York,	Poughkeepsie, N. Y.
1903	Mr, Susan,	Rosario, S. A.,	Northwestern,	Chicago, Ill.
1903	Wheeler, Maude S.,	Peking, China,	Northwestern,	Lake Mills, Wis.
1903	Bartlett, Carrie M.,	Ngu-Cheng, China,	Des Moines,	Wall Lake, Ia.
1904	Betow, Emna J., M. D.,	Sieng Iu, China,	Cincinnati,	Louisville, Ky.
1904	fix, Edith M.,	Wuhu, China,	N astern,	Albion, Mich.
1904	Crooks, face A.,	Chin Kiang, China,	Northwestern,	Charlotte, Mich.
1904	Glassburner, Manie F.,	Ngu-Cheng, China,	Des Moines,	Charter Oak, Ia.
1904	Hewitt, Helen,	ufa, Mo,	Northwestern,	Elgin, Ill.
1904	Holland, Mrs. Alma II.,	Jubbulpore, India,	Des Moines,	Washington, Ia.
1904	Hu, May L.,	Foochow, China,	Des Moines,	Foochow, China.
1904	Koons, Sue L., M. D.,	Tai An Fu, China,	Philadelphia,	Harveyville, Pa.
1904	Lorenz, Frieda V.,	Kucheng, China,	Minneapolis,	Germany.
1904	Lossing, Mabel,	Khandwa, India,	Des Mes,	Dubuque, Ia.
1904	Morgan, Cora, da,	Naidad, India,	Topeka,	Wichita, Kan.
1904	Payne, Ella E.,	ufcl knw, India,	New England,	Malden, Mass.
1904	Peters, Alice,	Guanajuato, Mexico,	Philadelphia,	Ashland, Pa.
1904	Saxe, Agnes E.,	Nanking, China,	Northwestern,	Princeville, Ill.
1904		Muttra, India,	New York,	Walden, N. Y.

DIRECTORY OF MISSIONARIES.—Continued.

APPOINT-MENT.	MISSIONARY.	FOREIGN STATIONS.	BRANCH.	HOME ADRESS.
1904	Sia, Ruby,	Foochow, China,	Des Moines,	Foochow, China.
1904	Strow, Elizabeth M.,	Foochow, China,	New York,	Jersey City, N. J.
1904	Swan, Hilda,	Pakur, India,	Topeka,	Scandia, Kan.
1904	Thomas, Mary M.,	Hing Hua, China,	Cincinnati,	Lancaster, O.
1904	Toll, Evelyn,	Bangalore, India,	Northwestern,	Hamilton, Canada.
1904	Whittaker, Lotte. M.,	Rangoon, Burma,	Minneapolis,	Minneapolis, Minn.
1904	Waugh, Nra B.,	Moradabad, India,	Cincinnati,	India.
1905	Aaronsen, Hilma A.,	Calcutta, India,	Des Moines,	St. Louis, Mo.
1905	Austin, Laura F.,	Eat, India,	Columbia River,	Woodburn, Ore.
1905	Blackst ok, Isabella Thoburn	Lucknow, India,	Philadelphia, Pa.,	Lucknow.
1905	Bullis, Edith M,		Northwestern,	Englewood, Ill.
1905	Burt, Edith,	yo, Japan,	Northwestern,	Zurich, Switzerland.
1905	Crabtree, Margaret,	Rome, Italy,	Cincinnati,	Cleveland, O.
1905	Cody, Mary A.,	Manila, P. I.,	Cincinnati,	Cleveland, O.
1905	Creek, Bertha,	Nagasaki, Japan,	Northwestern,	Olney, Ill.
1905	Crowell, Bessie F.,	Darjeeling, India,	New England,	Portland, Me.
1905	Decker, Marguerite,	Allahabad, India,	Pacific,	Los Angeles, Cal.
1905	Finlay, Alice,	Manila, P. I.,	Cincinnati,	Coshocton, O.
1005	Gimson, Esther, M. D.,	Fukuoka, Japan,	Northwestern,	Chicago, Ill.
1905	Grandstrand, Pauline,	Bareilly, India,	Self-supporting,	Linstrom, Minn.
1905	Grove, Mrs. Harriet L. R,	Pakur, India,	North ern,	Chicago, Ill.
1905	Hill, Katherine Ledyard,	Poona, India,	Philadelphia,	Newport, R. I.
1905	Holland, Ary J.,	Lucknow, India,	Topeka,	Abilene, Kan.
1905	Hollister, Grace A.,	Bangalore, India,	Cincinnati,	Loda, O.
1905	*Holmes, Ada,	Mexico City, Mexico,		Carlisle, England.
1905	Hughes, Jennie V.,	Gujerat, India,	ia River,	an Grove, N. J.
1905	Ketring, Mary, M. D.,	Nan Chang, China,	New York,	Toledo, O.
1905	Logeman, Minnie Y.,	Chung King, China,	Cincinnati,	Chicago, Ill.
1905	Long, Hortense,	Cawnpore, India,	North ern,	East Syracuse, N. Y.
1905	Marker, Jessie B.,	Kagoskima, Japan,	New York,	Shipping Port, Pa.
		Seoul, Korea,	Cincinnati,	

DIRECTORY OF MISSIONARIES.—Continued.

Appoint-ment.	Missionary.	Foreign Stations.	Branch.	Home Address.
1905	*Newby, Alta,	Nanchang, China,	Des Moines,	Mt. Hamill, Ia.
1905	Simester, Mary A,	Chentu, China,	New England,	Wadsworth, O.
1905	Shibati, Suye,	Oita, Japan,	Topeka,	Japan.
1905	Swan, Hilda,	Pakur, India,	Topeka,	Scandia, Kan.
1905	Turner, Mrs. Maud N.,	Sironcha, India,	Topeka,	Denton, Texas.
1905	Wells, Annie My,	Chung King, China,	Des Moines,	Shenandoah, Ia.
1906	Bills, Grace Ada,	Muzzaffarpur, India,	Northwestern,	Evansville, Ind.
1906	Brethorst, Alice,	Tsicheo, China,	Minneapolis,	Lenox, S. D.
1906	Coffin, Sophia Jordan,	Old Umtali, Africa,	New York,	Stanley, Alberto, Canada.
1906	Crouse, Margaret D.,	Baroda, India,	Philadelphia,	Reading, Pa.
1906	Draper, Frances L., M. D.,	Sieng Iu, China,	Northwestern,	Jackson, Mich.
1906	Drummer, Martha A.,	Quessua, Africa,	Pacific,	Atlanta, Ga.
1906	Driesbach, Gertrude Irene,	Manila, P. I.,	Topeka,	Roper, Kan.
1906	Easton, Celeste,	Bareilly, India,	Pacific,	Riverside, Cal.
1906	Ericson, Judith,	Kolar, India,	Topeka,	Galesburg, Ill.
1906	Haynes, Emily Irene,	Pyeng Yang, Korea,	New York,	Rifel isle, N. J.
1906	Hoffman, Carlotta,	Phalera, India,	Northwestern,	Manistee, Mich.
1906	Holland, Harriet A.,	Kolar, India,	Northwestern,	Chicago, Ill.
1906	Honsinger, Welthy B.,	Nanchang, China,	New York,	Rome, N. Y.
1906	James, Phoebe,	Rangoon, Burma,	Topeka,	Burma.
1906	Kipp, Julia R.,	Aligarh, India,	Northwestern,	1 rann, Ill.
1906	Knox, Emma M.,	Tientsin, China,	Northwestern,	Chicago, Ill.
1906	Marsh, Jessie L.,	Montevideo, S. A.,	Northwestern,	Caw, Mich.
1906	Nelson, E, Lavinia,	Ajmere, India,	Topeka,	Oakland, Neb.
1906	Nelson, Lena C.,	Meerut, India,	Topeka,	Oakland, Neb.
1906	Nolele, Edith,	Mexico,	Minneapolis,	Centerville, S. D.
1906	Parrish, Rebecca, M. D.,	Manila, P. I.,	Northwestern,	Logansport, Ind.
1906	*Pugh, Ada,	Malacca,	Minneapolis,	England.
1906	Reynolds, Elsie,	Jubbulpore, India,	Des Moines,	Nodaway, Ia.
1906	Rank, Minnie L.,	Kuala Lumpur, S. S.,	Minneapolis	Minneapolis, Minn.

DIRECTORY OF MISSIONARIES.—Continued.

APPOINT-MENT.	MISSIONARY.	FOREIGN STATIONS.	BRANCH.	HOME ADDRESS.
1906	Simonds, Mildred,	Vikarabad, India,	Des Moines,	Nayette, Ia.
1906	Stixrud, Louise,	Dagupan, P. I.,	Minneapolis,	Minneapolis, Minn.
1906	Strawick, Gertrude,	Ing Chung, China,	Northwestern,	Butler, Pa.
1906	Sprowles, Alberta B.,	Hakodate, Japan,	Philadelphia,	Frankfort, Pa.
1906	Snavely, Gertrude E.,	Seoul, Korea,	Philadelphia,	Harrisburg, Pa.
1906	Tang Ilien,	Nanchang, China,	Minneapolis,	China.
1906	Wallace, Lydia Ethel,	Foochow, China,	Baltimore,	North Gower, Canada.
1906	Widney, May C.,	Lucknow, India,	Topeka,	Lynden, Kan.
1906	Albertson, Millie,	Seoul, Korea,	Cincinnati,	Columbus, O.
1907	Baker, Liu C.,	Hing Hua, China,	Cincinnati,	Pixy, Pa.
1907	Baugh, Evelyn B.,	Peking, China,	Pacific,	Petaluma, Cal.
1907	Betz, Blanche,	Pachuca, Mexico,	Northwestern,	Denver, Col.
1907	Boddy, Estie T.,	Peking, China,	Des Moines,	Ayrshire, Iowa.
1907	Borg, Jennie,	Chung King, China,	Topeka,	Lindsay, Neb.
1907	Brooks, Jessie,	Malacca, S. S.,	Minneapolis,	Minneapolis, Minn.
1907	Crawford, Mabel L.,	Manila, Philippines,	Des Moines,	Sioux City, Ia.
1907	Dudley, Rosa E.,	Manila, Philippines,	Columbia River,	Puyallup, Wash.
1907	Dyer, Clara P.,	Ch'ang Li, China,	New England,	Providence, R. I.
1907	Forsyth, Estella,	Phalera, India,	Northwestern,	Flint, Mich.
1907	Hallman, Sarah B.,	Pyeng Yang, Korea,	Baltimore,	Oil City, Pa.
1907	Held, Lu, M. D.,	Foochow, China,	Northwestern,	Chicago, Ill.
1907	Jones, Edna,	Foochow, China,	Baltimore,	Folsom, Cal.
1907	Liers, Josephine,	Khandwa, India,	Des Moines,	Dubuque, Ia.
1907	Manderson, Melissa, M. D,	North China,	Northwestern,	South Bend, Ind.
1907	McKinney, Alice,	Callao, Peru, S. A.,	New York,	Logan, Ia.
1907	Norberg, Eugenia,	Asansol, India,	North Garn,	Chicago, Ill.
1907	Powell, Alice M.,	Ray, China,	New York,	Washington, Pa.
1907	Robinson, Alvina,	Rangoon, Burma,	Des Moines,	Humeston, Ia.
1907	Russell, Helen M.,	Oba, Japan,	Pacific,	Poultney, Vt.
1907	Simpson, Cora,	Foochow, China,	Northwestern,	Guide Rock, Neb.

DIRECTORY OF MISSIONARIES.—Continued.

APPOINTMENT.	MISSIONARY.	FOREIGN STATIONS.	BRANCH.	HOME ADDRESS.
1907	Smith, Adelina N.,	Kiu Kiang, China,	Northwestern,	Spokane, Wash.
1907	Stout, Winifred L.,	Chentu, China,	Northwestern,	uHey, S. Dak.
1907	Sutton, Marianne,	Taiping,	Minneapolis,	Alexandria, Minn.
1907	Tite, Ora M.,	Chemulpo, Kore a	Cincinnati,	Norwalk, O.
1908	Ankeney, Josie V.,	Ngu-Cheng,	Des Moines,	Prescott, Iow a
1908	Ashbaugh, Adella,	Nagasaki, Japan,	Cincinnati,	Mt. Vernon, Ohio.
1908	Bunce, Thirza E.,	Taiping, China,	Northwestern.	Terre Haute, Ind.
1908	Carncross, Flora,	Central China,	Northwestern,	Wausau, Wis.
1908	Erbst, Whilhelmina,	Philippines,	Minneapolis,	St. Paul, Minn.
1908	Fonda, Edith L.,	China,	Northwestern;	Berwyn, Ill.
1908	Frazey, Laura,	Foochow, China,	Topeka,	Nickerson, Kan.
1908	Gabrielson, Winnie,	Northwest India,	Topeka,	Strumsberg, Neb.
1908	Gardner, Minnie,	China,	Topeka,	Baldwin, Kan.
1908	Golisch, Anna Lulu,	West China,	Des Moines,	Afton, Iowa.
1908	Huelster, Luella,	Nanking, China;	Minneapolis,	St. Paul, Minn.
1908	Jaquet, Myra,	North China,	Northwestern;	St. Paul, Minn.
1908	Muir, Winifred,	Chin Kiang, China,	Northwestern,	Rushville, Ind.
1908	Santee, Helen C.,	Yokohama,	Philadelphia,	Philadelphia, Pa.
1908	Seidlmann, Paula,	Sieng Iu, China,	Cincinnati,	Vienna, Austria.
1908	Sharp, Mrs. Robert,	Korea,	New York,	Port Maitland, Nova Scotia.
1908	Stryker, Minnie, M. D.,	Tai-an-fu, China;	Philadelphia,	West Pittsburg, Pa.
1908	Sutton, Daisy B.,	Nagasaki, Japan,	Cincinnati,	
1908	Tracey, Alethea,	Central China,	New York,	Tyrone, New York.
1908	Terrell, Linnie,	Brindaban, India,	Cincinnati,	Pomeroy, Ohio.
1908	Voigt, Mary,	Muzzaffarpur, India,	Northwestern;,	Kankakee, Ill.

DIRECTORY OF MISSIONARIES.—Continued.

ACCEPTED, NOT YET APPOINTED.

ACCEPTANCE.	NAME.	BRANCH.	HOME ADDRESS.
1904	Cantwell, Sarah C.,	Cincinnati,	Delaware, O.
1907	Dutton, Mrs. M. L.,	Cincinnati,	Bellefontaine, O.
1907	Search, Blanche F.,	Philadelphia,	Wilkesbarre, Pa.
1908	Oldroyd, Roxanna,	Topeka,	Kansas City, Kan.
1908	Richmond, Mary,	Topeka,	Toronto, Kan.

Entered into Rest.

APPOINTMENT.	MISSIONARY.	FOREIGN STATIONS.	DIED.
1875	Miss Letitia A. Campbell (Coleman),	Peking, China,	May 18, 1878.
1876	Miss L. H. Green, M.D. (Mrs. Cheney),	Bareilly, India,	September 30, 1878.
1878	Miss Susan B. Higgins,	Yokohama, J p a,	July 3, 1879.
1881	Miss Emma Michener,	Monrovia, Africa,	December 11, 1881.
1884	Miss Ella Gilchrist, M. D.,	Kiu Kiang, China,	April 23, 1884.
1871	Miss Beulah Woolston,	Foochow, China,	October 24, 1886.
1878	Miss Cecilia Guelf,	&to, S. A.,	1886.
1881	Miss Harriet Kerr,	Bareilly, India,	December 11, 1886.
1880	Miss Florence Nickerson,	Lucknow, India,	January 31, 1887.
1878	Miss Harriet Woolston, M. D.,	Moradabad, India,	1879.
1872	Miss Elizabeth M. Pultz,	Moradabad, India,	November 5, 1887.
1883	Miss Emma- J. Everding,	Nagasaki, J p a,	January 13, 1892.
1878	Miss M. E. Layton,	Cawnpore, India,	April 22, 1892.
1888	Miss M. E. V. Pardoe,	Tokyo, J pana	g*st 31, 1892.

DIRECTORY OF MISSIONARIES.—Continued.

Entered into Rest.

APPOINTMENT.	MISSIONARY.	FOREIGN STATIONS.	DIED.
1887	Miss Mary A. V nce (Mrs. Belknap).	Tokyo, J p na.	September 27, 1892.
1880	Miss Anna B. Sears,	Peking, China,	December 4, 1895.
1884	Miss Clara A. Downey,	Cawnpore, India,	January 4, 1896.
1888	Miss Mary E. Carroll,	Bombay, India,	June 12, 1897.
1884	Miss Linna M. Schenck,	Lovetch, Bulgaria,	March 22, 1898.
1881	Miss Phebe Rowe,	Lucknow, India,	April 13, 1898.
1889	Miss Maud E. Simons,	Yokohama, J pana	July 29, 1898.
1874	Miss Mary Hastings,	Pachuca, Mexico,	1899.
1876	Miss Nettie Ogden,	Mexico,	1899.
1887	Miss Mary A. Hughes (Mrs. Ernsberger),	Madras, India,	November 12, 1900.
1900	Miss Martha L. McKibben,	Mexico City. Mexico,	November, 19.
1895	Miss Florence Sterling (Mrs. Leuth),	India,	January 8, 1901.
1898	Miss Cora Zentmire (Mrs. Brewster),	Angola, Africa,	September 1, 1901.
1869	Miss Isabella Thoburn,	Lucknow, India,	ber 14, 1901.
1886	Miss Elia A. Fuller,	Sironcha, India,	
1884	Miss Mary De F. Loyd,	Mexico City, Mexico,	May 28, 1902.
1897	Miss Lillian Harris, M. D,	Pyeng Yang, Korea,	May 16, 1902.
1900	Miss Josephine an,	Quessua, Africa,	July 5, 1902.
1902	Miss Mabel Sia,	Ngu Cheng, China,	November, 1903.
1903	Miss Ida May Cartwright,	Lucknow, India,	April 9, 1904.
1893	Mrs. Anna C. Davis,	Nanking, China,	M y 3, 1904.
1904	Miss Anna Stone,	Kiu Kiang, China,	March 14, 1906.
1884	Miss Mary C. Robinson,	Chin Kiang, China,	April 20, 1906.
1904	Miss Lois M. Buck,	Moradabad, India,	April 17, 197.
1903	Miss Mary B. Tuttle, M. D.,	Pithoragarh, India,	June 22, 197.
1902	Miss Susanna Stumpf,	Jagdalpur, India,	January 26, 197.
1871	Miss Mary Q. Porter, (Mrs. Gamewell),	Peking, China,	November 27, 1906.
1895	Miss Kate O. Curts,	Godhra, India,	January 3, 1908.

RETIRED AFTER TWENTY-FIVE YEARS' SERVICE.

Missionary.	Foreign Stations.	Home Address.
Woolston, Sarah, ...	Foochow, China, . . .	Mt. Holly, N. J.

RETIRED AFTER TWENTY-SEVEN YEARS' SERVICE.

Swain, Clara A., M. D., .	India, ...	Castile, N. Y.

MISSIONARIES

Sent out from America or employed by the Woman's Foreign Missionary Society since its Organization.

m indicates Marriage; *s* Self-Supporting; *r* Retired; *dis*. Dismissed; *d* Deceased.
* Daughters of Missionaries. Name in italics is married name.
Abbreviations, in parenthesis, indicate Branch.

Date of App'm't.	Name and Branch.	Date of App'm't.	Name and Branch.
1905	Aaronsen, Hilma. (Des M.)	1907	Brooks, Jessie. (Minn.)
1901	Abbott, Anna Agnes. (N.-W.)	1899 m	Brouse, Louise T. (*Cook.*) (1905.)
1878 r	Abrams, Minnie F. (1898.)	1871 m	Brown, Maria. (*Davis.*) (1874.)
1900 s	Adams, Jeanette.	1891 r	Bryan, Mary E., M. D. (1897.)
1882 m	Akers, L. Stella, M. D. (*Perkins.*) (1885.)	1880 *	Budden, Annie. (N. Y.)
		1904 d *	Buck, Lois M. (Cin.)
1907	Albertson, Millie. (Cin.)	1905	Bullis, Edith M. (N.-W.)
1903	Alexander, Bessie. (Cin.)	1900 m	Bumgardner, Lucy E. (*Morton.*) (1903.)
1888–1907	Allen, Belle J. (N. E.)		
1894	Allen, Mabel. (Des M.)	1908	Bunce, Thirza E. (N. W.)
1894	Alling, Harriet S. (N.-W.)	1898 dis	Burman, Matilda O. (1903.)
1900	Anderson, Luella R. (Cin.)	1905 *	Burt, Edith. (N.-W.)
1908	Ankeney, Jessie V. (D. M.)	1879 r	Bushnell, Kate C., M. D. (1882.)
1908	Ashbaugh, Adella. (Cin.)	1894 m	Butcher, Annie. (*Hewes.*) (1896.)
1882	Atkinson, Anna P. (N. Y.)	1907 r	Campbell, Margaret, M. D. (Cin.)
1888 r	Atkinson, Mary.	1875 d	Campbell, Lettia A. (*Coleman.*) (1878.)
1905	Austin, F. Laura. (C. R.)		
1886	Ayers, Harriet L. (Cin.)	1876 m	Carey, Mary F. (*Davis.*) (1880.)
1907	Baker, Lulu C. (Cin.)	1898 m	Carver, Margaret B. (*Ernsberger.*)
1895 m	Barrow, Mrs. M. L., M. D. (*King.*) (1900.)	1888 d	Carroll, Mary E. (1897.)
1904	Bartlett, Carrie M. (Des M.)	1887	Carleton, Mary E., M. D. (N. Y.)
1890 s	Baucus, Georgiana.	1908	Carncross, Flora. (N. W.)
1907	Baugh, Evelyn B. (Pacif.)	1903 d	Cartwright, Ida May. (1904.)
1902 m	Beard, Bertha. (*Gasson.*) (1903.)	1874 r	Chapin, Jennie M. (1890.)
1900 m	Beazell, Laura E. (*Andres.*) (1903.)	1904 m	Chisholm, Emma Mae. (*Brown.*) (1906.)
1902 m	Beck, Edna L., M. D. (*Keisler.*) (1906.)	1884 r	Christiancy, Mary, M. D. (1891.)
		1894 m	Christinsen, Christine. (*Ashe.*) (1896.)
1889 r	Bender, Elizabeth R. (Balt.)		
1890 m	Bengel, Margaret. (*Jones.*) (1892.)	1879 r	Clemens, Mrs. E. J. (1881.)
1890	Benn, Rachel R., M. D. (Phila.)	1904 r	Clippenger, Frances. (1905.)
1901	Bennett, Fannie A. (N.-W.)	1900	Cody, Mary. (Cin.) (1904.)
1896	Benthein, Emma M. (N.-W.)	1906	Coffin, Sophia J. (N. Y.)
1882 m	Benton, J. Emma. (*Elmer.*) (1885.)	1895	Collier, Clara J. (N. E.)
		1901	Collins, Susan. (Pacif.)
1904	Betow, Emma J., M. D. (Cin.)	1894 m	Collins, Ruth H. (*Thoburn.*) (1899.)
1907	Betz, Blanche. (N.-W.)		
1906	Bills, Grace Ida. (N.-W.)	1873 m	Combs, Lucinda, M. D. (*Strittmater.*) (1878.)
1888	Bing, Anna V. (Cin.)		
1888 r	Black, Lillian A. (1889.)	1905 r	Cook, Celinda. (1907.)
1892	Blackburn, Kate B. (N. W.)	1905 r	Cook, Rosalie. (1907.)
1872 m	Blackmar, Louisa. (*Gilder.*) (1900.)	1884 m	Corey, Katherine, M. D. (*Ford.*) (1888.)
1887	Blackmore, Sophia. (Minn.)	1905	Crabtree, M. Margaret. (Cin.)
1889	Blackstock, Ella. (Minn.)	1892 m	Craig, Frances. (*Smith.*) (1895.)
1905	Blackstock, Isabella Thoburn. (Phila.)	1904	Crane, Edith M. (N.-W.)
		1907	Crawford, Mabel. (Des M.)
1888	Blair, Kate A. (Cin.)	1905	Creek, Bertha. (N.-W.)
1897	Bobenhouse, Laura G. (Des M.)	1904	Crooks, Grace A. (N.-W.)
1900 r	Bohannon, Ida. (N.-W.) (1908.)	1892 dis	Crosthwaite, Isabella. (1893.)
1888	Bonafield, Julia A. (Cin.)	1895 m	Croucher, Miranda. (*Packard.*) (1903.)
1907	Borg, Jennie. (Top.)		
1897 dis	Boss, Harriet. (1898)	1906	Crouse, Margaret D. (Phila.)
1888 m	Bowen, Mary E. (*Brown.*) (1898.)	1905	Crowell, Bessie F. (N. E.)
1906	Bowman, M. Rebecca. (Top.)	1895 d	Curts, Kate O. (1908.)
1897 m	Bowne, Ida May. (*Manfre.*) (1903.)	1893	Cutler, Mary F., M. D. (N. Y.)
		1880 r	Cushman, Clara M. (1889.)
1906	Brethorst, Alice. (Minn.)	1890 r	Daily, Rebecca. (1897.)

Date of App'm't.	Name and Branch.
1888 r	Danforth, Mary A. (1893.)
1897 s	Daniel, N. Margaret. (Des M.)
1895 m	Dart, Jennie M., M. D. (Dease.) (1898.)
1892 d	Davis, Mrs. Anna L. (1904.)
1900	Davis, Dora. (N.-W.)
1902	Davis, Joanna. (Des M.)
1902 m	Davison, Mabel. (Smart.) (1907.)
1888 m	Day, Martha E. (Abbott.) (1894.)
1896 m	Deaver, Ida C. (1897)
1908 m	Deavitt, La Dona. (Rosenberg.) (1907.)
1899 m	Decker, Helen M. (Beech.)
1905	Decker, Marguerite M. (Pac.)
1884 r	De Line, Sarah M. (1895.)
1891 r	De Motte, Mary. (Doering.)
1873 r	Denning, Lou B. (1890.)
1882 m	De Vine, Esther J. (Williams.) (1891.)
1888	Dickerson, Augusta. (Phila.)
1897 s	Dickinson, Emma E.
1893 r	Donahue, Julia M., M. D. (1897.)
1884 d	Downey, Clara A. (1896.)
1906	Draper, Frances L., M. D. (N.-W.)
1899 r	Dreibelbies, Caroline. (1906.)
1906	Driesbach, Gertrude I. (Top.)
1906	Drummer, Martha A. (Pacif.)
1907	Dudley, Rose E. (Col. R.)
1890 r	Dudley, Hannah. (1891.)
1891	Dunmore, Effie. (Phila.)
1907	Dyer, Clara P. (N. E.)
1894–06	Easton, Celesta. (Pacif.) (1900.)
1878 s	Easton, S. A. (Cin.)
1902	Eddy, Mrs. S. M. (Cin.)
1901	Edmonds, Agnes M., M. D. (Des M.)
1902	Edmunds, Margaret J. (Harrison.) (1908.)
1894	Elicker, Anna R. (Des M.)
1897 m	Elliott, Martelle. (Davis.) (1904.)
1879 m	Elliott, Margaret. (Wilson.) (1883.)
1895 d	Elliott, Mary C. (Stephens.) (1886.)
1886 r	Elliott, Mary J. (1890.)
1900 r	Ellis, Ida. (N.-W.) (1908.)
1884	English, Fannie M. (N. Y.)
1908	Erbst, Wilhelmina. (Minn.)
1906	Ericson, Judith. (Top.)
1899	Ernsberger, Emma, M. D. (Cin.)
1888 r	Ernsberger, I., M. D. (1900.)
1900	Estey, Ethel M. (N. Y.)
1895	Evans, Alice A. (Des M.)
1883 d	Everding, Emma J. (1892.)
1899 m	Ewers, Harriet C. (Lyons.) (1900.)
1903	Fenderich, Norma H. (Phila.)
1892 m	Ferris, Emma E. (Shellabear.) (1897.)
1887 r	Field, Nellie H. (1888.)
1888	Files, Estelle M. (N. Y.)
1887 r	Fincham, Ella B. (1894.)
1905	Finlay, Alice. (Cin.)
1884 m	Fisher, Elizabeth. (Brewster.) (1888)
1896	Fisher, Fannie F. (N.-W.)
1908	Fonda, Edith L. (N. W.)
1890 m	Forbes, Ella R. (Phillips.) (1894.)
1893 r	Foster, Eva M. (1895.)
1902	Foster, Carrie. (Des M.)
1898 m	Forster, Miriam. (N.-W.)
1908	Frazey, Laura. (Top.)
1889 m	French, Anna S. (Freyer.) (1895.)
1891 r	Frey, Cecelia M. (1894.)
1893	Frey, Lulu E. (Cin.)
1886 d	Fuller, Delia A. (1901.)

Date of App'm't.	Name and Branch.
1908	Gabrielson, Winnie. (Top.)
1906	Galbreath, Elizabeth. (Cin.)
1887	Gallimore, Anna. (1903.)
1894	Galloway, Helen R. (Des M.)
1908	Gardner, Minnie. (Top.)
1879	Gheer, Jean M. (N. Y.)
1878 r	Gibson, Eugenia. (Mitchell.) (1882.)
1881 d	Gilchrist, Ella, M. D. (1884.)
1905	Gimson, Esther, M. D. (N.-W.)
1896	Gilman, Gertrude. (N. E.)
1908	Glassburner, Mamie F. (Des M.)
1898 m	Glenk, Marguerite E. (Burley.) (1905.)
1885	Gloss, Anna D., M. D. (N.-W.)
1892	Glover, Ella E. (N. E.)
1900 m	Goetz, Adeline. (Guthrie.) (1901.)
1908	Golisch, Anna L. (D. M.)
1880 m	Goodenough, Julia E. (Hudson.) (1886.)
1895 r	Goodin, E. S. (1899.)
1905 s	Grandstrand, Pauline. (Minn.)
1894	Greene, Lily D. (N.-W.)
1876 d	Green, Lucilla H., M.D. (Cheney.) (1878.)
1899 s	Gregg, Mary E. (Des M.)
1889	Griffiths, Mary B. (Des M.)
1905 s	Grove, Mrs. H. L. R. (N.-W.)
1878 d	Guelphi, Cecilia. (1886.)
1908	Guthapfel, Minerva L. (Phila.)
1888 m	Hale, Lillian G. (Scott-Welday.) (1894.)
1890–97	Hall, Mrs. R. S., M. D. (N. Y.)
1885 r	Hall, Emma M. (1900.)
1907	Hallman, Sarah B. (Balt.)
1883 dis	Hamisfar, Florence N., M. D. (1886.)
1900 m	Hammond, Alice J. (Sharp.) (1903.)
1892 r	Hammond, Rebecca J. (1899.)
1881	Hampton, Mary S. (N. Y.)
1895	Hardie, Eva M. (Cin.)
1892 m	Harrington, Susan. (Cousland.) (1893.)
1895 d	Harris, Lillian, M. D. (1902.)
1891 m	Harris, Mary W. (Folwell.) (1894.)
1893 r	Harris, Nellie M. (1895.)
1904 m	Hart, Ma y Ames. (Briggs.) (1908.)
1887	Hartford, Mabel C. (N. E.)
1884	Harvey, Emily L. (N. E.)
1874 d	Hastings, Mary. (1898.)
1906	Haynes, Emily Irene. (N. Y.)
1891 r	Heafer, Louise. (1907.)
1893	Heaton, Carrie A. (N.-W)
1892 m	Hebinger, Josephine. (Snuggs.) (1894)
1884 m	Hedrick, M. C. (Miles.) (1890.)
1898	Hemingway, Edith A. (N. E.)
1901	Henkle, Nianette. (Des M.)
1904 dis	Henry, Mary. (1906.)
1884	Hewitt, Ella J. (Phila.)
1886	Hewett, Lizzie. (N.-W.)
1904	Hewitt, Helen. (N.-W.)
1878 d	Higgins, Susan B. (1879)
1905	Hill, Katherine Ledyard. (Phila.)
1900	Hillman, Mary R. (Cin.)
1905 m	Hitchcock, Frances H. (Ricker.) (1908.)
1872	Hoag, Lucy, M. D. (N. Y.)
1895 m	Hodge, Emma, M.D. (Worrall.) (1899.)
1906	Hoffman, Carlotta. (N.-W.)
1892	Hoge, Elizabeth. (Cin.)

Date of App'm't.	Name and Branch.
1901 r	Holbrook, Ella M. (Pacif.)
1878 m	Holbrook, Mary J. (*Chapman.*) (1890.)
1900	Holman, Charlotte T. (Pacif.)
1906	Holland, Harriet A. (N.-W.)
1905	Holland, Ary. (Top.)
1904	Holland, Mrs. Alma H. (Des M.)
1905	Holmes, Ada. (O. R.)
1905	Hollister, Grace. (Cin.)
1906	Honsinger, Welthy B. (N. Y.)
1877 m	Howard, Leonora, M. D. (*King.*) (1884.)
1887 r	Howard, Meta, M. D. (1889.)
1879 r	Howe, Delia A. (1882.)
1872	Howe, Gertrude. (N.-W.)
1881 m	Hoy, Ellen I. (*Lawson.*) (1884.)
1895	Hu, King Eng, M. D. (Phila.)
1904	Hu, May. (Des M.)
1908	Huelster, Luella. (Minn.)
1883 m	Hugoboom, Marion. (1884.)
1887 d	Hughes, Mary. (*Ernsberger.*) (1890.)
1905	Hughes, Jennie V. (N. Y.)
1883 m	Hyde, Laura, M.D (*Foote*) (1886.)
1888 m	Hyde, Minnie Z. (*Wilson.*) (1894.)
1897 m	Hyde, Nettie M. (*Felt.*) (1907.)
1898	Illingworth, Charlotte. (Phila.)
1889	Imhof, Louisa. (Top.)
1899 s	Ingram, Helen. (Minn.)
1902	Jackson, C. Ethel. (N.-W.)
1902 m	Jakobson, Alma. (*Keventer.*) (1904.)
1906	James, Phebe. (Top.)
1908	Jaquet, Myra. (N.-W.)
1884	Jewell, Carrie I. (Cin.)
1883	Jewell, Mrs. O. M. (N. Y.)
1907	Jones, Edna. (Balt.)
1908	Jones, Dorothy. (N.-W.)
1894 r	Johnson, Anna.
1888 m	Johnson, Ella. (*Kinnear.*) (1893.)
1896 *	Kahn, Ida, M. D. (N.-W.)
1886 m	Kaulbach, Anna L. (*Wilson.*) (1889.)
1892 m	Keeler, Anna C. (*Manson.*) (1899.)
1880 dis	Kelly, Luella. (1885.)
1891 r	Kemper, Harriet. (1895.)
1891 m	Kennedy, Mary E. (*Core.*) (1894.)
1881 d	Kerr, Harriet. (1886.)
1888-05	Ketring, Mary, M. D.
1894	Kidwell, Lola May. (Cin.)
1893 m	Kissack, Sadie E. (*McCartney.*) (1896.)
1900	Kneeland, Bertha E. (N. E.)
1881	Knowles, Emma L. (N. E.)
1906	Knox, Emma M. (N.-W.)
1904	Koons, Sue L., M. D. (Phila.)
1902 r	Kurtz, Alice W. (Phila.) (1903.)
1885	Kyle, Theresa J. (Phila.)
1896 dis	Lamb, Emma L. (1901.)
1884 r	Latimer, Laura. (1888.)
1892	Lauck, Ada J. (Des M.)
1885 m	Lauck, Sarah. (*Parson.*) (1888.)
1886	Lawson, Anna E. (Des M.)
1892	Lawson, Christine. (N. Y.)
1878 d	Layton, M. E. (1892.)
1898	Lebeus. Martha. (Cin.)
1894 m	Lee, Irene E. (*Ver Mehr.*) (1901.)
1903	Lee, Mabel. (Minn.)
1884	LeHuray, Eleanor. (N. Y.)
1873 m	Leming, Sarah. (*Shepherd.*) (1875.)
1898	Lewis, Amy G. (Balt.)
1891 r	Lewis, Ella A. (Balt.) (1904.)
1901	Lewis, Margaret D., M. D.(N.-W.)

Date of App'm't.	Name and Branch.
1897	Lilly, May B. (Col. R.)
1890	Limberger, Anna R. (Phila.)
1895	Linam, Alice. (N. Y.)
1897	Livermore, Melva A. (Top.)
1901 s r	Llewellyn, Alice A. (Phila.) (1906.)
1905	Logeman, Minnie. (N.-W.)
1905 *	Long, Hortense. (N. Y.)
1898	Longstreet, Isabella D. (N.-W.)
1898	Loper, I. Grace. (N. Y.)
1874 m*	Lore, Julia A., M. D. (*McGrew.*) (1876.)
1904	Lorenz, Frieda V. (Minn.)
1904	Lossing, Mabel. (Des M.)
1884 d	Loyd, Mary De. F. (1902.)
1890	Lyon, M. Ellen, M. D. (N.-W.)
1899	Manning, Ella. (D. M.)
1884 m*	Mansel, Hester V. (*Monroe.*) (1889.)
1904 r	Marble, Elizabeth Dana.
1894 m	Marks, Lillian R. (*Kelley.*) (1903.)
1905	Marker, Jessie B. (Cin.) (Pacif.)
1901	Marriott, Jessie A. (N. E.)
1906	Marsh, Jessie L. (N.-W.)
1897	Martin, Clara. (Minn.)
1900	Martin, Elizabeth E. (N.-W.)
1900	Martin, Emma E., M. D. (N.-W.)
1899	Maskell, Florence. (Des M.)
1874 m d	Mason, Letitia, M. D. (*Quine.*) (1875.)
1892 r	Masters, Luella, M. D. (1905.)
1888	Maxey, Elizabeth. (N. Y.)
1888 m	McBurnie, Susan. (*Bond.*) (1894.)
1886 r	McDowell, Kate, M. D. (1891.)
1893 m	McGregor, Kate, M. D. (*Boomer.*) (1895.)
1904 r	McHose, Lottie. (Cin.) (1904.)
1883 m	McKesson. (*Conkling.*) (1886.)
1900 d	McKibben, Martha L. (1900.)
1900 m	McKinley, Mary B. (*Younglove.*) (1906.)
1907	McKinney, Alice. (N. Y.)
1901	McKnight, Isabel. (Top.)
1871 m	McMillan, Carrie. (*Buck.*) (1872.)
1897	Means, Alice. (Cin.)
1896	Means, Mary. (Cin.)
1900 r	Meek, Mrs. Mary C. (1905.)
1900 d	Mekkelson, Josephine. (1902.)
1897	Melton, Mary E. (N.-W.)
1896	Merrill, Clara E. (N.-W.)
1894 r	Meyer, Fannie E. (1903.)
1880 d	Michener, Emma. (1881.)
1901	Miller, Lulu A. (N. Y.)
1900 m	Miller, Martha J. (*Jones.*) (1904.)
1886 dis	Miller, Oriel. (1889.)
1901 r	Miller, Sara H. (1903.)
1888 r	Mitchell, Emma L. (1906.)
1873 r	Monelle, Nancy, M. D. (*Mansell.*) (1874.)
1902	Montgomery, Urdell. (Top.)
1900 r	Moore, Alice M. (1903.)
1900 r	Moots, Mrs. Cornelia. (1902.)
1904	Morgan, Cora. (Top.)
1899	Moyer, Jennie E. (N. Y.)
1904 *	Mudge, Ada. (N. E.)
1908	Muir, Winnifred. (N.-W.)
1878 r	Mulliner, Clara. (1883.)
1892 r	Neiger, Lillian. (1895.)
1906	Nelson, E. Lavina. (Top.)
1906	Nelson, Lena O. (Top.)
1905	Newby, Alta. (Des M.)
1898 r m	Newton, Marion. (1902.)
1896	Nicholls, Elizabeth W. (N. Y.)
1894	Nichols, Florence L. (N. E.)
1880 d	Nickerson, Florence. (1887.)

Date of App'm't.	Name and Branch.
1899	Nicholaisen, Martha L. (Minn.)
1906	Nolele, Edith. (Minn.)
1903 *	Northrup, Alice M. (N.-W.)
1900 r	Norton, Anna J., M. D. (1905.)
1900	Odgers, Evaline A. (N.-W.)
1891	Ogborn, Kate L. (D. M.)
1876 d	Ogden, Henrietta C. (1889.)
1903	Olsen, Mary E. (Minn.)
1899	Organ, Clara M. (1905.) (N. E.)
1894 m	Otto, Alice M. (Selby.) (1900.)
1900	Pak, Esther K., M. D. (Phila.)
1904	Payne, Ella E. (Phila.)
1892	Paine, Josephine O. (N. E.)
1888 d	Pardoe, Mary E. V. (1892.)
1889 r	Parker, Theda A. (1893.)
1903	Parkes, Elizabeth. (Pacif.)
1899	Parkinson, Phoebe A. (Col. R.)
1906	Parish, Rebecca, M. D. (N.-W.)
1890	Perkins, Fannie A. (Des M.)
1888 m	Perrine, Florence. (Mansell.) (1894.)
1904	Peters, Alice. (N.-W.)
1903	Peters, Jessie I. (N.-W.)
1894	Peters, Mary. (N.-W.)
1888	Peters, Sarah. (N.-W.)
1889	Phelps, Frances E. (Des M.)
1897 m	Pierce, Nellie. (Miller.) (1905.)
1902 r	Pierce, Thirza M. (N.-W.) (1908.)
1900 *	Plumb, Florence J. (N. Y.)
1903	Pool, Lydia S. (Des M.)
1896 m	Porter, Charlotte J. (1901.)
1871 m d	Porter, Mary Q. (Gamewell.) (1882.) (1907.)
1906	Powell, Alice M. (N. Y.)
1886 r	Pray, Susan, M. D. (1887.)
1878 r	Priest, Mary A. (1880.)
1906	Pugh, Ada. (Minn.)
1872 d	Pultz, Elizabeth M. (1877.)
1895	Purdy, Caroline M. (Phila.)
1902 m	Pyne, Rosa M. (Berry.) (1906.)
1900 m	Rasmussen, Mrs. Helen E. (Springer.) (1905.)
1906	Rank, Minnie L. (Minn.)
1884	Reed, Mary. (Cin.)
1906	Reynolds, Elsie. (Des M.)
1900	Rigby, Luella. (Des M.)
1902	Robbins, Henrietta. (N. Y.)
1907	Robinson, Alvina. (Des. M.)
1902 *	Robinson, Helen. (N. Y.)
1884 d	Robinson, Mary C. (1906.)
1900 *	Robinson, Ruth E. (Balt.)
1889 m	Rodgers, Anna M. (Furness.) (1890.)
1887 r	Rothweiler, Louise C. (1898.)
1894 m	Rouse, Wilma H. (Keene.) (1905.)
1881 d	Rowe, Phoebe. (1898.)
1900 m	Rowley, Mary L. (Wilson.) (1904.)
1901	Ruddick, Elizabeth May. (N. E.)
1887 m	Rulofsen, G. M. (Thompson.) (1888.)
1879	Russell, Elizabeth. (Cin.)
1895	Russell, M. Helen. (Pacif.) (1897-1907.)
1899 m	Samson, Carrie J. (Sunder.) (1903.)
1908	Santee, Helen. (Phil.)
1904	Saxe, Agnes E. (N. Y.)
1884 d	Schenck, Linna M. (1892.)
1895 m	Schockley, Mary E. (Drake.) (1904.)
1874 m	Schoonmaker, Dora. (Soper.) (1879.)
1889	Scott, Frances A. (Cin.)
1896	Scott, Emma, M. D. (Cin.)
1885	Scranton, Mrs. M. F. (N. E.)

Date of App'm't.	Name and Branch.
1880 d	Sears, Annie B. (1895.)
1890	Seeds, Leonora H. (Cin.)
1902	Seeds, Mabel K. (N.-W.)
1908	Seidlmann, Paula. (Cin.)
1889 s	Sellers, Rue E. (Cin.)
1879 dis	Sharpe, Mary (1883.)
1908	Sharp, Mrs. Rob't. (N. Y.)
1887	Shaw, Ella C. (N.-W.)
1888 s	Sheldon, Martha A., M.D. (N.E.)
1890 m	Sherwood, Rosetta, M.D. (Hall.) (1892-1896.)
1905	Shibati, Suye. (Top.)
1902 d	Sia, Mabel. (1903.)
1904	Sia, Ruby. (D. M.)
1903 r	Siddall, Adelaide. (1904.)
1905	Simester, Mary. (N. E.)
1906	Simonds, Mildred. (Des M.)
1889 d	Simonds, Maud E. (1898.)
1907	Simpson, Cora. (N.-W.)
1893	Singer, Florence E. (Phila.)
1900	Singh, Lilavati. (N.-W.)
1891 *	Sites, Ruth M. (Brown.) (1895.)
1901	Slate, Anna B. (Phila.)
1885	Smith, Lida B. (N. Y.)
1907	Smith, Adelina. (N.-W.)
1906	Snavely, Gertrude E. (Phila.)
1896 r	Soderstrom, Anna. (1901.)
1903 *	Soper, E. Maud. (Phila.)
1900 r	Southard, Ada J. (1905.)
1870 r	Sparkes, Fannie J. (1891.)
1878 m	Sparr, Julia, M. D. (Coffin.) (1883.)
1902 r	Spaulding, Winifred. (Top.) (1907.)
1896 m	Spear, Katherine A. (Collier.) (1900.)
1880 m	Spence, Mattie B. (Perrie.) (1883.)
1896 r	Spencer, Clarissa H. (1901.)
1878	Spencer, Matilda A. (Phila.)
1906	Sprowles, Alberta. (Phila.)
1892	Stahl, Josephine. (N.-W.)
1895 m	Stanton, Alice. M. (Woodruff.) (1899.)
1900 m	Stearns, Mary P. (Badley.)
1889 r	Steere, Anna E. (N.-W.)
1892	Stephens, Grace. (Balt.)
1895 d	Sterling, Florence. (Leuth.) (1897.) (1900.)
1890	Stevenson, Ida B., M. D. (Top.)
1906	Stixrud, Louise. (Minn.)
1901 m	Stockwell, Emma. (Price.) (1903.)
1901	Stockwell, Grace. (Des M.)
1904 d	Stone, Anna. (1906.)
1896	Stone, Mary, M. D. (Des M.)
1907	Stout, Winifred. (N.-W.)
1906	Strawick, Gertrude. (N.-W.)
1904	Strow, Elizabeth M. (N. Y.)
1908	Stryker, Minnie, M. D. (Phil.)
1902 d	Stumpf, Susanna M. (1907.)
1888 s	Sullivan, Lucy. (Cin.)
1908	Sutton, Daisy B. (Cin.)
1907	Sutton, Marianne. (Minn.)
1869 r	Swain, Clara A., M. D. (1896.)
1905	Swan, Hilda. (Top.)
1878	Swaney, Mary F. (Top.)
1902	Swift, Edith T. (N.-W.)
1903 m	Swormstedt, Virginia R. (Coffin.) (1907.)
1895	Taft, Gertrude, M. D. (Pacif.)
1906	Tang, Ilien. (Minn.)
1889 m	Taylor, Martha E. (Callahan.) (1893.)
1903	Temple, Laura. (N. Y.)
1908	Terrell, Linnie. (Cin.)
1887	Terry, Edna G., M. D. (N.E.)

16

Date of App'm't.	Name and Branch.
1869 *d*	Thoburn, Isabella. (1901.)
1904	Thomas, Mary M. (Cin.)
1903	Thomas, Hettie (Cin.)
1889 *m*	Thompson, Anna. (*Stephens*.) (1895.)
1890 *r*	Thompson, E.
1871 *m*	Tinsley, Jennie M. (*Waugh*.) (1876.)
1901	Tippet, Mrs. Susan. (Balt.)
1895	Todd, Althea M. (N. E.)
1897 *r*	Todd, Grace. (1898.)
1904	Toll, Evelyn. (N.-W.)
1908	Tracy, Alethea W. (N. Y.)
1874 *m*	Trask, Sigourney, M.D. (*Cowles*.) (1885.)
1903	Travis, Grace B. (N. Y.)
1889	Trimble, Lydia A. (Des M.)
1895 *r*	Tryon, Elizabeth. (1900.)
1890 *m*	Tucker, Grace. (*Tague*.) (1896.)
1905	Turner, Mrs. Maud N. (Top.)
1881 *r*	Turney, Mrs. L. M. (1882.)
1903 *m*	Turner, Sarah B. (*Parker*.) (1904.)
1903 *d*	Tuttle, Mary B.. M. D. (1907)
1907	Tuttle, Ora B. (Cin.)
1889 *m*	Van Dorsten, Amelia. (*Lawyer*.) (1894.)
1887 *d*	Vance, Mary A. (*Belknap*.) (1892.)
1881	Van Petten, Mrs. Carrie. (N.-W.)
1898	Varney, Elizabeth W. (Top.)
1891 *r*	Vickery, M. Ella. (1906.)
1908	Voigt, Mary. (N. W.)
1896 *r*	Waidman, Isabel. (1899.)
1906	Wallace, L. Ethel. (Balt.)
1908	Walker, Susan. (N.-W.)
1890 *m*	Walton, Ida B. (*Multer*.) (1891.)
1880 *m*	Warner, Ellen. (*Fox*.) (1885.)
1873 *m*	Warner, Susan N. (*Densmore*.) (1892.)
1883	Watson, Rebecca J. (Top.)
1904 *	Waugh, Nora Belle. (Cin.)
1902	Weaver, Georgia. (N. Y.)
1905	Wells, Anna May. (Des M.)
1901	Wells, Elizabeth J. (Des M.)
1895	Wells, Phebe. (N. Y.)
1902	Westcott, Pauline E. (N.-W.)
1881 *	Wheeler, Frances. (*Verity*.) (1893.)

Date of App'm't.	Name and Branch.
1908 *	Wheeler, Maud. (N -W.)
1891	White, Laura M. (Phila.)
1876 *m*	Whiting, Olive. (*Bishop*.) (1882.)
1904	Whittaker, Lottie M. (Minn.)
1906	Widney, May C. (Top.)
1896 *m*	Widdifield, Flora M. (*Chew*.) (1898.)
1892 *m*	Wilkinson. Lydia M. (*Wilkinson*.) (1905.)
1901 *m*	Williams, Christiana. (*Hall*.) (1902.)
1900	Williams. Mary E. (Phila.)
1896 *m*	Wilson, Fannie G. (*Alexander*.) (1900.)
1889	Wilson, Frances O. (Des M.)
1889 *m*	Wilson, Mary E. (*Buchanan*.) (1896.)
1893	Wilson, Minnie E. (N.-W.)
1894 *	Wilson, Mary E. (N.-W.)
1901	Winslow, Annie M. (Top.)
1885	Wisner, Julie E. (Cin.)
1905 *m*	Witte, Helena. (N.-W.)
1903 *m*	Wood, Bertha L. (*Robbins*.) (1906.)
1892	Wood, Catherine A. (Des M.)
1889 *	Wood, Elsie. (N. Y)
1901	Woods, Grace M. (N. Y.)
1880 *m*	Woodsworth, Kate. (*Quinn*.) (1883.)
1871 *d*	Woolston, Beulah. (1886)
1878 *d*	Woolston, Henrietta, M.D. (1879.)
1871 *r*	Woolston, Sarah H. (1896.)
18·5	Wright, Laura S. (N.-W.)
1880 *r*	Yates. Elizabeth U. (1885.)
1892	Young, Effie G. (N. E.)
1897	Young, Mariana. (Cin.)
1898 *d*	Zentmire, Cora. (*Brewster*.) (1900.)

Missionaries	568
Medical	57
Married	118
Retired	81
Self-supporting	13
Daughters of Missionaries	21
Deceased	44
Dismissed	9

CONSTITUTION

Woman's Foreign Missionary Society of the Methodist Episcopal Church.

ARTICLE I.—NAME.

This organization shall be called "THE WOMAN'S FOREIGN MISSIONARY SOCIETY OF THE METHODIST EPISCOPAL CHURCH."

ARTICLE II.—PURPOSE.

The purpose of this Society is to engage and unite the efforts of Christian women in sending missionaries to the women in foreign mission fields of the Methodist Episcopal Church, and in supporting them and native Christian teachers and Bible readers in those fields and all forms of work carried on by the Society.

ARTICLE III.—MEMBERSHIP.

The payment of one dollar annually shall constitute Membership, and twenty dollars Life Membership. Any person paying one hundred dollars shall become a Manager for Life, and the contribution of three hundred dollars shall constitute the donor a Patron for Life.

ARTICLE IV.—ORGANIZATION.

The organization of this Society shall consist of a General Executive Committee, Co-ordinate Branches, District Associations, Auxiliary Societies, to be constituted and limited as laid down in subsequent articles.

ARTICLE V.—GENERAL EXECUTIVE COMMITTEE.

The management and general administration of the affairs of the Society shall be vested in a General Executive Committee consisting of a President, Vice-president, Recording Secretary, Treasurer, the Corresponding Secretary the member of the Home Board and two delegates from each Branch, or such other persons as the Constitution of the said Society shall hereafter from time to time provide.

The President, Recording Secretary, Treasurer, and Secretaries of German and Scandinavian Work shall be elected annually by the General Executive Committee. The two delegates and reserves shall be elected at the Branch annual meetings. Said committee shall meet in Boston the third Wednesday in April, 1870, and annually, or oftener, thereafter, at such time and place as the General Executive Committee shall annually determine.

SEC. 2. The duties of the General Executive Committee shall be:

First—To take into consideration the interests and demands of the entire work of the Society as presented in the reports of the Branch Corresponding Secretaries and in the estimates of the needs of mission fields; to ascertain the financial condition of the Society; to appropriate its money in accordance with the purposes and method therein indicated;

to devise means for carrying forward the work of the Society; fixing the amounts to be raised, employing new missionaries, designating their field of labor, examining the reports of those already employed, and arranging with the several Branches the work to be undertaken by each.

Second—To transact any other business that the interests of the Society may demand, provided all the plans and directions of the Committee shall be in harmony with the provisions of the Constitution.

ARTICLE VI.—Permanent Committee of Woman's Foreign Missionary Society.

Reference Committee.

1. The Committee of Reference shall be composed of the President of the Woman's Foreign Missionary Society and the Branch Corresponding Secretaries.

2. It shall meet immediately after the adjournment of the General Executive Committee and organize by the election of a Chairman and Secretary.

3. All cases of emergency that would come before the General Executive Committee, arising in the interim of its sessions, shall be submitted to this Committee, and decided by a majority vote.

4. The Chairman shall send each resolution that is submitted to the committee to each member, and when all have returned their votes, the Recording Secretary shall declare the result, and record both resolutions and votes.

5. The Committee shall present a full report of its action during the year, to the General Executive Committee for approval and permanent record.

6. This committee shall hold a semi-annual meeting, at such time and place as shall be designated by the Chairman and Secretary. The expenses of this meeting shall be paid from the general treasury.

ARTICLE VII.—Co-ordinate Branches.

Section 1. Co-ordinate Branches of this Society, on their acceptance of this relationship under the provisions of the Constitution, may be organized in accordance with the following general plan for districting the territory of the Church:

Name.	States Included.	Headquarters.
New England Branch		Boston, Mass.
	New England States.	
New York Branch		New York, N. Y.
	New York, New Jersey.	
Philadelphia Branch		Philadelphia, Pa.
	Pennsylvania and Delaware.	
Baltimore Branch		Baltimore, Md.
	Maryland, District of Columbia, Eastern Virginia, North and South Carolina, Georgia, and Florida.	
Cincinnati Branch		Cincinnati, O.
	Ohio, West Virginia, Kentucky, Tennessee, Alabama, and Mississippi.	
Northwestern Branch		Chicago, Ill.
	Illinois, Indiana, Michigan, Wisconsin.	

Name.	States Included.	Headquarters.
Des Moines Branch	Iowa, Missouri, Arkansas, and Louisiana.	Des Moines, Iowa
Minneapolis Branch	Minnesota, North and South Dakota.	Minneapolis, Minn.
Topeka Branch	Kansas, Nebraska, Colorado, Wyoming, Utah, Texas, New Mexico, and Oklahoma.	Topeka, Kan.
Pacific Branch	California, Nevada, Arizona, and Hawaii.	Los Angeles, Cal.
Columbia River Branch	Montana, Idaho, Washington, and Oregon.	Portland, Ore.

This plan, however, may be changed by an affirmative vote of three-fourths of the members of the General Executive Committee present at any annual meeting of the same.

SEC. 2. The officers of each Branch shall consist of a President, one or more Vice-Presidents, a Recording Secretary, a Corresponding Secretary, a Treasurer, an Auditor, and such other officers as shall be necessary for the efficient work of the Branch. These, with the exception of the Auditor, shall constitute an Executive Committee for the administration of the affairs of the Branch, nine of whom shall be a quorum for the transaction of business. These officers shall be elected at the annual meeting of the Branch, and shall continue in office until others are chosen in their stead.

SEC. 3. The Executive Committee shall have supervision of the work assigned to the Branch by the General Executive Committee, provide for all the needs, and receive reports from all forms of work carried on by the Society, which, by the plan of the General Executive Committee, are to be supported by the Branch,

SEC. 4. Each Branch shall appoint a Standing Committee of not less than five, of which the Branch Corresponding Secretary shall be Chairman, who shall investigate the case of any candidate within the limits of the Branch, and shall supply such candidates with blanks for health certificate and constitutional questions, to be filled out and answered by her; and, when practicable, a personal interview shall be had with the woman by two or more of the Committee before her papers are forwarded to the Reference Committee, or the Committee appointed at the General Executive meeting. The Corresponding Secretary of the Branch presenting missionary candidates shall have a personal interview w th each woman presented before her final appointment to a foreign field.

SEC. 5. No Branch shall project new work, or undertake the support of new missionaries, except by the direction or with the approval of the General Executive Committee.

SEC. 6. Each Branch may make such By-Laws as may be deemed necessary to its efficiency, not inconsistent with this Constitution.

ARTICLE VIII.—DISTRICT ASSOCIATIONS.

District Associations shall be formed wherever practicable; said associations to have supervision of all Auxiliaries within their limits.

ARTICLE IX.—Auxiliary Societies.

Any number of women who shall contribute annually, may form a Society Auxiliary to that Branch of the Woman's Foreign Missionary Society of the Methodist Episcopal Church, within whose prescribed territorial limits they may reside, by appointing a President, one or more Vice-Presidents, a Recording Secretary, a Corresponding Secretary, a Treasurer, and Supervisor of Children's Work, who, together, shall constitute a local Executive Committee.

ARTICLE X.—Relating to the Missionary Authorities of the Church.

Section 1. This Society shall work in harmony with and under the supervision of the authorities of the Missionary Society of the Methodist Episcopal Church. The appointment, recall, and remuneration of missionaries, and the designation of their fields of labor, shall be subject to the approval of the Board of Managers of the Missionary Society of the Methodist Episcopal Church, and annual appropriations to mission fields shall be submitted for revision and approval to the General Missionary Committee of the Methodist Episcopal Church.

Sec. 2. All missionaries sent out by this Society shall labor under the direction of the particular Conference or Mission of the Church in which they may be severally employed. They shall be annually appointed by the President of the Conference on Missions, and shall be subject to the same rules of removal that govern the other missionaries.

Sec. 3. All the work of the Woman's Society in foreign lands shall be under the direction of the Conferences or Missions and their committees, in exactly the same manner as the work of the Missionary Society of the Methodist Episcopal Church, the Superintendent or District Superintendent having the same relation to the work and the person in charge of it that he would have were it a work in charge of any member of the Conference or Mission.

Sec. 4. The funds of the Society shall not be raised by collections or subscriptions taken during any of our regular Church services, nor in any Sunday-school, but shall be raised by such methods as the Constitution of the Society shall provide, none of which shall interfere with the contributions of our people and Sunday-schools for the treasury of the Missionary Society of the Methodist Episcopal Church; and the amount so collected shall be reported by the pastor to the Annual Conference, and be entered in a column among the benevolent collections in the Annual and General Minutes.

Sec. 5. Section 4 of this Article shall not be so interpreted as to prevent the women from taking collections in meetings convened in the interests of their societies; nor from securing memberships and life memberships in audiences where their work is represented, nor from holding festivals, or arranging lectures in the interest of their work.

ARTICLE XI.—Change of Constitution.

This Constitution may be changed at any annual meeting of the General Executive Committee by a three-fourths vote of those present voting, notice of the proposed change having been given at the previous annual meeting; but Article X shall not be changed except with the concurrence of the General Conference of the Methodist Episcopal Church.

BY-LAWS.

I.—Officers.

The officers of the Woman's Foreign Missionary Society shall be a President, Vice-president, Recording Secretary, Treasurer, and such other officers as shall be now or hereafter provided for according to the Constitution in Article V. These officers shall be elected annually by the General Executive Committee.

II.—Duties of Officers.

It shall be the duty of the President to preside at all meetings of the Society, and have authority, with the Recording Secretary and Treasurer, in the interim of the General Executive Committee, to transact all business that requires immediate action.

Of the Vice-president to: (a) Perform all duties of the President in her absence; and (b) render assistance when needed.

Of the Recording Secretary to: (a) Give notice of all meetings of the General Executive Committee.

(b) Keep a full record of all its proceedings, placing the same in the safe of the Publication Office.

(c) Present a report of the year's work at the anniversary of the Society; and

(d) Forward to Foreign Treasurers a copy of the appropriation for each Mission as soon as practicable after the adjournment of the General Executive Committee.

(e) To prepare and print the Annual Report of the Woman's Foreign Missionary Society, including the Minutes of the General Executive Committee.

(f) Prepare and present a Quadrennial Report to the General Conference.

Of the Treasurer to: (a) Receive all money from bequests, gifts, donations, or legacies made to the Woman's Foreign Missionary Society, and, unless otherwise specified by the donor, shall pay the same to the Treasurer of the Branch within whose bounds the donor resided at the time of death.

(b) Receive all money paid into the General Fund by the several Branches, and disburse the same subject to the order of the General Executive Committee.

III.—Duties of Branch Officers.

1. *President.*—(A) There shall be a President and one or more Vice-presidents in each Branch.

(B) It shall be the duty of the Branch President to: (1) Preside at all meetings of the Branch and of its Executive Committee.

(2) Be ex-officio member of all standing committees.

2. *Branch Corresponding Secretaries.*—(A) There shall be a Corresponding Secretary elected by each Branch at its Annual Meeting. These Corresponding Secretaries, together with the President of the Woman's Foreign Missionary Society, shall constitute the Foreign Department of the General Executive Committee to: (1) Consider estimates and make appropriations for the foreign work.

(2) To conduct the official correspondence with the missionaries, and

with missions assigned for such official correspondence; and to present a full report of the same to the General Executive Committee.

(3) Give careful consideration to the requests of missionaries.

(4) Examine and report upon all the testimonials of missionary candidates that are presented by the various Branches.

(5) To consider all matters that may be brought before the General Executive Committee relative to native assistants and workers.

(6) Each Corresponding Secretary shall present to the General Executive Committee a full report of her work, which shall include the following items:

The number of missionaries, Bible-women, boarding-schools, orphans, and other work supported by her Branch, and furnish a copy of the same, together with a report of the receipts and disbursements of the Branch treasury for publication in the Annual Report of the Woman's Foreign Missionary Society.

(B) It shall be the duty in each Branch for the Corresponding Secretary to: (1) Superintend all interests of the Branch pertaining to the foreign field.

(2) Conduct the correspondence of the Branch with foreign missionaries and missionary candidates.

(3) Sign all orders on the Branch Treasurer, including foreign remittances, in accordance with the appropriations.

(4) Give to the Branch all foreign communications, plans, and business of the Branch, essential to the furtherance of the work.

(5) Attend and present a report of her work to all Branch Annual and Quarterly Meetings, and submit an annual report for publication in the Branch Annual Report.

(6) Perform such other duties as the Branch may define.

3. *Branch Associate Secretaries.*—(A) There shall be an Associate Secretary elected by each Branch at its Annual Meeting. These Associate Secretaries, together with the Vice-president of the Woman's Foreign Missionary Society, shall constitute the Home Department of the General Executive Committee to: (1) Superintend the interests of the Home Department, including all publications, the work of the Special Secretaries, and all other interests pertaining to this department.

(2) Present to the General Executive Committee nominations for these offices, and, in each case where salaries are paid, to designate the amount.

(3) To present to the General Executive Committee the annual report of the home work, with statistics by Branches.

(4) To have charge of literature for meetings held outside of the country, and the expenses therefor shall be paid from the General Fund.

(B) The Home Department shall be divided into committees on the various sections of its work.

(C) It shall be the duty *in each Branch* for the Associate Secretary to: (1) Endeavor to advance the interests of the Woman's Foreign Missionary Society "as the necessities of the work require."

(2) To conduct the correspondence: (a) With the Special Secretaries; (b) With Conference Secretaries; (c) With Branch Superintendents and Chairmen of Standing Committees.

(3) Serve as an ex-officio member of all Branch Standing Committees.

(4) Assist in the preparation of the Branch Annual Report.

(5) Attend and present a report of the home work at all Branch Annual and Quarterly Meetings, and submit an annual report, including

statistics by Conferences for publication in the Branch Annual Report, and as required for the Annual Report of the Woman's Foreign Missionary Society, and for the *Woman's Missionary Friend.*

(6) Perform such other duties as the Branch may define.

4. Branch Treasurers.—(A) There shall be a Treasurer elected by each Branch at its Annual Meeting.

(B) It shall be the duty of each Branch Treasurer to: (1) Receive all funds of the Branch.

(2) Make and promptly forward the quarterly foreign remittances according to the appropriations, upon the written order of the Branch Corresponding Secretary.

(3) Disburse other funds under the direction of the Branch Executive Committee, upon the written order of the Branch Corresponding Secretary.

(4) Furnish quarterly reports to the *Woman's Missionary Friend.*

(5) Present full items of receipts and disbursements annually and quarterly to the Branch, and furnish a copy to the Branch Corresponding and Associate Secretaries.

(6) Prepare an itemized report for the Branch Annual Meeting and for publication in the Branch Annual Report; and,

(7) Perform such other duties as each Branch may define.

5. Branch Superintendents of Literature.—(A) There shall be a Superintendent of Literature elected by each Branch at its Annual Meeting.

(B) It shall be the duty of each Branch Superintendent of Literature to: (1) Advance the interest and increase the sale of the literature and publications.

(2) Have charge, in connection with the Branch Committee on Literature and the Agent of Supplies, of the exhibition and sale of Woman's Foreign Missionary Society publications at the various public gatherings and conventions throughout the country, the expenses to be borne by the Branch within whose bounds the meeting is held.

6. Branch Superintendent of Young People's Work.—(A) There shall be a Superintendent of Young People's Work elected by each Branch at its Annual Meeting.

(B) It shall be the duty of the Branch Superintendent of Young People's Work to: (1) Superintend and devise plans in her department, under the leadership of the Secretary of Young People's Work, and in harmony with the Conference Secretaries.

(2) Conduct correspondence with and receive reports from Conference Superintendents.

(3) Send to the Secretary of Young People's Work an annual statistical report, which shall correspond with the one presented at the Annual Meeting.

(4) Attend and present reports at the Branch Annual and Quarterly meetings.

(5) Provide material in the *Branch Quarterly* for her department.

(6) Perform such other duties as the Branch may require.

7. Branch Superintendent of Children's Work.—(A) There shall be a Superintendent of Children's Work elected by each Branch at its Annual Meeting.

(B) It shall be the duty of the Branch Superintendent of Children's Work to: (1) Superintend and devise plans in her department, under the leadership of the Secretary of Children's Work, and in harmony with the Conference Secretaries.

(2) Conduct correspondence with and receive reports from Conference Superintendents.

(3) Send to the Secretary of Children's Work an annual statistical report, which shall correspond with the one presented at the Annual Meeting.

(4) Attend and present reports at the Branch Annual and Quarterly Meetings.

(5) Provide material in the *Branch Quarterly* for her department.

(6) Perform such other duties as the Branch may require.

IV.—SPECIAL SECRETARIES FOR THE GENERAL WORK.

There shall be a Secretary of Young People's Work, a Secretary of Children's Work, a Secretary of German Work, a Secretary of Scandinavian Work, and a Secretary of the General Office, nominated by the Home Department, and elected annually by the General Executive Committee. Field Secretaries shall be employed as required by the Home Department.

1. *Duties of the Secretary of Young People's Work.*—It shall be the duty of the Secretary of Young People's Work to: (1) Superintend and devise plans for the work of this department.

(2) Conduct correspondence with Branch Superintendents of Young People's Work.

(3) Receive from Branch Superintendents an annual statistical report, which shall correspond with the one presented to the Branch Annual Meeting.

(4) Prepare annual report of department for General Executive Committee, showing statistics by Branches.

(5) Represent the department in significant gatherings.

(6) Provide material necessary for periodicals and press reports; and,

(7) Perform such other duties as the Home Department may define and the General Executive Committee approve.

2. *Duties of the Secretary of Children's Work.*—It shall be the duty of the Secretary of Children's Work to: (1) Superintend and devise plans for the work of this department.

(2) Conduct correspondence with Branch Superintendents of Children's Work.

(3) Receive from Branch Superintendents an annual statistical report, which shall correspond with the one presented to the Branch Annual Meeting.

(4) Prepare annual report of department for General Executive, showing statistics by Branches.

(5) Represent the department in significant gatherings.

(9) Provide material necessary for periodicals and press reports; and,

(7) Perform such other duties as the Home Department may define and the General Executive Committee approve.

3. *Duties of the Secretary of German Work.*—It shall be the duty of the Secretary of German Work to: (1) Superintend and devise plans for the work of the women, young people, and children in the German Methodist Churches.

(2) Conduct correspondence throughout the German constituency.

(3) Receive reports from the German Conference Secretaries and Treasurers, and present an annual statistical report to the General Executive Committee.

(4) Represent her constituency in significant gatherings.

(5) Provide material necessary for periodical and press reports.

(6) She shall be a member of the Home Department of the General Executive Committee.

4. *Duties of the Secretary of Scandinavian Work*.—It shall be the duty of the Secretary of Scandinavian Work to: (1) Superintend and devise plans for the work of the women, young people, and children in the Swedish Methodist Churches.

(2) Conduct correspondence throughout the Swedish constituency, receive reports from Swedish Conference Secretaries and Treasurers, and present an annual statistical report to the General Executive Committee.

(3) Represent her constituency in significant gatherings.

(4) Provide material necessary for periodical and press reports.

(5) She shall be a member of the Home Department of the General Executive Committee.

5. *General Office at New York*.—There shall be a General Office at New York.

The purpose of its maintenance shall be to: (a) Serve as a bureau of general information regarding the work of the Woman's Foreign Missionary Society at home and abroad.

(b) Serve as a central agency for those interests common to all Branches, which can be more effectively and economically conducted through such a center.

(c) Form the point of contact between the Woman's Foreign Missionary Society and other organizations of related interest in our own Church and other denominations; and also to,

(d) Serve in other lines as determined by the Home Department.

6. It shall be the duty of the Secretary of the General Office to express the purpose of the General Office under the direction of the Home Department.

V.—Foreign Treasurers.

A. There shall be a Foreign Treasurer for each mission where the Woman's Foreign Missionary Society supports work.

B. It shall be the duty of each Foreign Treasurer to: (1) Forward receipt immediately upon receiving remittances from the Branch Treasurer.

(2) On January 1st and July 1st of each year forward to the Branch Corresponding Secretary itemized statements showing balance in United States currency.

(3) Apply the funds of the Society only for the purpose designated by the General Executive Committee. This rule shall be interpreted to mean that no expenditure shall exceed the appropriation.

(4) Pay appropriations for buildings and for salaries of missionaries on the basis of United States gold, and all other appropriations on the basis of the local currency of the country, any surplus therefrom by exchange shall accrue to the treasury of the Branch remitting.

(5) Report in the semi-annual statements all surplus funds arising from unused appropriations, exchange, or other source, and hold said funds subject to the order of the Corresponding Secretary from whose Branch said funds accrue.

(6) Forward estimates approved by the Field Reference Committee, and printed, to the Corresponding Secretary of each Branch to insure arrival on or before September 1st.

(7) Pay money for buildings, on presentation of properly audited bills only.

VI.—Missionary Candidates.

Each person who offers herself as a missionary candidate shall: (a) Declare her belief that (1) she is divinely called to the work of a foreign missionary; (2) that she is actuated only by a desire to work in accordance with the will of God; and (3) that she intends to make foreign missionary work the service of her effective years.

(b) Be not less than twenty-five, nor more than thirty years of age. A special facility in acquiring languages or a call to English work may be considered a sufficient reason for deviating from this rule.

(c) When accepted, be under the direction of the General Executive Committee, and, if not sent out within the year, her case shall be presented for reconsideration at the ensuing session of the General Executive Committee by the Corresponding or Foreign Secretary in whose Branch she resides.

(d) Fill out required application blanks and sign the contract in duplicate for file record with the Branch Foreign Secretary, and in the General Office.

VII.—Missionaries.

Each missionary shall: (1) On acceptance by the Woman's Foreign Missionary Society, be under the control of the General Executive Committee, directly amenable to the Corresponding Secretary of the Branch employing her.

2. Devote her entire time and attention to her appointed work.

3. Consider the regulations of the Society named in the Constitution and By-laws as binding as the terms of the contract, and failure to conform to them on the part of the missionary shall release the Society from all financial liability.

4. Enter into the following contract by and with the Woman's Foreign Missionary Society through the Corresponding Secretary of the Branch employing her:

CONTRACT.

"I, —— ——, Corresponding Secretary of the —————— Branch of the Woman's Foreign Missionary Society of the Methodist Episcopal Church, covenant and agree on the part of the Woman's Foreign Missionary Society to pay the traveling expenses of —— ——, a missionary in the employ of the ——————Branch, from her home to her field of labor and her salary from the time of reaching the field at the rate of $—— for the first year, and thereafter at the rate of $—— per annum. I further agree to pay her return passage and home salary as provided in the By-laws relating to those matters."

"I, —— ——, a missionary, agree to give at least five years of continuous service as a single woman to the work of the Woman's Foreign Missionary Society in any field to which I may be sent, and, failing in this, to refund the amount of outfit and passage money. I also agree to conform to all the rules and regulations of said Society while in its employ."

5. Be limited to five years for the first term of service, and six years to each succeeding term; and present a physician's certificate in order to remain longer in the field than the specified time.

6. Report each quarter to the Corresponding Secretary of the Branch employing her, and to the Superintendent of the district in which her work is located.

7. Furnish the Official Correspondent with all facts as required.

8. Incur no expense which has not been authorized by the General Executive Committee, and shall credit to the Society all donations received for the support of the work, and annually report the same with her financial statement.

9. Not apply to private sources for financial aid without the sanction of the General Executive Committee. All solicitations for funds shall be made through the proper official authorities.

10. Report and credit in financial statements made January 1st and July 1st of each year, all sums received for the support of the work in her charge.

11. Send annual communications for patrons supporting Special Work.

12. Keep a clear record of all special work, including Bible-women, scholarships, etc., in her charge under the Branches supporting them, and on her removal or furlough transfer it to her substitute or successor.

13. Present estimates and all other matter requiring the action of the General Executive Committee through the Field Reference Committee of the Conference in which her work is located.

14. Include in her estimates for Bible-women and zenana workers all expenses of conveyances, munshis, and teachers, and in those for scholarships, the cost of fuel, lights, medicines, and the minor expenses necessary in the maintenance of the school.

15. Medical missionaries shall keep an itemized account of all receipts and disbursements, and report them quarterly to the Treasurer of the mission, any surplus being remitted to the Woman's Foreign Missionary Society. Medical outfit provided by the Society shall be the property of the Society.

16. No missionary in the employ of the Woman's Foreign Missionary Society shall adopt any child as her own, nor bring foreign-born girls or helpers to this country except upon the recommendation of the Field Reference Committee of the Conference in which they reside, and with the permission of the Foreign Department of the Woman's Foreign Missionary Society.

17. Any missionary of another Board on the field seeking admission to the Woman's Foreign Missionary Society must present suitable recommendations from her Board; serve at least three years in the Woman's Foreign Missionary Society, and be recommended by the Conference where she has labored, presenting such credentials as are required of other candidates before she is eligible to membership in the Woman's Foreign Missionary Society.

18. The acceptance as missionaries of assistants or native workers shall be in the hands of the Reference Committee, which, in reaching a conclusion, shall take into consideration: (a) the testimonials required in the regulations relating to candidates, including health certificates.

(b) A certificate showing three years of service under the Woman's Foreign Missionary Society.

(c) The recommendation of the Bishop in charge of the Conference.

19. *Salaries.*—(a) The salaries of missionaries going to the field after October, 1901, either as new or returned missionaries, shall include all expenses hitherto classed as incidentals, and shall be, in Africa, $500; Bul-

garia, $600; Foochow and Hing Hua, $600; North, Central, and West China, $650; India, $600; Italy, Japan, and Korea, $700; Malaysia, $600; Mexico, the Philippines, and South America, $750. The first year's work of a new missionary shall be so planned by the mission that the major part of her time shall be given to the study of the languages, and the first year's salary shall be one-sixth less than the full regular amount, except in the case of those whose full salary does not exceed $500. Medical missionaries shall, from the first, receive full salary.

(b) When beginning service, she shall be provided by the Society with not less than $100 for personal outfit, and also, if necessary, $100 for furniture, which shall be the property of the Society.

(c) On furlough, if her home is not in the United States, she shall receive full salary, in which case no furlough expenses will be paid by the Society. This provision shall apply only to missionaries in satisfactory relation to the Society, and for the term of furlough authorized by the General Executive Committee through the Branch employing her.

(d) The liability of the Society for the necessary traveling expenses of furlough or home leave shall depend upon conformity to the regulations.

(e) If proved manifestly unfit for missionary labor, she shall receive three months' notice by the Foreign Committee, at the expiration of which time, the General Executive Committee may cancel its obligation to the missionary. Return passage will be paid by the Society only at the expiration of the three months.

(f) In all cases where the relations of the missionary to the Society are harmonious, her home salary the first year shall be $350. If her health requires her to remain longer in this country, the second year's home salary shall be $300. If her detention for a longer period is necessary, her case shall be in the hands of her Branch for adjustment.

20. *Furlough.*—(a) In case of emergency demanding immediate return home, she shall bring a certificate of disability from a physician and from the Superintendent of the mission.

(b) If she contemplates returning home for any other reason than ill-health, secure permission of the General Executive Committee through the Corresponding Secretary of the Branch employing her, upon the recommendation of the Field Reference Committee.

(c) Accompany her application for return to the field after home leave with a new medical certificate. The recommendation of the Corresponding Secretary of the Branch employing her and a majority vote of the Foreign Department shall be authority for her return.

(d) Attend the first session of the General Executive Committee held after her return from the foreign field, and her traveling expenses to and from the place of meeting shall be paid from the same fund as those of members of that body.

21. *Rules.*—All rules pertaining to the relations of the Woman's Foreign Missionary Society of the Methodist Episcopal Church with its missionaries shall be published in the general Annual Report.

VIII.—FIELD REFERENCE COMMITTEE.

Each foreign Conference or Mission shall have a Field Reference or Finance Committee, of not less than three or more than seven representative members, who shall be elected by ballot annually by the missionaries of the Woman's Foreign Missionary Society, and by wives of missionaries in charge of work, whose duty it shall be to: (a) Prepare estimates and other matters requiring the action of the General Executive Committee.

(b) Approve of all contracts for new buildings, and of all extensive repairs before they are undertaken.

(c) Consider the furloughs of missionaries and forward its recommendations concerning the individual cases to the same.

(d) Decide immediately upon the departure of a missionary on furlough, either in meeting or by correspondence, whether her return to the field is desired, and communicate such decision to the Corresponding Secretary of the Branch supporting her.

(e) Consider all matters of general interest arising during the interim of their Annual Meetings.

(f) Perform such other duties as the General Executive Committee, through its Foreign Committee, shall require.

IX.—FOREIGN BUILDING COMMITTEE.

There shall be a Foreign Building Committee elected in the same manner as the Field Reference Committee, whose duties shall be to: (a) Superintend all matters relative to the purchase of property, erection of new buildings, and extensive repairs for which appropriations have been made.

(b) To audit and order paid all bills for the same.

X.—PUBLICATION DEPARTMENT.

1. The periodicals of the Woman's Foreign Missionary Society shall be known as the *Woman's Missionary Friend, Children's Missionary Friend, Der Frauen Missions Freund,* and *The Study.*

2. The literature of the Society shall include all other publications not specified in Section 1.

3. The Editors and Publisher of the periodicals and literature shall be elected annually at the General Executive Committee, when their reports shall be received, and a copy thereof submitted for publication in the Annual Report of the Woman's Foreign Missionary Society.

4. The Editors and Publisher shall be entitled to floor privileges on matters concerning their work.

5. In the interim of the General Executive Committee the management of the Society's publications shall be under the control of the Home Department.

6. Sample copies of all publications issued by the Society shall be sent to the President, Secretary, and Treasurer of the Woman's Foreign Missionary Society, and to such other officers and exchanges as may be deemed essential to the progress of this department.

XI.—ZENANA PAPER.

1. The Foreign Department shall take charge of the funds raised for the endowment of the Zenana Paper, and control of their investment and expenditure, and have the general supervision of the interests of the paper.

2. The Corresponding Secretary of each Branch shall have the control of the investment of the funds raised for the support of the Zenana Paper within the bounds of her Branch, with the approval of the Foreign Department, the interest on investment to be paid semi-annually to the Treasurer of the Zenana Paper.

3. The Woman's Conference in India shall nominate a Committee consisting of five persons, three women and two men, one of whom shall be the Publisher, to supervise the interests of the paper and arrange with the Press Committee for editing and publishing the Zenana Paper

in the various languages and dialects required; these nominations to be subject to the approval of the Foreign Department of the General Executive Committee.

4. The Official Correspondent of the Woman's Foreign Missionary Society in India shall send an annual report of the Zenana Paper to the Chairman of the Foreign Department, with the amount of circulation and items of interest, in time to be presented to the Annual Meeting of the General Executive Committee in America.

5. The Treasurer in India of the funds of the Zenana Paper shall furnish the Foreign Department an annual report of the receipts and expenditures of said paper, in time to be presented to the General Executive Committee meeting in America.

6. A report of the Zenana Paper shall be published in the Annual Report of the Woman's Foreign Missionary Society.

7. The Treasurer of the Zenana Paper funds in America shall send the interest on the investments direct to the Treasurer of the Zenana Paper in India, only upon the order of the Chairman of the Foreign Department.

XII.—FUNDS.

(a) 1. All money raised under the auspices of this Society belongs to the Woman's Foreign Missionary Society of the Methodist Episcopal Church, and shall not be diverted to other sources.

2. The Reserve Fund, a capital of $5,000, shall be retained in the treasury of the Society's publications, and in no case shall said amount be used in publishing interests or for any other demands.

3. Gifts, bequests, donations, and other moneys received from donors residing outside of the United States shall be paid into General Treasury, and credited as "received from the Society at large."

4. Proceeds on the foreign field, accruing rates of exchange, surplus from remittances made under appropriations and other sources, shall belong to the Branch supporting the work, and shall be reported January 1st and July 1st of each year, and held subject to the order of the Foreign Secretary in whose branch they accrue.

(b) There shall be a General Fund created by the payment by each Branch of one per cent annually of its total receipts, into the treasury of the Woman's Foreign Missionary Society.

XIII.—EXPENSES.

1. From the General Fund shall be paid: (a) Postage for the General Office and Special Secretaries of the Woman's Foreign Missionary Society.

(b) Traveling expenses to and from the meeting of the General Executive Committee, for the officers of the Woman's Foreign Missionary Society. Corresponding Secretaries, Associate Secretaries, Secretaries of German and Scandinavian Work, missionaries, Special Secretaries, and two delegates from each Branch.

(c) Traveling expenses to and from the mid-year meeting of the President of the Woman's Foreign Missionary Society and Corresponding Secretaries.

(d) Expense of the General Office.

2. The postage and traveling expenses of the Editors and Publisher to and from the meeting of General Executive Committee shall be paid from the receipts of the publication office.

XIV.—Delegates.

Delegates to the General Executive Committee shall be appointed to service on nomination by their respective Secretaries.

XV.—Order of Business.

The order of business for the General Executive Committee shall be as follows.

1. Calling the roll.
2. Appointment of Committees.
3. Reception of Memorials, Petitions, and proposed changes in the By-laws.
4. Reports of the Associate Secretaries by Branches.
5. Report of the Home Department.
6. Reports of the Foreign Department by Branch Corresponding Secretaries.
7. Reports of Official Correspondents.
8. Report of Editors and Publisher.
9. Fixing place of next meeting.
10. Election of President, Vice-president, Secretary, Treasurer, Special Secretaries, and other officers, who shall continue in office until the appointment of their successors.
11. Election of Editors and Publisher.
12. Notice of Constitutional amendments.

DAILY ORDER OF BUSINESS.

1. Roll call.
2. Minutes.
3. Reports of Committees.
4. Miscellaneous business.
5. Introductions.

Each session shall open and close with devotional exercises. All resolutions to be discussed shall be presented in writing. No member shall be granted leave of absence except by vote of the entire body.

XVI.—Fiscal Year.

The fiscal year of the Society shall begin October 1st.

XVII.—Meetings.

1. The General Executive Committee shall convene annually not later than the last week in October, at such places as the said Committee shall elect.

2. The date and arrangements for the Anniversary exercises of the General Executive Committee shall be made by the President, the Corresponding and Associate Secretaries of the Branch within whose bounds the meeting of the General Executive Committee is to be held.

3. The members of the Foreign Department shall assemble not less than three days earlier, to consider their work, and shall hold a mid-year meeting at a time and place agreed upon by themselves.

4. A majority of the members of the General Executive Committee shall constitute a quorum for the transaction of business.

17

XVIII.—By-Laws.

These By-laws may be changed or amended at any meeting of the General Executive Committee by a two-thirds vote of the members present and voting.

OFFICIAL RELATIONS OF MISSIONARIES.

1. Definition of relations of the Woman's Foreign Missionary Society, as given by the Bishops in May, 1881.

"To the ladies of the Woman's Foreign Missionary Society:

"To your questions we respectfully reply as follows:

"1. We take the liberty to refer you to our action bearing date November 22, 1877, a copy of which is as follows:

TEACHERS IN MISSION SCHOOLS.

"1. In the judgment of the Bishops it is not within the right of the Superintendent of the mission to remove lay teachers from the schools to which they have been appointed, nor to interfere authoritatively with the internal arrangements of the schools, unless such right be expressly granted by the missionary authorities at New York.

"2. In case of difference between appointee and the Mission (including the Superintendent), which can not be adjusted between the parties without unreasonable delay, we recommend that such difference, with the papers and facts, be referred by the parties to the Bishop in charge for final decision.

"3. It is our judgment that the missionaries sent by the Woman's Foreign Missionary Society should be permitted to be present at the meetings of the mission and to speak on all matters relating to their work. Most respectfully and sincerely,
"WILLIAM H. HARRIS."

ACTION TAKEN BY THE DELEGATED CONFERENCE IN INDIA IN 1881 AND ACCEPTED BY THE WOMAN'S FOREIGN MISSIONARY SOCIETY.

WHEREAS, Certain usages have grown up and been found acceptable and successful in connection with our older mission field in India, we deem it expedient to formulate the same in the following rules:

1. In general: The position of a lady missionary, placed in charge of work in connection with any of our circuits or stations, is the same as that of a second missionary or "junior preacher" to whom special work is assigned.

2. In particular: The general plan of work, such as establishing new schools, employing and dismissing head teachers, arranging terms of tuition, board, etc., and preparing a course of study, when these matters are not fixed by the Educational Committee, selecting classes of people among whom work may be more successfully carried on, arranging dispensaries and deciding the proportion of medical work to be given to natives and Europeans, Christians and non-Christians, etc., all such *general plans* shall be arranged by the lady in charge of the special departments of work, after free consultation with the Superintendent or Presiding Elder.

3. The missionary in charge of the work has full liberty to do the work assigned her in her own way, and to carry out the internal

arrangements of her department in the manner which she deems best adapted to secure success.

4. The relations of the Superintendent or Presiding Elder to the work under the charge of a lady is the same as it would be were it under the charge of a member of Conference—he having a general advisory supervision, auditing the accounts (when not done by trustees), making suggestions, etc., exactly as with all the other work of his district.

5. Lady missionaries in charge of work, and all missionaries of the Woman's Foreign Missionary Society, are appointed by the President of Conference, at the same time and in the same manner that the appointments of Conference are made. Should, however, a President of Conference at any time decline to appoint, the Superintendent or Presiding Elder in council will arrange the same.

6. All new buildings or expensive repairs or changes shall receive the sanction of Superintendent or Presiding Elder, even though no appropriations of money be asked.

7. A class of laborers is employed in our work known as "assistants." In the employment or dismissal of these ladies, the consent of the Superintendent of Mission or of the Presiding Elder must be secured. They may be transferred by the Presiding Elder, with the consent of the lady in charge of the department in which they are employed. When these lady assistants, being members of our Church, by several years of faithful service, have come to be received as belonging permanently to our body of laborers, they may, on the recommendation of the Woman's Society, when such exists, or by Quarterly Conference, be formally recognized by Conference, and appointed the same as are women missionaries.

8. In case of a transfer of a woman missionary or an "assistant" from one Conference or charge to another, written permission shall be secured, signed by the Superintendent or Presiding Elder in whose jurisdiction the person may be employed, when, according to the condition in Rule 7, the engagement may be completed.

CONSTITUTION FOR AUXILIARY SOCIETIES.

Auxiliaries are expected to labor in harmony with, and under the direction of, the Branch.

ARTICLE I.—NAME.

This organization shall be called The Woman's Foreign Missionary Society of.............Auxiliary to the ....Branch of the Woman's Foreign Missionary Society of the Methodist Episcopal Church.

ARTICLE II.—PURPOSE.

The purpose of this Society shall be to aid its Branch in interesting Christian women in the evangelizing of heathen women and in raising funds for this work.

ARTICLE III.—MEMBERSHIP.

Any person paying a regular subscription of two cents a week, or one dollar per year, may become a member of the Woman's Foreign Missionary Society. Any person contributing five dollars per quarter for one year, or twenty dollars at a time, shall be constituted a Life Member.

ARTICLE IV.—FUNDS.

All funds raised under the auspices of this Society belong to the Woman's Foreign Missionary Society, and shall not be diverted to other causes.

Remittances shall be forwarded quarterly to the Conference Treasurer.

ARTICLE V.—OFFICERS AND ELECTIONS.

The officers of this Society shall be a President, one or more Vice-Presidents, a Recording Secretary, a Corresponding Secretary, a Treasurer, and Supervisor of Children's Work, who shall constitute an Executive Committee to administer its affairs. Managers and Superintendents of departments of work may be added as needed. These officers shall be elected at the annual meeting of the Society.

ARTICLE VI.—CHANGE OF CONSTITUTION.

This Constitution may be changed at any annual meeting of the General Executive Committee of the Woman's Foreign Missionary Society by a three-fourths vote of those present and voting, notice of the proposed change having been given to the Branches before April 1st of that year.

CONSTITUTION FOR YOUNG PEOPLE'S SOCIETIES.

ARTICLE I.—NAME.

This organization shall be called The Young Woman's Foreign Missionary Society, or Standard Bearer Company of the Woman's Foreign Missionary Society of the.........Church, Auxiliary to the......... Branch of the Woman's Foreign Missionary Society of the Methodist Episcopal Church.

ARTICLE II.—Purpose.

The purpose of this organization is to interest young people in Foreign Missions and to support the work of the Woman's Foreign Missionary Society of the Methodist Episcopal Church.

ARTICLE III.—Membership.

Any person may become a member of this organization by paying not less than five cents a month, or may enroll as a Standard Bearer by signing the following pledge:

"In remembrance of our Father's love and in loyalty to the great commission of our King, I will give five cents a month as dues to the Woman's Foreign Missionary Society of the Methodist Episcopal Church to aid in sending the Gospel to the Christless millions."

The payment of fifteen dollars shall constitute Life Membership.

ARTICLE IV.—Badge.

The badge of this organization shall be the Church pennant pin. Members paying one dollar per year may wear the Woman's Foreign Missionary Society badge if preferred. Neither badge should be, worn by any person not paying dues.

ARTICLE V.—Funds.

Funds raised under the auspices of this Society belong to the Woman's Foreign Missionary Society and shall not be diverted to other causes. Remittances shall be forwarded quarterly to the Conference Treasurer.

ARTICLE VI.—Officers and Elections.

The officers of this organization shall be a President, two or more Vice-Presidents, a Recording Secretary, a Corresponding Secretary, and a Treasurer, who shall be elected at the annual meeting of the organization and constitute an Executive Committee to administer the affairs of the same. Superintendents of departments may be added as needed.

ARTICLE VII.—Change of Constitution.

This Constitution may be changed at any annual meeting of the General Executive Committee by a three-fourths vote of those present and voting, notice of the proposed change having been given to the Branches before April 1st of that year.

CONSTITUTION FOR KING'S HERALDS.

ARTICLE I.—Name.

This organization shall be called the King's Heralds of the Methodist Episcopal Church, and be under the supervision of the Auxiliary of the Woman's Foreign Missionary Society in the said Church, if any exist; otherwise under the especial supervision of the District Secretary of the Woman's Foreign Missionary Society.

ARTICLE II.—OBJECT.

The object of this organization shall be to promote missionary intelligence and interest among the children and to aid in the work of the Woman's Foreign Missionary Society of the Methodist Episcopal Church.

ARTICLE III.—MEMBERSHIP.

Any child between the ages of eight and fourteen may become a King's Herald by the payment of two cents a month. The payment of ten dollars shall constitute a child's life membership.

ARTICLE IV.—OFFICERS.

The officers of this organization shall be a Superintendent, President, two Vice-Presidents, Recording Secretary, Corresponding Secretary, Treasurer, and Agent for the *Children's Missionary Friend.*

ARTICLE V.—MEETINGS.

Meetings of this organization shall be held on the.........of each month. The officers shall be elected semi-annually at the September and March meetings.

ARTICLE VI.—BADGE.

The badge of this organization shall be a silver button with "King's Heralds" in blue lettering.

PLAN OF WORK FOR LITTLE LIGHT BEARERS.

Children under eight years of age may be enrolled as Little Light Bearers by the payment of twenty-five cents annually, receiving the enrollment card as a certificate of membership.
The payment of ten dollars shall constitute Life Membership.

DIRECTIONS.

The Superintendent elected by the Woman's Auxiliary shall have charge of the work for Little Light Bearers and plan for the collecting of dues, remitting and reporting quarterly through the regular channels, arrange for the annual public meeting, keep an accurate record in the Little Light Bearers' Record Book, and report regularly to the Woman's Auxiliary.

CONSTITUTION FOR DISTRICT ASSOCIATION.

ARTICLE I.—NAME.

This association shall be called The .... District Association of the Woman's Foreign Missionary Society in the ....Conference of the Methodist Episcopal Church.

ARTICLE II.—Purpose.

The purpose of this Association shall be to unite the Auxiliaries of the District in an earnest effort for the promotion of the work of the Woman's Foreign Missionary Society.

ARTICLE III.—Membership.

All members of the Woman's Foreign Missionary Society in .... District shall be considered members of this Association.

ARTICLE IV.—Officers.

The officers of this Association shall be a President, three or more Vice-Presidents, a Corresponding Secretary, a Recording Secretary, a Treasurer, and Superintendent of Young Woman's Work and of Children's Work, who shall constitute the Executive Committee to administer the affairs of the District.

ARTICLE V.—Meetings.

There shall be an annual meeting of the District Association, when reports shall be received from all Auxiliaries in the District, missionary intelligence be given, and necessary business transacted.

ARTICLE VI.—Change of Constitution.

This Constitution may be changed at any annual meeting of the General Executive Committee of the Woman's Foreign Missionary Society by a three-fourths vote of those present and voting, notice of the proposed change having been given to the Branches before April 1st of that year.

ACT OF INCORPORATION.

State of New York, } ss.
City and County of New York, } ss.

We, the undersigned, Caroline R. Wright, Anna A. Harris, Sarah K. Cornell, and Harriet B. Skidmore, of the City of New York, and Susan A. Sayre, of the City of Brooklyn, being all citizens of the United States of America, and citizens of the State of New York, do hereby, pursuant to and in conformity with the Act of the Legislature of the State of New York, passed on April 12th, 1848, entitled "An Act for the incorporation of benevolent, charitable, and missionary societies:" and the several acts of the said Legislature amendatory thereof, associate ourselves together and form a body politic and corporate, under the name and title of "The Woman's Foreign Missionary Society of the Methodist Episcopal Church," which we certify is the name or title by which said Society shall be known in law. And we do hereby further certify that the particular business and object of said Society is to engage and unite the efforts of Christian women in sending female missionaries to women in foreign mission fields of the Methodist Episcopal Church, and in supporting them and native Christian teachers and Bible readers in those fields.

That the number of managers to manage the business and affairs of said Society shall be seventeen, and that the names of such managers of said Society for the first year of its existence are: Lucy A. Alderman, Sarah L. Keen, Ellen T. Cowen, Hannah M. W. Hill, Mary C. Nind, Elizabeth K. Stanley, Harriet M. Shattuck, Isabel Hart, Caroline R. Wright, Harriet B. Skidmore, Rachel L. Goodier, Annie B. Gracey, Harriet D. Fisher, Sarah K. Cornell, Anna A. Harris, Ordelia M. Hillman, and Susan A. Sayre.

That the place of business or principal office of said Society shall be in the City and County of New York, in the State of New York.

Witness our hand and seal this 20th day of December, A. D. 1884.
[Seal.]

> CAROLINE R. WRIGHT,
> ANNA A. HARRIS,
> HARRIET B. SKIDMORE,
> SUSAN A. SAYRE,
> SARAH K. CORNELL.

ACT OF INCORPORATION.

State of New York, } ss.
City and County of New York, } ss.

On the 20th day of December, 1884, before me personally came and appeared Caroline R. Wright, Anna A. Harris, Harriet B. Skidmore, and Sarah K. Cornell, to me known, and to me personally known to be the individuals described in and who executed the foregoing certificate, and they severally duly acknowledged to me that they executed the same.

ANDREW LEMON,
[Notary's Seal.]   Notary Public (58),
New York County.

City of Brooklyn, }
State of New York, County of Kings, } ss.

On the 22d day of December, A. D. 1884, before me came Susan A. Sayre, to me known, and known to me to be one of the individuals described in and who executed the foregoing certificate, and duly acknowledged to me that she executed the same.

F. G. MINTRAM,

[Notary Seal.]   Notary Public of Kings County.

State of New York, } ss.
County of Kings, }

I, Rodney Thursby, Clerk of the County of Kings and Clerk of the Supreme Court of the State of New York, in and for said county (said court being a Court of Records), do hereby certify that F. G. Mintram, whose name is subscribed to the Certificate of Proof, or acknowledgment of the annexed instrument and thereon written, was at the time of taking such proof or acknowledgment, a Notary Public of the State of New York, in and for said County of Kings, dwelling in said County, commissioned and sworn, and duly authorized to take the same. And, further, that I am well acquainted with the handwriting of said Notary, and verily believe the signature to the said certificate is genuine, and that said instrument is executed and acknowledged according to the laws of the State of New York.

In Testimony Whereof, I have hereunto set my hand and affixed the seal of the said County and Court, this 24th day of December, 1884.

[Seal.]

CERTIFICATE OF INCORPORATION, DECEMBER 27, 1884.

I, the undersigned, one of the Justices of the Supreme Court of the State of New York, for the First Judicial District, do hereby approve the within certificate, and do consent that the same be filed, pursuant to the provisions of an Act of the Legislature of the State of New York, entitled, "An Act for the Incorporation of Benevolent, Charitable, Scientific and Missionary Societies," passed April 12th, 1848, and the several acts extending and amending said act. Dated New York, December 26, 1884.   ABM. R. LAWRENCE, J. S. C.

State of New York, }
City and County of New York, } ss.

I, James A. Flack, Clerk of the said City and County, and Clerk of the Supreme Court of said State for said County, do certify that I have compared the preceding with the original Certificate of Incorporation of the Woman's Foreign Missionary Society of the Methodist Episcopal Church, on file in my office, and that the same is a correct transcript therefrom, and of the whole of such original. Endorsed, filed, and recorded, December 27th, 1884, 1 hour and 25 minutes.

In Witness Whereof, I have hereunto subscribed my name, and affixed my official seal, this 12th day of November, 1888.

[Seal.]   JAMES A. FLACK, Clerk.

BOARD OF MANAGERS OF THE CORPORATION, 1896-97.

HARRIET B. SKIDMORE,	HELEN V. EMANS,	JULIA L. McGREW,
SUSAN A. SAYRE,	SARAH K. CORNELL,	ETTIE F. BALDWIN,
ELLIN J. KNOWLES,	MARY H. BIDWELL,	ANNA A. HARRIS.
ORDELIA M. HILLMAN,	ANNIE R. GRACEY,	

AMENDED ACT OF INCORPORATION.

CHAPTER 213.

AN ACT to Authorize the Woman's Foreign Missionary Society of the Methodist · Episcopal Church to Vest its Management in a General Executive Committee.

Became a law April 12, 1906, with the approval of the Governor.

Passed, three-fifths being present.

The people of the State of New York, represented in Senate and Assembly, do enact as follows:

SECTION 1. The Board of Managers of the Woman's Foreign Missionary Society of the Methodist Episcopal Church is abolished.

SEC. 2. The management and genèral administration of the affairs of the said Society shall be vested in a General Executive Committee, to consist of the President, Recording Secretary, General Treasurer, Secretary of German Work, Secretary of Scandinavian Work, and the Literature Committee of said Society, together with the Corresponding Secretary and the two delegates from each co-ordinate Branch of said Society.

SEC. 3. The President, Recording Secretary, General Treasurer, Secretaries of the German and Scandinavian Work and the Literature Committee, now in office, shall be members of the General Executive Committee, which shall meet on the third Wednesday in April, in the year nineteen hundred and six; and, thereafter, such officers and Literature Committee shall be elected annually by the General Executive Committee. The Corresponding Secretary and two delegates of each co-ordinate Branch shall be elected annually by such Branch.

SEC. 4. Meetings of the General Executive Committee shall be held annually, or oftener, at such time and place as the General Executive Committee shall appoint, and such place of meeting may be either within or without the State of New York. .

SEC. 5. This act shall take effect immediately.

State of New York,   } ss.
Office of the Secretary of State, }

I have compared the preceding with the original law on file in this office, and do hereby certify that the same is a correct transcript therefrom, and the whole of said original law.

Given under my hand and the seal of office of the Secretary of State, at the City of Albany, this sixteenth day of April, in the year one thousand nine hundred and six.   HORACE G. TENNANT,

[Seal.]   Second Deputy Secretary of State.

ACTION OF 1908.

CHAPTER 91.

AN ACT to amend chapter two hundred and thirteen of the laws of nineteen hundred and six, entitled "An act to authorize the Woman's Foreign Missionary Society of the Methodist Episcopal Church to vest its management in a general executive committee," relative to the membership and election or appointment of such General Executive Committee:

Became a law April 6, 1908, with the approval of the Governor.

Passed, three-fifths being present.

The People of the State of New York, represented in Senate and Assembly, do enact as follows:

Section 1. Sections two and three of chapter two hundred and thirteen of the laws of nineteen hundred and six, entitled "An act to authorize the

Woman's Foreign Missionary Society of the Methodist Church to vest its management in a general executive committee," are hereby amended to read, respectively, as follows:

Sec. 2. The management and general administration of the affairs of the said Society shall be vested in a general executive committee to consist of the President, Recording Secretary, and Treasurer of said Society, together with the Corresponding Secretary of each co-ordinate branch of the said Society; and one .or more delegates to be chosen by such co-ordinate branches; and such additional or different members as may be now or hereafter provided for by the Constitution of the said Society.

Sec. 3. The President, Recording Secretary, and Treasurer of said Society shall be members of the general executive committee; and hereafter such officers shall be elected annually by the general executive committee. The Corresponding Secretary and one cr more delegates of each co-ordinate branch shall be elected annually by such branch; and such other members of such general executive committee as shall hereafter be created by the Constitution of said Society shall be .elected or appointed in the manner which shall be prescribed by the said Constitution.

Sec. 4. This act shall take effect immediately.

State of New York, } ss.
Office of the Secretary of State. }

I have compared the preceding with the original law on file in this office and do hereby certify that the same is a correct transcript therefrom, and of the whole of the said original law.

JOHN S. WHALEN,
Secretary of State.

FORMS OF WILL, DEVISE, AND ANNUITY.

FORM OF BEQUEST.

I hereby give and bequeath to the "Woman's Foreign Missionary Society of the Methodist Episcopal Church," incorporated under the laws of the State of New York, ... dollars, to be paid to the Treasurer of said Society, whose receipt shall be sufficient acquittance to my executors therefor.

FORM OF DEVISE OF REAL ESTATE.

I hereby give and devise to the "Woman's Foreign Missionary Society of the Methodist Episcopal Church" (describe land, etc., intended to be given to the Society) and to their successors and assigns forever.

Miss Florence Hooper, 2201 Maryland Ave., Baltimore, Md., is the Treasurer of the Woman's Foreign Missionary Society, with power to sign release to executors through whom the Society may receive bequests and to perform such other acts as are required by the Act of Incorporation, and which can not be legally executed by Branch Treasurers.

Note.—Prompt notice of all bequests and devises should be given to the Corresponding Secretary of the Branch within which the donor resides.

Note.—In each of the above forms the name of the Branch to which the bequest or devise is made shall be inserted immediately before the words, "Woman's Foreign Missionary Society," whenever such Branch is incorporated. The name of the State under the laws of which said Branch is incorporated shall also be inserted.

Incorporated Branches: New England under the laws of Massachusetts; Baltimore under the laws of Maryland; Cincinnati under the laws of Ohio; Northwestern under the laws of Illinois; Des Moines under the laws of Iowa; Minneapolis under the laws of Minnesota; Pacific under the laws of California; Columbia River under the laws of Oregon.

FORM OF ANNUITY.

Whereas, ..., of ...., has donated to and paid into the treasury of the .... Branch of the Woman's Foreign Missionary Society of the Methodist Episcopal Church the sum of .... dollars.

Now, therefore, the said Branch of the Woman's Foreign Missionary Society of the Methodist Episcopal Church, in consideration thereof, hereby agrees to pay to said .... during .... natural life interest on the aforesaid sum at the rate of .... per cent per annum, payable semi-annually, said payments to cease on the death of said ...., and the said sum donated by .... as aforesaid is to be considered as an executed gift to said Society and to belong to said Society from this date, without any amount or liability therefor.

.... Branch of the Woman's Foreign Missionary Society of the Methodist Episcopal Church, by ....

RATES OF ANNUITIES.

Where it is practical, in the place of making a bequest, it is far better to convert property into cash and place the same in the treasury of the Missionary Society at once, on the annuity plan. By so doing all possibility of litigation is avoided, and a fair income is assured. The Woman's Foreign Missionary Society does not spend money so contributed while the annuitant lives, unless so requested by said annuitant, but invests it in good securities in this country.

The following rates are given:

To persons from 50 to 55 years of age......................4 per cent.
To persons from 56 to 60 years of age.....................4½ per cent.
To persons from 61 to 65 years of age.....................5 per cent.
To persons from 66 to 70 years of age.....................5½ per cent.
To persons 70 years and over.............................6 per cent.

Special cases shall be arranged for by the Branch Committee having in charge bequests and annuities.

This plan removes all risk of broken wills through skill of lawyers and uncertainty of courts.

AFTER DEATH BOND.

In consideration of my interest in, and love for the Woman's Foreign Missionary Society of the Methodist Episcopal Church, I hereby bind myself, my heirs, devisees, and representatives, to pay to the .... Branch, through the Treasurer of .... Conference of said Society, ... dollars, which said sum shall be paid at or before my death, without any relief whatever from valuation or appraisement laws.

[SIGNED.]
ATTEST:

MISSIONARY BENEFIT ASSOCIATION.

President—MRS. S. F. JOHNSON, 520 Oakland Ave., Pasadena, Cal.
Treasurer—MR. WILLIAM E. BLACKSTONE, Los Angeles, Cal.
Financial and Corresponding Secretary—MRS. J. A. BURHANS, 2401 Magnolia Ave., Edgewater, Chicago, Ill.
Auditor—MR. F. P. CRANDON, Evanston, Ill.

The object of the Association is to "assist any of its members who may be in need," and any missionary regularly appointed by the Woman's Foreign Missionary Society of the Methodist Episcopal Church is eligible to membership on the payment of an annual fee of $10.

Four members have received help during the year. One of them writes: "I can not tell how thankful I have been this year for the Missionary Benefit Association. If it were not for the help I expect to receive I would have to seek some employment to help pay expenses, and could not be free to bend every energy to getting well for China's sake."

All remittances and correspondence should be addressed to the Financial and Corresponding Secretary, Mrs. J. A. Burhans, 2401 Magnolia Ave., Edgewater, Chicago, Ill.

MEMBERSHIPS AND SCHOLARSHIPS IN THE WOMAN'S FOREIGN MISSIONARY SOCIETY.

The payment of one dollar a year, or two cents a week, constitutes membership.

The payment of twenty dollars constitutes life membership.

The payment of one hundred dollars constitutes an honorary life manager.

The payment of three hundred dollars constitutes an honorary life patron.

Bible women's salaries vary from twenty to one hundred dollars, according to experience in work and time given.

Scholarships vary from twenty to eighty dollars, according to the country.

Scholarships in India vary from twenty to forty dollars.

Scholarships in China are thirty dollars.

Scholarships in Mexico are fifty dollars.

Scholarships in Japan are forty dollars.

Scholarships in Korea are thirty-five dollars.

Scholarships in South America are eighty dollars.

POSTAGE TO FOREIGN LANDS.

The rates of postage to Mexico are the same as in the United States. To all other points where our missionaries are stationed letters weighing an ounce are five cents for the first ounce; three cents for ounce or fraction thereof additional. Newspapers, one cent for each two ounces; and on all printed matter the same as in United States; postal cards, two cents. Foreign postal cards may be procured at any postoffice. All foreign postage must be fully prepaid.

FOREIGN MONEY.

INDIA.—A pice is one-fourth of an anna, or about two-thirds of a cent. An anna is worth one-sixteenth of a rupee. The rupee varies in value, and is worth about 33 cents.

JAPAN.—A yen, whether in gold or silver, is one-half the value of the gold and silver dollar in the United States. There are one hundred sen in the yen.

CHINA.—A cash is one mill. The tael is worth in gold about $1.15. The Mexican dollar is also used in China.

SOME FIRST THINGS OF THE SOCIETY IN THE FOREIGN FIELD.

The Woman's Foreign Missionary Society Sent Out—

1869—The first woman physician, Miss Clara A. Swain, M. D., to non-Christian women, Lucknow, India.

1873—The first woman physician to China, Miss Lucinda Combs, M. D., Foochow.

1887—The first woman physician to Korea, Miss Metta Howard, M. D., Seoul.

1900—The first woman physician to the Philippines, Mrs. Anna J. Norton, M. D., Manila.

The Society Opened—

1874—The first hospital for women in Asia; Bareilly, India.

1875—The first hospital for women in China, Foochow.

1889—The first hospital for women in Korea, Seoul.

The Society Founded—

1887—The first Christian Woman's College in Asia, Miss Isabella Thoburn, Lucknow, India.

1890—The first Industrial Training School in Asia, Miss Ella Blackstock, Tokyo, Japan.

1892—The first Protestant Woman's College in Italy, Miss M. Ella Vickery, Rome.

1897—The first Christian woman's magazine in Japan, Miss Georgiana Baucus, Yokohama.

1904—The first Training School for Nurses in Korea, Miss Margaret J. Edmunds, Seoul.

1906—The first College for Women in Mexico, Miss Laura Temple, Mexico City.

AT HOME.

1870—District meeting first held Albion, Mich., Mrs. H. F. Spencer, Miss S. D. Rulison.

1871—Bequest, Sarah Kemp Slater, Grand Rapids, Mich.

1873—Proposed plan for Missionary Readings, Mrs. F. D. York.

1876—Conference Secretaries first elected, Michigan, Mrs. F. D. York, Mrs. Mary T. Lathrop.

1877—Missionary Leaflets, originated by Mrs. D. D. Lore and Mrs. J. T. Gracey.

1881—Thank-offering first observed, Lansing District, Mich., Mrs. H. E. Taylor.

1883—Thank-offering first observed by Branch, Northwestern.

1883—Missionary Lesson Leaf, Miss Sallie Ann Rulison.

1886—Children's Missionary Leaf, Frances J. Baker.

1889—Conference Treasurers first appointed, Northwestern Branch.

1890—Secretary of Home Department first appointed, Northwestern Branch, Mrs. M. Meredith.

1891—Little Light Bearers, Mrs. Lucie F. Harrison, Worcester, Mass.

1901—Standard Bearers, Miss Clara M. Cushman, Southbridge, Mass.

1901—Badge, seal and crest proposed by Miss Hodgkins in *The Friend,* and adopted in 1902; Committee, Miss Hodgkins, Miss Carnahan, and Mrs. R. E. Clark.

1905—College Department, Mrs. S. J. Herben, Northwestern Branch.

The Woman's Foreign Missionary
❦❦❦❦ Society ❦❦❦❦

General Office:
Room 611, 150 Fifth Avenue, New York City,
Miss Elizabeth R. Bender, Office Secretary.

Publication Office:
36 Bromfield Street, Boston, Mass.
Miss Annie G. Bailey, Publisher.

Send all Orders for Periodicals to the Publication Office.

Depots of Supplies:

New England Branch:
  Miss F. Addie Farnham, Room 18, 36 Bromfield St., Boston, Mass.
New York Branch:
  Miss Anna L. Cole, · · Room 401, 150 Fifth Ave., New York City
Philadelphia Branch:
  Miss Hannah Bunting, · · · · · · 1018 Arch St., Philadelphia, Pa.
Baltimore Branch:
  Miss Florence Allen, · · · · · · · 516 Park Ave., Baltimore, Md.
Cincinnati Branch:
  Miss Alice M. Startsman, 220 W. Fourth St., Room 84, Cincinnati, O.
Northwestern Branch:
  Miss Marie Winterton, Room 808, 57 Washington St., Chicago, Ill.
Des Moines Branch:
  Miss Mary Q. Evans, · · · 105 N. Mulberry St., Maryville, Mo.
Minneapolis Branch:
  Miss Sarah E. Mason, 3400 University Ave., S.E., Minneapolis, Minn.
Topeka Branch:
  Miss M. D. Thackara, · · · · · · · 1303 T St., Lincoln, Neb.
Pacific Branch:
  Miss Carrie M. Leas, · · · · · 531 W. Fifth St., Los Angeles, Cal.
  Miss Josephine Marston, · · 2534 Piedmont Ave., Berkeley, Cal.
Columbia River Branch:
  Mrs. L. C. Dickey, · · · 293 E. Thirty-fourth St., Portland, Ore.
German Work:
  Miss Freda Cramer, 273 Southern Ave., Mt. Auburn, Cincinnati, O.

Woman's Missionary Friend

Editor, ... MISS ELIZABETH C, NORTHUP

Subscription Price, 50 cents

Frauen-Missions-Freund

Editor, ... MISS A. M. ACHARD

Subscription Price, 25 cents

Children's Missionary Friend

Editor, ... MRS. O. W. SCOTT

Single Copy, 20 cents.
Ten or more copies to one address, 10 cents each

The Study

For use of Auxiliaries in connection with the monthly topic

Editor, ... MRS. MARY ISHAM

Price—One dozen copies each month for one year, 30 cents

Subscriptions should be sent for the above Publications to

MISS ANNIE G. BAILEY, - - - *Publisher,*

36 Bromfield St., Boston, Mass.

Zenana Papers

Rafiq-I-Niswan (Urdu). Abla Hitkarak (Hindi).

Editor, . . . MISS LILAVATI SINGH, Lucknow, India

Mathar Mithiri (Tamil).

Editor, ... MISS GRACE STEPHENS, Madras, India

Mahila Bandhub (Bengali).

Editor, MRS. J. P. MEIK, 46 Dharamtala St., Calcutta, India

Marathi.

Editor, . . MISS HELEN E. ROBINSON, Bombay, India

Japanese Friend. The Tokiwa.

Editor, MISS GEORGIANA BAUCUS, Yokohama, Japan

Subscription price, 50 yen.

The Folts Mission Institute

A Woman's Training-school for Home and Foreign Missionaries, Pastors' Assistants, and Other Christian Workers.

BIBLE DEPARTMENT
KINDERGARTEN DEPARTMENT

Herkimer, New York